Other Books Currently Available
in the Dove on Fundraising Series:

Other Nonprofit Resources from Jossey-Bass:

CONDUCTING A SUCCESSFUL MAJOR GIFTS AND PLANNED GIVING PROGRAM

The Dove on Fundraising Series is a library of premier resource guides that combine practical instruction with real-world examples. In response to the ever-changing challenges nonprofits face, Kent E. Dove, the Indiana University Foundation, and Jossey-Bass have come together to develop and advance professional standards for fundraisers everywhere. Built on the successful fundraising model developed by veteran fundraiser and series editor Kent Dove, these publications provide a flexible campaign-based approach that recognizes fundraising as both a science and an art.

Clustered around the comprehensive *Conducting a Successful Fundraising Program,* each publication examines a key aspect of fundraising, and all authors bring years of experience and knowledge to their topics. Together, these guides present an integrated framework validated by research and practical results. **The Dove on Fundraising Series** seeks to provide nonprofit leaders, fundraisers, consultants, and students with not only time-tested principles, but also successful examples, strategies, and publications that readers can use to shape their own development programs.

CONDUCTING A SUCCESSFUL MAJOR GIFTS AND PLANNED GIVING PROGRAM

A Comprehensive Guide and Resource

Kent E. Dove
Alan M. Spears
Thomas W. Herbert

JOSSEY-BASS
A Wiley Company
www.josseybass.com

Published by

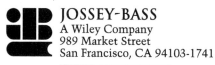

JOSSEY-BASS
A Wiley Company
989 Market Street
San Francisco, CA 94103-1741

www.josseybass.com

Jossey-Bass books and products are available through most bookstores. To contact Jossey-Bass directly, call (888) 378-2537, fax to (800) 605-2665, or visit our website at www.josseybass.com.

Substantial discounts on bulk quantities of Jossey-Bass books are available to corporations, professional associations, and other organizations. For details and discount information, contact the special sales department at Jossey-Bass.

We at Jossey-Bass strive to use the most environmentally sensitive paper stocks available to us. Our publications are printed on acid-free recycled stock whenever possible, and our paper always meets or exceeds minimum GPO and EPA requirements.

Jossey-Bass also publishes its books in a variety of electronic formats. Some content that appears in print may not be available in electronic books.

Readers should be aware that Internet Web sites offered as citations or sources for further information may have changed or disappeared between when this book was written and when it is read.

Credits are on page 558.

Library of Congress Cataloging-in-Publication Data

Dove, Kent E., date.
   Conducting a successful major gifts and planned giving program:
a comprehensive guide and resource / Kent E. Dove, Alan M.
Spears, Thomas W. Herbert.—1st ed.
          p. cm.
Includes bibliographical references and index.
   ISBN 0-7879-5707-0 (alk. paper)
   1. Fund raising—United States. 2. Deferred giving—United
States. 3. Nonprofit organizations—United States—Finance.
I. Spears, Alan M., date. II. Herbert, Thomas W. III. Title.
   HV41.9.U5 D68 2002
   658.15'224—dc21

2001008666

HB Printing   10 9 8 7 6 5 4 3 2   FIRST EDITION

CONTENTS

To my loving wife, Donna. Her love and support have meant everything to me in my life and my career. And to my parents, Glen and Jewell Spears, who raised me right and continue to be a great source of guidance and wise counsel. Also, my thanks to Kent Dove, who has been a wonderful mentor and an example to me as a development professional.

Alan M. Spears

To my wife, Kirsten Roberts, for her unconditional love and patience that has been an immeasurable source of support in my life. To my son, Zachary, who is a blessing and a miracle. To my parents, T. Walter Herbert Jr. and Marjorie Millard Herbert, whose love and sacrifice created the foundation for the life I enjoy today. To the following true professionals who have given me opportunities and guidance over my career: Carl J. Bendorf, David Dierks, Rick Eason, Don Ireland-Schunicht, Jack R. Ohle, Nancy Perazelli, Marc Rainey, Jake B. Schrum, and Curtis R. Simic. Last but not least, to Kent E. Dove and Alan M. Spears, for their mentorship and for the example of true fundraising excellence they set for me every day.

Thomas W. Herbert

PREFACE

This is the fifth book in a five-volume, foundational series about fundraising. The series, completed over the past thirty months, concludes with a focus on the most important gifts a nonprofit organization receives—major gifts and planned gifts.

In this book new thinking about the critical intersection, the clear interdependence, between major gifts and planned giving is affirmed, and ways for every nonprofit to enter into an integrated major gifts and planned giving environment are outlined.

My career has been spent working in the major gifts area, but I am not an attorney and do not profess deep knowledge of the intricacies of planned giving vehicles and techniques. To address these matters I am pleased to introduce two Indiana University colleagues who are more than qualified. Alan M. Spears is executive director of the Office of Major Gifts and Planned Giving Services at the Indiana University Foundation (IUF), and Thomas W. Herbert is executive director of development and alumni programs at the Indiana University College of Arts and Sciences. Both are extraordinary professionals. Someone once said to me, "so you have six lawyers in your planned giving office," and I replied, "No, I have six professional fundraisers who happen to also have law degrees." Alan and Tom are two of those fundraisers who are also lawyers. As you read the pages that follow, you'll come to know both, too, as consummate fundraising professionals with enormous knowledge and command of the law as it pertains to planned giving options, knowledge they are able to convey in comfortable, easy-to-understand ways. What I hope can also be read between the lines is that each one cares more about the best interests of the prospect than he does about the techniques used to close major planned gifts.

Audience

Conducting a Successful Major Gifts and Planned Giving Program is written for two primary audiences. It is intended to serve as a constant companion for those who work actively in the areas of major gifts and planned giving in service to the nearly 775,000 registered nonprofit organizations in the United States, for the countless others who work in nonprofit groups that are not registered, and also for our friends and colleagues outside the United States who engage in these activities. Tax laws vary from country to country, but the principles of research, cultivation, soliciting, and stewardship detailed here do not, nor do the organizational ideas for implementing and marketing a program. Staff, board members, top leaders, and volunteers all can benefit from this book.

The second audience is students. This book is written to serve as a textbook too. Moreover, one of the aims of this book and of its companions in this series is to serve as an encouragement to the teaching of the subject of fundraising in educational settings across the country.

Overview of the Contents

Conducting a Successful Major Gifts and Planned Giving Program is divided into two parts. Part One has two sections. Section One opens with a look at the established patterns and principles that have guided major gift prospect identification, cultivation, solicitation, and stewardship over time. The six chapters in this section cover the latest research techniques and the securing of high-end lead gifts. The growing importance of major gifts to the success of any nonprofit is made crystal clear. And a new perspective is introduced. We contend that the major gifts effort and planned giving program are, or should be, inextricably joined and that every nonprofit can successfully engage in a major gifts program using planned giving techniques.

Chapter One is a step-by-step look at the processes involved in identifying, researching, and rating major gift prospects. Chapter Two follows closely on this theme by introducing a system to manage the cultivation and solicitation process and discussing in detail how to solicit major gifts.

Chapter Three climbs to the pinnacle of major gift fundraising and describes how to secure lead major gifts. It tells who makes these gifts and why, how to solicit these gifts successfully, and how to steward the donors after the gifts are closed. Rodney P. Kirsch, vice president for development and alumni relations at Penn State University, and Martin W. Shell, senior associate dean for external relations and chief operating officer at the Stanford Law School, authored this chapter.

The pivotal chapter in this book is Chapter Four. It describes first the inevitable link between the successful solicitation of major gifts and the artful use of planned giving techniques. These are not two separate and discrete functions. They are so closely tied they might be considered a single function. This chapter then shows how every nonprofit can establish at least an elementary planned giving program using bequest expectancies.

Chapter Five takes the development of a planned giving program to the next level. It describes how to involve the organization's governing board in the program and how to craft a gift acceptance policy. It then examines how to manage the program, develop a budget, and set goals. It concludes by discussing the resources needed to succeed in a planned giving program, including the use of consultants.

Now you're ready to market your program to prospects. Chapter Six tells you how, covering the use of print materials, seminars, Web sites, and more.

Section Two of Part One gives you a detailed look at the various planned giving options. It provides an understanding of each option and its potential uses and also discusses the tax considerations attached to each.

Chapter Seven covers outright giving vehicles—tangible personal property, real estate, securities, and life insurance.

Chapter Eight covers life income gifts—charitable gift annuities, charitable remainder trusts, and pooled income funds.

Chapter Nine covers estate gifts—bequests, qualified retirement programs, and U.S. Savings Bonds.

Chapter Ten introduces some advanced planned giving techniques—charitable lead trusts, gifts of business interests, gifts of intellectual property, donor advised funds, and supporting organizations.

The authors' text concludes at the end of Chapter Ten, but this book does not end there. Part Two presents a large number of resources. One of the aims of this book is to provide a visual example to support each of the major points addressed in the text. This is a feature common to all the books in this series. We believe it is important not only to tell readers how to do things but also to show them how. Too often, busy people do not really have time to begin a task with a blank piece of paper. They can be much more effective when they have a tool, a guide that can quickly and easily be adapted to their own needs. In this series, providing both the necessary information and the tools to use that information effectively has been one of our chief goals.

Acknowledgments

This book and the four previous books in this series did not get compiled and written by one person alone. It was a large team effort. Although space does not permit mentioning everyone who assisted, some must be named here for their essential contributions.

The board of directors of the Indiana University Foundation and Curtis R. Simic, its president, deserve special mention. The board approved this enterprise with the full understanding that it would require the time, energy, effort, and resources of the very busy people who are responsible for conducting a $100-million-a-year program on a daily basis. The board feels this series is worthwhile for what it promises to share with the larger nonprofit community, thus helping to fulfill the commitment of everyone at Indiana University to encourage best practices in fundraising whenever possible. Without board permission this series could not have been undertaken. We thank the board members for their support.

Three people did the laborious, tedious task of word processing, and constantly revising, the text. Beth Gillespie, who assists Alan, Bliss Isom, who assists Tom, and Trisha Moutardier, who keeps my office running.

This text, like all the books in the series, is resource rich. Again, a number of people contributed to this effort, and I must mention here two who were especially helpful as we gathered the many exhibits and resources that fill the following pages: Nancy Perazoli, gift planning officer at Drake University, and Jim Marshall, president, Endowment Development Services.

As always, I also thank the editorial team for the Nonprofit and Public Management Series at Jossey-Bass. We've now done five books together in the past thirty months. I think I talk to them more than I do to my own family.

Finally, and most important, thanks to my wife, Sandy, and children, Jason and Kerrye. Doing a project like this requires focus, discipline, determination, and sacrifice. The greatest sacrifice I have made is taking time away from my family. That ends here. The series is complete.

Bloomington, Indiana   Kent E. Dove
January 2002

THE AUTHORS

KENT E. DOVE is the author of five books that comprise the foundation of the Dove on Fundraising series, a collaborative effort between Dove, the Indiana University Foundation (IUF), and Jossey-Bass. In addition to the present book, they are *Conducting a Successful Capital Campaign* (2nd ed., Jossey-Bass, 1999), proclaimed as the leading guide to planning and implementing a capital campaign; *Conducting a Successful Fundraising Program* (Jossey-Bass, 2000); *Conducting a Successful Annual Giving Program* (with Jeffrey A. Lindauer and Carolyn P. Madvig, Jossey-Bass, 2001); and *Conducting a Successful Development Services Program* (with Vicky L. Martin, Kathy K. Wilson, Mary M. Bonk, and Sarah C. Beggs, Jossey-Bass, 2001).

Dove's career began shortly after his graduation from Indiana University when he joined the Indiana University Foundation staff as a publications writer for the University's 150th birthday campaign. He also directed annual giving programs for several of the university's professional schools. Over the next decade he moved to progressively more responsible positions at other institutions—director of annual giving, assistant director of development, director of development—leading to his appointment as vice president of development, coordinating the offices of development, alumni relations, public relations, and government relations. At thirty-four years of age, he was the youngest chief advancement officer at a major U.S. university at that time. Six years later he became counsel to and resident director of the then-largest capital campaign for a public university in America while also serving as a consultant to the largest campaign ever undertaken in Canada to that point in time.

Dove's career spans five decades, and he has been described as "the preeminent fundraising practitioner working in America today." He currently serves as vice president for development at the IUF, where he returned in 1993 to serve as executive director of capital campaigns to manage a six-year, $350 million endowment campaign for Indiana University–Bloomington, the largest campaign ever undertaken by the university. The campaign surpassed its goal in the summer of 1999, more than a year ahead of schedule, with $373 million raised. It concluded on December 31, 2000, with $504 million. Dove was named vice president for development in 1997, and in 1999, the Council for Advancement and Support of Education (CASE) recognized Indiana University with its highest award of excellence for overall fundraising performance for the period from 1993 to 1998. CASE accorded IU the same recognition in 2000 for its performance for the period from 1994 to 1999.

Dove previously held various educational fundraising management positions at Rice University, the University of California–Berkeley, Drake University, the University of Alabama, Northwestern University, the University of Tennessee Center for the Health Sciences, and West Virginia University.

From June 1989 to December 1993 he operated Kent E. Dove & Associates, a small firm designed and organized to offer highly personal, specialized attention to a select client base. His areas of interest are assessment of institutional development programs, institutional planning, market surveys, management and supervision of capital campaigns, staff and board training, and management of nonprofit organizations.

Dove has served three terms on the CASE Educational Fundraising Committee and one term on the board of directors of the National Society of Fund Raising Executives (now the Association of Fundraising Professionals, AFP). In 1986 he received the CASE Steuben Glass Apple Award for Outstanding Teaching.

ALAN M. SPEARS is the executive director of the Office of Major Gifts and Planned Giving Programs for the Indiana University Foundation, a position he has held since 1998. He holds B.A., M.A., and J.D. degrees from Indiana University. Prior to his arrival at the IUF, he managed the trust department of a major bank in his hometown of Richmond, Indiana. He is a member of the National Committee on Planned Giving, the Planned Giving Group of Indiana, and the Hoosier Hills Estate Planning Council.

THOMAS W. HERBERT joined the Indiana University Foundation in April of 1998 as associate director of Planned Giving Services. In July of 1999 he was promoted to director of Planned Giving Services, becoming at age thirty-two the youngest director of a planned giving program at a major research university in America. He is now executive director of development and alumni programs at the Indiana University College of Arts and Sciences. Prior to joining the foundation staff, he spent three years as a gift planning officer with Drake University in Des Moines, Iowa. While at Drake he served as the annual conference chair and president of the Mid-Iowa Planned Giving Council. He is currently a member of the National Committee on Planned Giving, the Planned Giving Group of Indiana, and the Hoosier Hills Estate Planning Council. Prior to entering the field of planned giving, he was an account supervisor with the advertising firm of Bently, Barnes and Lynn in Chicago. He holds a B.A. degree in history from Northwestern University and a J.D. degree from Chicago-Kent College of Law.

INTRODUCTION

In 1999, a total of $203.45 billion was contributed to U.S. charities. The great majority of this amount, eighty-five cents of each dollar, came from individuals, through both living donors and bequests. *Giving USA, 1999* (American Association of Fund-Raising Counsel [AAFRC] Trust for Philanthropy, 1999a), reporting on giving in 1998, listed nearly four hundred gifts of $1 million or more from individuals to every part of the nonprofit sector in 1998—religion, education, health care, human services, the arts, the environment, and more.

In *Giving USA, 2000* (AAFRC Trust for Philanthropy, 2000), which reports 1999 gifts, gone was the list of gifts of $1 million and higher. That list had grown too long. In its stead appears a list of gifts of $5 million and higher. One hundred and fifty such gifts are listed, the largest $2.4 billion. Also chronicled are four gifts of $100 million or more, eleven between $50 and $100 million, and eighteen between $25 and $50 million. Total giving grew to $190.16 billion in 1999, a 9 percent increase in one year alone. The 2001 edition of *Giving USA* again only lists gifts of $5 million and more. It includes 227 entries; two gifts of $5 billion are included.

As we enter the twenty-first century, nonprofit organizations are coming to a clear understanding that the key to their continued success is a strong major gifts program. Major gifts are defined as the top 10 to 20 percent of gifts received by an organization that result in 70 to 80 percent or more of the organization's fundraising revenues. In large organizations a major gift may be defined as $100,000 or more. For smaller nonprofits or those just getting started, major gifts may be defined as $2,500 to $5,000 or more. The definitions used by a majority of non-profits are between those two extremes. For these organizations the definition of a major gift will range from $5,000 to $100,000, with the exact figure depending on the particular circumstances of the nonprofit.

Fundraising is critical to virtually every nonprofit organization's ability to sustain itself at the highest level, and major gifts are indispensable to all highly successful development programs. At their highest levels, major gifts will often be a defining gift for both the donor and the recipient organization; such a major gift may represent the single largest gift ever made by the donor or received by the organization. All effective development programs have appropriate staff and budget resources dedicated to raising major gifts.

Major gifts do not have to be made with cash or as outright gifts. They can be structured over a defined period of time, such as a pledge period of five years, or be deferred, and they may employ a variety of assets, such as cash, securities, or real property.

They are generally made by older donors (see Chapter Four). Individuals go through life cycles as they age. In their early years they acquire. In the next phase they maintain and sustain what they have acquired. Eventually those who amass wealth come to a point where the children are educated and out of the house, the mortgage(s) are paid, and they have as many personal possessions as they desire. Now they begin to think about their mortality—how they want to distribute their amassed net worth, how they want to be remembered. It is at this point that large-scale charitable giving often enters their lives. A large majority, although not all, of major donors are forty-something or older.

A major gift is usually not the first gift the donor makes to a nonprofit. These gifts are the result of relationship building. Securing major gifts is a process stretching over time, unlike the straightforward one-on-one visit or call or written appeal resulting in an immediate response that characterizes most annual giving efforts.

When one thinks in terms of sheer size, it is easily understandable why major gifts carry such might. They can make a big difference in and of themselves, and they can also help a nonprofit absorb the cost of fundraising and balance it across the development effort. Unlike annual giving programs that can legitimately cost fifty to seventy-five cents or more on each dollar raised, major gift and planned giving programs can be maintained for pennies on the dollar raised.

Major gifts inspire effort on the part of nonprofit staff and instill confidence in other prospective donors. They raise the sights of other donors. They provide legacies for the people who make them. But, most of all, each major gift validates a nonprofit. It shows that people believe in the nonprofit's mission and that they believe in it deeply. Major gifts are the stuff of which both fundraising myth and fundamental change for the better are made. Their impact truly can be major.

PLANNING AND IMPLEMENTING YOUR MAJOR GIFTS AND PLANNED GIVING PROGRAM

TABLES, FIGURES, AND EXHIBITS IN PART ONE

Tables

Figure

Exhibits

IDENTIFYING, RESEARCHING, AND RATING MAJOR GIFT PROSPECTS

It is impossible to overemphasize the importance of major gifts to the success of any fundraising program. But major gifts do not just happen; someone makes them happen. They are the result of a well-thought-out plan that often involves years of strategic planning and many interactions between the donor and a number of organizational representatives. To obtain major gifts an organization must involve itself in the process of identifying, cultivating, and soliciting major donors. This opening chapter sets the stage for this process by describing some general characteristics of major donors and some common distinctive characteristics of women and people of color who make major gifts. It concludes with an in-depth look at the ways organizations can conduct productive prospect research.

Characteristics of Major Donors

Many major donors share certain traits. Although there will always be exceptions to the general patterns, here are some helpful guidelines.

Gibson (1999) identifies the following characteristics of lead gift donors (see Chapter Three): most are self-made, have a history of giving, have personal ties to the organizations they support, are sixty-five years of age or older, and are passionate about the causes they fund.

Major donors typically have strong values and deep beliefs, according to Campbell (1985). They believe in people and have great respect for knowledge. They often desire to provide others with opportunities they did not themselves have, to help the less fortunate, to improve the quality of life, to solve problems in society, and to preserve and perpetuate values of humankind, especially those values that they hold dearest. Major gift donors are frequently quite religious, have a deep belief in the free enterprise system, and are generally conservative.

They know someone in or something about the nonprofit organization they are supporting. Someone in the nonprofit or something about it has made an impression on them. They have come to believe in someone—the chief executive officer, a member of the board, a volunteer, a professional staff member—or in some part of what the organization stands for. Major donors have values that are comparable to the organization's, and they are probably already regular donors to the organization or to one that is similar. Major donors tend to stay with programs and activities that have been of interest to them over a long period.

Major donors usually view giving as an investment, and through such investments they desire to solve a problem or issue and to express themselves (to attain self-actualization). They also expect to see and understand the "return" on their investment. They will not seek but will usually accept (and in fact often expect) recognition, either for themselves or to honor or memorialize someone else. They have the resources to make a major gift, even though these resources may not be liquid at the moment. Their spouses and families are usually involved in the gift decision.

Seeking to quantify the traits that motivate wealthy people to make charitable contributions, Price and File (1994) studied more than eight hundred individuals and developed seven basic profiles (see Exhibit 1.1). The general perspective on philanthropy embodied in each profile suggests that different kinds of nonprofit organizations may take specific and unique approaches to fundraising, but does not fully account for human complexities, which can subtly or obviously make a particular individual fail to fit the profile absolutely.

Women's Expanding Role

According to Gwinn Scott ("Exploring Women and Philanthropy," 1998), for more than a century women philanthropists have been bringing dramatic change about in America, whether they were creating colleges, as Sophia Smith did in 1871 with a gift of $393,000, or working to save the planet, as Harriet Bullitt and Patsy Bullitt Collins did when they announced in 1994 that they would give most

EXHIBIT 1.1. THE SEVEN FACES OF PHILANTHROPY.

The Communitarians: Doing Good Makes Sense

Communitarians, the largest segment (26.3 percent), give because it makes good sense to do so. Communitarians are typically local business owners who find that service on boards and committees of local nonprofits can be good for business, because of the relationships that often develop in such settings. The other reason Communitarians believe active philanthropy makes good sense is that they help their own communities prosper by supporting local charities.

The Devout: Doing Good Is God's Will

The Devout are motivated to support nonprofits for religious reasons: they say they believe it is God's will for them to help others. Almost always members of a local church, which is part of a regional or national religious group, the Devout channel nearly all (94.6 percent) their giving to religious institutions. The Devout make up the second largest group (20.9 percent) of major donors.

The Investor: Doing Good Is Good Business

Investors are affluent individual donors who give with one eye on the nonprofit cause and one eye on personal tax and estate consequences. Investors calibrate their giving to take advantage of tax and estate benefits and therefore want to work with nonprofits that understand these concerns. To achieve their tax, estate, and philanthropic interests, Investors donate to a wide range of nonprofits and are the segment most likely to support umbrella nonprofits such as community foundations (22.5 percent). About 15.3 percent of major donors are Investors.

The Socialite: Doing Good Is Fun

Socialites consider social functions benefiting nonprofits an especially appealing way to help make a better world and have a good time doing it. Socialites are members of local social networks with which they interact to select nonprofits for support and to leverage in fundraising activities. They seek opportunities to create fundraisers and social events benefiting nonprofits and are less interested in participating in the day-to-day operations of the nonprofit or activities directed at constituents. Socialites, who tend to support the arts and education as well as religious nonprofits, make up 10.8 percent of major donors.

The Altruist: Doing Good Feels Right

Altruists embody the popular perception of the selfless donor—the donor who gives out of generosity and empathy to urgent causes and who modestly "wishes to remain anonymous." Altruists give because they believe it is a moral imperative and because it helps them grow as human beings or evolve spiritually. Altruists make giving decisions without the input of advisers and are not usually interested in active roles in the nonprofits they support. A far greater proportion of Altruists than any other group focus their philanthropy on social causes. Nine percent of major donors are Altruists.

EXHIBIT 1.1. THE SEVEN FACES OF PHILANTHROPY, Cont'd.

The Repayer: Doing Good in Return

Repayers tend to have been constituents first and donors second. A typical Repayer has personally benefited from some institution, often a school or medical center, and now supports that institution from a feeling of loyalty or obligation. Repayers concentrate their philanthropy on medical charities and educational institutions. Repayers are 10.2 percent of major donors.

The Dynast: Doing Good Is a Family Tradition

Unlike other segments, Dynasts typically inherit their wealth. The philanthropic motivation of Dynasts stems from their socialization. Giving is something their family has always stood for, and they believe it is expected of them to support nonprofits. However, younger Dynasts will seek out different philanthropies than their parents. Although Dynasts have been significant figures in philanthropy for some time, they now comprise 8.3 percent of major donors.

Source: Price and File, 1994, pp. 14–16.

of their $375 million fortune to fund environmental causes. In fact, women have long responded to a wide variety of needs and given to all kinds of institutions and organizations, and yet only recently have they begun to realize their full potential as philanthropists—and only recently have many nonprofits taken action to identify and cultivate women as key sources of financial support. Scott finds that women tend to prefer outright gifts over multiyear commitments, are driven more by causes than by competition between and among themselves, base their choices on where they can have the most impact, are moved to respond to cases that stir their hearts and evoke passion, are more likely than men to give anonymously or to name things for others, and give most readily to organizations that include women as board members, on staff, as volunteers in the life of and decision-making processes of the organization, and target programs toward women.

The role that women play in all phases of philanthropy is growing and will continue to grow. Women have long controlled the majority of wealth; they outlive men on average. Only in the past twenty-five years, however, have they emerged in large numbers as an active, independent force in philanthropy. Today's nonprofit boards are heavily populated, in some cases dominated, by women. Corporate boardrooms are seeing more and more women too. Women in growing numbers are rising to the topmost rungs of the corporate ladder, and they are populating the executive and staff ranks of nonprofit organizations and development programs as well.

Women are now giving big as well. For example, Miller and Nayyar (1998) report on a recent Princeton University study (Capek, 1997) showing that the number of women whose net worth exceeds $600,000 increased 28 percent between 1992 and 1995, and on research by INDEPENDENT SECTOR (1996) showing that average charitable contributions by women increased 26 percent between 1993 and 1995. The correlation here is not that because women now have more money they are giving big. Interest in the nonprofit organization's case and involvement with the organization remain the predominant reasons that both men and women make large gifts. The point is that women now have the ability and feel empowered to give big when such interest and involvement are present.

According to the Women's Philanthropy Institute (1999):

- 43 percent of Americans with assets greater than $500,000 are women.
- Women own 36 percent of U.S. businesses. Women are starting new businesses at three times the rate of men.
- Companies owned by women employ 35 percent more people than the Fortune 500 firms employ worldwide.
- 29 percent of working wives make more than their husbands.
- 74 percent of men and 71 percent of women invest in stock funds, and both sexes allocate 46 percent of their portfolios to equities.
- 78 percent of women business owners volunteer. Among all business owners, 56 percent volunteer.
- 88 percent of charitable dollars in the United States comes from individual donors.
- 71 percent of women and 65 percent of men gave to charity in 1995.
- Both men and women donate an average of 2 percent of their annual income to charity. In 1995, women's average annual gift was 93 percent as much as men's.
- $10 trillion will be passing to the baby boomers in the next thirty years, and women outlive men by seven years.
- In the first half of the twenty-first century, from 1998 to 2052, the intergenerational transfer is now estimated at $41 trillion.

Shaw and Taylor (1995) identify the "six C's" that typically motivate women: desire to change, create, connect, show commitment, collaborate, and celebrate.

Similarly, research shows that men typically give out of loyalty to the organization, support the traditions of the organization to which they give, are more likely to give before volunteering, and are generally comfortable talking about money. Women usually want their gift to make a difference. They are more likely to volunteer before giving, usually prefer private over public recognition, often prefer to work as part of a team toward a goal, and are generally uncomfortable talking about money.

Nonprofit organizations' donor education programs can help women become more comfortable with their potential or actual roles as philanthropists and also increase their sense of connection to the organization.

Giving by People of Color

Another frontier for mainstream philanthropy to address is giving by people of color. Little information is available in this area today, but organizations are paying increasing attention to it (see, for example, American Association of Fund-Raising Counsel, 1999b, a *Giving USA Update* devoted to this subject).

It is too early in the research cycle to make generalizations about the donor characteristics of people of color as a whole. Differences in income, length of time in the United States, extent of religious observance, and education are some of the factors that may contribute to differences between individuals within ethnic groups. In addition, different ethnic groups are likely to have a number of different characteristics. Here are some initial findings that reflect some of these differences.

In a study of ethnic philanthropy in the San Francisco Bay Area, Smith, Shue, Vest, and Villarreal (1994) note that sometimes, "subtle gift-giving rituals can signal appropriate degrees of honor and shame, reaffirm cultural precepts, and allow positive channels for 'face-saving' behavior. In such cultural contexts, giving a gift or being asked to give (particularly by a stranger) can easily create suspicion on the part of the potential donor or inadvertently create a situation in which the gift-giver perceives that he or she has been placed in a subservient position" (p. 7).

Berry (1999) notes that Native American cultures place a high value on sharing, exchange, reciprocity, and community involvement. Traditional give-away rituals can be key to building relationships and organizing social structures. Philanthropy, however, is often associated with receiving gifts from outside the community, reinforcing longstanding hierarchies of dependence on U.S. governmental programs.

The attitudes of many Latin immigrants toward philanthropy reflect the fact that in these individuals' home countries the government and the church—rather than nonprofit organizations—assume primary responsibility for dealing with social issues.

Researchers working in African American, Asian American, Latino, and Native American communities all report that addressing critical needs is the number one priority of donors. When crises occur in the family, extended family, or neighborhood, resources may be fully allocated there, and so they never reach the mainstream nonprofit sector. The U.S. Bureau of the Census (1999) describes almost 25 percent of African American households as "other families with children," in contrast to the category of married couples with children. This suggests that many African Americans are using their resources to care for children in their extended family or community at large—a generous act but not formal philanthropy.

The *Giving USA Update* mentioned earlier concludes that most minority communities have long traditions of charitable behavior and are strong supporters of the traditional nonprofit sector in the United States. Nevertheless, anecdotal and survey evidence suggests that many people of color are somewhat less involved in the formal nonprofit sector than their white counterparts. If people of color as a whole are to be included more fully in organizational philanthropy, the nonprofit sector must connect its fundraising practices to the giving patterns and cultures of a wide range of communities of color.

Identifying Your Prospects

Broad generalizations like those in the previous sections help a nonprofit focus on certain characteristics, qualities, and groupings and use them to inform the process of identifying major gift prospects. It is the role of prospect research to bring the organization's best prospects into clearer focus and identify and address their motivations for giving.

Proactive Research

With the world of nonprofit fundraising becoming more competitive every day, research has become more important than ever. "Prospect research is an important step in the process of increasing the philanthropic resources of an organization. We seek to identify the shared values between an organization and its prospective donors through the collection, organization, and presentation of significant information for development purposes," says Martha Murphy, director of prospect research at Valparaiso University (personal communication, Apr. 1996). *Proactive research* allows an organization to discover prospects and constituents who might have otherwise remained unknown to the organization. Methods for conducting proactive research are many and varied.

Screening the Database

One excellent way of identifying new prospects is to engage a vendor to perform electronic screening of your organization's existing database. Although electronic screening is not new, such services have become more sophisticated with the use of computer-based methods. According to Barth (1998), screening companies often use a combination of tools to provide data. One of these tools is *geodemographic screening*, which matches your organization's constituents with the characteristics of their neighborhoods and with models of consumer behavior in order to rate their probable interests, lifestyles, and philanthropic giving trends. Recognized companies that provide geodemographic screening include Grenzebach Glier, Marts & Lundy, and Econometrics.

Another tool is *asset screening*, which compares publicly reported stock holdings and property ownership to the names in your database. Companies that provide these sorts of data include Thomson Financial Wealth Indication (formerly CDA/Investnet), Prospect Identification Network (PIN), and Major Gifts Identification/Consulting (MaGIC).

It is understandable why larger organizations with sizable databases use such services, but even smaller organization that feel they know their donors well can find welcome surprises in the results of such screening. It takes only the discovery of one or two key prospects to make this process worthwhile.

Regardless of the type of demographic screening your organization uses, the data should enhance, not replace, its own information. Moreover, because such screening often increases the workloads of research staff, who must validate or negate the ratings for particular prospects, it is a good idea to ask questions like these before contracting with a screening vendor: What is the our purpose in using this service? What do we want to achieve? How will the results be processed? How much data can we process internally?

Once a round of prospect identification research has been completed, the development team (fundraisers, researchers, and others, including key volunteers) should review the results to determine whether all the needed information is there and which prospects actually belong in the major gift prospect pool. Prospects who do not belong can then be deleted from the list early in the review process, and their names given to the annual giving program instead.

Reviewing Print Media

Reviewing newspapers, magazines, and other print media and clipping pertinent articles is a beneficial, albeit time consuming, method of proactive prospect identification. Using this method usually requires familiarity with the names of existing prospects and close proximity to a computer with access to the organization's database so the researcher can look up names as they are found to determine whether the individuals are constituents of the organization. Some scanning can be done through Internet sites housing files of newspapers and other periodicals. However, experienced researchers feel that this method fails to uncover much valuable information. For those who are nevertheless inclined to review print media via the Internet, a few excellent sites for newspapers and periodicals are

American Journalism Review NewsLink: *http://www.ajr.org*

Dow Jones Interactive: *http://nrstg1s.dnjr.com*

Folio: The Magazine for Magazine Management: *http://www.foliomag.com*

Gebbie Press: *http://www.gebbieinc.com*

MagPortal: *http://magportal.com*

NewsDirectory: Newspapers and Media: *http://newsdirectory.com*

Using Push Technology

Push technology is a powerful proactive research tool that every nonprofit should consider using. It supplies you with information culled from the Internet in areas that you specify. You choose an Internet site (or several sites) that offer this service and establish the parameters (key words) for the kind of information you are seeking (see Resource 1). These sites usually require users to register, but the service is often free. Once you have determined the keywords you are interested in (such as the name of your organization, the name of an individual or corporation, and so forth), the site you are using will "push" information containing your keywords to you either via e-mail or within the site itself. Not all the information you receive will be useful, but many new prospects can be found using this technology. Push technology also helps you stay current with prospects your organization is already cultivating. A few excellent sites to use for this purpose are

http://www.10kwizard.com

http://www.freedgar.com

http://www.newsalert.com

Reactive Research

Reactive research is just what its name suggests—reacting to a request for information. Even though proactive research is more fun, especially when that special prospect is discovered who had previously gone unnoticed, the reality of most prospect research is responding to requests from development staff or key volunteers for further information on known prospects. The following sections discuss approaches to acquiring information about both new and known prospects' ability and inclination to give.

Estimating an Individual's Giving Potential

Once prospects are identified, the next step is to conduct in-house financial ratings. These ratings address prospects' *potential* to give (the range in which they would give if the organization were their number one philanthropic cause and they wanted to make the biggest gift of their lives) and their *probable* gift size (the gift they could pledge, without much solicitation, within the next eighteen months and payable over the next three to five years).

When giving potential is being considered, any information known to the organization about an individual's financial circumstances should play a part. Factors to be considered include accumulated or inherited wealth; stock and bond holdings; real and personal property; full or part ownership in business enterprises; access to family or other corporations, foundations, or trusts; annual income level; and participation on for-profit and nonprofit boards.

There are no absolute rules for determining how much an individual may be capable of giving on the basis of accumulated assets and income, but a useful framework is shown in Table 1.1. These guidelines should be used only as a starting point for organizational thinking about an individual's potential to make charitable gifts. Remember, at this point the organization is rating potential to give, not inclination to do so; measurements of inclination tend to be less precise and more subjective. Inclination factors to be considered include the prospect's level of interest as well as number of years of giving to the organization, involvement with the organization, and cumulative previous giving.

TABLE 1.1. GIFT-GIVING POTENTIAL.

Income Level	Assets Accumulated	Gift Rating
$2,500,000 or more	$250,000,000 or more	$60,000,000 or higher
2,500,000 or more	150,000,000–250,000,000	40,000,000–60,000,000
2,500,000 or more	100,000,000–150,000,000	25,000,000–40,000,000
2,500,000 or more	50,000,000–100,000,000	10,000,000–25,000,000
2,500,000 or more	25,000,000–50,000,000	5,000,000–10,000,000
2,500,000 or less	20,000,000–25,000,000	2,500,000–5,000,000
2,000,000 or less	10,000,000–20,000,000	1,000,000–2,500,000
1,000,000 or less	7,500,000–10,000,000	500,000–1,000,000
500,000–1,000,000	5,000,000–7,500,000	250,000–500,000
100,000–500,000	2,500,000–5,000,000	100,000–250,000
100,000–250,000	1,000,000–2,500,000	50,000–100,000
less than 100,000	less than 1,000,000	10,000–25,000

Methods of Rating and Screening

Susan Ruderman (2000), vice president of Veritas Information Services, explains that *peer screening* is a system using volunteers to indicate what information (financial and biographical) they know about prospects.

These evaluation sessions have a dual goal:

- To uncover fresh information about important prospects (first priority) and about all other prospects (second priority)
- To promote the cultivation and involvement of the volunteer evaluators who participate in the process

Other benefits may also accrue. For example, these sessions are often a valuable tool in staff training. They are a way of identifying suitable solicitors, they can raise the sights of volunteers who eventually will become donors, and they provide an opportunity to educate participants about the campaign.

During any rating and screening session conducted by or with volunteer evaluators, the sole criterion should be what a donor can do given his or her personal circumstances. Staff members should not participate in this evaluation other than to explain the purpose of the session, keep the session moving, and clarify and answer questions about form and procedure. Four rating session procedures are commonly used:

1. *Group discussion ratings.* Evaluators engage in roundtable discussion until they agree on a rating. A group leader should conduct this session. A professional staff member should be present to record observations but should not make any comments that could influence the ratings. This is the best method of evaluation, but its success depends on the group leader's ability to initiate discussion and on the group's willingness to participate openly and forthrightly as well as on the evaluators' ability to make informed ratings.

2. *Group/individual ratings.* Each member of the group is given a rating book and works individually, without discussion, to rate the prospects and offer appropriate written comments. A professional staff member collects the evaluations at the end of the rating session and tabulates the information after the meeting. The major disadvantage here is that the evaluators do not have the opportunity to exchange ideas or information. The advantage is that the ratings are more confidential, and this may lead the evaluators to provide more accurate (higher) evaluations as well as more pointed and useful comments. The success of this kind of session often depends on getting someone who is well known and well connected in the community to serve as host or hostess.

3. *Individual/one-to-one ratings.* A professional staff member meets individually with volunteer evaluators and goes through the prospect list with each one verbally, recording his or her pertinent comments about each prospect on an evaluation form. The advantage to this process is that the evaluator can feel completely assured of confidentiality: no one else will hear the comments or know the evaluator's personal feelings about the prospect. The disadvantage is that each evaluation is limited to the extent of the individual evaluator's knowledge. Moreover, the evaluator may not know a number of the prospects well enough to rate them. It will then be necessary to hold additional rating sessions with other evaluators.

4. *Individual/solitary ratings.* Evaluators are given a list of prospects and rating instructions and are left on their own. The evaluations are either picked up or mailed back by a mutually agreed-upon date. This procedure should be used only in special circumstances. Its advantage is that it gives the evaluator time to reflect on and consider the ratings and comments; properly used, it generally leads to very thoughtful, thorough evaluations. Its disadvantage is that individuals often put off doing the evaluations and thereby stall the process.

No matter which procedure is used, prospect evaluations should be done by knowledgeable individuals. Secondhand and hearsay information is of little or no value; speculation is just that. The best evaluators tend to be bankers, lawyers, investment counselors, financial planners, insurance executives, the socially prominent, and those actively involved in organized philanthropy in communities with organized efforts.

The evaluation of individual prospects should continue until an adequate database is established. For each prospect, many organizations acquire at least three gift valuations, preferably all falling within a fairly narrow range (say, $10,000, $15,000, and $12,000), before assuming that the prospect's rating has been validated. The entire process must be conducted with a high level of sensitivity for individual confidentiality. Rating sessions must be confidential, and raters' names and comments must not be revealed except on a need-to-know basis among the specific development officers working most closely with the prospects. Many times those who make the best raters will find themselves facing prospect names that they cannot discuss without potential or real conflicts of interest. Discussions and ratings that involve such real or potential conflicts of interest, that strain personal discretion or discernment, or that raise individual ethical concerns should be assiduously avoided at every point in this process. No one should be asked to do anything that gives him or her an uneasy feeling.

Ruderman (2000) observes that "regardless of the type of screening you conduct, remember that data is only data. Nothing replaces the personal contact and relationship with a prospect. Capacity, either real or imagined, is no substitute for inclination, although wealth and its identification are obvious prerequisites for a major gift. Screening may, however, help you decide where best to direct limited cultivation resources" (p. 12).

Keeping Evaluation Sessions Manageable

It is extremely important to keep evaluation sessions manageable from the standpoint of the volunteers. It can be counterproductive if too many prospects are expected to be evaluated in one sitting. No evaluation session should be scheduled to last more than one and a half hours. How many prospects can be rated in ninety minutes? The answer depends on the rating method being used, the level of the prospects being evaluated, and the ability of the evaluators. Some evaluators, working alone, can rate as many as 500 prospects in one session, whereas a group discussion may cover only 100 to 150 prospects. When evaluators are asked to rate too many prospects or when the session is too long, the level of concentration will drop off toward the end. Therefore it is generally recommended that staff keep all prospect lists as short as possible and if need be do multiple sessions of ninety minutes or less.

Storing the Information

The organization should retain the information from the rating sessions, storing it in a secure place. This confidential file should include the following information for each prospect:

- Prospect name
- Rater's name
- Suggested potential gift level
- Other rater comments
- Rater's ability to help with the cultivation and solicitation process

The ratings are also entered into the prospects' records and into the organization's database.

The LAI Approach to Researching Individuals

The Fund Raising School (1995) identifies the fundamental areas of research as linkage, ability, and interest, otherwise known as the LAI principle.

Linkage

Linkage concerns the ways the prospect is connected to your organization. Is he or she a board member, graduate, donor, volunteer, parent, service user, or member? In determining linkage, the first place you should look is within the organization itself, checking existing files and records for any contact information, and examining the database for a record of giving to the organization. However, a linkage may also exist in the form of a relationship with someone else already associated with the organization: that is, the organization may have a link to the prospect through a board member, volunteer, professor, and so forth.

Ability

This area of research asks whether the prospect has the *ability* to make a financial contribution and whether his or her current life circumstance permits or prohibits a contribution at this point in time. Besides using volunteer raters, as we have already discussed, organizations have the option of employing other methods of estimating major gifts.

There are two schools of thought with regard to estimating the net worth of an individual: for and against. Most organizations do not attempt to estimate an individual's net worth simply because it is impossible to know all the details of a prospect's assets and liabilities short of the prospect's telling you. However, some research offices do try to work out formulas to arrive at a ball park figure from which they can assume gift capacity. The University of Virginia, through much trial and error, has set the following formula for estimating a prospect's net worth and giving capacity (see Resource 2).

Total real estate holdings × 3 = estimated net worth
3 percent of estimated net worth = estimated giving capacity

The University of British Columbia suggests several methods for estimating a potential major gift; which one you use depends on the quality and quantity of information you have available:

1. 1 to 5 percent of net worth.
2. 20 × level of consistent annual giving.
3. 10 × largest annual gift.
4. 10 percent of annual income (2 percent per year for five years).
5. 1 to 4 percent of stock worth $1–$499,999; 5 to 9 percent of stock worth $500,000–$999,000; and 10 percent of stock worth $1 million or more.
6. "Standard formula": 5 × the total of four annual gifts to charities in the community (including your organization).

EXHIBIT 1.2. USEFUL BOOKMARKS
FOR DOING ON-LINE PROSPECT RESEARCH, Cont'd.

Outstanding Americans: *http://www.oyaawards.com*

LawOffice.com—Over One Million Lawyers and Information About the Law: *http://www.lawoffice.com*

General Information Sites

The Careful Donor: *http://donors.philanthropy.com*

Chambers of Commerce and Other Related Associations on the Internet: *http://www.indychamber.com/chambers.htm*

Council for Advancement and Support of Education Home Page: *http://www.case.org*

Guide to Understanding Financials: *http://www.ibm.com/FinancialGuide*

Indiana University Libraries Online Resources: *http://www.indiana.edu/~libfind*

KPMG Knowledge Management: *http://kpmg.interact.nl/publication/survey.html*

Lexis-Nexis Academic Universe: *http://web.lexis-nexis.com/universe*

Librarians' Index to the Internet: *http://sunsite.berkeley.edu/InternetIndex*

Primary Source Media: City Directories Online: *http://www.citydirectories.psmedia.com/index.html*

Prospect Research Online: *http://www.rpbooks.com*

Travelocity—Online Airfares, Hotel and Car Reservations: *http://www.travelocity.com*

TravelWeb: Hotel and Flight Reservations: *http://www.travelweb.com*

University of Virginia Prospect Research: *http://www.people.virginia.edu/~dev-pros/index.html*

Yahoo! Real Estate—Home Values: *http://realestate.yahoo.com/realestate/homevalues*

Search Engines

Alta Vista: *http://altavista.digital.com*

Dogpile: *http://www.dogpile.com*

Google: *http://www.google.com*

Source: Reprinted with the permission of Vicky L. Martin.

When Do You Stop Looking?

With the vast of amount of data readily available, much of it at the push of a button, it is easy to get caught up in an endless cycle of searching. Sometimes it is difficult to stop the search, especially if there is not much information about the prospect to be found. The information freeway beckons, teasing with the possibility that if the search continues it will eventually yield that one piece of information so desperately needed. This is a dangerous route to follow; it can easily make the research effort counterproductive. It is critical that those in the organization define the necessary levels of research. For example, on the one hand a brief profile might be defined as needing only address, phone, and business information verification, thus eliminating the need for extensive searching through various databases. On the other hand a request for an in-depth profile might justify time spent searching through various Web sites and funds expended on fee-based services, especially if the prospect has been identified as having major gift potential and the additional information is needed in order to develop an informed strategy for solicitation. Even then, however, the organization must establish research guidelines, and researchers must use self-discipline to avoid getting caught up in an endless cycle of searching and data gathering.

Sorting Through and Analyzing the Data

One outcome of the research should be a prospect profile. The format of the profile is not as important as the content. The following standard information, if it is available, should be included in every profile:

- Name, nickname
- Home address (all addresses if the prospect has multiple residences)
- Home phone (for all residences)
- Cell phone number(s)
- Fax number(s) (for all residences)
- Pager number
- E-mail address (home and business)
- Business title, address, and phone number
- Name of secretary or assistant
- Date and place of birth
- Education (secondary and higher, along with academic major)
- Academic awards and achievements
- Employment history
- Marital status
- Spouse's name
- Spouse's education
- Spouse's business affiliation
- Number, names, and ages of children
- Family connection to the organization
- Family connections to other organizations
- Honors and achievements

- Clubs and organizations
- Political affiliation
- Religious affiliation
- Personal interests
- Net salary
- Stock holdings
- Estimated net worth
- Estimated giving ability
- Directorships
- Family foundations
- Favorite charities
- Gift record
- Name of attorney
- Name of banker
- Names of close friends

A good rule of thumb when preparing a profile is to be sure to supply the sources for all information. Include also the name of the preparer, the date the profile was completed, and for whom it was completed. This is beneficial information, especially if there are multiple requests for information on the same prospect (see Resource 4).

Prospect research has become highly sophisticated over the years. It is no longer sufficient simply to type up a biographical profile of a prospect. It has become necessary for a researcher to be strategic: to analyze all the pieces of information available on a prospect, not only developing a comprehensive profile of an individual of the sort just outlined but also putting forth a strategy for involving the prospect in the life of the organization. There are still many nonprofits that do not use research findings in strategy development, but those that do reap many benefits. In a complete, well-prepared strategy, the information gleaned through the research effort (paper knowledge) is paired with that of the fundraiser (personal knowledge). An involvement strategy should contain this information:

- Prospect name
- Business title
- Address
- Telephone
- Strategy type (cultivation, solicitation, stewardship)
- Name of the volunteer who will implement the strategy
- Expected solicitation date
- Summary of analysis and objectives (action plan)

Researching Corporations and Foundations

Researching public companies has never been easier, thanks to the Internet. Most public companies have their own Web sites, and even better, all the tax forms that public companies are required to file by the Securities and Exchange Commission (SEC) are virtually free and easily accessible through the Web site known as EDGAR (*http://www.sec.gov/cgi-bin/srch-edgar*). The information contained in these SEC documents is invaluable in that it gives a much truer picture of a company's status than the annual corporate reports published for the general public.

To make the best use of this wealth of information, those who are researching public companies would do well to seek training in reading financial statements. One good resource for independent study is the "Guide to Understanding Financials," published by International Business Machines (IBM) and available on-line (*http://www.ibm.com/investor/financialguide*). Many of the tools needed to understand complex financial statements can be found in this guide. Other sources of training include consultations with a stock broker or financial analyst and the business schools of colleges or universities. Dun & Bradstreet periodically offers workshops in understanding financial statements.

Although the information available on public companies through the SEC is rich in detail, it is not the only place where good prospect research can be done. There are also many excellent books, CD-ROMs, and on-line resources available to aid in corporate research. A few favorites are listed here:

Books

> *The Corporate Directory of U.S. Public Companies*
>
> *Corporate Giving Directory*
>
> *Corporate Giving Yellow Pages*
>
> *Directory of Corporate Affiliations/U.S. Public*
>
> *Million Dollar Directory*
>
> *National Directory of Corporate Giving*
>
> *International Directory of Company Histories*
>
> *Standard & Poor's Register of Corporations, Directors and Executives*

CD-ROMs

> *Corporate Affiliations Plus*
>
> *Standard & Poor's Corporations On Disk*

Fee-Based Databases

Bloomberg

Dow Jones Interactive: *http://nrstg1s.dnjr.com*

Global Access, PRIMARK: *http://www.primark.com/ga*

Hoover's Online: *http://www.hoovers.com*

Prospect Research Online (PRO): *http://www.rpbooks.com*

Free Internet Sites

Companies Online: *http://www.companiesonline.com*

Business Credit USA: *http://www.businesscreditusa.com*

Hoover's Online: *http://www.hoovers.com*

EDGAR: *http://www.edgar-online.com/overview.asp*

Corporate Information: *http://www.corporateinformation.com*

Thomas Register of American Manufacturers: *http://www.thomasregister.com*

Bank Online: *http://www.bankonline.com/fidirectory.htm*

Yahoo!: *http://dir.yahoo.com/business/companies*

American Journalism Review NewsLink: *http://www.ajr.org*

Insider Trader: *http://www.insidertrader.com*

This list is by no means comprehensive, but it does contain some of the more popular tools for conducting research on public companies.

Researching private companies is not nearly as easy because they are not required to file with the SEC. However, there are still several good resources to consult (including some of the same ones useful for public companies):

Books

Directory of Corporate Affiliation, U.S. Private Companies

Million Dollar Directory

Manufacturers Directories

Standard & Poor's Register of Corporations, Directors and Executives

Ward's Private Company Profiles

Internet

Companies Online: *http://www.companiesonline.com*

Business Credit USA: *http://www.businesscreditusa.com*

Hoover's Online: *http://www.hoovers.com*

Corporate Information: *http://www.corporateinformation.com*

Thomas Register of American Manufacturers: *http://www.thomasregister.com*

Yahoo!: *http://dir.yahoo.com/business/companies*

American Journalism Review NewsLink: *http://www.ajr.org*

When the books and databases don't seem to offer much insight into a private company, other excellent resources include

Secretary of State, Corporation Division: all companies, public or private, must register with this governmental division in any state where they conduct business. The information to be found here is minimal but usually includes the address, telephone, and principal officers.

Chambers of Commerce: *http://www.worldchambers.com/frnote.shtml*

Finally, always try to determine whether the company, public or private, has its own Web site. To search for company Web sites visit *http://www.websense.com/locator.cfm*.

As in conducting research on individuals, at some point the researcher needs to make the decision to stop searching and to start analyzing the data and compiling it into a useful report.

Along with the data gleaned from the tools listed here and any others that may have been discovered along the way, there are additional pieces of information that nonprofits should search out in order to get a clear picture of a company's likelihood to give. Look at obligations to other nonprofit organizations. More important, closely study current interests and funding trends. In determining how much to ask for, think of the company as also representing sources of other income. A corporation may have five or six channels of potential funding (corporate contributions; a corporate foundation; a matching gift program; the departments of research and development, marketing, and advertising; and the discretionary budget of the executive office).

Research on corporate prospects needs to address four vital questions:

1. How financially healthy is the business?
2. What are its current products, and what are its interests in your organization?
3. What existing relationships could be used for moving the prospect to the next step of cultivation or solicitation?
4. How has the corporation supported your organization in the past, and why would it want to give support again?

The following basic information should be gathered on each corporate prospect:

- Full name and correct address
- Corporate assets
- Type of business
- Names of corporate officers and directors
- Names of corporate foundation officers (if a foundation exists)
- Sales volume
- Previous giving record
- Charitable giving decision-making process
- Gifts to other nonprofit organizations (more difficult to determine when there is no corporate foundation)
- Connections with your organization (educational institutions can seek alumni employed by the corporation, hospitals might identify past patients the corporation employs, and so forth)
- History of corporation dealings with your organization
- Local subsidiaries and the names of their officers
- Corporate gift committee names, connections, and kindred interests

From the standpoint of corporate and foundation relations, it is equally important to learn something about company products, research and development, and future marketing plans. An annual report can supply some of this information. Other possible sources are the organization's office of sponsored research (if it has one), which may be aware of research and development interests in the corporation. Philanthropic publications such as *Taft Giving Watch* and *Philanthropic Digest* list corporate contributions, which can be reviewed for trends in grants for research and development. In addition, several databases list awards of government contracts. Finally, newspapers and journals can provide a glimpse of the future. Articles in such magazines as *Fortune* and *Forbes* may provide a vision of the direction in which the corporate prospect is moving. Local newspapers are an equally valuable resource.

Working with the appropriate in-house staff, the researcher needs to expand on the basic questions about relationships with corporate prospects. Have any corporate employees benefited from your organization? Do any of your organization's staff serve on the corporation's advisory board or science advisory panel? Does the corporation in any way rely on your organization for services? If the organization has received previous funding from the corporation or from the corporate foundation, what are the details of that funding? Enlightened corporate self-interest is the basis of these relationships on the company's part, and so it is important to understand these components in planning an approach. Very often quid pro quo considerations (stockholder concerns, for example) determine the granting policies of national corporations. Moreover, except for a few national corporations and corporate foundations, this category of prospects has become more specialized in recent years. Corporations tend to lend their financial support in areas where they have plant operations and particularly headquarters. Corporations will also consider support when they have subsidiaries located in the service area of the nonprofit organization.

Besides major corporations, other sources for corporate support are local independent businesses, the organization's vendors, and businesses that are owned by or that employ people affiliated with the organization, whatever these businesses' geographical locations. In dealing with any major gift prospect, but especially a corporate or foundation prospect, an organization should never extend its boundaries beyond the circle represented by its volunteer leaders. This is a cardinal rule, but one that is often broken.

Foundations are the easiest of prospects to research in that they usually have specific funding interests that are known or that can easily be determined by potential applicants. For the most part these interests are dictated by policy and by the foundation's granting history. The information to be sought is basically the same as that needed for understanding a corporation, and it should include the following data about the foundation:

- Full, correct name.
- Precise street address and telephone number.
- Officers' or directors' names and professional connections.
- Brief historical sketch (when the foundation was created, by whom, and for what purpose).
- Current assets.
- Recent grant amounts by year and individual recipient.
- Decision-making process.
- Pattern of giving (to what kinds of organizations and for what programs, with specific examples).
- Best contact for your organization (the person to visit or send a proposal to).
- Connections with your organization.
- History of your organization's contacts with the foundation.
- Copy of a recent PF 990 tax form filed by the foundation, with a listing of income and grants made (copies of these filings are available by mail, fax, and e-mail through the Associates Program of The Foundation Center, a fee-based service. Recently, many PF 990s have become available via the Guidestar Web site for free (*http://www.guidestar.org*).

- Giving guidelines and any statements of interest published by the foundation
- Most recent annual report

In addition to the resources available through The Foundation Center, several other excellent sources of information exist. Four of the most widely used comprehensive references are

Prospector's Choice (CD-ROM)

FC [The Foundation Center] *Search* (CD-ROM)

The Foundation Directory (book)

Guidestar (Internet: *http://www.guidestar.org*)

These, along with the Associates Program of The Foundation Center, provide information about foundations' financial assets, interests, giving focus, grants to organizations, and requirements for submitting proposals. One valuable component of these references is their indexing of information according to a foundation's giving interests.

Many of these materials are also available on Dialog—an online-based information service that provides comprehensive sources of information to professionals. Their database includes files critical to fundraising like *The Foundation Directory* and *Grants Index*.

The best foundation prospects for a nonprofit organization are those geographically nearby; the likelihood of investment is much greater when the foundation is in the organization's local area, state, or region. A foundation is also more likely to support an organization when the foundation's philosophy is similar to that of the organization. It is important that there be a match between the organization's interests and the foundation's. If individuals associated with the foundation are directly or indirectly affiliated with the organization, and especially if they are on the organization's board, the chances are enhanced that it will receive favorable consideration. Any review of foundations requires a systematic study of all sources to locate those foundations that might have matching interests.

Remember to talk to members of your board and others close to the organization to see whether they can help establish links with the foundation. It is extremely important that the effort to secure gifts from foundations be focused on those foundations that are most likely to support the organization. In many instances the great majority of foundations will not be interested in a particular program, and it makes no sense to pursue those.

Researching Likely Donors for Projects

Many times, research is used to assist fundraising staff in developing a list of potential individual, corporate, or foundation donors to a particular project or program. This can be a fairly time consuming task if not approached correctly. The researcher can simplify the task by having a thorough conversation with the requestor. In order to provide the best results possible, the researcher needs this information:

- Copy of the business plan for the project or a program description.
- Appropriate keywords for the project; requestor and researcher should agree on these words. (Resource 1 lists typical key words.)
- Amount of funding the requestor is seeking.
- Other funding already obtained (amount and funder).

Once equipped with this information, the researcher has a choice of several databases that allow keyword searching for funding opportunities. A few favorite databases are

Prospector's Choice (CD-ROM)

FC [The Foundation Center] *Search* (CD-ROM)

Sponsored Programs Information Network (SPIN)

COS [Community of Science] *Funding Opportunities*

Prospect research and rating is vital to gaining an understanding of the prospective donor and his or her interests and capabilities. It is also essential to developing a cultivation pattern designed to lead to a successful solicitation of a major gift, the topic addressed in Chapter Two.

CULTIVATING AND SOLICITING MAJOR GIFTS

Cultivation leading to solicitation is a continuous process. It often takes several steps over a period anywhere from a few months to several years to obtain a major gift from a prospect. Experienced major gifts officers say that it now takes, on average, twenty-four to thirty months to cultivate and negotiate major gifts successfully. Because the process is often long and sometimes complex, nonprofit organizations should establish a systematic framework to monitor and prompt prospect cultivation and solicitation activity. Chapter Two first addresses developing an approach to managing prospects systematically and then discusses the techniques of effective cultivation and solicitation that lead to the securing of major gifts.

Developing a Prospect Management System

Bringing in major gifts is a matter of hard work, imagination, and good taste. Certainly major gifts occasionally come from unexpected sources, but usually many cultivation contacts by staff or volunteers are necessary to bring prospects to the point of making major gifts. Therefore the pursuit of the extraordinary gift should be a well-planned, properly funded, adequately staffed part of any fundraising effort.

Objectives of Prospect Management

Prospect management is a systematic approach to identifying and tracking major gift prospects. Prospect management systems—whether they use large and complex databases, straightforward word processing programs, manual systems, or a combination of all these methods—rely on and encourage careful planning and follow-through. When it systematically records vital information on major gift candidates and donors, an organization knows at any given time who its best prospects are and where it stands in relation to them.

According to Baxter (1987), today's use of detailed prospect management has been "made possible by the widespread use of technology in fundraising." This technology "has revolutionized gift processing, acknowledgment, and record keeping," allowing nonprofit organizations to focus in great detail "on individuals and organizations that hold the most promise for major gifts."

Baxter states:

A well-designed and -maintained prospect management system can improve major gift fundraising and help an organization to improve the effectiveness of its development program. It can provide detail on a single prospect, select all prospects with a common trait, or give an overall view of a campaign's progress.

The objectives of most tracking systems are:

- To manage effectively cultivation and solicitation processes that are highly individualized
- To identify and quantify measures of progress in the cultivation and solicitation process
- To maintain momentum over long periods of time
- To provide information that will educate, motivate, and reward volunteers and staff involved in the major gifts effort
- To focus attention on top prospects
- To facilitate regular reporting to volunteers and staff
- To develop a written history of prospect cultivation that will provide an institutional memory of communications with major supporters

Choosing Technologies

When it comes to selecting equipment and programs for a prospect management system, Baxter (1987) points out that the selection criteria include

Size of major prospect pool, size of development staff, complexity of fundraising program, existing computer capability, and budget. Systems developed for prospect management need not be complex, but they should accommodate all of the data needed for identifying, assigning, and tracking major prospects. . . . An institution should consider its information needs, the size of its file, and its hardware and software. If the system is already in place in the office—both computer (hardware) and programs (software)—this will have an effect on the data and number of records that can be tracked. Ideally, the first two considerations—needs and size—should determine the kind of equipment selected.

Lange and Hunsaker (1999) reinforce these points, noting that

In setting up a system, an institution should plan for the kinds of routine reports needed as well as for the data it will need to call up at any given moment. Plan for growth, and, if possible, select a system that is flexible enough to allow for modifications and newly identified information needs. Include all important data fields, but do not clutter the system with unnecessary data. Remember, the more fields in the system, the more maintenance required. An elaborate system that has outdated information or empty data fields is almost worse than no system at all.

Lange and Hunsaker describe some of the more traditional systems, observing that "organizations have three main options when they select a system: homegrown systems, comprehensive systems, and off-the-shelf modules."

The homegrown option is traditionally adopted by smaller shops, which generally have less complex prospect tracking needs than the larger nonprofits, limited budgets, and little or no staff. They can adequately track and maintain their prospect pools working with a PC-based word processor, spreadsheet, and database.

Several vendors provide the comprehensive systems that typically serve larger, more complex organizations. These systems have modules and screens available for storing, manipulating, and reporting volumes of data. The information handled by the various modules ranges from the basic biographical data, to major gift prospecting, to very sophisticated gift processing, which is becoming more critical due to higher and stricter reporting standards. Most comprehensive systems allow the information systems staff to build interfaces to other applications to further tailor information to the user's needs.

Then there are a variety of off-the-shelf modules. Many larger organizations use these as stand-alone prospect management and tracking systems, which can interface with a homegrown or comprehensive system. Off-the-shelf systems usually have the ability to store prospect call reports and reminders, track wealth indicators, and document next steps. However, these systems do not always have the flexibility needed to add site-specific implementations.

Baxter (1987) notes that "most development software vendors have prospect management modules. If one of these meets an institution's specifications for data, file size, and system cost, it will save developing a system from scratch."

Lange and Hunsaker (1999) also spell out the issues in using existing computer systems to perform prospect management and tracking.

> If an institution's system is flexible, a means of flagging major prospects and the addition of a few fields may be all that is needed. However, it is not always feasible for institutions with very large master databases to add the prospect management feature, since it focuses on such a small percentage of the file. Since it is a system tailored to an institution, the most important consideration is to provide the information that is essential to its development program. This will vary from institution to institution and may mean simply an alphabetical list of major prospects and a few details about them, something that can be managed easily on a word-processing system. If, on the other hand, it is important to be able to select prospects by geographic region, by staff or volunteer assignment, by rating, gift target or a combination of elements, a more complex system will be required.

Finally, though fundraising principles often remain fairly constant, technologies are continually changing. One of today's evolving opportunities is to outsource the technological side of prospect management to application service providers (ASPs). For those with limited budgets, staff, or technology expertise, this is becoming an attractive option.

Data Elements

Baxter (1987) emphasizes that for the prospect management system to be a useful tool, prospect information must constantly be relayed to the person or department responsible for data entry and system maintenance. This means that staff and volunteers must document all contact between the organization and major gift prospects and forward the information to the system, submitting any additions or deletions, and keeping the system manager apprised of changes in a prospect's status. Regular reports from the system can identify any information gaps or highlight errors.

Baxter suggests that prospect management systems be set up to handle the following data elements. These are of course suggestions rather than hard-and-fast requirements, because each organization has unique characteristics that will influence its system design.

Data Element	*Comments*
Identification	If possible, should be consistent with master file ID number.
Name	Prefix (title), last, first, middle, suffix.
Address, phone	Can allow for home, business, second home, and so on, but must keep in sync with master file.
Title	Business or professional position.
Salutation	Needed where prospect management system has word-processing capabilities.
Geographic region	Useful for institutions with constituents spread out over a large area, where location determines staff assignment, and for planning cultivation/solicitation trips and visits.
Source	Type of prospect (alumnus, trustee, parent, corporation, foundation, and so on).
Wealth code	For those institutions whose lists have been screened by an outside vendor or through peer review.
Class/degree	For educational institutions.
Gift rating	Prospect's capacity to give, usually a range of figures.
Interest rating	Prospect's involvement with the institution (readiness for solicitation).
Status	Where prospect is in solicitation cycle (cultivation, solicitation, stewardship, and so on).
Giving areas	The project, campaign, or type of gift the prospect is targeted for or given clearance for (can be multiple occurrences).
Staff	Staff member assigned to manage the prospect.
Volunteer	Nonstaff volunteer assigned to prospect.
Moves	Contacts between institution and prospect, generally a date and brief description of each contact. Systems can be designed to accommodate numerous entries, to

	record last contact and next move, or to have comment fields that summarize past activity and future plans.
Solicitation	Request date, amount, purpose, solicitor (if other than volunteer); response date, amount, purpose.
Connections	Other ties to institution: spouse, family, classmates, business associates, and so on.
Identifiers	Institutional codes that identify special populations (sometimes called list or select codes).
Tickler	Date for staff or volunteer to conduct follow-up.
Comments	Free-form text to flag special circumstances or provide additional information.

Whatever the choice of data elements, and whatever the system's configuration, fields should be set up to allow for swift and easy information searches.

Prospect Management Subsystems

The prospect management system is an integral part of a comprehensive approach to pursuing the extraordinary gift. It should be designed to ensure that an organization's best prospects are identified, cultivated, and solicited according to a master plan and that all activities involving the prospect are monitored. Used conscientiously, it can measurably help those who have responsibility for the success of major campaigns. Five subsystems are usually found in a prospect management system for major donors: a rating system, a priority system, an accountability system, an approach system, and a report system.

Rating System. Step one in a program to obtain extraordinary gifts is identifying priority prospects. This system places a great deal of importance on the research function. Research and rating go hand in hand, and a solid records and research system is the foundation of any fundraising program. If not already in place, a research capability that will yield prospect ratings must be developed. The end result of a rating process should be not one but two rating codes: the prospect's giving capacity and the prospect's interest in the organization. A prospect's giving capacity is a collective best judgment, after a review of all the pertinent rating and file information, of how much the prospect could contribute to the organization over three to five years, if so inclined. The interest rating is a collective judgment of the prospect's interest in and concern for the organization. This rating is based on personal information, the prospect's giving record, and file information on hand. Table 2.1 shows the numerical rating codes that might be used in a typical system.

TABLE 2.1. PROSPECT RATING CODES.

Giving Capacity Code	Estimated Giving Capacity	Interest Code	Description
1	$2,500–5,000	1	Not involved, no record of interest
2	5,000–10,000	2	Minimal interest, occasional donor, attends meetings infrequently, and so on
3	10,000–25,000		
4	25,000–50,000	3	Moderately active or formerly very active
5	50,000–100,000	4	Very active, major donor, club member, committee person
6	100,000–250,000	5	Member of governing board, other boards, or executive groups
7	250,000–500,000		
8	500,000–1,000,000		
9	1,000,000 or more		

Priority System. By adding the two numerical ratings (capacity and interest), an organization can determine each prospect's priority rating. The higher the rating, the higher the prospect's priority. The higher the prospect's priority, the more cultivation moves (structured contacts designed to bring a prospect closer to making a major gift) an organization will want to make on the prospect in a given period, usually a calendar year.

As a guide to determining how much cultivation a prospect gets, organizations can use the cultivation quota—the sum of the two numerical ratings multiplied by two. This quota represents the minimum number of cultivation moves an organization should hope to make on a prospect each year. For example, consider one prospect who is rated 3/1 (that is, who has a capacity rating of 3 and an interest rating of 1) and another who is rated 1/3. Both have a cultivation quota of 8 ([3 + 1] × 2 = 8). At the moment, the first is a rather unlikely prospect for a $10,000 gift; the second is a fairly likely prospect for a $2,500 gift. Although their cultivation quotas tell the organization to plan for eight cultivation moves in a year, the organization may have to decide which prospect will get its attention first: with the first prospect, a longer cultivation period may result in a larger gift; with the second, a smaller gift is likely to be more readily realized.

Cultivation quotas are flexible guidelines. Staff and volunteers should have the authority to make more or fewer than the recommended number of contacts, as circumstances may dictate. Another important point is that ratings—and therefore cultivation quotas—may change during the year. To return to the previous example, in the opinion of the organization the person rated 3/1 has a gift potential of $10,000 to $25,000 but has not demonstrated much past interest in the organization. But then a staff member who calls on the prospect discovers that the prospect has become much more interested. This discovery changes the prospect's interest rating to 3, and this change in turn increases the cultivation quota to 12. Now, four additional contacts are called for over a year.

It must be clearly understood that ordinarily a nonprofit's top leaders should be assigned to cultivate and solicit those with both the greatest capacity to give and the greatest interest. It is equally important that the entire organizational team stay focused throughout on the best donor prospects. Little time should be given to prospects rated 1/1, but what about prospects rated 9/1 or 8/2? Should time be spent on them? Yes—but it must be a measured amount of time, and the effort should be disciplined. It usually takes a series of steps to move a prospect from the point of clearly having little or no interest to the point where he or she serves on the organization's governing board. This kind of cultivation is not accomplished in one leap. Hence, even where great ability to give exists, the proclivity to give needs to be developed, and that often takes more time than is available in a limited-term, movement-intensive fundraising environment. Leave some time for such long shots, and give some effort to their cultivation, but reserve the bulk of the effort for prospects with major gift potential who are already more involved.

Accountability System. Each major gift prospect should be assigned to a member of the staff whose duty it is to see that a personalized campaign is waged to get the best gift possible. In order to effectively carry out this responsibility, a strategy needs to be developed for each prospect. A good strategy plan will contain a long-term goal to be achieved with the prospect and specific steps to be taken toward that goal. It will be designed to lead to major gift solicitation and will contain an expected solicitation date (see Exhibit 2.1). Each staff member becomes an account executive and acts as a catalyst, providing the initiative and the strategy. The organization should attempt to assign most prospects to one or more volunteers for the actual cultivation and solicitation, and it should strive to give its volunteers the feeling that they are responsible for their prospects. However, in some cases a prospect will be assigned to a staff member for cultivation and solicitation because the staff member truly is the better choice.

Approach System. Types of contact include phone calls, letters, and personal visits by staff, by the chief executive officer, and by volunteers; prospect attendance at organizational functions and leadership retreats; prospect involvement in key

EXHIBIT 2.1. INDIVIDUALIZED STRATEGY PLAN FORM.

Submitted by: _____   Date submitted: _____

Prospect name: _____   Capacity to give: _____

ID number: _____   Primary manager: _____

Title: _____   Co-managers: _____

Business: _____   _____

Address: _____   Strategy type: *(check one)*

_____   ___ Cultivation

_____   ___ Solicitation

_____   ___ Stewardship

Telephone: _____   Volunteer: _____

          Prospect for: *(unit/project)*

INDIVIDUAL PLAN

Expected solicitation date: _____

Summary of analysis and objectives:
(12- to 24-month summary of actions planned and considered)

_____

issues and programs; publications; firsthand briefings and information given to prospects on important events; and recognition events. In most systems, contacts are weighted according to significance, importance, and impact. A typical weighted system looks like this:

Cultivation Contact	*Contact Points*
Letter from a staff member	1
Phone call from a staff member	2
Letter from a volunteer	2
Invitation to a major event	3
Phone call from a volunteer	3
Phone call from chief executive officer	3

Visit by a staff member	4
Letter from chief executive officer	4
Attendance at an organizational activity (off-site)	4
Visit by a volunteer	5
Attendance at an organizational event (on-site)	5
Firsthand information about important events	6
Meeting with the chief executive officer	7
Personal recognition	7
Leadership retreat	7

Report System. For accountability and for results, follow-through is absolutely necessary after making contacts with major donor prospects. There is no substitute for persistence tempered by patience.

First, a call report should be filed after every phone call or visit (see Exhibit 2.2). A good call report begins with a clear, concise, meaningful summary—something that quickly tells the readers if this is relevant to their specific fundraising activities and whether this contact needs their detailed attention. The report then lists these details:

- Date of contact
- Name of development officer or volunteer who made the contact
- Identifying information on the prospect (whatever identifies the prospect within the organization's information system)
- Distribution (the people who need to see the report)

Then, every two to four weeks, staff and volunteers should report on their gift prospect assignments. These reports should list all prospects (individuals, foundations, and corporations) for whom the person is responsible, the number of cultivation and of solicitation contacts that the master plan indicates should be made with each prospect during the year, and the number of contacts made to date. By reviewing these reports, the nonprofit can readily see which prospects need attention and can plan accordingly.

It is also a useful management technique to require staff members to identify their top ten prospects, and then, during a regular staff meeting, ask each staff member to report on what is being done to move these prospects closer to making major gifts, who has the initiative, and what the next step is. At subsequent staff meetings, each staff member reports any progress or difficulty in carrying out cultivation plans and discusses the next sequence of steps to be taken.

EXHIBIT 2.2. PROSPECT CALL REPORT FORM.

This is a confidential *record.*

Prospect name: _____

ID number: _____

Title: _____

Contacted at: _____ Home _____ Business

Address: _____

_____

_____

Phone number: _____

Contact date: _____

Degrees (years obtained): _____

Cross-reference: _____

Volunteer names and IDs:

_____

_____

Reported by: _____

Type of contact: *(check one)*

___ Visit ___ Phone ___

___ Other *(specify)*

Purpose of contact: *(check one)* ___ Cultivation ___ Solicitation ___ Evaluation
___ Stewardship ___ Feasibility study ___ Volunteer recruitment
___ Volunteer follow-up ___ Committee meeting

SUMMARY OF CONTACT _____

DETAILS OF CONTACT _____

_____

Reminders and dates:

Next action:

Staying Focused on Results

With its five subsystems, the prospect management system for soliciting major donors is a control mechanism that ensures big gift prospects are rated, given priority, assigned to staff members and volunteers, cultivated and solicited according to a master plan, and reported on. The system should be designed to get results, not to stimulate scoring points because points need to be scored. It should encourage well-thought-out, appropriate strategic moves that the organization feels will bring its prospects closer to making major gifts.

No one can know for sure how many contacts it will take to bring a prospect to the point of making a gift. The average is generally thought to be seven to ten. Nevertheless, to work strategically with prospects, an organization needs to use something, such as cultivation quotas, as a guide. It is appropriate to rely on a guidance system that is a tool for bringing human factors into play because, after all, human factors are the most important elements in helping the prospect get ready to give.

Prospect tracking and management help an organization monitor its involvement with major prospects. Once someone is identified as a prospect, it is imperative that the organization involve that person in its life. Involvement precedes and often begets investment, and investment is the endgame in the fundraising campaign.

Soliciting Major Gifts from Individuals

Securing major gifts is both the natural and the hoped-for result of the cultivation process. Cultivation begins when the prospective donor first hears about a particular organization. It reaches its highest point when the donor asks, "How much will it cost?" Because tangible results are not usually obtained in a few weeks or months, cultivation demands a sensitive balance of patience and persistence.

Philanthropy is the act of expressing love for others, and so major gifts are much more than money contributed to meet an organization's needs. They represent a person's opportunity for investment, and they are based on his or her commitment. Solicitation is the delicate presentation of an opportunity to invest material assets in a way that brings intangible rewards and a sense of fulfillment. Solicitation is not begging; it is a high form of seeking investments.

One advantage of the capital campaign is that it necessitates asking for major gifts within a definite time frame. An organization can seldom successfully jump immediately from identifying a project to asking for a major investment. Nevertheless, more gifts have probably been lost through waiting for the perfect time than through asking too soon. *It is better to act, even imperfectly, than to wait forever for the perfect time.* Some factors to consider in timing are length of cultivation, date of the prospect's last major gift, his or her age and health, and the urgency of the project for which funds are sought.

Preparing to Make the Major Gift Call

Each negotiation is a campaign in itself, according to Campbell (1985). Do the necessary homework. Know the prospect—his or her needs, wants, hopes, and ambitions. Get all the help available. Find out who the prospect's family members, friends, and advisers are and which people at the organization the prospect knows and respects. Meet with those people and learn all they can tell you about the prospect. Identify at least two possible projects that correspond to the prospect's interests. Document the need for each project and the benefits that will accrue if it is funded. Prepare a presentation—flip chart, proposal, or letter—to take to the meeting with the prospect, and perhaps leave it with the prospect. Bring the prospect to the organization regularly. Candidly discuss opportunities, issues, and problems. Ask for the prospect's counsel and advice. Follow up, report back, and show appreciation whenever it is possible to do so. (Exhibit 2.3 shows how one institution breaks the solicitation process into steps for its volunteers; also see Resource 5).

Select solicitors who have made major gifts themselves. Teams of solicitors, most commonly two or three people, usually work better than individuals on major gift calls. Develop a strategy for each major gift prospect, and review this strategy with these solicitors. If necessary, give them a script, and rehearse it with them until they have internalized it.

Telephone the prospect or visit in person to ask for time to talk about the organization's case for support and opportunities for investment. Then confirm this appointment in writing. It may be useful to send the prospect some easy-to-read information about the organization's plans along with the confirmation letter. Select the meeting site where the prospect will be most comfortable. Avoid noisy, congested sites. Reconfirm the meeting by phone shortly beforehand.

Large gifts from individuals do sometimes result from personal conversations alone, without the aid of formal written presentations, but usually only when a donor is very closely identified and involved with the organization. Even then, a follow-up presentation in writing often helps firm up the appeal. The written presentation may be anything from a letter to a highly individualized—and occasionally quite extensive—published document. Ordinarily, however, a typewritten proposal with a cover letter is adequate. The length of the proposal may vary from one page to many, with extensive supporting appendixes. Usually, however, a statement of three to ten pages in length is all that is necessary. The written proposal should cover at least these four items:

1. Statement of the opportunity or need
2. Proposed action for meeting the need or fulfilling the opportunity
3. Financial data, including information about costs, other funds available, and the amount being requested
4. A summary statement of the benefits the donor will derive from the gift

Asking for large gifts should never be a hit-or-miss proposition, nor should such solicitations be made in casual conversations. This is a serious mission that

EXHIBIT 2.3. SEVEN STEPS TO A MAJOR GIFT.

Step 1: Identify the Prospect.

Purpose: To discover a new or newly qualified prospect.

Questions: Does the prospect have the financial capacity to make a major gift? What form of assets might the prospect use to make a gift?

Step 2: Research and Qualify the Prospect.

Purpose: To gather and analyze relevant information about a prospect.

Questions: What are the prospect's potential interests and priorities? Does the prospect currently have a relationship with Indiana University? What information is still needed to build a gift strategy? Who is the best potential volunteer?

Step 3: Strategize with Staff.

Purpose: To develop a plan for contact, cultivation, and solicitation.

Questions: What is a realistic gift target? Which of the prospect's interests best match the priority goals of the Campaign? What does the prospect need to know, feel, and experience to bring about a major commitment?

Step 4: Involve the Prospect: Make the First Call.

Purpose: To build a bridge between the prospect and Indiana University Bloomington.

Questions: What are the prospect's attitudes and concerns about Indiana University Bloomington? Which of the prospect's interests and needs can be satisfied by meaningful participation in the Campaign? How much future involvement/cultivation will be required before the ask?

Step 5: Make the Ask.

Purpose: To invite the prospect to consider an investment in the Endowment Campaign.

Questions: What is the prospect's reaction to the ask? What are the crucial objections or concerns? What needs to be done to facilitate an actual gift or pledge commitment?

Step 6: Make the Close.

Purpose: To lead the prospect to a commitment.

Questions: What further attitudes and concerns must be addressed? What alterations may be necessary to the original request? What professional help is needed (legal counsel, investment advice, etc.)?

Step 7: Follow Up.

Purpose: To express appreciation and thanks.

Questions: What kinds of personal attention can be shown to the donor? Where should ties to Indiana University Bloomington be strengthened? What further interests and needs of the donor may be served by another gift?

Five Prospect Attitudes and Reactions

1. Agreement—Proceed to the next step.

2. Misunderstanding—Clarify the misunderstanding; gently correct with facts.

3. Indifference—Use "closed-ended" questions to discover needs and interests.

4. Skepticism—Overcome with an "expert witness."

5. "Real objections"—Use the four-step process:

   a. Clarify the objection to make sure you understand it.

   b. Meet the objection but never beat it. Restate the objection as a question; use further questions to narrow the objection to one specific, manageable issue.

   c. Minimize the impact of the objection; try to emphasize the greater good or bigger picture.

   d. Try to gain a neutral position. Ask if the objection will keep the prospect from joining in the Endowment Campaign. Summarize graciously and move on.

Source: The Capital Campaign Volunteer's Kit, Indiana University Foundation. Reprinted with the permission of Indiana University Foundation.

requires preparation and planning before visits, an understanding of the techniques to be employed during visits, and the willingness to follow up after visits.

Making the Visit

During a visit allow an initial period for conversation on topics of mutual interest, and then introduce the reason for the visit. Present the background that has led to the occasion of this presentation. Do not let the conversation become a monologue; allow ample opportunity for the prospective donor to participate. Ask questions. Listen carefully to everything that the prospect says. Finally, ask for the prospect's participation, and be clear about how much the organization is hoping to receive.

Be aware of your body language—dress, actions, eye contact. First impressions are important. Consider the prospect's objections and criticisms as opportunities for discussion and indications of interest. Deal with them as such, but never enter into an argument with a prospect.

Take ample time in a solicitation. Arouse interest to the point where the prospect asks, "How much do you want?" Remember, people give to help people. Sell the organization's programs and concepts, not the costs. Logic, emotion, and enthusiasm are the best motivators. Tax advantages seldom play a part in major gift decisions. They are most often a secondary benefit.

Ask for the gift! Keep the prospect's sights up, and be specific about the amount. If you can, cite some other lead gifts in the major gifts range. It is not uncommon to ask for two to four times what it is thought a prospect will actually give, and there is no known case of a volunteer or a staff member being shot for asking for too much. A large request, if it is within the giving ability of the prospective donor, is usually flattering.

Should the donor's no become evident, listen carefully to the reasons. Find out what must be done before a gift can be secured. Then leave the meeting without closing, and plan a strategy for the next visit. Gifts that are made in haste or that are made by an unconvinced donor tend to be minimal. Clearly establish the next move, including a date for a possible follow-up meeting. It is better not to leave the pledge card with the prospect. Although some solicitors do this and some prospects insist on it, if the pledge card is left with the prospect, the solicitor loses a primary reason to follow up, and it is possible that the prospect will either file the card or make only a minimal gift.

In discussing a major gift with a prospect, emphasize that the gift can be made not only as an outright gift but also in the form of securities and other property and that a gift can return a lifetime income if the donor so desires. In most fundraising campaigns, unless they are solely for construction purposes, bequests are generally welcomed, too.

During many solicitations the prospect will raise objections. The reasons behind some objections are not immediately obvious. For instance, some elderly donors who are alone or lonely will object to closing not because they have an objection to the case or reservations about investing but because they fear that after a gift decision is announced the organization will cease giving them the attention inherent in cultivation and solicitation. Most objections are more straightforward, however. For example, prospects may say, "This is a bad time for us financially. All our assets are currently illiquid," or, "I do not agree with your chief executive officer's priorities."

Whatever the objection, hear it out completely. In discussing the objection with the prospect, restate it, and make sure you understand it in context. Explore ways that the objection could be overcome. Never let the objection lead into an argument, however, and do not make the objection bigger than it is. Respond to it with facts, but never make excuses. If the objection is weak, deal with it as quickly as possible, and move on. It is perfectly legitimate to compromise on objections if in fact they will not be a hindrance to reaching the major goal.

Determine whether the prospect will donate if the objection can be overcome. If so, do what reasonably can be done to remove it. Always remember that objections are really questions, and that the prospect's investment in the project will help overcome the objections. Remembering this fact will help you convert objections into reasons for giving. If an objection cannot be overcome, then move along to another prospect; do not waste time on prospects who for whatever reason are absolutely not going to give.

After the visit, write a short note of thanks for the prospect's time and interest. As appropriate, draft a further note of thanks from the chief executive officer and perhaps from the board chair. Prepare a complete summary report on the visit, with particular attention to new information on the potential donor's special interests, background, and idiosyncrasies. Be sure to include at least the following information:

- Name of company, foundation, or individual visited, date visited, and place of meeting
- If a foundation or corporation, names and positions of people visited
- Names of the staff and volunteers who went on the visit
- The purpose of the visit
- The points that were to be highlighted or conveyed during the visit, and whether this was done successfully
- As much detail as possible about what happened at the meeting (what comments were made by whom and the responses to those comments)
- Lists of any materials distributed during the meeting (state whether there are copies in the development office's research files)

- Mention of any pre- or postmeeting correspondence of which others should have copies
- The concerns (if any) that were voiced by the prospect, and the positive comments that were made in response
- Whether a request for funding or assistance was made and, if so, the details of that request
- Whether additional action or follow-up is needed, and if so, what types, by when, and by whom
- Whether other people should be alerted to the fact that this visit was made, and if so, who they are
- As appropriate, thoughts and recommendations on the best strategies or approaches for cultivating and soliciting the prospect

The Public Management Institute (Conrad, 1978) has identified the fourteen most common major errors that are made in soliciting a major gift:

1. Not asking for the gift
2. Not asking for a large enough gift
3. Not listening; talking too much
4. Not asking questions
5. Talking about the organization and its approach rather than about the benefits to its clients
6. Not being flexible, and not having alternatives to offer the prospect
7. Not knowing enough about the prospect before the solicitation
8. Forgetting to summarize before moving on
9. Not having prearranged signals between solicitation team members
10. Asking for the gift too soon
11. Speaking rather than remaining silent after asking for the gift
12. Settling on the first offer that a prospect suggests, even if it is lower than expected
13. Not cultivating the donor before soliciting
14. Not sending out trained solicitors

Study this list. These mistakes are all avoidable with the right preparation, approach, and presentation to the prospect.

Being asked to contribute has a powerful and positive effect on giving. In 1993, fully 84.1 percent of the households surveyed by INDEPENDENT SECTOR had been asked to contribute, and 76.9 percent of those that were asked had done so; in contrast only 38.1 percent of the households that had not been asked contributed anything. This pattern has been observed consistently over the four surveys that INDEPENDENT SECTOR has conducted since 1987. Moreover, in 1993, respondents reported on how specific kinds of asking might affect their giving frequency. Being asked to give by someone the respondent knows well or being asked by clergy are the most significant factors that lead to higher giving levels; other methods of solicitation, although eliciting giving, are less effective (INDEPENDENT SECTOR, 1996). This finding strongly suggests that nonprofits need to plan the type of contacts to be made and by whom and how frequently they should be made.

Obtaining major gifts is a process—a cycle—open to everyone. Most of all, everyone must give this activity top priority in day-to-day and week-to-week efforts. Nothing must be allowed to divert attention from the greatest source of support for an organization: major donors.

Soliciting Major Gifts from Corporations and Foundations

Most of this discussion about major gifts has centered on individual donor prospects, and about 85 percent of the money given to all nonprofits does come from individuals rather than from foundations or corporations. But the process of identifying, cultivating, and soliciting major gift prospects can and should be used effectively for corporations and foundations, too.

Understanding Donor Priorities

As Richard K. Dupree, executive director of development at the Indiana University's Kelley School of Business, and Tracy A. Connelly, director of corporate and foundation relations at the Kelley School of Business, point out (personal communication, July 1999), corporations and corporate foundations give to what they know. They know their local communities, local and state educational organizations, and local nonprofit organizations. They also know their business—pharmaceuticals, accounting, or technology, for example—both in their local community and throughout the world.

Most corporations and corporate foundations still prefer to give to organizations located in the geographical area where they operate. There are several possible reasons for this:

- They know the organization and its leadership (they read about it in the newspaper; they attend events sponsored by the organization; corporate executives may serve on the nonprofit organization's board).
- They feel a sense of obligation to the community in which they are located and do business.
- They want to reinvest in the community to help meet short- and long-term business or community objectives (workforce development, neighborhood improvement, diversity).

- They can easily monitor the impact of their giving, by visiting the organization and meeting with local organizational leaders.
- They can effect more change on this smaller scale than they could if they spread philanthropic dollars more thinly across wide areas.
- They vastly increase the goodwill and public relations impact of their philanthropy among employees, customers, suppliers, and community members who know the corporation.

Corporations and corporate foundations that give outside their geographical areas do so because they know the organizations they are supporting. They know that either there is no local nonprofit organization that can carry out their objective in the same way or the organization outside their area has expertise beyond that of local nonprofits. Corporation and foundation giving officers are often extremely knowledgeable about nonprofits that address areas of endeavor in which they have a special interest, whether these nonprofits are within their geographical areas or beyond. For example, a California-based technology corporation may make a gift to a midwestern college or university because the school is a leader in education and research. That same corporation might also decline a proposal from a college or university in its own community if the school is not a leader in the field or does not meet a specific business objective of the corporation. Conversely, that corporation would be more likely to support a human services organization in its own community and to decline a proposal from a similar organization in the Midwest.

Foundations give truth to the adage "Charity begins at home." Some give regionally, a few give nationally, and a handful give internationally, but the vast majority of foundations give within their own communities or geographical areas. The largest concentration of foundations, both in terms of size and number, is housed on the island of Manhattan in New York City. They give the majority of their support to organizations within a 250-mile radius of the city. Another cluster of large foundations calls Texas home. The vast majority of these foundations do not make grants outside the state of Texas. It's a strong reminder to keep the home fires burning.

Understanding Proposals

A distinctive characteristic of corporations and foundations is that they often require a solicitation for a major gift to be submitted in the form of a proposal, a formal request. It is most often written, although it may be a verbal request: verbal requests are usually accompanied by or supported by a written document, however. A written proposal may be a simple one-page letter (see Resource 6) or a comprehensive, elaborate presentation (see Resource 7).

Outline of a Full Proposal

1. Cover Letter (very important; use it to emphasize key ideas in the proposal)

2. Proposal Cover and Title Page

3. Table of Contents

4. Executive Summary (no longer than one page for a long proposal, one paragraph for a short proposal)

    Grant amount requested

    Specific purpose of the grant

    Anticipated results

5. Introduction (in short proposals the executive summary may be the introduction)

    The issue

    The nonprofit's plan

    The amount requested

    Discussion of the issue

6. What's Wrong

    Why it is important to address the issue

    How the nonprofit proposes to address the issue (what it will do, what others have done, why its way is better)

7. Solution

    What the nonprofit will accomplish

    How the nonprofit will accomplish it

    What it will take to address the issue (people, money, other resources)

8. The Nonprofit Organization's Qualifications

    What the nonprofit has done in the past

    What the nonprofit is doing now

    What the nonprofit is contributing (talent, time, space, money)

    What the nonprofit will do next

9. Methods (ways in which the nonprofit intends to accomplish the goal)

10. Evaluation Plan (how the organization and others will know the goal has been accomplished)

11. Future Funding Plans (how the project will survive in the future, when the grant is gone)

12. Budget (as complete and detailed as possible, with narrative)

13. Conclusion

14. Summary

15. Thanks

16. Appendixes (as brief and informative as possible)

      Evidence of tax-exempt status

      Supportive documents

      Letters of commitment, commendations, support, and so forth

      Other specific information

      Other general information

The Fund Raising School (1995) cites these twelve primary reasons why proposals do not get funded:

- Project has not been documented properly.
- Project does not strike reviewer as significant; statement of the project does not stimulate interest.
- Prospective client groups have not been involved in planning and determining project goals.
- Proposal is poorly written or hard to understand.
- Proposal objectives do not match objectives of funding source.
- Proposal budget is not within range of funding available.
- Proposed project has not been coordinated with other individuals and organizations working in the same area.
- Funding source has not been convinced that the individuals submitting the proposal are capable of carrying it out.
- Project objectives are too ambitious.
- Proposal writer does not follow guidelines provided by funding agency.
- Insufficient evidence that the project can sustain itself beyond the life of the grant.
- Evaluation procedures are inadequate.

A proposal should be designed to do two things:

- To make a potential donor aware that the nonprofit organization has a program or a project that will accomplish something that the donor wants done
- To invite the potential donor to invest in this program or project, thus filling the potential donor's need to get that something done

Don't think about how a foundation or corporation can help you achieve your goals; rather consider how your organization can help the foundation or corporation achieve its goals, and present your proposal accordingly.

Also be aware that proposals, at least those that get funded, seldom arrive unannounced and uninvited. The same principles that apply to the cultivation of individuals apply to the cultivation of corporations and foundations. Letters of inquiry, telephone calls, e-mail exchanges, and personal visits are the precursors to the submission of a proposal that gets funded. It has been said, although it is not proven, that more than 75 percent of grants made by foundations go to institutions and organizations with whom one or more members of the foundation board have personal involvement or close associations. The two most significant reasons why people give money to causes are belief in the cause and involvement with the organization. Foundation and corporate giving guidelines direct decisions, but board members and chief executive officers make the decisions.

It is also important to follow the guidelines provided by the potential funding source. Deviations from these requirements usually will trigger penalties and may cause your proposal to be dropped from consideration. Foundations and corporations receive far more qualified proposals than they can fund. Some report as many as ten to fifteen proposals for every grant made. One method of pruning the list is to eliminate from consideration those proposals that do not follow guidelines.

The format to be used will also depend on the nature of your organization's relationship with the potential funding source. And you may find that corporate or foundation giving officers are willing to answer questions as the proposal is developed. This assistance can be critical to your success.

Proposal Writing Style

Speaking in your organization's distinctive voice is important. At the same time, the principles that apply to good writing in general, making effective presentations, and preparing marketing materials apply equally to publications and proposals.

Paul La Rocque (1992) offers these writing style guidelines:

- Keep to one idea per sentence.
- Keep sentence length low. Vary lengths, but consider a sentence that runs past twenty-three words a long sentence. If you must use a long sentence, place a short one before and after it.
- Don't have more than three numbers of any kind in one sentence.
- Don't have more than three prepositional phrases in any sentence. If the phrases run consecutively or have the same preposition, even three are too many.

- When unraveling an unclear sentence, find the subject-verb-object relationship. Don't fall unnecessarily into the passive voice.
- Reduce difficult words to single-syllable or simple terms. Recast jargon and journalese, and pretentious or repetitive phrasing, into everyday words.
- Don't back into a sentence with unnecessary clauses or clauses that delay the subject and should come later in the sentence if at all.
- Prune all deadwood and redundancy from the sentence. (Use "now" instead of "at the present time"; "soon" instead of "in the immediate future.")
- Don't pack the lead. Specificity is wonderful, but where you can't be specific without burdening the beginning, you should choose a general, clear statement and support it with details later.
- Maintain a graceful, conversational word order. Read the work aloud to yourself to check rhythm and readability.
- Choose concrete over abstract terms.
- Use single strong verbs instead of several weak ones. (Use "they decided" instead of "they made a decision"; "they tried" instead of "they made an effort"; "they intend" instead of "they have the intention.")

Fundraising literature and proposals too often contain a good deal of specialized language—professional jargon that is familiar to educators, medical staff, or seminary scholars but a deep mystery to almost everyone else. Try to avoid it. Keep in mind that many foundation and corporate decision makers will be laypeople who respond best to plain language, short sentences, and familiar usage. One rule of good writing that particularly applies to proposals is to avoid generalities and look for specifics. Every organization has its own history, achievements, and vital statistics. Know them, and include them in the writing.

David W. Barton Jr., retired president of Barton Gillet, is fond of reminding people that the characters in Mark Twain's *Huckleberry Finn* speak in five distinct dialects. He mentions that Twain pointed to this phenomenon in the book's introduction because he had taken pains to get the dialects right: the characters speak authentically, and Twain wanted the reader to appreciate what he had accomplished. What he wrote is a masterpiece because he respected his characters enough to get their language right. In the same way, every organization speaks in a different voice, with a different tone and a different stylistic emphasis. If an organization can capture its own flavor and essence in its proposals and other literature, its constituents will respond to it. The difference between the right word and the nearly right word is the difference between lightning and a lightning bug; it's only the right word and the right image aimed at the right person at the right time and in the right way that can produce lightning.

People Give to People

William L. Taylor (personal communication, Apr. 2001), director of planning and advancement for The Menil Collection, advises that

> Corporation and foundation work is essentially major individual gift work. There are key players who make decisions and they are swayed by the same considerations any individual of means is—reputation of the institution, fiscal probity, a convincing case, and preeminently who solicits. As competition increases, the peer volunteer committed and well versed becomes ever more the trump card in the deck. We all have good causes, and good institutions; but who believes in us and is willing to "turn to" for us makes all the difference. This is old news, but every day proves it out more and more.

Taylor sums it up neatly: foundations and corporations give "to established reputations and quality; to well-designed and convincing cases that present vision, not problems and solutions, not needs; to ideas that advance the community; and to solicitors who are peers and whom they cannot turn down."

For those nonprofits that fit Taylor's model, corporations and foundations can be a significant resource, and the potential for nonprofit growth and expansion in the first quarter of the twenty-first century will keep both in the mainstream of major gift philanthropy.

CHAPTER THREE

SECURING LEAD GIFTS

Rodney P. Kirsch
Martin W. Shell

L ead gifts are at the pinnacle of the major gifts range. Most of these gifts, although not all, come in the form of lead gifts to capital campaigns. This chapter focuses on the conditions needed to bring about lead investments from individuals and on ways of positioning and using the positive dynamics created by such magnificent investments. And these major acts of philanthropy are indeed investments. They result from deep and meaningful relationships that span the course of time, and they are as much "given" as "solicited." In this respect they represent the convergence of factors that go well beyond the mechanics of soliciting large gifts during campaigns. But there are also some cautions and considerations to be raised about how fundraisers work to achieve lead gifts, considerations that take account of the many personal complexities in donors' lives.

The American Association of Fund-Raising Counsel Trust for Philanthropy (2001) reports that there are now nearly 775,000 501(c)(3) organizations registered as charities with the Internal Revenue Service. The great majority of these will not see their donors listed in the *Forbes* annual roster of largest gifts. This is not terribly important. What matters is that your organization certainly can achieve success with lead gifts, a success to be measured less by your past achievements in this area than by the extraordinary potential you have to bring about change in the community you serve.

Defining a Leadership Gift

Before considering the optimal conditions for inspiring leadership gifts, let us define such gifts.

Traditional Views

There are three traditional definitions of *lead gifts*.

Inspirational Gift. Lead gifts and the donors who make them possess remarkable qualities. The impact of these gifts is to move a significant part of an organization or sometimes the entire organization forward in a single leap. They create synergy for further philanthropy and define for the entire constituency the importance and value one donor places on the organization. As one donor said about a lead gift, "It puts you [the organization] on the map. Others will now more carefully consider the important contributions your organization makes."

Indeed, as their name implies, these gifts set a standard of leadership, perhaps beyond any anticipated level. In many cases a lead gift can be truly historic, launching a new chapter in the life of the recipient organization. In this way leadership gifts are philosophical and inspirational. They are the kinds of investments to keep in mind as you consider major gifts. Adopting this thinking will raise your expectations and your donors' aspirations. Dare to dream big dreams!

Gift That Is a Significant Portion of Donor's Wealth. The public does not ordinarily know what portion of a donor's wealth a gift represents. Often insiders don't know either. Most professional development officers and volunteers consider a gift that represents 20 percent or more of an individual's net worth substantive, regardless of the gift amount, be it $50,000 or $50 million. Key volunteers, donors, and staff members must have a feel for the sacrificial nature of such substantive gifts and should use this knowledge wisely to encourage other donors, discreetly and strategically.

Gift Related to Other Large Gifts. Perhaps the most conventional way of defining a lead gift is by stipulating its amount. This amount will of course vary from organization to organization, but today a standard definition for a lead gift is 10 percent (or more) of the campaign goal.

Another traditional way to define lead gifts is to determine where they fit in relationship to other major gifts over the course of a campaign. Being among the top 2 or 3 percent in gift size would certainly qualify for recognition. But be aware that this definition is *comparative*; it is not necessarily related to the true potential of the donor and so may fall short of what might have been obtained under the previous two definitions.

Contemporary Definitions

Today three additional expressions are coming into common use in the discussion of lead gifts.

Legacy Gift. A *legacy gift* is the largest gift an individual makes to a nonprofit. It is usually made in the form of a life income arrangement or as a part of a bequest. It is often the last gift the donor makes. It generally is both the donor's largest and last gift to the nonprofit. The amount is not of major importance. This gift is defined by the donor's wish to leave a legacy with the organization. These gifts are almost always made for capital purposes—endowment or construction.

Threshold Gift. The largest gift a nonprofit has ever received, be it $5,000 or $50 million, represents its *threshold gift*. Threshold gifts are extremely important: they are the penultimate lead gift. They not only raise the sights of the organization and add to its financial well-being, but also make larger gifts "legitimate." Although the United States is noted for producing leaders, it produces far more followers, particularly in philanthropy. Individuals generally are reluctant to go it alone, to do something that singles them out, particularly when it involves giving extraordinary sums of money. The most difficult lead gift a nonprofit is seeking at any point in time is its next threshold gift, the one that leads it to a higher level of thinking and possibilities. A classic example of the transitive effects of a threshold gift occurred in a capital campaign in the 1980s. The nonprofit sought as the lead gift to its campaign a gift of $15 million, a dollar amount far higher than the amount of its previous threshold gift. Although prospects for such a gift were identified and aggressive cultivations were underway, all of the prospects were reluctant to be the first to give at this level. Finally, the nonprofit broke the dam. The first $15 million commitment came. Three more $15 million commitments followed in the next twelve months. Today that organization's threshold gift level is $50 million, an amount it received recently. It has received more than twenty gifts of $15 million or more since it crashed that barrier fifteen years ago.

Transformational Gift. The ultimate lead gift is the *transformational gift*. It does exactly what the name implies; it literally transforms a nonprofit. It is usually an eight-, nine-, or ten-figure gift. It can stabilize or even enlarge a nonprofit's financial base through an endowment gift to support programs or operations, or it can transform an organization by permitting capital expenditure to modernize or expand existing facilities and the programs they house. Few individuals are willing during their lifetimes to make gifts of such magnitude that they will have to alter their personal tastes, lifestyles, or living conditions. The thought of trading the penthouse for the poorhouse in one's golden years is not that appealing to most. Therefore virtually all transformational gifts are estate gifts. However, there are notable exceptions to this pattern. Walter H. Annenberg and Robert Edward "Ted" Turner III are two recent, high-profile examples of donors who have such tremendous wealth that they could make transformational gifts during their lifetimes without sacrificing their lifestyles.

Shared Purpose and Passion

A lead gift typically grows out of a close association between a donor and a nonprofit organization, an association based on a shared and deeply held vision, belief, or value. At first blush, this suggests that nonprofits should pay attention to creating persuasive case statements and program brochures. But these standard campaign vehicles are merely initial and at best superficial instruments for inspiring lead gifts. When engaging individuals in the lead gift process, each nonprofit organization should consider the constituencies it serves, the mission it holds dear, and the values it expresses. The organization's ability to articulate these important dimensions of its existence is essential to fostering an environment in which lead gifts become possibilities.

Experienced development professionals know, both from surveys and from personal experience and anecdotal evidence, that major philanthropy at its core is primarily an emotion-based enterprise. This is particularly true where lead gifts are concerned. Many individuals, often without much forethought, write modest checks every day for good causes. But lead gifts—the kind that transform an organization—are usually tied to deeply held beliefs in the purpose of a nonprofit and are given with passion. The donor does expect accountability after the gift is made, and surely the tax implications are thoroughly examined during the decision-making stage. Nevertheless the impulse to consult a financial adviser or concern over the measurable outcomes of a lead gift will stem from the donor's strong convictions about the purpose and the work of the organization. This kind of passion cannot be evoked by brochures or annual reports, which, from the donor's perspective, tend over time to make organizations seem more similar than different. Instead, a donor's passion for an organization's purpose comes from his or her genuine involvement in the life of the organization. Therefore the heart of the matter in securing lead gifts is the development of meaningful, personal relationships with prospects and donors.

The most successful organizations find myriad ways of bringing individual donors inside, where they can help shape policy, test their values and interests against the organization's, fully understand the organization's mission, appreciate the organization's impact, and ultimately discover the right channels for expressing, through philanthropy, their passion for the organization's work. Involvement of this type does indeed beget significant investment, and organizations have the ability to choose just how and to whom they wish to extend this special level of involvement. It should be done with the understanding that practical considerations (time constraints, governing structures, budgetary limitations, program activities, and the like) allow for only a precious few individuals to see the organization in this special way. Therefore those few should be carefully chosen. They will discover lead donors for your organization, make lead gifts themselves, or do both.

Mature, Ongoing Relationships

Lead gifts from total strangers are wonderful but exceedingly rare. How many times have you been named beneficiary of a will drawn up by someone unknown to you? Lead gifts come almost invariably from individuals who have known an organization for a long time.

Endeavor daily to develop ever-deepening relationships with key stakeholders. The process of genuine engagement with volunteers is one that must be extended to a broader circle of interested parties. This is a process of selection, one whereby the donor selects the organization and the organization selects the donor for a long-term and even, one hopes, lifetime relationship. Nevertheless, one of the most critical errors made in securing lead gifts is failing to look beyond the immediate campaign to the lifetime value of a donor's relationship with the organization. The concept of a lifelong relationship, like the attitude of valuing lifetime friendships with donors, is central to creating an environment for lead gifts. Thinking about relationships with volunteers, donors, and other stakeholders in a long-term context brings several fundamental ideas into focus.

First, quality is more important than quantity. Creating a positive climate for lead giving, in and beyond the context of a campaign, is hardly a mass production, assembly-line process; indeed, according to an unpublished Federal Reserve technical paper (analyzed by the *Left Business Observer* and cited by United Auto Workers, 1997), the richest 0.5 percent of the population owned 27 to 28 percent of the wealth in America in 1995. Organizations are best advised to focus their time on and build mature relationships with individuals who can ultimately make the kinds of high-impact gifts that this chapter describes. This need not be a cold, calculating activity; rather, the organization's role is to serve as a catalyst in these relationships, and facilitating them is a process that is both consuming and rewarding—time intensive but worthy of the organization's investment. It is more essential than ever to focus attention on building high-quality relationships with a few individuals instead of seeking many relationships that never go beyond the superficial level. (If you do not believe this, read, or reread, Chapter Six of this book.)

Second, multiple relationships between the prospect and the organization add value. The best volunteers and the most generous donors are those who extend their involvement in multiple ways. Over time they may serve on different committees, contribute to different organizational programs, and form numerous relationships, whether with the chief executive officer or with clients served by the organization. For example, several years ago one institution discovered that over time a prospective major gift donor had directed gifts of modest size to nearly twenty separate purposes within the organization. Needless to say, this donor had established multiple interests and many personal relationships at different levels, and these relationships contributed to the donor's broad understanding of the organization's mission as well as to the impact that the organization had on the donor. When the time came for a multimillion-dollar lead investment in a single program, it was clear that this donor's many relationships had played a role in his continuing interest in the organization and in his willingness to make a transformational gift—which he did, at the level of more than $20 million. In any organization, large or small, the focus should be on managing and, as appropriate, even creating multiple relationships inside the organization. Too often, however, an organization's first instinct is to direct prospects to its priority program rather than allowing them to explore their own interests. Organizations should encourage rather than restrict multiple contacts and connections.

Third, past donors are most likely to be future investors. Treat them well. There is nothing more fundamental than remembering past and current donors. The typical nonprofit organization, however, if it were to candidly examine where it places its priorities, would probably discover that it is much busier looking for the next big prospect than stewarding the last major donor. One college president, for example, complained that his staff relied too heavily on the "*Casablanca* method" of fundraising—"rounding up the usual suspects," as he put it—instead of broadening the base of donors. Every organization surely must find new friends in order to stay vibrant and keep moving forward, but an environment conducive to lead gifts evolves from careful stewardship of relationships with past and current donors. The challenge for those in the nonprofit sector is to focus as much energy on stewardship as on solicitation, thus creating an appropriately balanced environment for continuous lifetime giving.

Asking for the Gift

In April 1998, Joan and Sanford Weill announced a gift of $100 million to name Cornell University's Medical Center. Mr. Weill, asked how he and his wife had decided to make this gift, pointed to Cornell's president and medical dean and said, "They asked" (Arenson, 1998). The circumstances surrounding this gift are private of course, but it can be surmised that the decision was not quite so simple. And yet Mr. Weill's brief, spontaneous answer is poignant. It teaches once again the age-old lesson of fundraising at any level: the single biggest mistake in major gift fundraising is failing to ask for the gift; therefore, asking for the gift is the most important thing to do.

This seems obvious, but asking cannot be taken for granted. How many lead gifts have never materialized for your organization because the request was not made, even though all the other factors were in place? How many lead gifts went to another organization because that nonprofit made a request and yours did not? How many gifts never reached their maximum potential because the basis of your strategy was insufficient thought and too little homework?

The elements of a successful solicitation call and ways to deal with the typical objections encountered in such meetings are discussed elsewhere in this book (see especially Chapter Two). Our intention in this chapter is to underscore the significance of actively, directly, and aggressively seeking philanthropic investments of the highest possible magnitude. If the proper steps are taken to develop an environment and culture conducive to lead giving, then the achievement of significant gift commitments will naturally follow.

Exploring donors' values, fostering mature relationships, engaging volunteers in meaningful ways, personally involving the organization's top leader—all these activities play a part in getting a donor ready to say yes to a direct proposal or to respond to a vision by asking, "How much will it take?" None of this can happen, of course, without your organization's firm commitment to sustained, focused contact with volunteers and donors.

Every lead gift solicitation is unique. Each prospect represents a minicampaign requiring specialized attention, creative approaches, and a solicitation grounded in the right strategy. The solicitation of lead gifts is nothing more than choosing the right volunteer to ask the right prospect for the right amount for the right purpose at the right time and in the right form. But deciding which elements are right cannot be done in a vacuum. Successful decisions evolve from high-quality interactions with volunteers, past and current donors, and prospective donors. Establishing lead gift solicitation strategies requires a significant investment of time by people in the organization. The process is labor intensive and very personalized, and the organization must devote ample budgetary resources to it. Budgetary investments that enhance direct contacts with prospects will create the most favorable conditions for lead giving.

In discussing the act of asking, one more element deserves emphatic mention: the need to challenge the donor, in terms of both the amount and the purpose of the gift. Stay within the bounds of reason and good professional judgment of course, but do challenge the donor's competitive spirit by asking the donor to stretch, not just financially but also intellectually and emotionally. The most emotionally and intellectually committed lead gift prospects will expect nonprofit organizations to present them with concepts that respond to their own strong impulses to transform organizations through philanthropy.

Listening to the Donor

Those who pursue large gifts, be they volunteers or staff, like the major gift prospects they cultivate and solicit, use a variety of talents and skills to achieve success. Although there is no one ideal prototype that describes the quintessential major gift solicitor, these solicitors do frequently have some traits in common. First and foremost they believe in the cause they represent, often as passionately as the prospective donors they are courting—or even more passionately. And *courting* is often an apt description of the relationship that develops. This is a second common thread—they develop relationships. The art forms of romance are commonly employed in appropriate ways throughout a successful cultivation and solicitation process. Thoughtful gestures, special attention, timely appropriate actions, and proper advances are all incorporated. Major donors are people, not automatic cash machines. Their giving is personal and often emotional. This makes the personal interaction between solicitor and prospect more than a casual or business relationship. Good solicitors are generally attentive, sensitive, thoughtful, thorough, responsive, and respectful of their prospect's needs, wants, and desires. In all these areas probably the most underrated and clearly important factor is one more trait—they are good listeners.

Experts identify five levels of listening:

- Ignoring
- Pretending
- Selective listening
- Attentive listening
- Emphatic listening

Using the first three levels will not result in major gift fundraising success. *Attentive listening* is critical to obtaining big gifts, but it is *emphatic listening*, listening with the intent to understand, and seeing the world the way the prospective donor sees it, that identifies the truly extraordinary solicitor. Emphatic listening, it is important to note, is not necessarily agreeing with but rather completely understanding your prospect, both emotionally and intellectually. It is appropriate to describe this type of emphatic listening in the fundraising context as *advancement listening,* because it is this type of listening that can truly advance the cause you champion.

For example, consider the story of one extremely committed donor from whom an organization sought a lead gift. The organization's relationships with this donor had followed the classic development track—initial identification of the donor, a visit from the development officer, a strong relationship with the chief executive officer. (The donor was not, however, a member of the organization's board.) Throughout the evolution of this relationship the donor's giving had increased. When the chief executive officer began to talk about an investment at the lead gift level, the need to grow the organization's endowment was stressed. Every time the subject was raised, however, the donor listened intently but kept turning the conversation to a specific building project that was also on the drawing board. The building was important—it would be needed within five years—but it was not the organization's highest priority. After repeated conversations, however, the advancement officer and the chief executive officer decided that they should listen to the donor. This act of advancement listening netted a $2 million building gift—the donor's single largest gift ever, by a factor of ten, with tremendous potential for more. In this case the organization chose to subordinate a higher priority to an opportunity to match a donor's interest with another worthy but less immediate project. This decision will probably net the nonprofit organization millions of additional gift dollars in the years ahead, and the next lead gift from this donor is likely to be for endowment purposes.

Not every act of emphatic listening ends so positively. Sometimes a nonprofit organization must retreat from a gift discussion because the donor's wishes are incompatible with the organization's needs. Such cases illuminate an important side of the relationships between donors and institutions: donors make tremendous investments in organizations, but they do not run them. The chief executive officer and the organization's governing body determine which gifts can be accepted and for what purposes; they set the priorities. It is vital for any organization, regardless of its financial condition, to maintain its integrity with respect to the gifts that it does and does not accept. Fortunate is the organization that is not financially dependent on its next lead gift!

Stewardship

Having to turn away gift support is a rarity at most organizations; a much larger challenge is proper stewardship of the gifts that are accepted.

There are several concepts of what stewardship means, yet they have important elements in common. The original concept predates the Bible but has been codified in biblical language. It is that all possessions belong to God and that humanity is responsible for managing those resources while on earth. In feudal Europe, a steward was the person who ran the manor house, particularly the financial affairs of the estate. The green movement of the past few decades also uses the term, emphasizing our need to be stewards of the earth's natural resources. An underlying element in each concept is high moral quality and responsible management. A proper steward is one who is morally responsible and trustworthy.

Many nonprofit organizations may not have specifically thought of stewarding donors as a moral obligation, but it is an important concept. Donors have chosen to invest in your organization. They give time, energy, resources, and talents. Like the steward of the manor, the organization has a responsibility to use those gifts wisely and to properly account for those uses. Donors place high trust in organizations, and so organizations should be systematic about telling donors how their money is used. Donors should receive immediate responses to inquiries about how gifts and other assets are managed. Good stewardship also requires communication with donors when organizational needs change, and when those changes affect donors' gifts.

There are also some extremely practical reasons for being a good steward. No reasonable person would continue sending money to a financial institution that failed to report regularly on the investment. If you want your most committed stakeholders to remain committed, be forthright and regular in reporting on the rich dividends that their gifts are paying at your institution.

Good stewardship leads quite naturally to stronger existing relationships between donor and organization and to the development of new ones. Donors are investors, and they are interested in seeing a return on their investments. The stewardship requirement for lead gift prospects and donors goes far beyond sending an annual report on endowment performance or having the organization's chief executive officer pay an annual visit. Good stewardship is a personal process that is carefully managed. It aims not simply to maintain a donor's satisfaction but to increase that satisfaction to the point where the donor asks, "What more can I do?" Good stewardship is not the end of the solicitation cycle; it is the beginning of a new and higher level of donor involvement.

Positioning Lead Gifts in a Campaign Context

In the 1980s, when capital campaign goals exceeded the billion-dollar mark, some speculated that campaigns could not sustain themselves at such rarefied heights. In the 1990s, with the record-breaking bull market and the growth of worldwide wealth, we began to wonder whether there is any ceiling at all to campaign goals.

Whether there is or not, campaigns will remain part of the fundraising landscape for one simple reason: they work; they raise money. And lead gifts have never been more important to campaigns. Transformational gifts represent huge percentages of campaign totals. Capital campaigns' goals continue growing at a feverish pace because lead gifts are escalating exponentially.

Do donors really care about goals? Do campaigns provide a genuine opportunity to ask for unprecedented gifts? Twenty years ago, donors might not have cared as much about the details of capital campaigns. Today, however, they often care deeply about making gifts in the context of a campaign. Why is this so?

The decision to make a campaign gift does not always reflect a donor's desire to be included in a mass appeal for funds. Rather, it reflects the evolving role of campaigns and the programs that those campaigns seek to fund. It also reflects donors' increased sophistication. A successful capital campaign today is a direct outgrowth of the nonprofit organization's strategic planning process. Organizational needs are not simply brought to the chief executive officer's desk and converted into a campaign brochure. The needs, goals, ambitions, and mission of the organization should be debated, discussed, and determined. The campaign then can be an outgrowth of the organization's strategic thinking. Lead gift donors increasingly want to know that their gifts will be used for specific strategic purposes. For example, in February 1998, the University of Pennsylvania law school announced the largest outright gift ever to a law school for construction and endowment purposes, and in May 1998, the Wharton School at the University of Pennsylvania announced the largest single gift ever to a U.S. business school (in this instance an unrestricted gift). In both cases the donors were key volunteers who had taken a hand in shaping institutional directions and ambitions.

Involving key volunteers and donors in strategic planning is also vital to a campaign's success. Committed outsiders bring a real-world perspective to the planning process. Such donors become much more committed to the process, and once committed, they have a greater investment in its successful outcome. Donors actually cultivate themselves through this planning involvement, becoming much more familiar with the strengths and needs of the organization. This is not to suggest that the planning process should be turned over to donors and volunteers—organizational representatives ultimately must develop and implement the strategic plan—but the involvement of key constituents will make finding resources much easier when it is time to fund the strategic initiatives. Donors do care about campaigns when the case for support has been clearly developed and can be backed by strategic analysis.

Capital campaigns provide a framework that makes securing lead gifts much easier. Campaigns set deadlines, benchmarks, and goals. Deadlines make decision making more efficient; thus donors will be more efficient with their gift decisions when deadlines are set. The deadline concept is further refined in many campaigns, too. Most campaigns do not go public until a certain percentage of the goal has been committed—usually between 40 and 60 percent—and lead gifts represent the bulk of the money raised during this quiet phase. Asking lead donors to make their gift commitments early, before the campaign goes public, creates another deadline that can encourage gift decisions. Skillful campaign leaders often set several minideadlines as a way to benchmark progress and help solicitors close gifts.

Campaigns also provide a bandwagon effect, and campaign-conditioned donors often expect to play a part in it. Some donors will not make a gift decision unless they know it will be part of a larger organizational fundraising effort; as one donor said a few years ago, "I don't want to be a lone wolf." Donors at the lead gift level want their gifts to be counted among other large contributions. Campaigns provide a way for that to happen, and this "rising tide" then encourages others to join. Donors also want to associate themselves with successful organizations, and successful campaigns suggest successful organizations.

Campaigns also offer a formal structure for recognizing philanthropy. Campaigns provide opportunities for regular stewardship and public relations events (donor recognition dinners, news releases, periodic campaign updates), and the campaign format increases the visibility of a donor's gift and at the same time provides a larger audience for it. Gift announcements let organizations reinforce the campaign's overarching goals and highlight how the donor's investment supports the organizational mission. Donor recognition undergirds the stewardship process because it provides another way to thank the donor for the gift. It also encourages others to get on the bandwagon.

Not every donor prefers this kind of recognition, however. That was the situation recently when an organization received a very large gift—a record breaker—but both the gift and the donor's identity had to remain unknown; the donor did not want to make headlines with his act of philanthropy. This attitude is uncommon—even refreshing, given our world of hype and advertising—but when it does appear, the opportunity to publicize the gift so as to encourage the donor's peers and others to raise their sights for giving to the institution is lost.

Some major donors give for reasons other than simple altruism. Ego gratification is often a very important consideration. A major donor may want regional and national publicity for a commitment. The donor may want peers and other volunteer leaders in the organization to know of the donor's generosity and may also want his or her family and social set to be aware of the gift. Often major donors, highly successful in their business and professional lives, have developed a strong competitive spirit, and the same drive is often at least part of their motivation to make major gifts and feel challenged to make even larger commitments. Lead gifts may become a vehicle through which these highly competitive, successful individuals, whose egos are often equally well developed, can make a statement to the business and philanthropic worlds.

Donors like these can and should be exacting about the publicity they receive for their gifts. Organizations cannot guarantee media coverage of gift announcements of course. Some donors expect this coverage, however, and capital campaigns often help in achieving it. Campaigns provide a context for a gift announcement and complementary messages; these campaign messages give the media something to report in addition to the donor's gift and how it will be used. Campaign publications can also be used to tell others about the gift. They are no substitute for prominent news coverage, but they do ensure that the message is delivered to the audience you choose and at the time that you set.

An important consideration in announcing lead gifts is the staging, sequencing, and pacing of these announcements around campaign events and meetings. This strategy can have a strong motivational impact on both internal and external audiences. For example, asking a donor couple to personally announce their gift to peers has a tremendous emotional effect on those who have not yet given. Donors' personal testimonies and the life stories behind them can be exemplary in raising the standard for the next cycle of campaign gifts.

One final word about press releases on gifts: keep the donor well informed. It is vital to stay in touch with the donor throughout the gift decision process, but it is equally important to keep the donor informed about announcement strategies. It is better to err on the side of giving the donor too many opportunities to change a news release or the circumstances surrounding an announcement. Putting up with some inconvenience is far preferable to angering a donor because he or she feels insufficiently consulted about the publicity surrounding a lead gift that is, after all, an extremely personal matter.

Other Considerations

In addition to working with a lead donor or a lead donor couple, organizations often work with a donor's associates. This group may include spouses, significant others, children, other heirs, administrative staff, and financial and legal advisers.

These individuals can play a crucial role in the gift decision process and in the subsequent stewardship activity; they may be either advocates or adversaries in the giving process. The best rule is to involve them as early as possible: the organization benefits when its representatives understand the importance of involving people associated with the donor.

Family and heirs present special issues in the negotiation of major gifts. They often have a personal stake in the donor's commitment and believe that they have a vested interest in the process. It is up to the organization—and sometimes the donor—to demonstrate that the gift decision is in the donor's best interest. Often, by using creative vehicles for planned giving, an organization can design a strategy that benefits the donor, his or her heirs, and the organization itself.

Negotiating such gift arrangements may involve the donor's financial and legal counsel, and organizational representatives are often called upon to validate the donor's intended gift for these advisers. This is especially true when an adviser is looking for reasons to stop the donor from making the gift. Organizational representatives should have a working knowledge of the financial and tax implications of charitable gifts or have ready access to people who do. Most donors make lead gifts for reasons other than the tax and estate benefits, but the tax laws do provide real opportunities for people with an interest in making charitable contributions. Never has this been so true as in today's financial markets, where millions of new fortunes—and potential major donors—have been created with the dramatic increase in the value of equity markets.

Today, gifts of appreciated securities are becoming the currency of choice for major donors, and organizational staff must be well versed in the nuances of stock gifts. Sometimes a donor will make a gift decision when a stock reaches a specific value, or the donor may time a gift to occur in conjunction with a capital event (such as the takeover of a company or an initial public offering). Gifts of stock in a donor's publicly traded corporation can also create special challenges and opportunities. For example, high-profile executives or board members who use corporate stock as their gift vehicle often worry about a possible adverse market reaction to their liquidation of stock for gift purposes. Some corporate insiders will not make significant stock gifts because they fear that the market will misinterpret their intent in giving away the securities. In work with donors and their advisers, each donor's circumstance requires flexibility and creativity.

Most people are living longer than their parents did and will be much more active later in life. Therefore another consideration for most donors is the maintenance of a certain standard of living. Longer life expectancy also holds the possibility of costs associated with long-term care for the donor, the donor's spouse, or both, and this possibility can place tremendous pressure on donors to hold onto resources that otherwise might be given. Despite the old fundraising saw that "no one protects the donor's wallet like the donor," concerns about longer life expectancy are real and must be treated with respect and honesty. The ethics of our profession require us to maintain a fiduciary relationship with donors, especially older ones, and we must work with all major donors to craft gift arrangements that benefit both them and our organizations.

Philanthropic work achieves the greatest joy and the most good when it moves beyond the mechanics of fundraising and "sealing the deal." Fundraisers will attain greater success when they adopt a long-term view of their work and recognize that leadership investments are about building lasting relationships that offer meaning and value to the donor first and benefits to the organization second. Placing the donor's interests and vision above the organization's needs unleashes the potential to move organizations forward through philanthropy.

CHAPTER FOUR

CONNECTING MAJOR GIFTS AND PLANNED GIVING

Major gifts are almost always made from a donor's noncash assets. This is due to the fact that even very high income major gift donors are unlikely simply to write a check for five or six figures. Major gift donors are savvy enough to approach a donation of this size with an eye toward how it fits within their overall financial planning. They take a sophisticated approach that includes considering the tax deductions and other benefits that can be reaped from a noncash asset donation compared to an income donation. Table 1.1 illustrates the potential gift ranges associated with different levels of assets that generally inform modern discussions about donors' ability, but not proclivity, to give a major gift.

Accepting the premise that major gifts will be, at least to some degree, planned gifts, might lead an organization to the conclusion that it need not concern itself with the process of developing major gifts. Why not concentrate on touting the benefits of planned gifts as a way to create large donations? Because it won't work.

Donations of any size, and especially major gifts, are usually not solely or even primarily motivated by the tax and other benefits planned giving provides. Most donors, first and foremost, are motivated by an organization's mission—to do good, to make a difference—not by an opportunity to take advantage of the tax code. Philanthropy is the act of expressing love for others, and so major gifts are much more than money contributed to meet an organization's needs. They represent a person's opportunity for investment, and they are based on his or her commitment. White (1995), in his book *The Art of Planned Giving*, put it this way:

"The language of philanthropy speaks to a person's heart and soul before it speaks to anything else. It must. If it did not, the tax benefits and the increased income so often touted as the incentives to make a planned gift would add up to no incentive at all" (p. 8). Simply put, even though 95 percent of major gifts will be planned gifts, the techniques of planned giving can never replace the process of cultivating and soliciting major gifts.

How do these two pieces of the puzzle fit together? How do you marry all the technicalities of planned giving with the realities of the major gift process? By seeing planned giving as the facilitator of the major gift. Take the following example:

A local business owner who has one fourteen-year-old child has contributed to and been involved for several years with a nonprofit we'll call the City Medical Center. Her history with City Medical Center and position in the community makes her a natural candidate for a major gift to the organization's campaign. She has been cultivated effectively so that the staff person working with her knows her ambitions and passions and how those feelings can be matched with City Medical Center's initiatives. The major gift solicitation is consummated effectively, and she is asked for $150,000, the largest request ever made of her. Her initial reaction to the ask is both positive and reserved. Her heart tells her she would love to be involved at that level, but her head and her pocketbook wonder if it is financially prudent or feasible.

The development work has been effective to this point because it has produced an excited major gift prospect who wants to be involved. Also the amount asked was correct because it raised her sights somewhat without being completely unreasonable. In short, the nonprofit has done an excellent job of major gift cultivation and solicitation. It is now appropriate to address planned giving.

The donor shares her feelings with the organization. She believes deeply in the cause and wants to contribute $150,000 but isn't certain she can do so. Enter planned giving. Listening carefully, the organization learns that her business is expanding, and the costs are affecting her cash flow. Also, her son is fourteen years old, and she is preparing for college expenses. However, she does have a large individual retirement account (IRA) and some common publicly traded stock that has appreciated greatly in the last five years. Working with her advisers, the organization forwards two options. One is to put some of the appreciated stock into a charitable trust. The trust would provide the donor with income toward her son's college expenses and then collapse and pay its remaining proceeds to City Medical Center. The second alternative is to list City Medical Center as a remainder beneficiary of her IRA. This will help her avoid the taxes these retirement plan assets incur when the owner of the asset dies. Either option establishes a planned gift that allows the donor to make the $150,000 gift to City Medical Center and also to use her appreciated assets effectively, working within her overall tax and financial planning. The end result is that City Medical Center receives both this major gift and an enhanced relationship with a happy donor.

As this example demonstrates, planned giving techniques can problem solve for the donor and thus facilitate the major gift. Conversely, imagine what might have happened if the nonprofit had presented the planned giving option to the donor without any prior major gift cultivation. The organization's solicitors might have spoken only about the tax and income benefits available to the donor if she gave $150,000 to City Medical Center. The donor, like many in that situation, would have quickly become bored with tax code intricacies and might have begun wondering why she should give to this nonprofit. She might conclude that "all City Medical Center wants is my money; it does not care about me or my interests." In fact, after this type of meeting she might even call some other local nonprofit, one that has been effectively cultivating her and that has also asked her for a major gift, and ask if it can work with planned gifts! Planned giving is the instruction manual that guides the major gift investment from a donor. It only facilitates the gift and cannot replace the major gift process.

Planned giving is also important for facilitating a donor's final and ultimate gift to an organization, as the following example demonstrates.

An eighty-year-old donor who is a widower with two grown children has been involved with City Medical Center for many, many years and in several different capacities. He makes regular annual gifts, has served on City Medical Center's board, and made a major gift during its last campaign. He now spends much of his time volunteering for City Medical Center and advocating for this nonprofit in the community. A City Medical Center staff member visits with him often. During one such visit, she speaks to him about leaving a legacy at City Medical Center through his estate plan, one that would honor his long-standing involvement with the organization. The donor expresses an interest in exploring this possibility. The staff member suggests that he visit with a planned giving professional on City Medical Center's staff. He agrees.

This example is different from the first in that the cultivation and solicitation of this donor are part of ongoing effective stewardship rather than a planned and executed major gift approach. The donor's long association with City Medical Center makes this approach possible and also enables the ensuing discussion of a legacy or estate gift.

Then the planned giving representative, who may be a qualified board member or volunteer in organizations without paid professional staff, visits with the donor. He listens carefully to the donor's desire to leave something for his two children and his concerns about their spending habits. The donor also shares that he owns some stock investments, a life insurance policy, and a pension from his employer. His single largest asset is his home, and he wants to explore possible charitable uses for it. After speaking with the donor's attorney and CPA, the planned giving representative offers two alternatives. The first is for the donor to give his home to City Medical Center now in the form of a retained life estate. This means the donor will pass ownership of the home to City Medical Center while retaining the right to live in the home as long as he wants. The second option is to create a charitable trust in the donor's estate plan that will receive the home at his death. The trust will sell the home and then pay an income to the donor's two children for as long as they live. This addresses the donor's concerns regarding his children's spending habits by providing the children with an income stream over their lifetimes. Once the children pass on, the trust will collapse and direct the remaining proceeds to City Medical Center. Either alternative will establish a gift that is substantial and leave a fitting legacy at City Medical Center for a donor who was connected to the organization for so many years.

Although the major gift approach is different here, planned giving's role is the same. By listening carefully and bringing his expertise to bear, the planned giving representative facilitates the estate gift that the donor has in his heart.

Again, planned giving provides the means to create the major gift.

How to Begin a Planned Giving Effort: Start with Bequests

Major gifts are critical to the future well-being of any nonprofit organization, and planned giving facilitates these major commitments from donors. But planned giving is highly technical and demands critical expertise. Any nonprofit that hires a planned giving professional should insist the individual have in-depth knowledge of planned giving vehicles as well as the communication skills needed to relay it to donors and their advisers. Suppose, however, an organization has a one- or two-person development office working full-time to acquire annual cash gifts. Or perhaps it relies entirely on the chief executive officer and volunteers. How can this nonprofit obtain planned gifts too? It can start small, and look to its friends.

If this is your organization, first look to internal resources that can be marshaled toward the effort. Is there an estate planning attorney on your board or somehow involved in your mission? If so, is he or she willing to volunteer some assistance and oversight to your planned giving initiative? Is there an estate planning council in your area where attorneys, CPAs, trust officers, and financial advisers meet regularly? Does your organization know anyone on the council? These are the kinds of questions a small nonprofit must ask to learn what friends it has who can assist it. These volunteers can oversee the copy in planned giving marketing materials and be a resource for answers to technical questions donors may ask in the planned giving context. Sometimes the work of these volunteers can be formalized through bringing them together in a *planned giving advisory committee* (see Chapter Five). When starting small, however, delay forming a committee until other aspects of the start-up planned giving effort are in place.

The first kind of giving a planned giving program should seek is the *bequest*. Bequests, sometimes referred to as *bequest expectancies*, are revocable gifts made most commonly through a donor's will (see Chapter Nine). The main advantage of encouraging bequests is that they are easy for a donor to understand and they do not create an administrative and legal responsibility for the organization (as becoming the trustee of a charitable remainder trust does, for example).

Furthermore, bequests are the most common planned gift and provide the most support for nonprofits. The American Association of Fund-Raising Counsel Trust for Philanthropy (2001) reports that in 2000, $16.02 billion was received by nonprofits through bequests. This figure will grow because the United States will have an increasingly aged population over the next twenty-five to thirty years. Opportunities for bequest gifts abound and should be pursued by every nonprofit. The importance of promoting and receiving bequests to the long-term health of any fundraising organization cannot be overstated. Even if your nonprofit makes no other information or literature on planned giving available to prospects, it should have materials about how to make a will (see Exhibit 4.1).

Promoting Bequests

Promoting bequests to donors takes some effort and planning. The first step is to make a presentation to the nonprofit's board about bequests and their importance to the organization's future. A friend from the board or from the financial planning community might assist by answering estate tax questions that board members might have. Also, board members themselves should be asked to establish bequests for the organization's benefit. Their leadership in this area is as critical as in any other and will help the organization deliver the bequest message to other prospects.

Once the governing board recognizes the importance of bequests, it should be encouraged to create a bequest recognition society for the organization. The recognition society can offer donors such special benefits as mementos or perhaps an annual dinner. Board members should be charter members of this society, so that planned giving can be presented to others as a growing success story within the organization. The organization can create some simple promotional material that introduces the recognition society to prospects, explains how bequests support the mission of the organization, lists the benefits members receive, and names the charter members (if they have agreed to be included). This material should also include an enrollment mechanism permitting prospective members to share information about their bequest gifts (see Exhibit 4.2). This assists the organization in tracking its bequest expectancies.

Once the board is enlisted and a special recognition society created, the organization is ready to begin cultivating bequests among other donors. The first step is

EXHIBIT 4.1. HOW TO MAKE A WILL BROCHURE.

Keep the
music going
with your gift!

P⊘PS

Bloomington
POPS

EXHIBIT 4.1. HOW TO MAKE A WILL BROCHURE, Cont'd.

The gift of music. . .

The Bloomington Pops is now able to accept gifts in many forms.
Below are two new gift options available to our supporters.
Please take a moment to review the following and to see if these
methods can work for you. Your gift may be made as a memorial
designation for a loved one.

1. Gift to the Bloomington Pops through your Will or Living Trust

One of the most common ways individuals leave a legacy at charitable organizations is through a bequest in their Will or Living Trust. At the Bloomington Pops these types of gifts are especially meaningful because they provide the long-term support that will be needed to meet future challenges.

Bequests come in many forms. Here are a few methods to consider:

- **Specific bequest**
  A specific bequest provides that the Bloomington Pops will receive a specific dollar amount.

- **Residuary Bequest**
  A residuary bequest provides that the Bloomington Pops will receive all or a stated portion of your estate after all other bequests, debts, taxes, and expenses have been distributed.

- **Contingent Bequest**
  A contingent bequest can ensure that if circumstances make it impossible to carry out your primary provisions (such as when your spouse or other heirs do not survive you), your assets will then pass on to the Bloomington Pops rather than to unintended beneficiaries.

EXHIBIT 4.1. HOW TO MAKE A WILL BROCHURE, Cont'd.

2. Gift of Life Insurance to the Bloomington Pops

The Bloomington Pops can now be supported through gifts of "paid up" life insurance. Often individuals own policies that no longer need premium payments, and are no longer needed. These types of policies can be transferred to the Bloomington Pops. The Bloomington Pops will cash in the policy to support our current programming. Such gifts are very meaningful to the Pops, and provide generous income tax charitable deductions to donors.

In order for the Bloomington Pops to accept a gift of life insurance, and for a charitable income tax deduction to be generated for the donor, the following things are needed:

- The ownership of the policy must be transferred to Bloomington Pops;

- The Bloomington Pops must become the sole beneficiary of the policy;

- The policy documents must be transferred to our office.

NOTE: Please be advised that these types of gifts are somewhat technical. If you decide you want to support the Bloomington Pops through either a bequest in your Will or Living Trust, or through a paid up life insurance policy, speak with your own attorney or tax advisor first. They are in the best position to assess your personal situation and provide guidance. Gifts are 501(c)(3) non-profit tax deductions.

We hope you will consider supporting the Bloomington Pops through these methods. Please know that whatever form your gifts may take, they are deeply appreciated and make our organization possible. Thank you for your ongoing generous support and for considering the options above. For information please contact Mike Walsh at 336-8747.

Source: Douglas M. Wilson, Bloomington, Indiana. Reprinted with permission.

EXHIBIT 4.2. BEQUEST RECOGNITION SOCIETY MATERIAL.

THE TRAILING ARBUTUS *(epigaea repens) is a beautiful trailing evergreen whose name and image are one of Indiana University's cherished traditions. Usually found in the wild in areas of acid soil where pine trees thrive, its fragrant pink or white flowers grace many of Indiana's wooded hillsides. First discovered by Professor Hermann B. Boisen on "Arbutus Hill" east of Bloomington, the arbutus is the official flower of Indiana University. The yearbook, founded in 1894, is named for it, and it is part of the design on the jewel of office worn by all new University presidents during inauguration ceremonies.*

INDIANA UNIVERSITY
FOUNDATION

Arbutus Society / P.O. Box 500 / Bloomington, IN 47402

EXHIBIT 4.2. BEQUEST RECOGNITION SOCIETY MATERIAL, Cont'd.

ARBUTUS
SOCIETY

The generosity of our donors deserves to be recognized. The Arbutus Society honors those who inform us that they are including Indiana University Foundation in their estate plans. This can be through a bequest, a charitable gift annuity, a charitable remainder trust, or any other planned giving arrangement.

INFORMING US OF YOUR PLANS is a good idea for several reasons. First and foremost, it lets you ensure that we understand your wishes so that your gift will be used exactly as you intend. Second, it allows us and the University to make note of your gift as we plan for the future. And finally, it lets us honor you and show you our appreciation by including you in the roster of donors to Indiana University and in such recognition groups as the Arbutus Society.

NAMED FOR THE OFFICIAL FLOWER OF INDIANA UNIVERSITY, the Society organizes an annual event exclusively for its members. During the year, members are also invited to lectures, exhibits, receptions, performances, and other special events. New members also receive, with their confirmation letter, a supply of note cards featuring the Maryrose Wampler rendering of *The Trailing Arbutus.*

TO ENROLL IN THE ARBUTUS SOCIETY, simply fill out and return the enclosed reply card. Briefly describe your gift plan and/or attach the relevant page(s) from your will or other document. All gift information is confidential; however, we will assume that we can inform the appropriate University officials of your planned gift, unless you tell us otherwise.

INDIANA UNIVERSITY FOUNDATION

EXHIBIT 4.2. BEQUEST RECOGNITION SOCIETY MATERIAL, Cont'd.

SECURING THE FUTURE
of Indiana University

EXHIBIT 4.2. BEQUEST RECOGNITION SOCIETY MATERIAL, Cont'd.

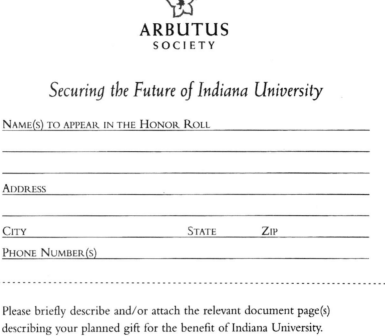

ARBUTUS
SOCIETY

Securing the Future of Indiana University

NAME(S) TO APPEAR IN THE HONOR ROLL

ADDRESS

CITY   STATE   ZIP

PHONE NUMBER(S)

Please briefly describe and/or attach the relevant document page(s) describing your planned gift for the benefit of Indiana University.

SIGNATURE   DATE

○ *You may publish my name as a member of the Arbutus Society.*
○ *I prefer to remain anonymous.*

INDIANA UNIVERSITY FOUNDATION

Source: Indiana University Foundation. Reprinted with permission.

EXHIBIT 4.2. BEQUEST RECOGNITION SOCIETY MATERIAL, Cont'd.

DRAKE HERITAGE SOCIETY

Membership Enrollment Form

__ YES! I/we confirm that I/we have made a planned gift to Drake.

__ I/we give my/our permission to Drake University to publicly recognize my/our membership in the Heritage Society.

Name(s): _____

Print as you would like your name(s) listed in Drake's publications.

Address: _____

City: _____ State: _____

Zip code: _____

College/School: _____ Grad. Year: _____

Signature: _____ Date: _____

Please return your confidential response in the enclosed postage paid envelope. You may also call the Gift Planning Office at 515-271-3171 or call our toll-free number, 1-800-443-7253, Extension 3171.

Source: Drake University, Drake Heritage Society.

to identify those donors who are logical prospects. These donors are the ones familiar with an organization's mission and already convinced of its stability. They are generally older people and have a history of supporting the nonprofit (see Figure 4.1 and Table 4.1). They have been visited many times before and feel closely connected. Solid cultivation has already taken place, and they can be logically and easily introduced to the ways that further support can be provided through a bequest.

Nonprofits can promote bequests in a variety of ways. Face-to-face visits and conversations with identified prospects work best. The promotional material can be shared and left with the donor. During these personal visits it is important to spend time listening to any concerns about estate planning that the donor chooses to discuss. If the donor already has advisers, recommend that the donor visit with them to address these concerns. If the donor does not have an adviser, be prepared to recommend at least three friends of your organization who are qualified to help. You can also refer donors to the local bar association for recommendations. These face-to-face visits are the method most likely to produce success, and you will probably learn about some bequests to your organization already in place. Too, it is incumbent to continue with identifying and doing the major gift cultivation of bequest prospects so the number of donors making a charitable bequest will continue to grow.

FIGURE 4.1. CONTINUOUS LIFETIME GIVING: THE GIVING LIFE CYCLE.

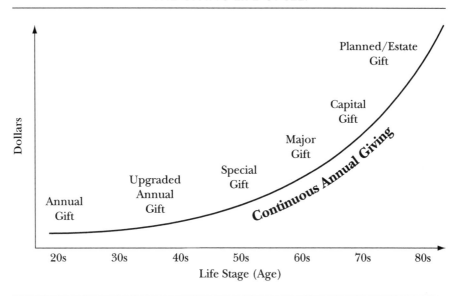

TABLE 4.1. CONTINUOUS LIFETIME GIVING PROGRAM—BROAD OUTLINE.

Type of Giving	Age of Prospects										
	20–25	25–30	30–35	35–40	40–45	45–50	50–55	55–60	60–65	65–70	70+
Annual gifts											
less than $1,000	X	X	X	X	X	X	X	X	X	X	X
$1,000–4,999			X	X	X	X	X	X	X	X	X
$5,000–24,999					X	X	X	X	X	X	X
$25,000+							X	X	X	X	X
Special gifts											
Programs, events (for example, reunions)			X		X			X		X	
Major and planned gifts						X	X	X	X	X	X
Wills and bequests							X	X	X	X	X
Capital gifts							X	X	X	X	X

Beyond personal visits are some other techniques nonprofits often employ to grow their bequest expectancy lists. One of the most popular is the *will seminar,* which teaches constituents the importance of having a will or updating an existing will (see Resource 8). Because many people die without a will or with one that is out of date, hosting a free will seminar is a service to donors and prospects as well as an opportunity for the nonprofit to introduce the idea of including charitable bequests in one's will. Again, look to friends to conduct this seminar. If possible, have an estate planning attorney who is connected to your organization—perhaps as a board member—lead the seminar. The speaker's credentials should assure the people invited of the expertise to be shared and may increase the audience too. At the seminar be certain to share material on your bequest society, and give audience members an evaluation of the seminar that they can complete and return. One question on the evaluation should ask whether a personal visit to discuss a charitable bequest to your organization would be welcome. People who answer yes should be visited as soon as possible so they know their interest is not taken lightly.

Another step that a small organization can take to promote bequests is to send a special direct mail appeal. This is especially appropriate when the nonprofit's donors are spread across a large geographical area and cannot easily be visited or brought together for a seminar. The cover letter should be signed by a high-profile board member, volunteer, or donor who has already made a charitable bequest for the nonprofit's benefit. That way, the letter functions as a testimonial in addition to discussing the importance of charitable bequests and encouraging constituents to make such a bequest. The letter should also thank those who have already made a charitable bequest. And it should include a reply card so that prospects can request further information or alert you that they already have a bequest for your organization in place. This permits you to have conversations with prospects who are considering a bequest to encourage their interest and helps you acknowledge donors with bequests in place (see Exhibit 4.3).

Maintaining Contact

Bequests are revocable gifts; anyone can change his or her will at any time. Therefore it is imperative that bequest donors continue to feel closely connected with the nonprofit after their bequest is established. Simply filing the paperwork to record commitments will not realize the same future dollars from bequests as continuing to pay close attention to this group of donors. Bequest recognition societies help, but they are only one part of a stewardship program. Keep the personal visits and appropriate tokens of appreciation coming to further ensure that donors will not change their wills at a later date to exclude your organization.

EXHIBIT 4.3. BEQUEST APPEAL LETTER.

March 25, 2000

Dear [Name]:

Now's your chance.

As you probably know, IU Bloomington is conducting an endowment campaign. The campaign is in its final months—June 30 is the deadline—and the School of Optometry is still some distance from its goal. We know that it sometimes takes a last-minute push to get over the top: now is the time to start pushing.

We need our alumni to act.

If you are like many, you would love to give something back to the School. It gave you your start, it trained you to excel in your field, and its continued distinction reflects well on you as a graduate. But perhaps you have hesitated, feeling you cannot afford to be as generous as you would like.

We have a solution. It is one of the easiest ways to contribute to the School's campaign, it has great tax advantages, and, best of all, it puts no crimp in your current budget: a charitable bequest.

Obviously, your first priority is to provide for your loved ones after you are gone. Having accomplished that goal, however, providing for the School of Optometry is another way to leave a meaningful legacy. The beauty of a charitable bequest is that it allows you to retain control and full use of your assets during your lifetime, yet still leave a something for your alma mater—at a level you might never have managed otherwise.

If you decide, as Andrya and I have, to include the School of Optometry in your estate plans, we thank you for your thoughtfulness and ask that you notify us with the enclosed card. Doing so allows us to recognize you and your gift as part of the School's endowment campaign. It will also give us the chance to talk with you about how you'd like your eventual gift used at the School.

We hope to hear from you very soon—June 30 is closer than you think.

Sincerely,

Dean Gerald E. Lowther, OD, MS, PhD

P.S. If you have specific questions about making a gift to the School, or other ways to make a gift, please contact Eileen Savage at the IU Foundation (812) 855-6391 or (800) 558-8311.

Source: Indiana University-Bloomington, School of Optometry. Reprinted with the permission of Indiana University Foundation.

CHAPTER FIVE

IMPLEMENTING A PLANNED GIVING PROGRAM

Chapter Four discussed the intersection of major and planned gifts, why a planned giving program is necessary, and how every nonprofit can begin one. This chapter expands on the introduction of planned giving to a nonprofit's environment and explores how a planned giving program can be further developed.

Involving the Governing Board

The level of board commitment will determine whether a planned giving initiative is successful. The board of any nonprofit organization must be committed to a planned giving initiative and continually involved in its progress. Board involvement is critical because initiating a planned giving program requires investing current resources for future benefit. It means hiring staff, accepting liability, and perhaps waiting years before revenues from planned gifts arrive. An organization's board must understand these realities and be willing to support the investment over a period of time long enough to produce tangible results. This does not mean that productivity, measured in terms of both activity and closed gifts, cannot be measured from the beginning. This can be done and should be, but holding the realized results in hand will take longer.

Organizational staff may have to work to convince the board members that planned giving is important to the nonprofit's future. You will probably begin at the top. Arrange a meeting with the chairperson to explain the objectives of the program. If possible, invite one or two peers of the chair or planned giving professional colleagues from nonprofits that already have planned giving programs. They can help you convince the chairperson that planned giving is important to securing major gifts. Bring a strategic plan summarizing expenses associated with organizing the program (developing a budget will be covered later in this chapter) and a projection of the results (see Resource 9).

Once the chairperson is convinced of the program's worth, he or she can take the issue to other board members. The makeup of the board and the personalities involved will dictate the best method of sharing program information. For example, on the one hand it may be appropriate to send a letter that raises the issue and presents the strategic plan. On the other hand it may be more appropriate to have personal discussions between key members of the board and the chairperson, who will lead the discussions.

After board members have been introduced to the idea informally, they will need to discuss it at a board meeting. If the chairperson is sufficiently committed and articulate he or she may make the sales presentation. Alternatively, he or she may introduce the topic, say a few words about it, and then turn to the chief executive officer, chief development officer, or a designated board member to summarize the strategic plan for the other board members. This meeting is critical. Be prepared for serious questions about whether this initiative is warranted.

Although issues of funding and return on investment will be paramount to the board, the issues of gift acceptance and liability will be a close second. Planned giving involves many legal technicalities, so be prepared to discuss how the organization will deal with them. Governance over these issues should be provided by a planned giving committee of the board that is charged with reviewing planned giving's efforts and progress. The committee should include one or more estate planning professionals who can advise the organization in specific gift situations. Its membership should not exceed five people so it can be nimble enough to provide guidance quickly. Finally, it should be fully involved in developing the organization's gift acceptance policy.

Establishing a Gift Acceptance Policy

Once there is board support for a planned giving program, the next step is to develop a gift acceptance policy that says what types of gifts the organization is and is not willing to accept. Gift acceptance policies set parameters on a host of liability issues associated with certain assets and speak to the gift administration issues that are rampant in planned giving. Moreover, establishing a policy immediately will educate development staff and board members on this topic at the program's inception. This is a healthier approach than making decisions about policy ad hoc when prompted by a prospective gift. With a policy already in place, an organization will have the guidance and can impose the discipline to refuse a gift if necessary.

Developing a gift acceptance policy must be a collaborative effort between the board's planned giving committee members, the development staff, and the chief executive officer. Outside legal counsel should also be involved if such expertise is not available on the board's planned giving committee. This combination of participants will provide the legal expertise, the development insight, and the organizational knowledge necessary to draft a workable policy.

Adoption of the gift acceptance policy must involve the entire governing board. Send a draft of the policy to each board member, and allow ample time for discussion at the subsequent board meeting. It may be that the policy will need to be redrafted and reintroduced at a future meeting. This process of debate and revision is healthy. If the passage of the policy is not immediate, this should not be perceived as a failure.

Issues to Be Addressed

A gift acceptance policy should address several specific issues (see Resource 10). The policy should begin by stating its purpose, and how it relates to the mission of the organization. A gift acceptance policy should also state clearly that the organization always encourages the donor to seek his or her own legal or tax counsel prior to making a planned gift. This is critical: a nonprofit organization must avoid the conflict of interest that would occur if it both functioned as the donor's adviser and received the donor's gifts. Furthermore, a nonprofit cannot involve itself in the unauthorized practice of law. Because the opportunity for these undesirable situations often arises with donors who have a close affiliation with the charity, the policy should clearly state that donors should seek independent representation before making a planned gift.

Gift acceptance policies should also speak to the issue of gift restrictions. Most of the planned gifts an organization receives will be restricted. What types of restrictions the nonprofit will and will not allow should be stated in the policy. How rigid and specific an organization should be regarding restrictions is a decision made between the administrative staff and the board. However, a gift acceptance policy should always state that gifts will be refused if they are not consistent with the organization's mission or if they exceed its scope.

Gift acceptance policies should also designate the persons who are empowered to negotiate a planned giving arrangement with a donor. They are normally individuals within the organization who can sign the legal documents that create the gift. This generally includes the organization's chief executive officer, chief development officer, chief financial officer, and the planned giving professional(s) who are knowledgeable and skilled in the area. The gift acceptance policy thus sends a clear message to constituents and staff about who is responsible for negotiating planned gifts, and limits the organization's liability for the actions of others.

Types of Gifts to be Accepted

The types of gifts an organization accepts are also an important component of a gift acceptance policy. The gifts an organization can accept depend on its ability to manage those gifts. Some gifts, such as bequests, are relatively easy for any organization to handle. However, most deferred gifts are complex, and thus a careful assessment of the organization's resources is a critical step in creating a gift acceptance policy. An organization may not want to accept gifts of real estate if it is not staffed to manage and dispose of the property. This may also be true for gifts of tangible personal property, such as furniture or stamp collections. Establishing and administering a gift annuity program is costly and labor intensive, as is managing gifts of life insurance. Does the charity want to take on the necessary responsibilities for those gifts? It is important for an organization to do a careful self-assessment as part of developing this portion of the policy.

Once that assessment is completed, the policy should list the types of gifts the organization will accept and those it will not. The policy should also state how gifts will be managed, disposed of, or invested after they are accepted. For example, it may be appropriate for the policy to state that gifts of marketable securities and real estate may be sold immediately upon receipt. Finally, the policy should clarify when the nonprofit will use the gift. This is especially important with planned gifts because the gift proceeds are generally not available until after the donor's death.

One type of gift that requires careful study is closely held stock. Because closely held stock is a security not publicly traded, its value is difficult to determine. If an organization decides to accept such gifts, the policy should state that their value must be established by the donor through an independent appraisal. The policy should also specify that prior to acceptance a review of a proposed gift of closely held stock will be performed to make certain there are no restrictions on selling the stock and that there is an available market for it.

If an organization decides to accept gifts of real estate, guidelines for those gifts should be included in the gift acceptance policy. The policy should notify prospective real estate donors that an appraisal of the property provided by the donor will be required. The issues in setting real estate gift policy are similar to those for gifts of closely held stock. Will the policy be to hold real estate for investment or to sell it immediately? Who in the organization will assess the property's marketability? If the real estate isn't deemed marketable, is the gift refused outright, or will the organization negotiate regarding improvements to the property? Is the organization both willing and able to carry certain costs such as insurance and mortgages or notes associated with property? Will the donor be required to make a separate gift to cover the expenses? All these issues need to be addressed in the policy.

Real estate gifts have the additional issues of environmental liability, zoning compliance, and easements. A nonprofit that owns real estate with environmental problems may be required to clean it up under the federal Comprehensive Environmental Response, Compensation and Liability Act (CERCLA). Therefore it is important that an environmental audit be performed before a property is accepted—especially if the property has been previously used commercially. This should be articulated in the policy so donors understand this requirement.

Does your organization wish to accept tangible personal property such as jewelry, cars, boats, and equipment? If so, it must be able to receipt those gifts properly and be certain to determine the marketability of the items. The acceptance policy should address these types of gifts and should include an appraisal requirement for the donor and the requirement that the gift be assessed for the organization's prospective use, maintenance, storage, and other costs as well as the gift's marketability, before it is accepted.

Acceptance of Various Gift Vehicles

Gift vehicles should also be addressed in the policy, and here too an assessment of the organization's strengths and abilities is critical. Does the organization wish to initiate a charitable gift annuity program? Gift annuities are wonderful gifts, but an organization must clearly understand the liability created in issuing the annuity. A nonprofit must register with the state insurance commission where required by state law in any state where it solicits gift annuities. State laws often require nonprofits to have segregated reserves on their books to cover payments due to annuitants. If a nonprofit decides to establish a gift annuity program, the gift acceptance policy should define the minimum size gift annuity the organization will offer. It should also set a minimum age requirement and describe the types of property that can be accepted in exchange for an annuity. Deferred gift annuities should be articulated separately in the policy. There may be gifts of real property the organization would accept for a deferred gift annuity that it would not accept for one that requires payments to begin immediately. The policy should also discuss how annuities will be managed and list the states where they will be offered.

Another gift vehicle that requires attention is the charitable remainder trust. Does the organization wish to accept the trustee appointments and the fiduciary responsibility these gifts entail? If the nonprofit offers itself as trustee, are there specific instances where it would refuse to accept that responsibility? For example, suppose a donor wishes to establish a charitable trust that benefits multiple charities, but wants your organization to manage it. Will you do so, and under what circumstances? These issues need to be clarified and written into the organization's gift acceptance policy. Other issues to be addressed include setting the minimum gift amount required to establish a charitable trust and determining the percentage of the trust principal that must accrue to the organization if a donor wants to benefit multiple charities.

Gifts of life insurance policies are another area to explore carefully. If an organization chooses to accept these gifts, the policy should set conditions on the types of life insurance vehicles the organization will accept. For example, if an organization accepts only whole life policies must they be paid up, meaning no further premiums are due, or not? If not, does the charity intend to bill the donor for future premiums? If so, should the donor be required to sign a pledge agreement to ensure that the future premiums are paid? Does the organization plan to accept gifts of life insurance in order to cash them in upon receipt so that it receives the cash surrender value immediately? These questions should be answered in the gift acceptance policy so donors are informed. The policy should also state the minimum life insurance face value the organization is willing to accept, what type of insurance products it will assume, and some rating minimum that the insurance company offering the policy must meet, such as a specific AM Best or Standard & Poor's rating.

Ethical Standards

Gift acceptance policies should also include the Model Standards of Practice for the Charitable Gift Planner (see Exhibit 5.1). The Model Standards, promulgated by the National Committee on Planned Giving, establish ethical standards for everyone involved in the planned giving profession. For example, the Model Standards state that a charitable gift planner must make every effort to give the donor a full explanation of all aspects of the proposed planned gift. They also state that charitable gift planners should suggest donors seek independent counsel whenever they are considering a planned gift. Including the Model Standards in your gift acceptance policy will incorporate those ethical standards into your gift planning operation.

EXHIBIT 5.1. MODEL STANDARDS OF PRACTICE FOR THE CHARITABLE GIFT PLANNER.

Preamble

The purpose of this statement is to encourage responsible gift planning by urging the adoption of the following Standards of Practice by all individuals who work in the charitable gift planning process, gift planning officers, fund raising consultants, attorneys, accountants, financial planners, life insurance agents and other financial services professionals (collectively referred to hereafter as "Gift Planners"), and by the institutions that these persons represent.

This statement recognizes that the solicitation, planning and administration of a charitable gift is a complex process involving philanthropic, personal, financial, and tax considerations, and often involves professionals from various disciplines whose goals should include working together to structure a gift that achieves a fair and proper balance between the interests of the donor and the purposes of the charitable institution.

I. Primacy of Philanthropic Motivation

The principal basis for making a charitable gift should be a desire on the part of the donor to support the work of charitable institutions.

II. Explanation of Tax Implications

Congress has provided tax incentives for charitable giving, and the emphasis in this statement on philanthropic motivation in no way minimizes the necessity and appropriateness of a full and accurate explanation by the Gift Planner of those incentives and their implications.

III. Full Disclosure

It is essential to the gift planning process that the role and relationships of all parties involved, including how and by whom each is compensated, be fully disclosed to the donor. A Gift Planner shall not act or purport to act as a representative of any charity without the express knowledge and approval of the charity, and shall not, while employed by the charity, act or purport to act as a representative of the donor, without the express consent of both the charity and the donor.

IV. Compensation

Compensation paid to Gift Planners shall be reasonable and proportionate to the services provided. Payment of finder's fees, commissions or other fees by a donee organization to an independent Gift Planner as a condition for the delivery of a gift is never appropriate. Such payments lead to abusive practices and may violate certain state and federal regulations. Likewise, commission-based compensation for Gift Planners who are employed by a charitable institution is never appropriate.

V. Competence and Professionalism

The Gift Planner should strive to achieve and maintain a high degree of competence in his or her chosen area, and shall advise donors only in areas in which he or she is professionally qualified. It is a hallmark of professionalism for Gift Planners that they realize when they have reached the limits of their knowledge and expertise, and as a result, should include other professionals in the process. Such relationships should be characterized by courtesy, tact and mutual respect.

EXHIBIT 5.1. MODEL STANDARDS OF
PRACTICE FOR THE CHARITABLE GIFT PLANNER, Cont'd.

VI. Consultation with Independent Advisers

A Gift Planner acting on behalf of a charity shall in all cases strongly encourage the donor to discuss the proposed gift with competent independent legal and tax advisers of the donor's choice.

VII. Consultation with Charities

Although Gift Planners frequently and properly counsel donors concerning specific charitable gifts without the prior knowledge or approval of the donee organization, the Gift Planner, in order to insure that the gift will accomplish the donor's objectives, should encourage the donor early in the gift planning process, to discuss the proposed gift with the charity to whom the gift is to be made. In cases where the donor desires anonymity, the Gift Planner shall endeavor, on behalf of the undisclosed donor, to obtain the charity's input in the gift planning process.

VIII. Description and Representation of Gift

The Gift Planner shall make every effort to assure that the donor receives a full description and an accurate representation of all aspects of any proposed charitable gift plan. The consequences for the charity, the donor and, where applicable, the donor's family, should be apparent, and the assumptions underlying any financial illustrations should be realistic.

IX. Full Compliance

A Gift Planner shall fully comply with and shall encourage other parties in the gift planning process to fully comply with both the letter and spirit of all applicable federal and state laws and regulations.

X. Public Trust

Gift Planners shall, in all dealings with donors, institutions and other professionals, act with fairness, honesty, integrity and openness. Except for compensation received for services, the terms of which have been disclosed to the donor, they shall have no vested interest that could result in personal gain.

Adopted and subscribed to by the National Committee on Planned Giving and the American Council on Gift Annuities, May 7, 1991. Revised April 1999.

Source: Reprinted with permission, copyright 1991, National Committee on Planned Giving®.

Gift Acceptance Committee

The best efforts of any organization will not produce a gift acceptance policy that will anticipate everything. Therefore, it is important that the policy establish a gift acceptance committee in the organization. This committee should be separate from the planned giving committee of the board. It is typically composed of staff who represent such organizational functions as business affairs, gift administration, and development. At smaller nonprofits this committee may be composed of the executive director, development director, and a board member from the organization's finance committee, one who is very familiar with the charity's fiscal circumstances. The purpose of the gift acceptance committee is to review proposed gifts that are not defined in the gift acceptance policy or that have special circumstances. This committee should be small enough to respond to proposed gifts on a timely basis.

The gift acceptance committee should have access to outside legal counsel, and the availability of this counsel should be stated in the gift acceptance policy. Outside legal counsel can advise and protect the nonprofit when gifts with unusual legal ramifications are proposed, such as gifts of closely held stock with buy-sell agreements or other restrictions and gifts governed by contracts such as bargain sales. By stating that counsel will be engaged when appropriate, the policy enables the organization to seek necessary information while leaving the final decision on acceptance in the committee's hands.

Finally, there may be times when the gift acceptance committee needs to make recommendations to the entire board regarding a gift. The decision to go to the board should be reached by the committee in concert with its legal adviser. The gift acceptance policy should establish a procedure for accessing board expertise and approval when necessary.

Annual Review

Once a gift acceptance policy is adopted, it should be reviewed annually by the board's planned giving committee to maintain the policy as a centerpiece of the planned giving effort. This annual review is also an opportunity to amend the policy in the event of tax law changes or changed circumstances in the organization. Any such revisions or adjustments to the policy should come as recommendations for adoption from the planned giving committee to the board.

Managing a Planned Giving Program

Once a planned giving program has been established and an acceptance policy approved, it must be managed. One of the first steps is to develop a record-keeping system to track planned gifts. Staff should put an inventory and filing system in place to track bequests, annuities, charitable remainder trusts, insurance policies, gifts in kind, estates in probate, and anticipated estate distributions.

One of the elements most critical to the long-term management of planned gifts is a *gift agreement*. This is a legal document that sets forth the donor's intentions and the organization's responsibilities. It provides guidance for administering the gift, now and in the future, when the donor and the organizational representatives who worked with the donor are no longer available to answer questions that arise (see Resource 11). In the case of deferred gifts, this agreement is of the utmost importance.

Developing a Budget

Establishing a budget for a planned giving program is a challenging management exercise. It is a given that it takes money to raise money, but how much it takes is often up for debate. This is doubly true with planned giving because there is no immediate return from the investment. Because the planned giving seeds planted today may not be harvested for many years, it is sometimes difficult to justify current expenditures. Moreover, it is important to remember that no two planned giving programs are alike. The nonprofit's location, constituency, breadth of services, quality of services, reputation, number of years in existence, and board composition will all affect its ability to realize planned gifts.

Developing a planned giving budget begins with knowing what expenses will be charged to it. Certain items—phones or office supplies, for example—may fall within the overall organizational budget, but others will not. Once it is known what expenses the planned giving effort must bear, budget preparation can begin.

Ashton (1991) describes one useful system for establishing a planned giving budget. She recommends first identifying expenses that are essentially stable and predictable, such as memberships in regional planned giving committees and subscriptions to planned giving newsletters. Second, allocate funds for variable items, such as special events or mailings, travel expenses for donor visits, and thank-you gifts for donor stewardship.

When developing this budget, it is important to keep the core goals of your program front and center. Those goals should be discovery, cultivation, and solicitation of planned giving prospects. Once you get beyond fixed costs, allocate the remaining budget to means of accomplishing these three things, and your effort will be focused in the right direction (see Exhibit 6.1).

Setting Specific Goals

Setting specific goals for a planned giving program is another important aspect of initiating the effort and then guiding program management. Without specific goals, a program will lack direction and a sense of urgency to accomplish its mission. These goals should not be set in terms of amounts raised, but rather in terms of objectives achieved. Dollar goals lose meaning quickly in planned giving because the amount of money a program closes will fluctuate from year to year. This is especially true of new programs. A new program may meet with early success by establishing bequests from board members the first year, but then experience a second and even a third year without closing many gifts. This doesn't mean the program is ineffective. It merely reflects the reality that cultivating a planned gift takes time with prospects who are not already closely connected to an organization. Setting goals based on dollars raised ignores this reality.

The specific goals, or objectives, to target are donor contacts and creation of effective marketing material. These donor contacts should be meaningful, significant face-to-face visits that are recorded in the organization's files for future reference. Donor visits are the backbone of any major gift and planned giving effort, and the number to be achieved per month, per quarter, per half year, or per year should be an essential goal set for any program. The target number of face-to-face visits that is set will depend on the staffing and age of the program. For example, during a new program's first year, staff will have to spend some time educating board members and establishing a gift acceptance policy. In subsequent years, as the program matures, they can spend more time on donor identification and visits. Goals should reflect this reality too.

The program should have a marketing plan involving newsletters, special events, and direct mail appeals (see Chapter Six), and specific goals should be defined for these efforts as well. The organization might need to decide, for example, how many editions of the newsletter will be sent during the year, how many events will be sponsored for stewardship or cultivation, and whether a special letter will be sent soliciting a specific type of gift. These decisions will depend on resources and staffing, but the marketing of planned gifts should be incorporated into clear goals at the start of the program and every year thereafter.

Critical Resources

Several resources are essential for any planned giving program, regardless of its size and budget. Without a commitment to these critical elements a program should not be initiated.

First, the person responsible for planned giving at a nonprofit should have membership in the National Committee on Planned Giving (NCPG) and its respective local council. NCPG is a national network of planned giving professionals that provides indispensable resources for planned giving programs. The local affiliated councils are places for continuing education and for sharing ideas with others in the field. Most local councils hold meetings that feature speakers on planned giving developments. NCPG also hosts a national conference annually that is an excellent resource for information on all aspects of planned giving. NCPG can be contacted easily regarding a local affiliated planned giving council in your area at the following address:

National Committee on Planned Giving
233 McCrea Street, Suite 400
Indianapolis, IN 46225
Phone: (317) 269-6274   Fax: (317) 269-6276
E-mail: ncpg@iupui.edu
Web site: www.ncpg.org

A second critical resource is computer software for producing planned giving illustrations for donors (see Exhibit 5.2). These graphic tools can illustrate a donor's charitable deduction or expected income and clarify gift design. They can produce a variety of charts and graphs to help articulate the prospective gift. These software packages as not inexpensive, but they are necessary for any serious planned giving

EXHIBIT 5.2. GIFT PLANNING SOFTWARE PROVIDERS.

Crescendo Planned Gifts Software
1601 Carmen Drive, Suite 103
Camarillo, CA 93010
Contact: Ardis Schultz
Vice President/Marketing
800/858-9154
FAX: 805/388-2483
E-mail: crescendosoft@hotmail.com
Web site: www.crescendosoft.com
• Crescendo Pro
• Crescendo Estate
• Crescendo Lite
• Crescendo Plus

PG Calc Incorporated
129 Mount Auburn Street
Cambridge, MA 02138
Contact: Tina Yelle
Vice President
888/497-4970
FAX: 617/497-4974
E-mail: info@pgcalc.com
Web site: www.pgcalc.com
• Gift Planning Software:
   Planned Giving Manager
   Mini Manager

EXHIBIT 5.2. GIFT PLANNING SOFTWARE PROVIDERS, Cont'd.

- Gift Administration Software:
  GiftWrap
  Pooled Fund Organizer
  Universal Sub-Account Organizer

Planned Giving Seminars/Services
2048 Garden Avenue
St. Paul, MN 55113
Contact: Robert A. Evenson, CFRE
President
651/646-0317
FAX: 651/646-0317
E-mail: reven29@aol.com
Web site: http://members.aol.com/pgss1997/index.html
- Program design and implementation
- Program evaluation
- Technical assistance with individual gifts
- Trustee Seminars
- Gift Planning Software: The Planned Giving Companion
- Professional Training/Education: A Brisk Walk Through the Basics

SunGard Trust Systems, Inc.
551077 Center Drive
P.O. Box 240882
Charlotte, NC 28224-0882
Contact: John Bingham
Vice President, Not-for-Profit Solutions
704/527-6300
FAX: 704/527-9741
E-mail: john.bingham@sungardtrust.com
Web site: www.sungardtrst.com
- Trust Accounting Software

BIPSTER International LLC
P.O. Box 3022
Salem, MA 01970
Contact: Susan DameGreene, Managing Member
Phone: 978-744-3180 or 888-588-BIPS (2477)
FAX: 978-744-0319
E-mail: susan@bipster.com
Web site: www.bipster.com
- Bequest Processing Software (BIPS)
- Start-up of bequest programs
- Training and support for collection of bequests

Source: Reprinted with permission, *NCPG Directory of Council Members,* copyright 2001, National Committee on Planned Giving®.

effort. Without them program staff and volunteers will lack the sophisticated aids that will give the program credibility as they converse with donors and their advisers.

A third critical element is sufficient staff support. The person responsible for identifying, cultivating, and closing planned gifts cannot be also responsible for creating files, reviewing and copying correspondence, setting appointments, and other administrative duties. A planned giving professional saddled with these responsibilities will not have sufficient time and organization to produce an effective program.

A fourth critical element is resource material for the planned giving office. Resource books that contain the legal nuts and bolts of planned giving should be available to provide answers to questions that will arise in this context (see Exhibit 5.3). Vendors who sell these materials also provide updates so that when the law changes the resources are kept up to date. Having these materials on hand enables staff and volunteers to speak knowledgeably about issues with donors and their advisers. This in turn inspires confidence in the program among those most able to help through their financial support. Please keep in mind, however, that the planned giving professional cannot serve as a donor's attorney. Ultimately, donors must rely on their own counsel to provide the legal advice they need to move forward with a gift.

The final critical elements are patience and hard work. Planned giving involves equal measures of both if a program is to be successful. The planned giving message must be sent to donors again and again before it will bear fruit.

EXHIBIT 5.3. GIFT PLANNING LEGAL RESOURCES.

Kallina & Ackerman, LLP
6507 York Road
Baltimore, MD 21212
Contact: Emil Kallina, II, Esquire
410/377-2170
FAX: 410/377-2179
E-mail: kallacker@home.com

Estes Associates
41 Spoke Drive
Woodbridge, CT 06525
Contact: Ellen G. Estes, LL.B.
Attorney & Planned Giving Consultant
203/393-3159
FAX: 203/393-3857
E-mail: ellen.estes@juno.com

Sinclair, Townes & Company
230 Peachtree Street NW
Suite 1601
Atlanta, GA 30303

EXHIBIT 5.3. GIFT PLANNING LEGAL RESOURCES, Cont'd.

Contact: Rick Billingslea, Marketing Manager or
Molly Bagett, Associate Consultant
404/688-4047
FAX: 404/688-6543
E-mail: info@sinclairtownes.com
Web site: www.sinclairtownes.com

Winton Smith & Associates
2670 Union Extended, Suite 1200
Memphis, TN 38112
Contact: Winton Smith, Jr., Owner
800/727-1040 or 901/327-2700
FAX: 901/327-5875
E-mail: winton@wintonsmith.com

Mellon Private Asset Management-Charitable Gifts Office
One Boston Place
Boston, MA 02108
Contact: Linda R. Fitzpatrick
First Vice President
617/722-7649
FAX: 617/722-7362

Conrad Teitell
13 Arcadia Road
Old Greenwich, CT 06870
Contact: Sally-Ann O'Shea, Chief of Staff
203/637-4553
FAX: 203/637-4572
E-mail: info@taxwisegiving.com
Web site: www.taxwisegiving.com

Endowment Development Services (EDS)
2511 E. 46th Street, #R7
Indianapolis, IN 46205
Contact: James R. Marshall, President
317/542-9829
FAX: 317/549-9470
E-mail: 75762.2443@compuserv.com

Pentera, Inc.
8650 Commerce Park Place, Suite G
Indianapolis, IN 46268
Contact: Douglas A. Weaver
Assistant to the President/Marketing
317/875-0910
FAX: 317/875-0912
E-mail: PenteraInc@aol.com

Source: Reprinted with permission, *NCPG Directory of Council Members,* copyright 2001, National
Committee on Planned Giving®.

Planned gifts arrive based on a donor's timetable, not that of the charitable organization. In many months no gifts will close even though multiple proposals are put forth. When those times occur, keep focused on your core objectives and maintain patience with your effort. Only a long-term, sustained effort will bear meaningful results, so keep at it and celebrate your successes as they arrive.

Use of Consultants

A planned giving effort can be enhanced by the use of outside consultants, and they are available in a variety of planned giving areas. Some consultants focus on marketing, whereas others have expertise in the area of financial management (see Exhibit 5.4). How those consultants can help depends on the needs of the program and its level of development.

Planned giving programs that are just beginning may use a consultant to help guide the process who provides advice on developing planned giving guidelines, giving presentations to the board, and initiating the marketing effort. Such external expertise gives the initial effort a greater chance to succeed.

More mature planned giving efforts use consulting services in a variety of ways. For example, if an organization decides to begin offering gift annuities, a consultant can assist in organizing the financial and legal aspects of the effort. This would include ensuring that the organization complies with the various state laws regulating gift annuities. The consultant might also help the nonprofit to create procedures for the accounting of gift annuity payments and the investment of the gifts to make the payments.

Selecting a consultant is an important process. It should involve the nonprofit's planned giving professional, chief executive officer, and chair of the planned giving committee of the board. These three should interview prospective consultants to judge how their experience will fit with the organization's specific needs. Once they are employed, their performance should be assessed on a regular basis.

Although planned giving consultants can be an enormous benefit, they are not a critical element for success. If your organization is not prepared or able to hire a consultant, do not be distressed. Many planned giving initiatives have succeeded without them. Asking for advice from planned giving colleagues is an excellent way to move forward without hiring a consultant. There are also numerous seminars available that can provide much of the same guidance a planned giving consultant would on all areas of planned giving, including marketing, gift administration, and gift design. The challenge then is to take the knowledge gained from others and apply it specifically to your organization.

EXHIBIT 5.4. PLANNED GIVING CONSULTANTS.

Alice A. Pinsley, Ph.D., CFP, Planned Giving Consultant
141 Woodbine Road
Stamford, CT 06903
Contact: Alice Pinsley
203/329-9850
FAX: 203/329-9851
• Program design and implementation
• Marketing plans
• Program evaluation
• Technical assistance with individual gifts
• Volunteer seminars
• Trustee seminars
• Donor seminars
• Custom planned giving ads

Barrett Planned Giving, Inc.
2000 L Street, N.W., Suite 200
Washington, DC 20036-4907
Contact: Richard D. Barrett
President
202/416-1667
FAX: 202/416-1668
E-mail: barrettplan@compuserve.com
Web site: www.barrettplannedgiving.com
• Program design and implementation
• Marketing plans
• Program evaluation
• Technical assistance with individual gifts
• Volunteer seminars
• Trustee seminars
• Donor seminars
• Professional publication: *Planned Giving Essentials: A Step-by-Step Guide to Success*

Carr Real Estate for Charities
A Division of Carr Real Estate Services, Inc.
A Subsidiary of CarrAmerica
3611 S. Harbor Blvd., Suite 230
Santa Ana, CA 92704
Contact: Chase V. Magnuson
Vice President
714/557-2277
FAX: 714/557-4829
E-mail: cmagnuso@carramerica.com
Web site: realestateforcharities.com
• Technical assistance with individual gifts
• Real estate services

EXHIBIT 5.4. PLANNED GIVING CONSULTANTS, Cont'd.

Currie, Ferner, Scarpetta & DeVries
401 Second Avenue South
Suite 102
Minneapolis, MN 55401
Contact: David C. Ferner
Managing Partner
612/340-9810
FAX: 612/333-6672
• Program design and implementation
• Marketing plans
• Program evaluation
• Technical assistance with individual gifts
• Volunteer seminars
• Trustee seminars
• Donor seminars

Davidson Gift Design
3940 Walcott Late
Bloomington, IN 47404
Contact: Pamela Jones Davidson, JD
President
812/876-8646
FAX: 812/876-9484
E-mail: pjdavidson@giftplanners.com
Web site: www.giftplanners.com
• Program design and implementation
• Marketing plans
• Program evaluation
• Technical assistance with individual gifts
• Volunteer seminars
• Donor seminars

Estes Associates
41 Spoke Drive
Woodbridge, CT 06525
Contact: Ellen G. Estes, LL.B.
Attorney & Planned Giving Consultant
203/393-3159
FAX: 203/393-3857
E-mail: ellen.estes@juno.com
• Program design and implementation
• Marketing plans
• Program evaluation
• Technical assistance with individual gifts
• Volunteer seminars
• Trustee seminars
• Donor seminars
• One-day seminars—"Planned Giving—Plain and Simple"—for development officers,
  board members, volunteers, allied professionals and other staff people

EXHIBIT 5.4. PLANNED GIVING CONSULTANTS, Cont'd.

Gift Planning Associates
731 Market Street, #600
San Francisco, CA 94103
Contact: Richard Lamport
Principal
415/243-9175
FAX: 415/284-0150
E-mail: giftplaner@compuserve.com
• Program design and implementation
• Marketing plans
• Program evaluation
• Technical assistance with individual gifts
• Volunteer seminars
• Trustee seminars
• Donor seminars

John Brown Limited, Inc.
46 Grove Street, PO Box 296
Peterborough, NH 03458-0296
Contact: John J. Brown
President
603/924-3834
FAX: 603/924-7998
E-mail: jblnh@aol.com
Web site: jblnh.com
• Program design and implementation
• Marketing plans
• Program evaluation
• Technical assistance with individual gifts
• Volunteer seminars
• Trustee seminars
• Donor seminars

Kathryn W. Miree & Associates, Inc.
PO Box 130846
Birmingham, AL 35213
Contact: Kathryn W. Miree
President
205/939-0003
FAX: 205/939-3781
E-mail: kwmiree@giftplanners.com
Web site: www.giftplanners.com
• Program design and implementation
• Marketing plans
• Program evaluation
• Technical assistance with individual gifts
• Volunteer seminars
• Trustee seminars
• Donor seminars
• Professional publications: *Building a Planned Giving Program*—3 book series

EXHIBIT 5.4. PLANNED GIVING CONSULTANTS, Cont'd.

Laura Hansen Dean and Associates
PO Box 36386
Indianapolis, IN 46236
Contact: Laura Hansen Dean
President
317/823-2302 or 812/876-8646
FAX: 317/823-6396 or 812/876-9484
E-mail: lhdean@giftplanners.com
Web site: www.giftplanners.com
• Program design and implementation
• Marketing plans
• Program evaluation
• Technical assistance with individual gifts
• Volunteer seminars
• Trustee seminars
• Donor seminars
• Charitable Gift Planning

Mangone & Co.
12687 West Cedar Drive, Suite 350
Lakewood, CO 80228
Contact: Betsy A. Mangone
President
303/980-0800
FAX: 303/980-9158
E-mail: bmangone@aol.com
Web site: www.giftplanners.com
• Program design and implementation
• Marketing plans
• Program evaluation
• Technical assistance with individual gifts
• Volunteer seminars
• Trustee seminars
• Donor seminars
• Executive search

Marts & Lundy, Inc.
1200 Wall Street West
Lyndhurst, NJ 07071
Contact: John G. Lewis, Jr.
Senior Consultant
800/526-9005
FAX: 201/460-0680
E-mail: vermontlew@aol.com
Web site: martsandlundy.com
• Program design and implementation
• Marketing plans
• Program evaluation
• Technical assistance with individual gifts
• Volunteer seminars

EXHIBIT 5.4. PLANNED GIVING CONSULTANTS, Cont'd.

- Trustee seminars
- Donor seminars

Merrill Lynch Nonprofit Financial Services
800 Scudders Mill Road, Section 1F
Plainsboro, NJ 08536
Contact: operator referral to a consultant
888/NPFS-555
Web site: www.plan.ml.com/prodservs/ep-pfs.html
- Program design and implementation
- Program evaluation
- Technical assistance with individual gifts
- Volunteer seminars
- Trustee seminars
- Donor seminars

Planned Giving Services
3147 Fairview Avenue East, Suite 200
Seattle, WA 98102
Contact: Frank Minton
President
206/329-8144
FAX: 206/329-8230
E-mail: Plangiv@aol.com
Web site: www.plannedgivingservices.com
- Program design and implementation
- Marketing plans
- Program evaluation
- Technical assistance with individual gifts
- Volunteer seminars
- Trustee seminars
- Donor seminars
- Gift Annuity State Certifications
- Cross border gifts (Canada-US)

Planned Giving Specialists, Inc.
1359 E. 27th St.
Brooklyn, NY 11210
Contact: David G. Clough
President
718/338-1766
FAX: 718/338-8070
E-mail: dgcpgs@aol.com
- Program design and implementation
- Marketing plans
- Program evaluation
- Technical assistance with individual gifts
- Volunteer seminars
- Trustee seminars
- Donor seminars

EXHIBIT 5.4. PLANNED GIVING CONSULTANTS, Cont'd.

PNC Private Bank
Charitable and Endowment Management
Two PNC Plaza, 25th Floor
620 Liberty Avenue
Pittsburgh, PA 15222-2719
Contact: Bruce Bickel, Sr. Vice President and Manager Charitable Endowment Fund or
Sylvia Myers Maurin, Vice President and Manager Charitable Planning Services
Bickel: 412/762-3502 or
Maurin: 412/762-3806
FAX: 412/705-1043
E-mail: bruce.bickel@pncbank.com or
sylviamyers-maurin@pncbank.com
Web site: www.pncbank.com
• Program design and implementation
• Marketing plans
• Program evaluation
• Technical assistance with individual gifts
• Volunteer seminars
• Trustee seminars
• Donor seminars

Robert F. Sharpe & Company, Inc.
5050 Poplar Avenue, Suite 700
Memphis, TN 38157
Contact: Barlow T. Mann
Chief Operating Officer
800/238-3253
FAX: 901/761-4268
E-mail: info@rfsco.com
Web site: www.rfsco.com
• Program design and implementation
• Marketing plans
• Program evaluation
• Technical assistance with individual gifts
• Volunteer seminars
• Trustee seminars
• Donor seminars

Sinclair, Townes & Company
230 Peachtree Street NW
Suite 1601
Atlanta, GA 30303
Contact: Rick Billingslea, Marketing Manager or
Molly Bagett, Associate Consultant
404/688-4047
FAX: 404/688-6543
E-mail: info@sinclairtownes.com
Web site: www.sinclairtownes.com

EXHIBIT 5.4. PLANNED GIVING CONSULTANTS, Cont'd.

- Program design and implementation
- Marketing plans
- Program evaluation
- Technical assistance with individual gifts
- Volunteer seminars
- Trustee seminars
- Donor seminars

Strategies for Planned Giving
15300 Pearl Road, Suite 203
Cleveland, OH 44136
Contact: Peggy Wallace Bender
President
440/572-4790
FAX: 440/572-7734
E-mail: giftplan@aol.com
Web site: www.s4pg.com
- Program design and implementation
- Marketing plans
- Program evaluation
- Technical assistance with individual gifts
- Volunteer seminars
- Trustee seminars
- Donor seminars

Wilson & Krause
3224 Basil Court
Dallas, TX 75204
Contact: Cynthia Wilson Krause
President
214/823-8729
FAX: 214/824-8409
E-mail: cwkrause@giftplanners.com
Web site: www.giftplanners.com
- Program design and implementation
- Marketing plans
- Program evaluation
- Technical assistance with individual gifts
- Volunteer seminars
- Trustee seminars
- Donor seminars

Winton Smith & Associates
2670 Union Extended, Suite 1200
Memphis, TN 38112
Contact: Winton Smith, Jr., Owner
800/727-1040 or 901/327-2700
FAX: 901/327-5875
E-mail: winton@wintonsmith.com

EXHIBIT 5.4. PLANNED GIVING CONSULTANTS, Cont'd.

- Program design and implementation
- Marketing plans
- Program evaluation
- Technical assistance with individual gifts
- Volunteer seminars
- Trustee seminars
- Donor seminars

Planned Giving Seminars/Services
2048 Garden Avenue
St. Paul, MN 55113
Contact: Robert A. Evenson, CFRE
President
651/646-0317
FAX: 651/646-0317
e-mail: reven29@aol.com
Web site: http://members.aol.com/pgss1997/index.html
- Program design and implementation
- Program evaluation
- Technical assistance with individual gifts
- Trustee Seminars
- Gift Planning Software: The Planned Giving Companion
- Professional Training/Education: A Brisk Walk Through the Basics

Mellon Private Asset Management-Charitable Gifts Office
One Boston Place
Boston, MA 02108
Contact: Linda R. Fitzpatrick
First Vice President
617/722-7649
FAX: 617/722-7362
- Technical assistance with individual gifts
- Trustee seminars
- Donor seminars

Conrad Teitell
13 Arcadia Road
Old Greenwich, CT 06870
Contact: Sally-Ann O'Shea, Chief of Staff
Phone: 203/637-4553
FAX: 203/637-4572
E-mail: info@taxwisegiving.com
Web site: www.taxwisegiving.com
- Volunteer seminars
- Trustee seminars
- Publications: *AMICUS*— the quarterly financial guide for donors
  Taxwise Giving— a monthly newsletter for professionals
  Booklets: professional and donor booklets and publications

EXHIBIT 5.4. PLANNED GIVING CONSULTANTS, Cont'd.

- Books: *Substantiating Charitable Gifts*
  Portable Planned Giving Manual
  Outright Charitable Gifts
  Planned Giving
  Deferred Giving
  Charitable Lead Trusts

Endowment Development Services (EDS)
2511 E. 46th Street, #R7
Indianapolis, IN 46205
Contact: James R. Marshall, President
317/542-9829
FAX: 317/549-9470
E-mail: 75762.2443@compuserv.com
- Program design and implementation
- Marketing plans
- Program evaluation
- Technical assistance with individual gifts
- Volunteer seminars
- Trustee seminars
- Donor seminars
- Newsletters for prospects and allied professionals
- Specialty booklets
- Videos for marketing and training
- Staff and volunteer training programs
- Client workshops and target group presentations
- Survey and focus group studies
- Consulting services
- Technical support

Pentera, Inc.
8650 Commerce Park Place, Suite G
Indianapolis, IN 46268
Contact: Douglas A. Weaver
Assistant to the President/Marketing
317/875-0910
FAX: 317/875-0912
E-mail: PenteraInc@aol.com
- Program design and implementation
- Marketing plans
- Program evaluation
- Technical assistance with individual gifts
- Volunteer seminars
- Trustee seminars
- Donor seminars
- *Financial Strategies*—quarterly newsletter for allied professionals

EXHIBIT 5.4. PLANNED GIVING CONSULTANTS, Cont'd.

R & R Newkirk
8695 S Archer, #10
Willow Springs, IL 60480
Contact: Wilma Carmichael
Marketing Director
800/342-2375
FAX: 708/839-9207
E-mail: newkirk2@aol.com
Web site: www.rrnewkirk.com
• Marketing plans
• Technical assistance with individual gifts
• Volunteer seminars
• Trustee seminars   ·
• Donor seminars
• Advisor newsletter: *Charitable Giving Tax Service Library*

The Stelter Company
10435 New York Avenue
Des Moines, IA 50322
Contact: Larry P. Stelter, President
800/331-6881
FAX: 515/278-5851
E-mail: onestandsout@stelter.com
Web site: www.stelter.com
• Newsletters for donors
• Seminar: Relationship Building Workshop
• Publication: *Charitable Planning Perspectives*

Source: Reprinted with permission, *NCPG Directory of Council Members,* copyright 2001, National Committee on Planned Giving®.

CHAPTER SIX

MARKETING PLANNED GIFTS

A planned giving program must be marketed both internally and externally. Both kinds of marketing are essential to the success of every planned giving program. This chapter discusses why this is so and examines the ways to market a program effectively.

Internal Marketing

Marketing planned gifts begins by convincing the nonprofit organization of their significance. The board's and the staff's agreement to initiate a planned giving program is only the beginning of this process, however. Effective internal marketing of planned gifts requires a continuous effort to emphasize and reemphasize planned giving's effectiveness and its importance. It also involves continual training about planned giving vehicles and about recognizing planned giving opportunities.

Planned gifts can be marketed in numerous ways, such as by direct mail, at seminars, and on Web sites. However, none of these techniques replaces visiting with donors individually. Unless it cultivates prospects and donors as individuals, a program will not be fully effective. Therefore, training board members, development staff, and key volunteers to carry the planned giving message to prospects on the individual level is as important as any marketing initiative undertaken.

Getting the Board Onboard

Keep planned giving information in front of the governing board. Board members are the most effective marketers an organization has. They traffic in the right social circles to spread the planned giving message to the potential donors a planned giving program must reach to be highly successful. Their word of mouth and personal commitment are key.

There are several ways to keep board members aware of planned giving. The easiest is to share success stories with them at regular board meetings. The planned giving committee of the board should report on aggregate numbers at regular intervals, but it is equally as important for the committee members to share an individual story or two with other board members, whenever one is available to tell. Without divulging the donor's name (unless the donor has agreed in advance that his or her name can be used), a committee member can take five or ten minutes to describe how this individual came to make a planned gift. A good narrative will describe what assets were considered, how they were discussed, and how the final plan for the gift was created. It will detail the tax benefits and the income stream generated for the donor. And it will always conclude by summing up the human impact of the gift—more students educated through scholarships, for example, or more children inoculated against diseases. If this requires coaching the presenter in advance of the presentation, coaching should be done. Sharing these stories will make board members feel good about being a part of the organization and will keep them focused on planned gifts. An even more powerful and effective method is to have the donor tell the story himself or herself, on those occasions when the donor is willing to share personal thoughts.

Another technique is to bring in an outside planned giving expert to make a presentation to all or part of the board. It is preferable to do this at a breakfast or luncheon meeting at a time convenient for the board members. An outside speaker brings a certain cachet to the event. For best effect the presentation should focus on only one or two planned giving techniques and the group should be kept small. If the nonprofit has a large board, inviting a limited segment of the group provides the small-group atmosphere most conductive to discussion and allows more questions to be asked and answered. If the board includes members from a wide geographical area, consider hosting a luncheon or two at different sites. If a luncheon isn't workable, take advantage of a social occasion or a sponsored event. Even a ballet or a ballgame can be an appropriate occasion for a preperformance presentation. In these cases, however, it is imperative to be brief and to focus on a limited agenda. Of course the presentation must end in time to permit attendance at the event.

Educating Staff

In a larger organization, training frontline development staff in planned giving is imperative. They may be donors' primary contacts in the organization and have many opportunities for cultivation and stewardship. The staff's ability to spot planned giving opportunities and then react to them intelligently will have a major impact on any program's success.

Staff training should be a regular event. For example, your organization might hold a brown-bag lunch every two months or so, at which planned giving is discussed. Each meeting should focus on a specific planned giving vehicle or a specific prospect and should train staff to identify when and how to use the appropriate vehicle. This way staff learn not only to recognize planned giving opportunities but also how to discuss the appropriate planned gift vehicles when opportunities arise. The desired end is that staff develop the ability to see opportunities and develop strategies that will work in each case.

Nine common objections to planned gifts are shown next, followed by appropriate responses.

Objection	*Response*	*Solutions*
I don't have enough money.	What if I can show you a way to make a gift that won't require any money out of your pocket now?	Bequest, gift from qualified plan at death
I'm going to retire in a few years.	What if I could show you some gift plans that may actually increase your retirement income?	Charitable trust, charitable gift annuity, deferred charitable gift annuity, gift from qualified plan at death
I need to make sure my spouse is provided for.	What if we talk about gift plans that may help you provide income for your spouse and support the City Shelter?	Gift annuity, charitable trust, a qualified plan to establish a charitable trust at death
I want to make sure my children are provided for. I would love to make a large gift, but I don't want to disinherit them.	What if I could show you a plan that could provide income for your children or a plan that would ensure that your children would receive an inheritance?	Charitable remainder trust, charitable lead trust, wealth replacement trust, qualified plan to charity and other assets to children

I need to save for children's (or grandchildren's) education.	What if I could show you a plan that may help you with educational expenses, depending on your assets?	Charitable lead trust, charitable remainder trust
I'm not a wealthy person; charitable giving is for rich people.	Even if you aren't a wealthy person, you may still benefit from charitable gift plans that can reduce income and estate taxes. Let me give you more information about taxes and the tax benefits of charitable gift planning.	Estate planning inventory (available from City Shelter), annuity, gift from a qualified plan
I don't have any family. Why do I need to think about gift and estate planning?	If you don't have a plan, state laws will determine how your estate is divided. Even if you don't have family, you can have an estate plan that reflects the things you care about.	"City Shelter: Ways to Give" brochure
Planned giving is just too complicated.	We have professionals on staff who can sort out the complexities for you.	"City Shelter: Ways to Give" brochure
My adviser hasn't mentioned this.	Many times professional advisers see themselves as service providers who are paid to respond to their clients' needs. Thus gift planning might not come up unless your adviser knows about the charities you care about. You may want to share this information with your adviser and let him or her know that City Shelter has experts who can provide him or her with specific information about gift plans.	

Note: © 2000 Camilyn W. Kuhns. Used with permission.

Another way to train staff is to involve them in the development of planned giving print materials. Get their perspective on what will work with the donors they are visiting. Ask them to help with selecting effective illustrations, examples, or scenarios that illuminate the printed text. Having staff review these materials will reinforce their understanding of planned giving and help them identify specific possible planned gifts among their own group of prospects.

A third way to provide training is through presentations at staff retreats. These presentations might include role playing to demonstrate planned giving visits. Printed material that reinforces the presentation content and can serve as a reference in the future should always be distributed. Questions should be encouraged and fully discussed to stimulate involvement in the presentation. These presentations should be kept as brief as possible while still being thorough. Keep the details simple and the focus on donor interactions. Remember, staff members do not need to be experts, just knowledgeable enough to know when and how to discuss gift vehicles with their donors.

Educating Volunteers

If an organization depends on volunteers for fundraising assistance, it is important to inform them about planned giving techniques. This will make them comfortable with suggesting planned giving possibilities to prospects they are cultivating and give them the ability to do it successfully. Training volunteers resembles training staff. Holding training sessions over lunch, soliciting feedback on marketing materials, and offering in-depth presentations at volunteer retreats are all effective ways to communicate with them about planned giving. Moreover, such training will often motivate them to consider and complete their own planned gifts.

External Marketing: It's All About Segmentation

There are three keys to marketing planned gifts—segmentation, segmentation, segmentation. Marketing a planned giving program offers the same challenge as marketing anything else: How do you get your message to your target audience and motivate those in that audience to action? An approach that is sweeping all industries is to divide one's market up into logical segments whenever possible. This enables the organization to send a tailored message to specific people, one that resonates with their life situation.

According to Steenhuysen (1999), segmentation of the gift planning market typically happens along two separate lines: wealth and age.

Wealth

Let's look at segmentation by wealth first.

Super Affluent. Around 1 percent of the population is in the *super affluent* category. These families and individuals have mega-estates, managed with the assistance of the most sophisticated attorneys and advisers in the country. Their estates are so large that they will lose some money to the estate tax system no matter how much they plan. Therefore they generally look to maintain control, even if they can't maintain the wealth. Usually they are receptive to charitable planning vehicles like private foundations because through the foundation they can maintain a hand in how the wealth is distributed and thus maintain influence and prestige.

Second Tier. The second tier of wealth includes around 9 to 10 percent of the population. These families and individuals have average estates of around $5 million, but all have estates that are subject to estate taxes (the cut-off in 2002 and 2003 is $1 million) and thus have an estate tax problem. They are motivated to minimize the estate tax bite and can benefit from careful planning. Many of the tools at their disposal do not include giving, but charitable remainder trusts do fit well in this group's estate planning needs.

How will the Tax Act of 2001 affect those in these two tiers? The new tax law provides the following new exclusion amounts and tax rates:

Calendar Year	Estate Tax Exclusion[1]	Highest Estate Tax Rate
2002	$1 million	50%
2003	$1 million	49%
2004	$1.5 million	48%
2005	$1.5 million	47%
2006	$2 million	46%
2007	$2 million	45%
2008	$2 million	45%
2009	$3.5 million	45%
2010	"Repeal" = no tax	"Repeal" = no tax

The 2001 tax act expires; all changes enacted in 2001 vanish.

2011+	$1 million[2]	55%

[1] Estates smaller than the exclusion amount will not be subject to federal estate tax.

[2] The exclusion was to reach $1 million under pre-2001 law; therefore, it reverts to $1 million.

The fact is that the estate tax has been repealed only for those individuals who happen to pass away in 2010. However, all individuals who face estate tax consequences will have to plan for the possibility of passing away between now and 2009, a period that includes a wide range of exclusion amounts (and, therefore, planning variables), and plan for the possibility of living to the year 2011, when the estate tax is scheduled to return to 2001 levels. *Always* ask them to speak about this with their attorneys, accountants, and financial planners to ensure that they receive tax advice that is tailored to their specific situation.

Third Tier. The third tier of wealth contains the remaining population, which does not have estate tax problems because their estates are of a size that excludes them from paying estate taxes. Rather, meaning and mission motivate their planning. They construct their wills to make a meaningful final statement to their families about what treasured objects go to whom. When they leave a bequest to a charity, they are motivated by mission and by their emotional attachment to that mission. Estate planning techniques simply do not reach them.

Age

When organizations segment their donors and prospects by generation, they can consider these groups:

- Depression era generation
- World War II generation
- Eisenhower generation
- Baby boomers 1
- Baby boomers 2
- Generation X

Depression Generation. The *Depression generation* came of age from 1930 to 1939, during the hardest economic times this country knew in the twentieth century. Their lives and their relationship to wealth have been directly shaped by the Great Depression. Frequently they are big savers who feel as though a disaster that could devastate their wealth could occur at any time. They've seen it happen.

They are also typically touched by human need. During their formative years they saw many good people struggling because they were simply down on their luck, or they felt hard times themselves. They understand how much difference some financial assistance can make. An organization's mission is extremely important to them. Most of them give to their churches and to educational and human service agencies.

Usually they give from their earned income. Because they value security, bequests are popular with this group. They feel more able to make a large gift at their death (once they have provided for family and loved ones) than while they are living. They also like gift annuities because of the fixed, guaranteed payments. Marketing efforts for individuals in this group should appeal to their sympathetic souls, their thrifty sensibilities, and their need for security.

World War II Generation. The next generation to segment for marketing purposes is the *World War II generation.* These individuals came of age between 1940 and 1945 and are usually not as focused on savings as those who grew to adulthood in the Depression era. Having an external enemy fostered their sense of community and shaped their life experience. Their external enemy was conquered both in World War II and the subsequent Cold War, and they typically feel more secure than the previous generation with spending their assets to celebrate their lives' personal and communal victories. They are also concerned with maintaining their lifestyles at the level to which they have grown accustomed. They are not interested in losing ground.

Shaped by victories over common enemies, those in this group often want to perpetuate ideals and missions that are important to the common good. Focus marketing to members of this group on your nonprofit's mission and on how important your nonprofit is to society in general. One approach to rallying their support is to make the message resonate with their battle mentality.

Individuals in this group prefer to make planned gifts using charitable gift annuities and charitable trusts. They feel they are getting something in return when they receive the income these vehicles produce, thus keeping their lifestyles at the accustomed level. Their desire to win often leads them to compare rates among charitable organizations to be certain they receive the maximum return. This group is also typically open to bequests. They have seen their children enjoy better lifestyles than they did as young people; thus, when their children are doing comparatively well, they feel comfortable leaving a portion of their estates to charity.

Eisenhower Generation. Following the World War II generation comes a group referred to as the *Eisenhower generation.* These individuals were born between 1928 and 1945 and matured between 1949 and 1966. Because they came of age during the postwar industrial boom, they experienced greater financial success faster than any previous generation had. As a result, members of this generation usually spend more money on themselves than did the members of previous generations. Moreover, their relative good health means they are living longer to take advantage of their accumulated wealth. They are the ones with the bumper stickers on their expensive cars that declare, "I'm spending my kid's inheritance!"

This generation is motivated to assist worthy causes, but is also looking for a return on its charitable giving. Sometimes the return is a social one, such as provided by organizations like Rotary clubs, Kiwanis, or local arts groups. In terms of planned giving, this means members of this generation frequently have a strong interest in gifts that provide an income, such as charitable trusts and gift annuities. Due to their interest in seeking a high return, people of this generation will often actively compare charities to see which one can offer the better rate on a gift annuity. They will also closely watch the performance of a charitable unitrust. Marketing to this generation, therefore, should focus not just on a charity's community mission but also the services and benefits the nonprofit can offer the donor.

Baby Boomers 1. After the Eisenhower generation comes the first wave of *baby boomers*. This generation came of age between 1964 and 1972 and also enjoyed a postwar economy unprecedented in U.S. history. Consequently these boomers are often noted for their impulse to spend money on material objects. Even when limits are set, as they were during the energy crisis in the mid-1970s, for example, members of this group often refuse to become savers and instead take advantage of the increased availability of credit. Having toys is important to this generation, as is evidenced by the phrase popular in the 1980s: "The one who dies with the most toys wins."

The members of this generation are just moving into a time when planned gifts are becoming of interest to them. Their philanthropy is frequently marked by a high need to feel personal significance from giving. Planned gifts from these individuals will likely be motivated by the donors' continual personal contact with the charity. Planned gifts such as donor advised funds and the establishment of private foundations appeal greatly to this group because both allow donors to stay involved with their philanthropy. Marketing to these individuals, therefore, should stress establishing a personal legacy, and nonprofits should invite their input into the ways their gifts are applied to the nonprofit' mission.

Baby Boomers 2 and Generation X. The second wave of baby boomers and their followers, the members of *Generation X*, are still too young to consider planned gifts. For the most part these two generations are focused on the accumulation of wealth and make their charitable gifts from current income. There are exceptions, however, and if your budget allows, it is worthwhile to consider them. Given that these groups are known as "me" generations for their individual members' focus on themselves, it is never too early to establish contact with these exceptions, to begin to build long-term relationships, and to understand their needs clearly, and at the same time to embed your mission in their philanthropic thought processes.

These exceptions are usually entrepreneurs who have acquired their wealth building their own companies, often successful high-tech firms and dot-com startups. These individuals become excited by possibilities and desire a very high level of involvement in whatever they do. Marketing to these individuals should emphasize vision and partnerships. Deferred gifts from this group will often need to be designed to meet their future needs, such as sending children through college or supplementing retirement income. Flip unitrusts (see Chapter Seven) and deferred gift annuities (see Chapter Eight) are popular vehicles because they can be designed both to provide philanthropy and to give the donor assurance that his or her future obligations will be met.

Developing a Marketing Plan

Marketing plans vary from organization to organization, according to staffing and budget. However, the four essential features of any marketing plan will be the same for every nonprofit:

1. Constant and consistent promotion
2. Effective segmentation
3. Positioning and branding of the organization's mission
4. Effective personal follow-up

Frost (1995) describes the elements of an effective marketing plan. It has a short executive summary that identifies the market and outlines how that market will be approached. It details the organization's strengths and weaknesses, resources, and current donor base. It then lists the organization's marketing objectives, strategies, and tactics and describes how the success of those tactics is going to be measured. It also includes a timetable and a budget (see Exhibit 6.1).

EXHIBIT 6.1. PLANNED GIVING ANNUAL BUDGET.

5805–02	MEMBERSHIP DUES		
	FPA Dues		$ 225
	American Council on Gift Annuities		75
	National Committee on Planned Giving		150
		5805 Total	**450**
5810–02	TRAVEL EXPENSES		
	Parking $5 per month × 12		60
	Gas 12,000 miles at 20 mpg = 600 × $1.75		1,050
		5810 Total	**1,110**
5815–02	EXPENSES		
	Depreciation ($22,680 ÷ 84 months = $270 per month		
	Insurance $30 × 12		360
	Grease, Oil & Filter 5 × $20		100
	Maintenance		485
	License		135
		5815 Total	**1,080**
5820–02	INSTITUTIONS & SEMINARS		
	NCPG Seminar in Indianapolis		
	Fee		575
	Hotel—4 nights × $140		560
	Air Fare		340
	Food—5 days × $30		120
	Taxi & Tips		30
	IAFP Case Study		60
	MIPG Conference		75
		5820 Total	**1,760**

EXHIBIT 6.1. PLANNED GIVING ANNUAL BUDGET, Cont'd.

5825–02	SPECIAL MEETINGS/MEALS			
	Association Meals			
	FPA			150
	Board/Donor Education w/National Speaker Adviser Luncheon			1,000
			5825 Total	**1,150**
5830–02	PROMOTION/RECOGNITION			
	Planned Gift Event (donors invited to hospital events)			1,028
	Brochures (yearend, etc.)			504
	Miscellaneous			—
	Cards—Birthday, Anniversary			100
	Flowers (not Christmas) 6 × $35			210
	Christmas Cards			100
	New Planned Giving Recognition Brochure for IHF,			
	Blank, Lutheran, Methodist (under mailings)			—
	Donor Wall Update			350
	Recognition pieces 100 × $40			4,000
	Blank (included above)			—
	Lutheran (included above)			—
	Methodist (included above)			—
	IHF (included above)			—
	General Printing, Seminar Books, Brochures, etc.			504
			5830 Total	**6,796**
5842–02	PRINTING			
	Misc. cover letters, etc.			500
			5842 Total	**500**
5840–02	SUBSCRIPTIONS			
	Resource Material Update			150
			5840 Total	**150**
5872–02	SERVICE AGREEMENT			
	ABC Consultant			595
			5872 Total	**595**
5876-02	LEGAL			
	Trust Drafting & Counseling			3,000
			5876 Total	**3,000**
5879-02	CAPITAL			
	PGDC Web Site			3,000
			5879 Total	**3,000**

		Mailhouse	Printing	
5845–02	PRINTING & MAILHOUSE EXPENSES			
	Adviser Newsletter 600 × 4	600	2,310	2,910
	Planned Giving Newsletter 5,000 × 3	1,500	8,498	9,998
	Legacy Society Booklet	2,000	8,000	10,000
			5845 Total	**22,908**
5850–02	POSTAGE			
	Adviser Newsletter 600 × 4			2,400
	Planned Giving Newsletter 5,000 × 3			15,000
	Legacy Society Booklet			20,000
			5850 Total	**37,400**
			TOTAL 2000 BUDGET	**$79,899**

Source: Iowa Health Foundation, Des Moines, Iowa. Reprinted with permission.

The budget for the plan should be built around the organization's strategies and tactics for the planned giving program. This program-driven approach will produce a budget that is true to organizational objectives and give a measurable return on dollars invested. Marketing will be an major part of this budget. A 1998 survey of top fundraisers conducted by Michael Kateman (1999) and the University of Missouri revealed that over 50 percent of the respondents spent 50 percent or more of their annual planned giving budget on marketing planned gifts.

Marketing Surveys

If possible, incorporate marketing surveys into your plan. Surveying your donors about their needs and desires will serve you well as you create the program's marketing strategy. For example, you may discover through a survey that your donor base prefers receiving your direct mail appeal in September. This would direct you to establish your planned giving appeal at that time. Any information you are able to gather about your donors and prospects will be instrumental in crafting your organization's planned giving marketing message (see Exhibit 6.2).

Preparing Planned Giving Publications

Publications of many kinds are helpful tools in fundraising. By themselves they will not raise money; however, planned giving publications, building on the organization's identity, can set the tone for the planned giving program and bring the donor in for a closer look at the organization's mission.

Jana Wilson, director of development publications at the Indiana University Foundation (personal communication, Nov. 1999), says fundraising publications should be to the point—brief, simple, and clear. In an environment of high media exposure, the audience—unless they are keenly interested (and most will not be initially)—will not respond to lengthy prose; poor design; or low-quality photos, graphics, and printing. So the first thing you must know in creating a publication is its most important purpose. "No matter what the project is, you need to know what you have to say, who you're saying it to, and how you want to say it," says Wilson. She suggests having a *creative strategy* for every publication. This strategy has eight basic elements:

Objective: What do you want this piece to do?

Strategy: How are you going to use it?

Target audience: Who is the publication for?

Primary message (call to action): What do you want to say? (A single sentence should be enough. If the message can't be summed up briefly, you may be trying to do too much with one publication.)

Secondary message: What else needs to be said?

Tone: Is it light and festive? Warm and nostalgic? Edgy and high-tech? Everyone needs to be on the same wavelength.

Deadline: When does the publication have to go out to prospects? (Work backward from this deadline to figure out when the various parts need to be done.)

Budget: How much can you spend on it? (Know what the budget is; plan to stay in it. The budget will largely determine how the publication looks. Usually you get what you pay for.)

Newsletters

The most essential marketing tool used by the majority of organizations involved in planned gifts fundraising is the newsletter. Small organizations will have only one, a general newsletter. Planned giving stories and materials should be included in it. Larger organizations may have two newsletters—one with general stories and information and one targeted to planned giving donors and prospects.

Planned giving newsletters should be sent at least three times a year to segmented portions of the donor base. These newsletters allow an organization to present in-depth analysis of gift planning options—usually covering one option per issue. If possible, include real-life examples or testimonials that illustrate key points. Because planned giving can seem overwhelming and complicated, bringing the material down to an easily understood level is vital for communicating effectively with most donors (see Resource 12). These newsletters should also include a response device that allows prospects to ask for further information. For the prospect's convenience, the response form should be printed on a postage-paid postcard or there should be a postage-paid envelope for returning it.

Brochures

Brochures are another key marketing tool. The ideal is to have a different brochure for each planned giving vehicle, developing an inventory of brochures on wills and bequests, charitable gift annuities, charitable remainder trusts, and other vehicles, such as real estate and life insurance (see Resource 13). These brochures can, for example, be left with people after a cultivation visit and can also be used for replying to those who respond to the newsletter.

For smaller organizations, it may be more cost effective to design a single brochure that lists all the planned giving options. Brochures with this design format should always include several items in addition to the summary of planned giving options. First, they should present the mission statement of the organization. In addition, if a capital campaign is under way, this brochure is an effective place to briefly outline the case statement and discuss campaign goals and progress. A variety of gift levels should be listed to raise donor sights and to offer affordable

EXHIBIT 6.2. PLANNED GIVING SURVEY.

Tell Us What You Think We're now well into our second year of
Next Steps, the IU Foundation's newsletter designed to advise you about financial,
estate, and gift planning opportunities. We hope the information on planned
giving options is useful to you. Now we would like to know what you think.

Your views are very important to us. The following questionnaire takes only a few minutes to complete
and can be returned in the enclosed postage-paid envelope. Please let us hear from you.

1. How often do you read *Next Steps*?
   - ○ Every time I receive it
   - ○ Sometimes
   - ○ Seldom

2. Which area(s) of financial and estate planning are of most interest to you?
   - ○ Planning your will
   - ○ Minimizing income taxes
   - ○ Planning charitable gifts
   - ○ Increasing retirement income
   - ○ Minimizing estate taxes
   - ○ Reducing capital gains taxes
   - ○ Using life insurance more effectively
   - ○ Exploring trusts in financial planning
   - ○ Other _____

3. Has *Next Steps* prompted you to:
   - ○ Review your will
   - ○ Revise your will
   - ○ Consult your legal or financial advisor
   - ○ Include gifts to charitable institutions
   - ○ Review your overall estate plans
   - ○ Other _____

(Continued on next page)

EXHIBIT 6.2. PLANNED GIVING SURVEY, Cont'd.

4. Have you made any provisions for the Indiana University Foundation in your financial or estate plans?

    ○ Through your will
    ○ Life insurance
    ○ No plans at this time
    ○ May consider in the future
    ○ Have made other arrangements _____

5. What kind(s) of information would you like to see featured in future issues of *Next Steps*?

    ○ Will and bequest planning
    ○ Trusts in financial planning
    ○ Gifts that may increase your income
    ○ Planning with appreciated securities
    ○ Gift opportunities at the Indiana University Foundation
    ○ Other _____

Suggestions:

_____

_____

_____

Name _____

Address _____

City _____ **State** _____ **Zip** _____

Email _____

Please return your completed questionnaire in the confidential reply paid envelope.
Thank you for your time!

Source: Indiana University Foundation. Printed with permission.

opportunities to donors with various giving capacities. It's also important to include a listing of the assets the organization is able to accept; this is an effective way to open donor's minds to gift possibilities beyond checks from disposable income. Try to include one or more donor testimonials that involve the reader at a human level, moving him or her to action by demonstrating the human impact of the organization's work, thus connecting the donor to your mission in a meaningful way. Include a how-to section giving the bequest language donors should use and instructions for the transfer of stock or other assets. Finally, be certain the brochure includes a personal message from the board chair, chief executive officer, planned giving committee chair, or chief development officer. This message is an important personal touch, a way for the organization to put its best foot forward and thank donors for their support (see Resource 14).

Asset Inventory Booklets

Another effective print item for a planned giving program is a booklet that assists donors to draw up an inventory of their assets. Such booklets can be obtained through banks, insurance companies, and planned giving vendors. Supplying these books provides a service to the donor and is an excellent introduction to the conversation about personal finances. Once donors use this tool to get an accurate feel for their overall financial picture, they often feel more comfortable parting with some of their assets in a planned gift arrangement (see Resource 15).

Employing Outside Vendors

A nonprofit's brochure inventory will obviously depend on its budget, but there are many vendors who can produce brochures and other materials at a reasonable cost if they cannot be done in house. If your organization does not have a publications department in house (and most small nonprofits do not), or if it cannot achieve adequate quality and service, seriously consider hiring outside help to produce planned giving publications, especially the major pieces. Because planned giving can be complicated and is subject to legal restrictions and because the tax laws can change on a regular basis, many smaller organizations turn to companies that specialize in producing planned giving publications. Often these companies have, along with copyeditors and designers, staff writers with technical backgrounds in such areas as tax law. The services they offer range from simply providing technical copy on one or more topics to designing and producing complete newsletters or brochures using your organization's name and logo.

The decision to use an outside planned giving vendor should include a comparison between the costs and time involved in producing the material in house and the cost of the vendor. Quality newsletters can be costly to produce in house and take a great deal of staff time. If you decide to use an outside vendor, ask to look at its client list and find out if any of the clients are potential competitors. Ask if the vendor would consider not taking competitors in the future should you sign with the vendor. Your primary concern here is personalization. You want your prospects and donors, to the extent possible, to see your newsletter as distinctive, designed for, and directed to them. The same newsletter coming from multiple nonprofits probably will be noticed, and it may lessen the effect of being received only from you. It is not always possible to use a vendor no one else in your marketing sphere is using, but it is a consideration worth weighing. Also review some samples of the vendor's work, reading the copy to see if it is easy to read and understand. Look at the design to see that it is simple, uncluttered, and has type large enough for older eyes. A heavy component of planned giving audiences is older, and this should be considered.

There are a number of ways to find outside vendors who specialize in planned giving material. The first and best way is to ask other organizations with planned giving material that you like. Call or write to other organizations around town or around the country that may have similar audiences. The World Wide Web offers a wealth of information, and many companies now advertise their services on-line. Employ search engines, using key words such as *philanthropy and publications* or *planned giving and publications*. In addition, there are sites such as Planned Giving Today (*http://www.pgtoday.com*) that offer a publication for gift planning professionals and that may point you to some vendors of planned giving publications (see also Exhibit 6.3).

Integration of the Planned Giving Message into Other Fund Appeals

One of the most cost-effective ways to market planned gifts is to integrate the planned giving message into other organizational marketing methods. The main function of planned giving literature, or indeed any communication about the program, is to say and keep saying the same message over and over again. It is important that everyone connected with your organization understands the goals and carries the same message to prospective donors—even if that message is stated with different emphases for different audiences. Continuity is the business of all organizational communications, whether they are disseminated via brochures, magazines, newsletters, Web sites, or any other medium. Each piece deserves careful

EXHIBIT 6.3. PROMOTIONAL PUBLICATIONS VENDORS.

Endowment Development Services (EDS)
2511 E. 46th Street, #R7
Indianapolis, IN 46205
Contact: James R. Marshall, President
317/542-9829
FAX: 317/549-9470
E-mail: 75762.2443@compuserv.com
• Program design and implementation
• Marketing plans
• Program evaluation
• Technical assistance with individual gifts
• Volunteer seminars
• Trustee seminars
• Donor seminars
• Newsletters for prospects and allied professionals
• Specialty booklets
• Videos for marketing and training
• Staff and volunteer training programs
• Client workshops and target group presentations
• Survey and focus group studies
• Consulting services
• Technical support

Pentera, Inc.
8650 Commerce Park Place, Suite G
Indianapolis, IN 46268
Contact: Douglas A. Weaver
Assistant to the President/Marketing
317/875-0910
FAX: 317/875-0912
E-mail: PenteraInc@aol.com
• Program design and implementation
• Marketing plans
• Program evaluation
• Technical assistance with individual gifts
• Volunteer seminars
• Trustee seminars
• Donor seminars
• *Financial Strategies*—quarterly newsletter for allied professionals

R & R Newkirk
8695 S Archer, #10
Willow Springs, IL 60480
Contact: Wilma Carmichael
Marketing Director
800/342-2375
FAX: 708/839-9207
E-mail: newkirk2@aol.com
Web site: www.rrnewkirk.com

EXHIBIT 6.3. PROMOTIONAL PUBLICATIONS VENDORS, Cont'd.

- Marketing plans
- Technical assistance with individual gifts
- Volunteer seminars
- Trustee seminars
- Donor seminars
- Advisor newsletter: *Charitable Giving Tax Service Library*

The Stelter Company
10435 New York Avenue
Des Moines, IA 50322
Contact: Larry P. Stelter, President
800/331-6881
FAX: 515/278-5851
E-mail: onestandsout@stelter.com
Web site: www.stelter.com
- Newsletters for donors
- Seminar: Relationship Building Workshop
- Publication: *Charitable Planning Perspectives*

Alice A. Pinsley, Ph.D., CFP, Planned Giving Consultant
141 Woodbine Road
Stamford, CT 06903
Contact: Alice Pinsley
203/329-9850
FAX: 203/329-9851
- Program design and implementation
- Marketing plans
- Program evaluation
- Technical assistance with individual gifts
- Volunteer seminars
- Trustee seminars
- Donor seminars
- Custom planned giving ads

Currie, Ferner, Scarpetta & DeVries
401 Second Avenue South
Suite 102
Minneapolis, MN 55401
Contact: David C. Ferner
Managing Partner
612/340-9810
FAX: 612/333-6672
- Program design and implementation
- Marketing plans
- Program evaluation
- Technical assistance with individual gifts
- Volunteer seminars
- Trustee seminars
- Donor seminars

EXHIBIT 6.3. PROMOTIONAL PUBLICATIONS VENDORS, Cont'd.

Estes Associates
41 Spoke Drive
Woodbridge, CT 06525
Contact: Ellen G. Estes, LL.B.
Attorney & Planned Giving Consultant
203/393-3159
FAX: 203/393-3857
E-mail: ellen.estes@juno.com
• Program design and implementation
• Marketing plans
• Program evaluation
• Technical assistance with individual gifts
• Volunteer seminars
• Trustee seminars
• Donor seminars
• One-day seminars—"Planned Giving—Plain and Simple"—for development
  officers, board members, volunteers, allied professionals and other staff people

Gift Planning Associates
731 Market Street, #600
San Francisco, CA 94103
Contact: Richard Lamport
Principal
415/243-9175
FAX: 415/284-0150
E-mail: giftplaner@compuserve.com
• Program design and implementation
• Marketing plans
• Program evaluation
• Technical assistance with individual gifts
• Volunteer seminars
• Trustee seminars
• Donor seminars

Kathryn W. Miree & Associates, Inc.
PO Box 130846
Birmingham, AL 35213
Contact: Kathryn W. Miree
President
205/939-0003
FAX: 205/939-3781
E-mail: kwmiree@giftplanners.com
Web site: www.giftplanners.com
• Program design and implementation
• Marketing plans
• Program evaluation
• Technical assistance with individual gifts
• Volunteer seminars
• Trustee seminars
• Donor seminars
• Professional publications: *Building a Planned Giving Program*—3 book series

EXHIBIT 6.3. PROMOTIONAL PUBLICATIONS VENDORS, Cont'd.

Sinclair, Townes & Company
230 Peachtree Street NW
Suite 1601
Atlanta, GA 30303
Contact: Rick Billingslea, Marketing Manager or
Molly Bagett, Associate Consultant
404/688-4047
FAX: 404/688-6543
E-mail: info@sinclairtownes.com
Web site: www.sinclairtownes.com
• Program design and implementation
• Marketing plans
• Program evaluation
• Technical assistance with individual gifts
• Volunteer seminars
• Trustee seminars
• Donor seminars

Strategies for Planned Giving
15300 Pearl Road, Suite 203
Cleveland, OH 44136
Contact: Peggy Wallace Bender
President
440/572-4790
FAX: 440/572-7734
E-mail: giftplan@aol.com
Web site: www.s4pg.com
• Program design and implementation
• Marketing plans
• Program evaluation
• Technical assistance with individual gifts
• Volunteer seminars
• Trustee seminars
• Donor seminars

Winton Smith & Associates
2670 Union Extended, Suite 1200
Memphis, TN 38112
Contact: Winton Smith, Jr., Owner
800/727-1040 or 901/327-2700
FAX: 901/327-5875
E-mail: winton@wintonsmith.com
• Program design and implementation
• Marketing plans
• Program evaluation
• Technical assistance with individual gifts
• Volunteer seminars
• Trustee seminars
• Donor seminars

EXHIBIT 6.3. PROMOTIONAL PUBLICATIONS VENDORS, Cont'd.

Conrad Teitell
13 Arcadia Road
Old Greenwich, CT 06870
Contact: Sally-Ann O'Shea, Chief of Staff
Phone: 203/637-4553
FAX: 203/637-4572
E-mail: info@taxwisegiving.com
Web site: www.taxwisegiving.com
- Volunteer seminars
- Trustee seminars
- Publications: *AMICUS*—the quarterly financial guide for donors
  Taxwise Giving—a monthly newsletter for professionals
- Booklets: professional and donor booklets and publications
- Books: *Substantiating Charitable Gifts*
  Portable Planned Giving Manual
  Outright Charitable Gifts
  Planned Giving
  Deferred Giving
  Charitable Lead Trusts

Planned Giving Today®
100 2nd Avenue S., Suite 180
Edmonds, WA 98020
Contact: G. Roger Schoenhals, Publisher
Phone: 800-525-5748
FAX: 405-744-3838
E-mail: pgt@pgtoday.com
Web site: www.pgtoday.com
- *Planned Giving Today* (monthly newsletter)
- The PGT Marketplace (services, products, training/
  employment news)
- Gift Planning in Canada (monthly supplement for Canadians)
- PGT-CD 2001 (electronic library of back issues)
- Marketing articles, How-To Series, introductory books

Source: Reprinted with permission, *NCPG Directory of Council Members,* copyright 2001, National Committee on Planned Giving®.

planning so that it deliberately calls the donors' attention to the attainment of higher standards, the involvement of respected people, praise from outside the organization, and every other good thing that can make for donor confidence in the planned giving program.

When the nonprofit's annual fund is built around a direct mail appeal, it is easy to include a check-off box on the reply material and a courtesy reminder that allows donors and prospects to ask for information on wills, bequests, and trusts. This simple step will uncover prospects for cultivation (see Exhibit 6.4).

EXHIBIT 6.4. DIRECT MAIL REPLY CARD.

Indiana University Foundation
P.O. Box 500
Bloomington, IN 47402

(812) 855-8311 phone
(800) 558-8311 toll-free
(812) 855-0637 fax
iufoundation.iu.edu

Summary as of:

1 THANK YOU FOR YOUR PLEDGE. Please review the following account information.

Original Pledge Date	Total Pledge Amount	Amount Received	Amount Now Due	Installment Frequency

Account Name/Unit

PLEDGE SUMMARY

2 ○ My company will match my gift, and my matching gift form is enclosed.
(Note: form must accompany each pledge payment.)

○ Please send me information on wills, bequests, and trusts.

3 I wish to make this payment by *(choose one)*:

○ Check *(please make check payable to* INDIANA UNIVERSITY FOUNDATION *and return it with this card)*

○ **Credit Card** *Please charge my:* ○ **Visa** ○ **MasterCard**   Expiration Date

Amount Enclosed

Card Number

Signature

The IU Foundation is the designated fundraising agency for Indiana University. A small portion of funds and/or income therefrom may be used to defray direct costs of raising funds.

Source: Indiana University Foundation. Printed with permission.

Another natural place in which to integrate planned giving information is the organization's annual report. This is a place to list the planned giving program's fiscal year results and provide information on the range of planned giving options.

Printed donor honor rolls can include planned giving information, though the most effective way to use this form of recognition is to produce a special honor roll for donors who have made a planned gift. However, if the budget allows for printing only one honor roll, make a planned giving section within it. In either case, it is easy to incorporate some planned giving marketing, either as straightforward information or in the form of a donor testimonial (see Resource 16).

Finally, any newsletters or other print materials distributed regularly can be used to forward the planned giving message. If your nonprofit organization is conducting a campaign and you send its constituents a newsletter on campaign progress, be sure to include a planned giving column. This column might contain a donor testimonial or a question and answer section on how to make a certain type of planned gift. If the organization has a special magazine for its constituents, place planned giving material there as well. These methods are easy to carry out and will not tax the budget.

More Marketing Tools

Direct mail letters, advertisements, Web sites, seminars, and recognition societies are also effective marketing tools in any planned giving program.

Targeted Letters

Targeted letters are an excellent and cost-effective way to market planned gifts (see Exhibit 6.5). For example, an organization might send a targeted mailing about bequests or gift annuities to donors who came of age in the Depression era.

Targeted letters should be personalized as much as possible. They should be signed by a board member or volunteer who has used the planned gift technique being described. Typically they should begin by thanking the donor for past support and touching on the mission of the organization. The center section of the letter is a discussion of the type of planned gift being featured. This discussion should not be technical; instead it should simply highlight the planned gift's advantages. Close the letter with an additional thank-you and clear instructions on how to request follow-up material. If the budget permits, include a response card. If not, a listing of the person to contact in your organization and his or her phone number is sufficient. If an article that discusses the technique being marketed is available from a national publication, such as the *Wall Street Journal*, drop it in the letter as well. This will give further information and assurance to prospects and increase their response.

EXHIBIT 6.5. PLANNED GIVING SOLICITATION LETTER.

Dear [Name]:

Imagine how pleased we were to learn that by making a gift to the IU School of Education we could receive a lifetime income as well as immediate tax benefits. A Charitable Gift Annuity offers just that.

When Mary Margaret completed her EdD in 1983, we never dreamed that we would be in a financial position to help the IU School of Education. But we did our homework and we learned that you may contribute cash, stocks, bonds, or mutual fund shares to the IU Foundation. In exchange for your gift, the IU Foundation promises to pay you—and a second annuitant if you wish—a fixed amount each year for the rest of your life. Some of the income is even tax-free.

We have chosen to establish a series of Gift Annuities with the mandatory withdrawals from our qualified retirement funds. By doing so, we are funding graduate fellowships that will exist in perpetuity. We are proud to be part of the long and rich tradition of the School of Education, and we are happy to know that our assistance will play a role in supporting tomorrow's educational leaders.

If you would like a personalized illustration or simply more information on Charitable Gift Annuities, Just fill out and return the enclosed card. You may also call Sarah Baumgart, Director of External Relations at the School of Education at (877) 856-8021, or John Keith, Associate Director of Planned Giving Services at the IU Foundation, at (800) 558-8311. You may also learn more about Gift Annuities through the IU Foundation's Web site, iufoundation.iu.edu. Simply click on "Giving to IU" and then the "Pathways to Giving" links.

Sincerely,

Mary Margaret Webb   Denzil Webb

EdS '79, EdD '83

Please note that the minimum donation required for this program is $5,000.

Also, Gift Annuities are not available with the IU Foundation in all states.

Source: Indiana University Foundation. Printed with permission.

Advertisements

Planned giving advertisements have proven effective for nonprofits as well. They are especially effective for organizations that have an established brand identity among the general public, such as the American Red Cross or the American Cancer Society. These large, national organizations place ads in public media often, because they do not have an inherent constituency, such as an alumni body or church congregation.

Planned giving advertisements should be simple and eye-catching. Because the brand of the nonprofit is well established, the ad should focus on the financial benefits available from planned giving (see Exhibit 6.6). For example, an ad focusing on the rates available on immediate and deferred gift annuities is effective when interest rates are low on bank certificates of deposits and other fixed-income investments. Ads that discuss the tax benefits of giving appreciated stock are also quite effective.

EXHIBIT 6.6. PLANNED GIVING ADS.

Do Wonders *for* IU
AND GET A LITTLE SOMETHING BACK

WHAT YOU DO: Make a gift to IU through a charitable remainder trust. **WHAT YOU GET:** A regular payment from the trust; tax savings; the satisfaction of giving.

And because you can fund your gift with real estate or stock as well as cash, you can do greater things than you may have realized.

Wonders will never cease—thanks to you.

INDIANA UNIVERSITY FOUNDATION

A charitable remainder trust is just one of the many planned giving arrangements you can use to benefit Indiana University. For more information, contact the Office of Planned Giving Services at the Indiana University Foundation, **(800) 558-8311.**

Source: Indiana University Foundation. Reproduced with permission.

EXHIBIT 6.6. PLANNED GIVING ADS, Cont'd.

HOW
TO
LIVE
FOREVER.

The people you help may never know you but they'll never forget the legacy you leave.

As your partner in planned giving, we'll help you realize your financial goals now and carry on your charitable spirit in the years ahead. At American Red Cross, we know that both are equally important and deeply personal. That's why we'll talk with you about how best to meet your financial needs for life income and tax savings -- through gift annuities, charitable remainder trusts, gifts of stock and many other planned giving arrangements.

And whether you want your legacy to help around the world, throughout America or right in your own hometown, American Red Cross will put your gift to work giving help to people in need. In our minds that's a pretty good definition of immortality.

For more information about planned gift opportunities to support Red Cross services, please complete the form below or call 1-800-HELP NOW.

American Red Cross

Name _____

Address_____

City_____ State_____ Zip_____

Telephone _____ Birthdate _____

☐ Yes, I'd like information on Red Cross Charitable Gift Annuities.

++T

Mail your completed form to the American Red Cross, P.O. Box 37243, Washington, D.C. 20013.
For Internet information: http://www.redcross.org

CALL 1-800-HELP NOW

American Red Cross

We'll be there.

Source: American National Red Cross. Reproduced with the permission of the American National Red Cross.

EXHIBIT 6.6. PLANNED GIVING ADS, Cont'd.

REMEMBERING THE PAST

Since 1881, the American Red Cross has been there, serving countless individuals in times of war, disaster, and personal need.

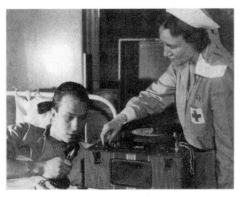

SECURING THE FUTURE

Every year, the American Red Cross touches the lives of one in six Americans. Now, you can help ensure the Red Cross can continue to provide its vital services – and guarantee yourself an ongoing source of personal income – through a Red Cross Charitable Gift Annuity.

Your donation of money or securities to the Red Cross in the form of a charitable gift annuity offers an outstanding combination of benefits:

- *Earn a guaranteed annual return rate of up to 12%*

- *Enjoy a large portion of your annuity income, tax-free*

- *Receive a charitable tax deduction*

If you are looking for a sound financial investment and would like to support the important work of the Red Cross, a charitable gift annuity might just be the solution for you. To find out more, please complete the form below or call 1-800-797-8022. Or visit our web site at http://www.redcross.org

❑ Yes, I'd like information on how a Red Cross Charitable Gift Annuity might work for me.

Name _____

Address _____

City _____

State _____ ZIP _____

Telephone _____ Birthdate _____

Mail your completed form to American Red Cross, P.O. Box 325, Washington, D.C. 20042

✚ American Red Cross

We'll be there.

P05S+PE+ +P28 SPB+++

Source: American National Red Cross. Reproduced with the permission of the American National Red Cross.

Web Site

The newest marketing tool is the Internet. Many large nonprofits are now placing planned giving information on their Web sites as a resource for their donors.

The information on the Web site should include donor testimonials that tell the story of a gift and how it supported your organization. Web sites lend themselves well to this approach because pictures can be easily used and stories easily updated. These donor testimonials will inspire your audience to look more closely at the nuts and bolts of making a planned gift. The Web page should include an easy way for a donor to send you an e-mail to ask for more information.

To view a Web site with planned giving marketing and other related development resources, visit *http://www.iuf.indiana.edu.*

Seminars

A seminar can also be an effective way to educate your prospects and donors on planned giving. If you haven't already segmented your market, the time you begin planning a seminar is the ideal time to do it. Once you have decided whom you wish to reach, the seminar should be designed to appeal specifically to that audience. If possible, personalized invitations should be sent, and the speaker selected must have appeal and credibility.

During the seminar, the planned giving material must be presented in lay language. The purpose is to clarify planned giving options for the participants. The presentation should provide take-home materials for the prospects to review and take to their own advisers. It should conclude with a reception of some kind so people have a chance to mingle and ask questions of the presenter and staff members in a one-on-one environment. Finally, the seminar materials should include an evaluation sheet for participants to complete and return. The information from the evaluations will allow you to fine-tune future events.

Recognition Societies and Donor Stewardship

Perhaps the most important marketing done is the stewardship of planned gift donors, because word-of-mouth marketing is always the most effective. If planned giving donors are pleased with the continued thanks and attention they receive, they will let others know. They also are very likely to make additional planned gifts, establishing second or third gift annuities or trusts, for example.

The key in stewarding planned giving donors is to create a separate recognition society. Their gifts are special and different from outright gifts and should be recognized as such. Establishing a society will create that recognition and make those donors feel special.

A donor recognition society should be named after something unique and lasting about your organization. It should also have its own annual event that brings members of the society together to thank and recognize them for their contributions. A special gift or token of appreciation that is unique to the society members is an effective stewardship step as well. Finally, be certain to publish the list of members (omitting those who request anonymity) whenever possible. This roster might be included in the annual report or in planned giving or regular newsletters. Routinely publishing the list will show the growth of the program to other prospects as well as recognize those who have made planned gifts.

External Marketing to Professional Advisers

It is critical for a planned giving program to extend itself to the community of professional advisers beyond the planned giving committee or the board. Planned gifts ideally occur in an atmosphere of teamwork, with the donor's own attorney or accountant playing a prominent role. The professional adviser community includes attorneys, trust officers, financial planners, accountants, stockbrokers, and insurance agents. These individuals have a donor's full financial picture and are in the best position to counsel the donor on the financial aspects of charitable giving.

Reaching out to this community is essential because it gives a program credibility. Any nonprofit that is well networked into the community of financial advisers will find that those advisers, in turn, will feel comfortable calling on the nonprofit for specific advice or information. They will also feel comfortable working with the nonprofit and its program when one of their clients is planning a gift. Finally, advisers often recommend charitable giving to clients as a tax strategy. If they know your organization, they may recommend it to the client contemplating a charitable gift in his or her estate.

Newsletters and Other Print Materials

Newsletters targeted to professional advisers work well in this outreach effort. A first step is to compile a mailing list of advisers in the local community. The local bar association can assist with a list of attorneys, and other professional organizations can you get in touch with CPAs and other professionals. Once the adviser mailing list is compiled, add it to the other lists of people who receive your planned giving publications. If possible, develop a separate newsletter for these advisers as well, one that provides the latest information on tax developments and in-depth analysis of planned giving techniques.

Newsletters for practitioners should be simple, direct, and to the point. This not a time to ask the reader to feel warm and fuzzy. Newsletters that are written for financial planners and advisers must be up-to-date on the tax and legal issues they discuss. Many organizations lack the expertise to write this kind of information and turn instead to large companies who create these newsletters with the organization's letterhead or logo. Whether you produce your own newsletter for advisers or use a vendor's product, this publication can enhance the credibility of your organization and raise its profile.

Web Site

One of the latest ways to reach professional advisers is on-line. Establishing a planned giving resource on its Web site is a very effective way for your organization to stay networked with this community. The Web site can be a strong resource that is easily accessible when the adviser needs it.

As opposed to the content designed for donors, the content on the Web site established for advisers must be in depth and should be updated constantly to take account of tax law changes and legislative developments. There is no need for donor testimonials here. The site should, however, include an easy way for advisers to contact you for further information.

Seminars

Seminars can be developed that target allied professionals. These seminars should be coupled with continuing education credit so that participants can satisfy their professional organization's requirements while attending. If you have a planned giving advisory committee in place, a committee member might present the planned giving material. He or she will benefit from increased visibility in the community and the resulting business referrals.

These seminars offer a chance to provide a service to allied professionals. They also position your organization in the community as a resource for further information, and build respect for your organization among important partners.

Networking Through Professional Organizations

Networking through professional organizations is the most effective way to build bridges to allied professionals in the community. Local chapters of the National Committee on Planned Giving offer outstanding opportunities for this type of interaction. Membership is inexpensive, and the nonprofit should take advantage of its networking potential.

Other professional organizations that should be investigated are local estate planning councils. These groups can be located through the local bar association. They offer access to the advisers who write most of the wills and put together the estate plans in a given community. Oftentimes these councils include CPAs and members of local trust companies as well. Those members should not be overlooked in their important role as advisers to clients on tax-wise strategies.

Partnering with Financial Institutions

Finally, every organization that is becoming involved in planned giving should explore strategic partnerships and affiliations with corporate entities in its local area. Relationships with banks or other financial institutions can be leveraged to assist an organization in becoming proficient in planned giving. For example, a small nonprofit could partner with a local bank's trust department to market charitable remainder trusts to the charity's donors. This way the nonprofit is approaching donors with a level of credibility it could not muster on its own. Another excellent opportunity may exist for small nonprofits to foster mutually beneficial relationships with community foundations for the receiving and administration of planned gifts. Such synergies should be actively explored. Ultimately, if the marketing methods discussed in this chapter are used with vision and ambition, any nonprofit can effectively secure planned gifts.

CHAPTER SEVEN

OUTRIGHT GIFTS

Outright gifts fall into five broad categories—gifts of tangible personal property, gifts of real property (real estate), gifts of intangible personal property, gifts of securities, and gifts of life insurance. This chapter defines each option and discusses the major considerations for donors and nonprofits in using each kind of gift, including the tax considerations.

Gifts of Tangible Personal Property

Tangible personal property is defined as property that can be held physically. Many different items are considered tangible personal property that may be used to make a gift. For example:

- Furniture
- Artwork
- Antiques
- Jewelry
- Coin collections
- Equipment
- Automobiles
- Aircraft

- Books
- Clothing
- Livestock

To transfer the ownership or the title of tangible personal property from the donor to the nonprofit requires the physical transfer of the property to the non-profit from the donor along with the formal acceptance of the property by the nonprofit. Usually a *deed of gift* is drafted to accomplish the transfer. The deed of gift is a writing that includes an identification of the property to be transferred and a statement of donative intent signed by the donor (see Exhibit 7.1). Certain types of tangible personal property have formal requirements for transferring title. For example, automobiles must be transferred from donor to donee at the appropriate state agency.

EXHIBIT 7.1. DEED OF GIFT.

_____ , 200__

_____ , DONOR, of _____ , hereby confirms that he is the legal owner of and does hereby irrevocably and unconditionally give, grant, and convey an absolute, unconditional, and undivided interest in the items described on the attached list, identified as Exhibit A, to the XYZ Charity for the benefit of _____ , hereinafter referred to as DONEE. Title to the items and all associated rights are hereby vested in DONEE, without reservation and free and clear of all encumbrances. DONOR understands and agrees that the items may be displayed, loaned, retained, disposed of, or otherwise employed at the sole discretion of DONEE.

EXECUTED by DONOR at _____ on _____ , 200__.

Donor _____

ACCEPTED: ATTESTED:
XYZ Charity

By: _____   By: _____
_____ , President   _____ , Corporate Secretary

Tax Considerations

One of the benefits of making a gift of tangible personal property is the charitable income tax deduction the donor receives (see Resource 17). The amount of the deduction for gifts of tangible personal property will depend on the nonprofit's use of the property. If the property has a use related to the exempt purposes of the organization, the amount of the donor's contribution is measured by the fair market value of the property. However, the donor's charitable deduction in the year of the gift is limited to 30 percent of the donor's adjusted gross income, assuming the property has been held by the donor for at least a year and a day to qualify as a long-term capital asset. A property has a use related to the exempt purpose of the nonprofit when it can be reasonably anticipated that the receiving organization will use the property in a way related to its mission. For example, artwork given to an art museum for display in its gallery has a related use.

If, however, the use of the gift is *not related* to the organization's mission, then the amount of the donor's contribution is measured by her cost basis in the property. For an unrelated use the donor may claim a deduction up to 50 percent of the donor's adjusted gross income. A consequence of this is that if the donor wants to make a gift of tangible personal property for which there is no related use, she may prefer to sell the property and make a gift of the proceeds from the sale in order to obtain a charitable income tax deduction for the property's fair market value. It should be noted that the donor is responsible for any capital gains tax due on the appreciation of the property. Long-term capital gain on tangible personal property is taxed at a 28 percent top rate (not the 20 percent rate of most other property), so making a gift saves the donor more tax on the same appreciation in this case. An example of a gift that does not meet the related use test is a gift made by a donor with the intent that the gift will be sold at an auction. In this instance the donor's charitable income tax deduction is limited to her cost basis in the gift.

As an alternative the donor can choose to make a bequest of tangible personal property, because such property given by bequest is not subject to related use restrictions or to the percentage limitations on deductions from adjusted gross income.

The Internal Revenue Service (IRS) requires that a donor obtain a *qualified appraisal* when the amount of a noncash gift reported as a charitable income tax deduction exceeds $5,000 (unless the donated property consists of publicly traded securities, non-publicly traded stock worth $10,000 or less, or property donated by a C Corporation). A *qualified appraiser* is defined as an individual who is in the business of making such appraisals. The donor is required to attach a completed appraisal summary to his tax return. If the donor claims an income tax deduction for a gift of art in excess of $20,000, he must attach a copy of the complete signed appraisal (not an appraisal summary) and provide an 8-by-10-inch color photograph or a 4-by-5-inch, or larger, color transparency of the item (as spelled out in Exhibit 7.2).

EXHIBIT 7.2. REQUIREMENTS OF A QUALIFIED APPRAISAL OF ARTWORK.

1. Appraisal Requirements

If the value of the artwork gift exceeds $5,000, the donor must obtain a qualified appraisal of the artwork.

- A fully completed appraisal summary must be attached to the income tax return on which the deduction for the contribution is first claimed.

- Written records documenting the information required for property contribution must be maintained.

2. Definition of Qualified Appraisal

A qualified appraisal is an appraisal document, which meets the following criteria:

- It must be made not earlier than 60 days before the date of the gift.

- It is prepared, signed, and dated by a qualified appraiser.

- It includes the following information:

    Description of the property and the physical condition of the property.

    The date or expected date of contribution to the charity.

    The terms of any agreement or understanding entered into between the donor and the charity relating to the use, sale, or disposition of the property.

    The qualifications of the appraiser who signs the appraisal, including his or her background, experience, education, and membership in any professional appraisal associations.

    A statement that the appraisal was prepared for income tax purposes.

    The date on which the property was appraised.

    The fair market value of the property on the date of contribution.

    The method of valuation used to determine the fair market value.

    The basis for the valuation, such as comparable sales transactions.

Notes: If the donor acquired the artwork from an art dealer, neither the art dealer nor persons employed by the dealer can be qualified appraisers of that artwork.

An appraiser who is regularly used by the donor or by the charity and who does not perform the majority of his or her appraisals for other persons cannot qualify as an appraiser for this transaction.

3. Appraisal Summary

An appraisal summary is a summary of the qualified appraisal. It is made on IRS Form 8283 and attached to the income tax return on which the deduction is claimed for the contribution.

EXHIBIT 7.2. REQUIREMENTS OF A
QUALIFIED APPRAISAL OF ARTWORK, Cont'd.

- The charity must sign the appraisal summary on IRS Form 8283 to acknowledge that the property described in the summary was received by the charity and that it was received on the date specified in the summary.
- For contributions of artwork valued at $20,000 or more, the donor must attach a complete copy of the signed appraisal, not the appraisal summary.
- For individual objects valued at $20,000 or more, an 8" × 10" color photograph or color transparency no smaller than 4" × 5" must be provided to the IRS upon request.

Notes: The donor may deduct the cost of the appraisal fee as a miscellaneous itemized deduction to the extent that the miscellaneous deductions for that tax year exceed 2 percent of adjusted gross income.

The donor must obtain a qualified appraisal for each separate item of property that is not included in a group of similar items of property.

The transfer is accomplished by executing a *deed of gift* between the donor and the nonprofit.

Substantiation of Gifts

When a noncash gift is made to a nonprofit, the IRS requires the gift to be substantiated. Both the donor and the nonprofit are required to follow certain procedures for reporting noncash gifts. IRS Form 8283 (see Exhibit 7.3) must be filed by donors who make certain gifts of noncash charitable contributions. The need to file this form depends on the status of the taxpayer and the size and type of gift:

- *Noncash gifts valued at $500 or less.* When a gift from an individual donor is valued at $500 or less, the donor need not complete Form 8283. However, when the donor has made a series of gifts in a given year, each of which is valued at $500 or less but with a total value exceeding $500, then the donor is required to complete Form 8283, Part A.
- *Noncash gifts valued between $501 and $5,000.* Gifts in this range must be reported on Part A of IRS Form 8283, which is then attached to the donor's federal income tax return. An appraisal is not necessary; however, the nonprofit should retain a copy of the completed Form 8283 for its records.
- *Noncash gifts valued over $5,000.* If the amount claimed as a charitable income tax deduction is in excess of $5,000, the IRS requires the donor to complete Part B of Form 8283. It is also necessary for the qualified appraiser and the donee charity to sign the form.

EXHIBIT 7.3. IRS FORM 8283.

Form **8283** (Rev. October 1998) Department of the Treasury Internal Revenue Service	**Noncash Charitable Contributions** ▶ **Attach to your tax return if you claimed a total deduction of over $500 for all contributed property.** ▶ **See separate instructions.**	OMB No. 1545-0908 Attachment Sequence No. **55**
Name(s) shown on your income tax return		Identifying number

Note: *Figure the amount of your contribution deduction before completing this form. See your tax return instructions.*

Section A—List in this section **only** items (or groups of similar items) for which you claimed a deduction of $5,000 or less. Also, list certain publicly traded securities even if the deduction is over $5,000 (see instructions).

Part I   Information on Donated Property—If you need more space, attach a statement.

1	(a) Name and address of the donee organization	(b) Description of donated property
A		
B		
C		
D		
E		

Note: *If the amount you claimed as a deduction for an item is $500 or less, you do not have to complete columns (d), (e), and (f).*

	(c) Date of the contribution	(d) Date acquired by donor (mo., yr.)	(e) How acquired by donor	(f) Donor's cost or adjusted basis	(g) Fair market value	(h) Method used to determine the fair market value
A						
B						
C						
D						
E						

Part II   Other Information—Complete line 2 if you gave less than an entire interest in property listed in Part I. Complete line 3 if conditions were attached to a contribution listed in Part I.

2 If, during the year, you contributed less than the entire interest in the property, complete lines a–e.

a Enter the letter from Part I that identifies the property ▶ _____. If Part II applies to more than one property, attach a separate statement.

b Total amount claimed as a deduction for the property listed in Part I: **(1)** For this tax year   ▶ _____ .
                                                                                   (2) For any prior tax years ▶ _____ .

c Name and address of each organization to which any such contribution was made in a prior year (complete only if different from the donee organization above):

Name of charitable organization (donee)

_____

Address (number, street, and room or suite no.)

_____

City or town, state, and ZIP code

_____

d For tangible property, enter the place where the property is located or kept ▶ _____

e Name of any person, other than the donee organization, having actual possession of the property ▶ _____

3 If conditions were attached to any contribution listed in Part I, answer questions a – c and attach the required statement (see instructions).

		Yes	No
a	Is there a restriction, either temporary or permanent, on the donee's right to use or dispose of the donated property?		
b	Did you give to anyone (other than the donee organization or another organization participating with the donee organization in cooperative fundraising) the right to the income from the donated property or to the possession of the property, including the right to vote donated securities, to acquire the property by purchase or otherwise, or to designate the person having such income, possession, or right to acquire?		
c	Is there a restriction limiting the donated property for a particular use?		

For Paperwork Reduction Act Notice, see page 4 of separate instructions.   Cat. No. 62299J   Form **8283** (Rev. 10-98)

EXHIBIT 7.3. IRS FORM 8283, Cont'd.

Form 8283 (Rev. 10-98)   Page **2**

Name(s) shown on your income tax return	Identifying number

Section B—Appraisal Summary—List in this section only items (or groups of similar items) for which you claimed a deduction of more than $5,000 per item or group. **Exception.** Report contributions of certain publicly traded securities only in Section A.

If you donated art, you may have to attach the complete appraisal. See the **Note** in Part I below.

Part I   **Information on Donated Property**—To be completed by the taxpayer and/or appraiser.

4   Check type of property:

☐ Art* (contribution of $20,000 or more)   ☐ Real Estate   ☐ Gems/Jewelry   ☐ Stamp Collections
☐ Art* (contribution of less than $20,000)   ☐ Coin Collections   ☐ Books   ☐ Other

*Art includes paintings, sculptures, watercolors, prints, drawings, ceramics, antique furniture, decorative arts, textiles, carpets, silver, rare manuscripts, historical memorabilia, and other similar objects.

Note: If your total art contribution deduction was $20,000 or more, you must attach a complete copy of the signed appraisal. See instructions.

5	(a) Description of donated property (if you need more space, attach a separate statement)	(b) If tangible property was donated, give a brief summary of the overall physical condition at the time of the gift	(c) Appraised fair market value
A			
B			
C			
D			

	(d) Date acquired by donor (mo., yr.)	(e) How acquired by donor	(f) Donor's cost or adjusted basis	(g) For bargain sales, enter amount received	(h) Amount claimed as a deduction	(i) Average trading price of securities
					See instructions	
A						
B						
C						
D						

Part II   **Taxpayer (Donor) Statement**—List each item included in Part I above that the appraisal identifies as having a value of $500 or less. See instructions.

I declare that the following item(s) included in Part I above has to the best of my knowledge and belief an appraised value of not more than $500 (per item). Enter identifying letter from Part I and describe the specific item. See instructions. ▶ _____

Signature of taxpayer (donor) ▶ _____   Date ▶ _____

Part III   **Declaration of Appraiser**

I declare that I am not the donor, the donee, a party to the transaction in which the donor acquired the property, employed by, or related to any of the foregoing persons, or married to any person who is related to any of the foregoing persons. And, if regularly used by the donor, donee, or party to the transaction, I performed the majority of my appraisals during my tax year for other persons.

Also, I declare that I hold myself out to the public as an appraiser or perform appraisals on a regular basis; and that because of my qualifications as described in the appraisal, I am qualified to make appraisals of the type of property being valued. I certify that the appraisal fees were not based on a percentage of the appraised property value. Furthermore, I understand that a false or fraudulent overstatement of the property value as described in the qualified appraisal or this appraisal summary may subject me to the penalty under section 6701(a) (aiding and abetting the understatement of tax liability). I affirm that I have not been barred from presenting evidence or testimony by the Director of Practice.

Sign Here | Signature ▶ _____   Title ▶ _____   Date of appraisal ▶ _____

Business address (including room or suite no.)	Identifying number

City or town, state, and ZIP code

Part IV   **Donee Acknowledgment**—To be completed by the charitable organization.

This charitable organization acknowledges that it is a qualified organization under section 170(c) and that it received the donated property as described in Section B, Part I, above on ▶ _____
(Date)

Furthermore, this organization affirms that in the event it sells, exchanges, or otherwise disposes of the property described in Section B, Part I (or any portion thereof) within 2 years after the date of receipt, it will file **Form 8282,** Donee Information Return, with the IRS and give the donor a copy of that form. This acknowledgment does not represent agreement with the claimed fair market value.

Does the organization intend to use the property for an unrelated use? . . . . ▶ ☐ Yes   ☐ No

Name of charitable organization (donee)	Employer identification number	
Address (number, street, and room or suite no.)	City or town, state, and ZIP code	
Authorized signature	Title	Date

⊕

- *Gifts of non-publicly traded stock.* Stock is defined as nonpublic when it is not listed on an exchange or regularly traded. If the donor makes a gift of non-publicly traded stock, Part B of Form 8283 must be completed. This is true regardless of the value of the stock. If the value of the stock exceeds $10,000, then a qualified appraisal is required.

If the nonprofit sells, exchanges, or disposes of donated property having a value of $5,000 or more, other than cash or marketable securities, within two years of the date of the gift, the organization must complete and file IRS Form 8282 and also send a copy to the donor. Form 8282 (see Exhibit 7.4) is used by the IRS to monitor potential fraud. Fraud may be suspected if the nonprofit sells the property for substantially less than the appraised value. To avoid the appearance of fraud, the donor's appraisal must be a realistic estimate of the true value of the item. (Exhibit 7.5 summarizes these requirements.)

Gifts of Real Property

Gifts of real property are one of the most common and generous types of gifts in charitable gift planning. However, making gifts of real property can be complicated, and the charity must exercise due diligence before accepting such gifts.

Real property is commonly defined as land and the structures that are permanently attached to it. Examples of real property are

- Undeveloped land
- Residential property
- Investment property, such as apartments, office buildings, and shopping centers
- Commercial property, such as industrial parks, hotels, and recreational parks
- Agricultural land used for the production of livestock or crops

It should be noted that real property also includes any natural resources on the land, such as timber, coal, oil and gas, and other minerals.

Types of Ownership

One of the key steps in evaluating a gift of real property is to determine how the property is owned. Generally, the ownership of real property falls into one of three categories:

- Fee simple
- Partial interest
- Indirect interest

EXHIBIT 7.4. IRS FORM 8282.

Form **8282**	**Donee Information Return**	OMB No. 1545-0908
(Rev. September 1998)	(Sale, Exchange, or Other Disposition of Donated Property)	
Department of the Treasury Internal Revenue Service	▶ See instructions on back.	Give a Copy to Donor

Please Print or Type	Name of charitable organization (donee)	Employer identification number
	Address (number, street, and room or suite no.)	
	City or town, state, and ZIP code	

Part I Information on ORIGINAL DONOR and DONEE Receiving the Property

1a Name(s) of the original donor of the property	1b Identifying number

Note: *Complete lines 2a–2d only if you gave this property to another charitable organization (successor donee).*

2a Name of charitable organization	2b Employer identification number
2c Address (number, street, and room or suite no.)	
2d City or town, state, and ZIP code	

Note: *If you are the original donee, skip Part II and go to Part III now.*

Part II Information on PREVIOUS DONEES—Complete this part only if you were not the first donee to receive the property. If you were the second donee, leave lines 4a–4d blank. If you were a third or later donee, complete lines 3a–4d. On lines 4a–4d, give information on the preceding donee (the one who gave you the property).

3a Name of original donee	3b Employer identification number
3c Address (number, street, and room or suite no.)	
3d City or town, state, and ZIP code	
4a Name of preceding donee	4b Employer identification number
4c Address (number, street, and room or suite no.)	
4d City or town, state, and ZIP code	

Part III Information on DONATED PROPERTY—If you are the original donee, leave column (c) blank.

(a) Description of donated property sold, exchanged, or otherwise disposed of (if you need more space, attach a separate statement)	(b) Date you received the item(s)	(c) Date the first donee received the item(s)	(d) Date item(s) sold, exchanged, or otherwise disposed of	(e) Amount received upon disposition

For Paperwork Reduction Act Notice, see back of form.　Cat. No. 62307Y　Form **8282** (Rev. 9-98)

EXHIBIT 7.5. APPRAISAL AND REPORTING SUMMARY.

Property Contributed and Amount	Qualified Appraisal Required?	Form 8283 Section A Required?	Form 8283 Section B[1] Required?	Form 8282 Required?
One item: Valued at $500 or less	No	No	No	No
One item: Valued at over $500 but not over $5,000	No	Yes	No	No
One item: Valued at over $5,000	Yes[2]	No	Yes	Yes
Multiple items: Combined value over $500 but not over $5,000	No	Yes	No	No
Multiple items: Combined value over $5,000 but with no one item or aggregation of similar items over $5,000	No	Yes	No	No
Similar items: Combined value over $5,000	Yes	No	Yes	Yes[3]
Publicly traded securities: Valued at over $500	No	Yes	No	No
Closely held securities: Valued at over $5,000 but not over $10,000	No	No	Yes[4]	Yes
Closely held securities: Valued at over $10,000	Yes	No	Yes	Yes
Artwork: Valued at over $5,000	Yes[5]	Yes	Yes	Yes
Inventory: If deduction taken exceeds donor's basis by more than $5,000	Yes	Yes	Yes	Yes

[1] Form 8283 Section B is often called the "Appraisal Summary" and is so captioned on the form itself.

[2] The $5,000 threshold for a qualified appraisal is raised to $10,000 for gifts of closely held stock. Qualified appraisals are not required for gifts of publicly traded securities regardless of the amount.

[3] Form 8282 generally is required if the charity sells the property within two years except for individual items valued at $500 or less at time of contribution.

[4] A "partially completed appraisal summary" (i.e., Parts I and II only of Form 8283 Section B) is required for gifts of closely held stock valued at over $5,000 but not over $10,000.

[5] The full qualified appraisal must be attached to the return when artwork is valued at over $20,000. People who donate artwork valued at $50,000 or more may wish to obtain a statement of value from the IRS prior to filing their tax return claiming the deduction. See Rev. Proc. 96-15.

Source: Printed courtesy of Endowment Development Services, Indianapolis.

Fee Simple. *Fee simple* is the most common type of individual ownership of real property. Fee simple means the owner has the largest possible estate in the real property. The owner of the fee simple enjoys all rights in the property during her lifetime, including possession, control, enjoyment, and disposition of the property. The owner also has the right to transfer her interest upon death.

Partial Interest. A *partial interest* in real property results when a property owner shares ownership of the property with another person or entity or when the rights normally associated with the fee simple are limited in some way. There are a number of forms of partial interest, including the following.

Tenancy in Common. *Tenancy in common* results when two or more persons own an undivided, fractional interest in a property. Owners may possess equal or unequal shares and may, unless contractually prohibited, dispose of their interest individually. Tenants in common also share in the income and expenses of the property according to their ownership share. When a tenant in common dies, his interest passes according to the terms of his will or estate plan. If he dies without a will, his interest passes according to his state's laws of intestate succession. If a person who owns property as a tenant in common transfers that interest by gift to a nonprofit, the nonprofit becomes a tenant in common with the remaining owners.

Joint Tenancy with Rights of Survivorship. Joint tenancy with rights of survivorship is distinguished from tenancy in common by several factors. Joint tenants all own equal interest, whereas tenants in common are permitted to own unequal shares. Most important, when one joint tenant dies, her interest passes in equal shares to the surviving tenants by operation of law. As a result, such transfers are not subject to probate administration of the estate of the deceased tenant. Because of this, any dispositions in the decedent's will or trust will have no effect on the transfer of property held in joint tenancy. Therefore, if a donor owns property as a joint tenant and the property is intended to be a charitable bequest, the charitable donee should also be a joint tenant.

Tax Considerations for Tenancy in Common and Joint Tenancy. Many people operate under the mistaken belief that joint tenancy allows the property owners to avoid estate taxes on the property. Although joint tenancy does avoid probate administration, the property held in such fashion remains a part of the owner's gross estate for purposes of calculating federal estate tax. It is often found that donors, relying on this misconception, have created joint tenancies during their lifetimes with their children or others, thinking the property will avoid estate taxation. However, what they have actually accomplished is the completion of a *lifetime gift*, which may create federal gift tax liability.

The tax code also stipulates unique treatment of the income tax basis of property held in joint tenancy. When a joint tenant dies, the decedent's interest receives a stepped-up cost basis; however, the surviving joint tenant's interest does not. Thus, if the surviving joint tenant sells his appreciated property, he may have to pay capital gains tax. This can be a consideration when the nonprofit receives an interest in a joint tenancy from the donor at the donor's death.

If the joint tenant sells his interest during his lifetime, the joint tenancy is severed and the purchaser of that interest becomes a tenant in common with the remaining owners.

Community Property. Several states (Arizona, California, Idaho, Louisiana, Nevada, New Mexico, Texas, and Washington) are *community property* states. Wisconsin has a system of marital property that operates similarly to community property laws.

Community property laws vary slightly from state to state; however, in general they provide that income earned and property acquired during marriage is to be shared equally by both spouses. This is true even if one spouse earns all of the income. However, the law also provides that property owned prior to marriage, plus gifts and inheritances, may remain as separate property provided it is maintained with separate assets and not commingled with the community assets.

Community property differs from property held in joint tenancy and tenants by the entirety (see the next section) in that it does not pass by operation of law to the surviving spouse; instead, it passes according to the terms of the deceased spouse's will or trust or by the laws of intestacy. In addition, community property receives a stepped-up cost basis for the entire property, unlike joint tenancy, which upon the death of the joint tenant receives a stepped-up cost basis for the decedent spouse's interest only. Therefore, if the surviving spouse subsequently sells community property, she will realize gain only for postdeath appreciation.

Tenancy by the Entirety. When a married couple takes title to property together, most states consider each of them to be owners of the entire property. This interest is referred to as *tenants by the entirety*. When property is held in this manner, neither spouse can dispose of his or her interest individually. In common with the joint tenancy, when one tenant dies, his or her interest passes automatically to the surviving tenant by operation of law. If the couple divorces, the tenancy by the entirety is severed, and the parties become tenants in common.

Life Estates and Remainders. Whereas the previous examples are forms of concurrent ownership of real property, *life estates* and *remainder interest* constitute consecutive ownership.

In a life estate agreement, the fee simple interest is divided among two or more persons. The life tenant is given the right of possession, control, and enjoyment of the property for a period usually measured by his life expectancy. However, his interest may also be measured by a term of years or by a combination of life and a term of years, so long as this period is expressly stated in the deed. After the conclusion of the measuring term, the property is transferred to the remainder beneficiary, who then holds the fee simple interest.

A gift of a remainder interest in a personal residence or farm occurs when a donor irrevocably transfers title in the property to a charitable organization while retaining the right to use the property for a term that is specified at the time of the gift. At the conclusion of the term, all rights in the property transfer to the charity as a remainder interest. The term of the gift can be measured by the life of one or more individuals, a fixed term of years, or by a combination of the two. However, these gifts are most frequently established to last for the term of the life or lives of the residents of the donated property. Therefore, these gifts are typically referred to as life estates. Life estate agreements work best for donors who desire to make a testamentary gift of real property to charity and also to receive a current income tax deduction for a charitable gift.

A *personal residence* is defined by the Internal Revenue Code as any property used by the taxpayer as a personal residence whether or not it is her primary residence. For example, a vacation home may qualify as a personal residence. The definition does not include household furnishings that are not fixtures of the residence. Therefore, if a donor desires to contribute the furnishings of the residence, they should be bequeathed to the nonprofit separately.

A *farm* is defined as land used by the taxpayer or by a tenant of the taxpayer for the production of crops, fruits, or other agricultural products for the sustenance of livestock, including cattle, hogs, horses, mules, donkeys, sheep, goats, fur-bearing animals, chickens, turkeys, pigeons, and other poultry.

The IRS does not provide specific guidance on how to complete a gift of a life estate interest. Ultimately the donor accomplishes the gift by transferring title to the property to the charity by a warranty deed (discussed later in this chapter). Prior to the transfer, the charity should consider many of the same issues that arise with any gift of real estate (also discussed later in this chapter), especially obtaining clear title and learning whether any environmental problems exist.

The deed should define the measuring term of the retained estate. If the term is measured by the lives of one or more individuals, it should identify these individuals in the order in which they will receive their interest. If the agreement is to be measured by a term of years, the deed should identify the primary tenants and also provide guidance regarding successor tenants should the primary tenants die prior to the expiration of the term of years.

The nonprofit should also document in writing the responsibilities to be retained by the donor. In most cases, the donor is required to maintain the property, insure the property against loss and liability, and repair the property in the event of damage. Furthermore the agreement should prohibit the donor from permitting any additional liens or encumbrances on the property without the express permission of the charity.

The agreement between the nonprofit and the donor may also provide options for the sale of the property. These may include the sale of the original property and repurchase of a new property with continuation of the retained estate, a division of the proceeds of the sale in accordance with the value of each party's interest, or some combination of these options. If the nonprofit and the donor agree to sell the property and divide the net sale proceeds, the present value of the nonprofit's remainder interest is calculated using the net sales proceeds on the date of the sale. Any expenses attributable to the life tenant, such as outstanding property taxes, are deducted from the life tenant's share of the sale proceeds. The present value of the remainder interest is distributed to the charity, and the remaining proceeds distributed to the donor. The donor will recognize capital gains based on his proportionate share of the sale proceeds. It is important to note that the decision to sell must be voluntary on the part of both the donor and the nonprofit. The nonprofit cannot be compelled to sell its interest prior to the expiration of the agreed-upon measuring term.

Another option is that the donor may eventually contribute the balance of his life estate, which would accelerate his gift of the remainder interest to the nonprofit. In this instance the donor receives an additional charitable income tax deduction based on the present value of his or her remaining life or the term of years. In these circumstances the present value of the remainder interest is calculated using the fair market value of the property on the date the retained life or term of years in the property is transferred to the nonprofit. The present value of the remainder interest is then subtracted from the fair market value of the property, which results in the amount that qualifies for the charitable income tax deduction.

Tax Consequences of Gifts of Remainder Interest. When a donor makes a gift of a remainder interest in a personal residence or farm, she is entitled to receive a charitable income tax deduction. This deduction is equal to the net present value of the charitable remainder interest. The guidelines for calculating this value are provided in the U.S. Treasury Regulations Section 1.170A-12 and include the following:

- Fair market value of the property on the date of the transfer
- Fair market value of any depreciable improvements attached to or depletable resources associated with the property at the time of the transfer
- Estimated useful life of depreciable improvements
- Salvage value of depreciable improvements at the conclusion of their useful life
- Measuring term of the agreement (life or term of years)
- Applicable federal midterm rate in effect the month of the transfer to charity or during either of the two preceding months

In most cases the gift of a remainder interest in a personal residence or farm will be made with property that the donor has held long-term and that has appreciated in value. As a consequence, the remainder interest is deductible against 30 percent of the donor's adjusted gross income, with a five-year carryover of any excess deduction.

Indirect Interest. Indirect interest, or ownership, exists when an individual does not hold title to the property itself but holds an interest in a legal entity that holds title to the property. Such entities are, for example, partnerships, corporations, limited liability companies, and revocable living trusts. Partnerships and corporations are discussed here. Limited liability companies are similar to corporations, and trusts in general are discussed in Chapters Nine and Ten.

Partnerships. Partnerships may be structured as general or as limited partnerships. In a *general partnership,* all partners are personally liable for the debts of the partnership. In a *limited partnership,* the liability of each limited partner is restricted to his investment. In this respect limited partners are similar to corporate shareholders. Also, limited partners have no voice in the day-to-day operation and decision making of the partnership, whereas in general partnerships the partners usually participate in management decisions. Partnerships are considered pass-through entities for income tax purposes. This means that items of income and expense, gain and loss, and indebtedness are considered owned by (passed through to) each partner according to his percentage interest in or share of the partnership.

When a nonprofit is considering whether to accept a gift of real property owned by a partnership, it should keep in mind that the partnership owns the property and the partner owns an interest in the partnership. Therefore care should be taken to read the partnership agreement to determine whether and under what conditions a partnership interest can be transferred to charity. Because partners are considered the owners of the partnership's income for income tax purposes, the nonprofit should also be careful to determine whether the partnership generates any unrelated business income. Unrelated business income can produce adverse tax consequences for the nonprofit. Furthermore, because partners are considered the owners of partnership debt, the transfer of a partnership interest in which the underlying assets are debt encumbered will be considered a bargain sale to the nonprofit (bargain sales and their tax consequences are discussed later in this chapter).

Because of the complexity of transferring a partnership interest, it may be preferable to first distribute the real estate from the partnership to the partners, who will then be tenants in common of that property. The partner making the gift can then donate his interest. An additional benefit of this option is that a distribution of real property by a partnership to a partner can be accomplished without constituting a taxable event for the partner.

Corporations. Frequently it is found that a donor has real property that is owned by a corporation in which the donor is a stockholder. This can be a particularly complicated transfer from a tax-planning perspective due to the presence of two tax-paying entities (the donor shareholder and the corporation) and two levels of tax. Thus it is critical for the nonprofit to determine who the donor should be and whether the corporation is involved with the gift.

If the corporation that owns the property is a C corporation, a gain or loss on sale or transfer is taxable initially at the corporate level. It does not matter whether the stock of the corporation is owned by a tax-exempt charity or a charitable remainder trust. If the corporation is classified as an S corporation, income tax treatment is more favorable because in most instances the corporate level of tax is eliminated. (For a fuller discussion of gifts involving assets owned by C and by S corporations, see Chapter Ten.)

Deeds

A donor's ownership of real property is evidenced by a written *deed,* the content and form of which are controlled by local law. The content and form vary depending on the title interest to be conveyed and the purpose the deed is to serve. For charitable gifts the types of deeds commonly used include

- Warranty deeds
- Grant deeds
- Quit claim deeds

Warranty Deed. *Warranty deeds* provide the greatest amount of protection to the nonprofit. The purpose of this type of deed is to create a continuing future obligation on the donor to guarantee the covenants contained in the deed. These covenants will normally include

- *Seisin* (sometimes spelled *seizin*): a guarantee that the donor is the owner of, has possession of, and has the right to give the property
- *Quiet enjoyment:* a guarantee that the donee charity will not be disturbed in its possession of the property
- *Encumbrance:* a guarantee that the property is not subject to any encumbrances other than those stated in the deed
- *Further assurance:* the donor's promise to procure and deliver any instrument (other than the deed) needed to transfer good title
- *Warranty forever:* an absolute guarantee by the donor to the donee of title and possession of the property

The nonprofit should bear in mind that even though a warranty deed provides the donor with assurances of good title, it does not guarantee that the nonprofit will have *marketable* title. Subsequent to the transfer, a third party may arise to make a claim to the rights and the property. Even though such claims may not violate any deed covenants or be sufficient cause for the donee charity to relinquish possession, they may cloud the charity's title to the property.

Grant Deed. Some states use *grant deeds* in place of warranty deeds. A grant deed warrants that the property has not been conveyed to another person. It further warrants the property to be free of any encumbrances, including liens, taxes, and assessments (other than those specifically referenced in the deed), made by the donor or any person claiming under her. A grant deed also describes any rights of way or other easements and also building restrictions. The key distinction between warranty and grant deeds is that a grant deed does not warrant good title.

Quit Claim Deed. The *quit claim deed* does not warrant possession to or any right of title to the property. It conveys only whatever rights the donor possesses at the time of the transfer to the nonprofit. For this reason, quit claim deeds offer charities the least amount of security. For charitable contribution purposes, quit claim deeds are the least desirable.

Transferring Title

The gift is not completed until title is transferred from the donor to the nonprofit. The process of transferring title includes the following:

- Title search
- Title insurance
- Property survey
- Physical inspection of property
- Evaluation of potential environmental hazards
- Property appraisal

Title Search. The *title search* is meant to determine whether there are any defects, liens, or other restrictions on a property's title. It is usually performed by a title company or an attorney. The title report will show any defects uncovered during the title search. These may include unpaid taxes, delinquent mortgage payments, or judgments against the owner. In addition, the title search should uncover any zoning restrictions or easements on the property and any defects that might delay the property's sale or disposition.

Title Insurance. It is recommended that even after conducting a title search, the nonprofit obtain *title insurance,* which guarantees that the title is marketable. Title insurance will protect the nonprofit from loss or damage as a result of any title defects. Title insurance will describe the property in detail and state what if any limitations there are to the nonprofit's ownership. Also, a title insurance policy may guarantee that the property is free of any undisclosed liens, disputes over the rights of ownership, or anything else that might cloud the nonprofit's title.

Property Survey. The title search reveals only those conditions shown in the recorder's office. It does not reveal whether the property has been encroached upon. For additional protection the nonprofit may have the property surveyed. A *property survey,* which should be conducted by a professional surveyor or civil engineer, will show the precise legal boundaries of a property along with the location of improvements, easements, rights of way, encroachments, and other physical features.

Property Inspection. The nonprofit should conduct its own *physical inspection* of the condition of the property before accepting it as a gift.

Evaluation of Environmental Hazards. As part of the inspection process the nonprofit should review the property for any *environmental hazards* in order to avoid being held liable for the cost of cleaning up the site after receiving the property. When even the remote possibility of an environmental hazard exists, the nonprofit should require an environmental audit prior to accepting the property. The first step in this audit is a Phase One Environmental Review, which researches prior owners and uses of the property. If this review turns up findings of concern, a Phase Two Review is conducted. In this next review a physical inspection and core sampling of the property is conducted. Today there are firms in most geographical areas that can conduct such environmental reviews.

Property Appraisal. If the donor intends to claim a charitable contribution income tax deduction in excess of $5,000 for her gift of real estate, a qualified appraisal must be performed by an independent qualified appraiser. The appraisal must be performed no earlier than sixty days prior to the transfer of the property and no later than the date on which the donor files the federal income tax return on which she claims the deduction. (See the definition of a qualified appraisal in Exhibit 7.2.)

Selling Contributed Property

Real property is best transferred to a nonprofit with the intent of an immediate sale. There may be occasions when contributed property can be put to use by the nonprofit or held for the production of income. The nonprofit should be wary, however. If the only means available to the donor to dispose of the real estate is to give it to a nonprofit organization, it is probably not a suitable piece of real estate to accept as a charitable gift.

If the real estate has appreciated since the donor purchased it, the gain on its sale is not attributable to the donor so long as he has given the property away prior to the sale. However, an exception to this rule takes effect when the donor retains direct or indirect control over the real estate or when there is an express or implied pre-arranged obligation on the part of the nonprofit to sell the property to a certain party.

Transfers of Real Estate to Life Income Vehicles

Donors can use a gift of real estate to fund life income vehicles. When planning these transfers, the nonprofit should take into consideration whether or not the property is compatible with the particular life income vehicle chosen, whether the property will be held or sold, and finally, whether the property needs to produce income. When these transfers are used effectively, real estate can be a valuable asset to fund life income vehicles. This section examines using real estate to fund charitable gift annuities, charitable remainder trusts, and pooled income funds.

Real Property Transfers in Exchange for a Gift Annuity. If a nonprofit offers charitable gift annuities, it should be cautious before accepting real estate to fund the gift annuity. The reason for this is that under an immediate payment gift annuity, the obligation to make the payments to the annuitant begins immediately, whether or not the nonprofit has sold the real estate that was contributed in exchange for the gift annuity. Moreover, some states (New York, for example) prohibit funding a gift annuity with real estate. If a nonprofit does decide to accept real estate in exchange for charitable gift annuities, it is recommended that it do so in each case only after a thorough examination of the property and its marketability. The nonprofit may even want to consider a possible reduction of its standard annuity rate or a discounting of the appraised value of the property used to determine the annuity payments. The discounts can compensate an organization for the liquidity risk it assumes when funding an immediate payment gift annuity with real estate.

Alternatively, a deferred gift annuity could be used. The deferral period can be structured to give the nonprofit sufficient time to sell the property and to use the sale proceeds to make the annuity payments. Again, the nonprofit may wish to reduce the deferred annuity rate from the recommended rate in order to reduce the risk.

Gifts of Real Property for a Charitable Remainder Unitrust. A charitable remainder unitrust is the recommended form of trust to use to accept gifts of real estate. There are four types of these trusts to choose from, each with its own payout format:

- Standard
- Net income
- Net income with makeup
- Flip unitrust

It is recommended that either the standard or flip unitrust be the preferred payout method. The flip and standard unitrusts can be invested by the governing board to satisfy long-term investment objectives of the income recipients of the trust and the remainder gift to charity (unitrusts are discussed further in Chapter Eight).

Transfers of Real Property to a Pooled Income Fund. Transfers of real property to pooled income funds can be problematic. The reason is that a gift of real property may dilute the value of units in the pooled income fund. When a donor makes a gift to a pooled income fund, the fund issues units to the donor, like a mutual fund. The income recipient of the units begins receiving her pro rata share of the total income of the fund whether or not the contributed property has produced any income or has been sold. If the fund is unable to sell the real estate for an extended period of time and the real estate produces no income, all the other participants in the pooled income fund will see their distributions reduced.

Therefore, if a nonprofit accepts real estate into its pooled income fund, it should do so only if the property produces income or can be readily sold.

Bargain Sales

A *bargain sale* results when a donor sells property to a nonprofit for less than its fair market value. In a bargain sale the nonprofit receives the benefit of the excess of the property's market value over its cost. The donor relinquishes the property and receives the sale price of the property in return. The donor may then deduct the difference between the fair market value and the sale price as a charitable contribution.

For example, if a donor has property with a value and cost basis of $10,000, and he sells it to the nonprofit for $6,000, he may deduct $4,000, the difference between the sale price and the purchase price. However, if a donor makes a bargain sale of appreciated property, it can produce a taxable gain, which the donor must report. A donor's cost basis is divided proportionally between the sale portion of the property and the gift portion. To determine the amount of gain to report, the donor subtracts the basis attributable to the sold part of the property from the price the nonprofit pays for the property. The taxable gain is the excess of the price the donor receives over the basis of the part sold. This means that if the sale price of the property is 40 percent of the property's value, 40 percent of the entire property's basis is used to determine the gain.

For example, a donor sells property worth $10,000, with a $5,000 basis, to a nonprofit for a price of $3,000. The nonprofit has received a $7,000 benefit, and that amount is deductible by the donor. However, because the donor has received $3,000, some tax must be paid on that gain. The $3,000 sale price is 30 percent of the property's value, so 30 percent of the $5,000 basis must be used to compute the gain as follows:

$3,000 purchase price = .30 basis proportion factor.

$10,000 value.

$5,000 as cost basis × .30 basis proportion factor = $1,500 basis for computation of the gain.

$3,000 − $1,500 basis for computation of gain = $1,500 taxable gain.

Bargain sales may be attractive to a donor who does not want to make a gift of all of a property's value. They have a disadvantage for the nonprofit because it must pay for part of the property rather than receiving it outright. Before entering into a bargain sale agreement, it is advisable for the nonprofit to obtain an appraisal to determine the true value of the property being offered for sale. A bargain sale paid for in installments can be an alternative to a gift annuity. In this case, however, the charity is not obligated to lifetime payments.

Gifts of Intangible Personal Property

Intangible personal property is property that has no intrinsic value; its value results from intangible qualities rather than from specific tangible (physical) factors. The Internal Revenue Code does not provide a specific definition of intangible personal property; however, it does provide some examples. Section 963(h)(3)(B) states that intangible personal property can take the form of a

- Copyrighted literary, musical, or artistic composition
- Patent, invention, formula, process, design, pattern, or know-how
- Trademark, trade name, or brand name
- Franchise, license, or contract
- Method, program, system, procedure, campaign, survey, study, forecast, estimate, customer list, or technical data
- Any similar item that has substantial value independent of the services of any individual

In the field of charitable gift planning, the intangible personal properties the gift planner will most often encounter will be copyrights, royalties, and patents. This section examines these types of gifts of intangible personal property and discusses the rules that apply to charitable tax deductions for income, gift, and estate tax purposes. The considerations surrounding gifts of intangible personal property are very complex, and your charity should not undertake to receive such a gift without advice from your own counsel. The donor should also be advised by his or her own counsel as to the proper method of transfer. Even though gifts of intangible personal property happen infrequently, they can be quite rewarding for your charity if properly handled.

As a general rule, gifts of intangible personal property are not subject to the same tax rules that apply to gifts of tangible personal property. The related use and future interest rules do not apply to gifts of intangible assets. However, the partial interest rule and Internal Revenue Code Section 170 reduction rules (which are applicable to contributions of ordinary income property) often will have an effect on gifts of intangible assets. With regard to gift and estate tax deductions, intangible personal property is subject to the same general rules that apply to tangible personal property and real property.

Copyrights

Title 17 of the *U.S. Code* provides that the holder of a copyright has the exclusive right:

- To reproduce the copyrighted work in copies or phono-records
- To prepare derivative works based upon the copyrighted work
- To distribute copies or phono-records of the copyrighted work to the public by sale or other transfer of ownership, or by rental, lease, or lending
- In the case of literary, musical, dramatic and other choreographic works, pantomimes, and motion pictures and other audiovisual works, to perform the copyrighted work publicly
- In the case of sound recordings, to perform the copyrighted work publicly by means of digital audio transmission

Generally, copyright protection is provided for original works of authorship, including literary works; musical works; dramatic works; choreographic works; pictorial, graphic, and sculptured work; motion pictures and other audiovisual work; sound recordings; and architectural works.

If a work was created on or after January 1, 1978, the duration of the copyright is for a term consisting of the life of the author plus another fifty years. In the case of a joint work, the copyright term is the life of the last surviving author plus fifty years.

If the copyrighted work was created before January 1, 1978, the copyright is for a term of twenty-eight years from the date it was originally secured. The *U.S. Code,* Title 17, Section 202 provides that ownership of a copyright, or of any of the exclusive rights under a copyright, is distinct from the ownership of any material object in which the work is embodied. Therefore the transfer of ownership of any material object in which the work is first fixed does not of itself convey any rights in that copyrighted work, nor, in the absence of an agreement between the parties, does transfer of the ownership of a copyright or of any exclusive rights under the copyright convey property rights in the material object. Bearing this in mind, the owner of a material object subject to copyright can contribute the object, the copyright (if she is also the holder of the copyright), or both.

Ownership of a copyright may be transferred in whole or in part by any means of conveyance or by operation of law and may also be given by bequest. Transfers must be evidenced in writing and signed by the copyright owner or the owner's agent. The final step in transferring the copyright involves sending the original or a certified copy of the original instrument of transfer to the Register of Copyrights, along with the applicable fee for recording. The document will be returned with a Certificate of Recordation (see *U.S. Code,* Title 17, Section 205A).

How the transfer of a copyright is treated in regard to its deductibility as a charitable contribution will depend on the answers to three questions:

- Is the copyright in the hands of the donor considered a capital asset or ordinary income property?
- Is the copyright subject to depreciation recapture?
- Does the contribution satisfy the partial interest rule?

According to U.S. Treasury Regulations Section 1.1221-1(c)(1), the copyright of a literary, musical, or artistic composition or similar property is excluded from the donor's capital assets if the composition was created by the donor's personal efforts. Similar property includes theatrical productions, radio programs, and any other property eligible for copyright protection. In short, a copyright is considered a capital asset unless it is owned by the taxpayer who created the copyrighted property. Therefore, if a copyright is transferred to your nonprofit and it is considered ordinary income property, the donor's charitable deduction on his income tax is limited to his adjusted cost basis, subject to the 50 percent deduction limitation. If the copyright is considered a long-term capital gain asset, the donor's deduction is based on the fair market value of the copyright, subject to the 30 percent deduction limitation on his adjusted gross income.

With respect to depreciation recapture, any depreciation previously claimed by the taxpayer is recaptured as ordinary income when the copyrighted property is transferred. For purposes of determining your donor's charitable deduction, the fair market value of the copyright is reduced by the amount of depreciation recaptured as ordinary income.

As discussed earlier, the partial interest rule can come into play with transfers of copyrights. An individual can contribute a copyright while retaining the material object or contribute the object while retaining the copyright. However, because of the partial interest rules set out in Section 170 of the Internal Revenue Code, a transfer of a copyright without the transfer of the underlying tangible asset is not deductible for income, gift, or estate tax purposes. This is because the transfer of the copyright without the underlying tangible asset constitutes a gift of less than the donor's entire interest. In order to qualify for a charitable tax deduction, the donor must transfer his entire interest in the copyrighted property. An exception to this rule occurs when the donor owns and transfers only the copyright, which then constitutes his or her entire interest in the property and qualifies as a completed gift eligible for the charitable tax deduction.

Patents

Title 35 of the *U.S. Code* sets out the patent laws that protect the intellectual property rights of anyone who invents or discovers any new useful process, machine, manufacture, or composition of matter, or any new and useful improvement on the same. Patents are issued in the name of the United States of America, under the seal of the Patent and Trademark Office. The patent grants to the recipient or her heirs or assigns the right to exclude anyone else from making, using, offering for sale, or selling the property subject to the patent throughout the United States and from importing the property into the United States.

Patents are granted for a term that begins on the date the patent is issued and ends twenty years from the date on which the application for the patent was filed in the United States.

The *U.S. Code*, Title 35, Section 261 states that an allocation of a patent or of any interest therein is assignable in law by a written instrument. The applicant, patentee, or her agent or legal representative may grant and convey an exclusive right under her application for a patent. A certificate of acknowledgment by the hand and official seal of a person authorized to administer oaths in the United States is required as evidence of an assignment, grant, or conveyance of a patent or application for a patent from a donor to a nonprofit. This transfer must be recorded in the patent and trademark office within three months from its date or it will become void.

As with copyrights, the deductibility of a gift of a patent depends on whether or not the patent is considered a capital asset or ordinary income property to the donor, whether any gain is subject to depreciation recapture, and whether a gift of the patent satisfies the partial interest rule.

Internal Revenue Code Section 1235 states that a transfer of a patent by the patent holder is to be considered a transfer for sale or exchange of a capital asset held for more than one year. Therefore, a charitable gift of the patent is considered a transfer of capital gain property. The donor will receive a charitable income tax deduction based on the fair market value of the patent, subject to the 30 percent limitation. Patents are also subject to depreciation recapture over their remaining useful life. The recapture includes the various government fees, costs of blueprints and models, attorney fees, and other expenditures related to obtaining the patent. When donating a patent to charity, the fair market value of the patent is reduced by the amount that would have been recaptured as ordinary income had the donor sold the patent instead. Finally, so that a gift of a patent may avoid violating the partial interest rule, the donor must transfer all of her substantial rights in the patent (or an undivided fractional interest in the same).

Royalty Interest

A royalty is defined as amounts received for the privilege of using patents, copyrights, formulas, goodwill, trademarks, trade brands, franchises, and similar property. It is important to remember that the royalty is a payment for the right to use one of the aforementioned property rights. Unless otherwise specified, the transfer of a royalty does not include the property or copyright that produces it. For example, a work of art is separate from its copyright, so a royalty received by the copyright owner for the right to produce and sell reproductions of the artwork is to be distinguished from the copyright on the artwork itself.

To determine the deductibility of a charitable contribution of a royalty interest, you must first define the tax status of the royalty. Most royalties are considered ordinary income assets; however, some others, such as certain mineral royalties, are considered interest in real property and therefore are treated as capital assets.

Gifts of Securities

Securities are among the most popular assets used to make gifts. Securities include publicly traded stocks, mutual funds, Treasury notes, and closely held stock. As many donors have seen the value of their stock portfolios and mutual funds increase tremendously in the bull market of the 1990s, they have increasingly used publicly traded stocks and mutual funds to make gifts. They are using securities to make outright gifts as well as to fund life income vehicles.

Stock Transfers

The process of transferring securities to a nonprofit depends on how the securities are held by the donor. When the securities are held by the donor's stockbroker, the donor or the broker should call to inform the nonprofit that a gift of securities is about to be made. The nonprofit then provides the donor's broker with its tax identification number and delivery instructions. As an alternative, the nonprofit may establish an account with the donor's broker in the nonprofit's name and transfer the stock from the donor's account to the new nonprofit account. Stock can then be sold directly from this account, with the proceeds delivered in the form of a check to the nonprofit, less the broker's commission. The donor's broker should always be instructed not to sell the securities until they are in the nonprofit's account, otherwise the donor will incur a capital gains tax on any appreciation of the securities.

Electronic transfer through the Depository Trust Company (DTC) is another method for receiving gifts of stock. It moves securities from one account to another without any physical exchange of stock certificates. The nonprofit must notify its account manager to be on the alert for a transfer of securities via DTC so that the transfer may be properly credited to the nonprofit's account.

Oftentimes the donor has physical possession of the stock certificates that are to be used to make the gift. To accomplish this transfer, the donor signs a stock power for each stock certificate that will be transferred to the nonprofit. Stock powers can be obtained from a broker or a bank; some nonprofits keep a supply of these forms on hand. The stock power allows the nonprofit to sell the securities once it possesses the actual certificates.

If the donor is mailing the stock certificates, the stock powers should be sent to the nonprofit in a separate envelope. If the certificates and the stock powers are sent together and then lost or stolen, whoever ends up with the securities would have the ability to sell them. Once the nonprofit has received both the stock powers and the stock certificates, it is then able to negotiate the sell.

It is also possible for the donor to make the gift by endorsing the back of each stock certificate, which results in the certificate being immediately negotiable. This method should be used only when the donor is hand delivering the certificates to the nonprofit.

Valuation

The value of a gift of securities to a nonprofit is determined by averaging the high price and the low price of the security on the date of the gift. If a gift is made on a Saturday, Sunday, or holiday, the average of the mean values on the preceding and succeeding business days must be used.

The date of the gift depends upon the method of delivery. If the donor sends the gift through the mail, the date postmarked on the envelope is the date of the gift. If the donor hand delivers the securities to the nonprofit, the date of delivery is the date of the gift. If the securities are transferred by a broker from the donor's account to the nonprofit's account, the date the securities are actually delivered to that account is the date of the gift.

Gifts of Life Insurance

Most planned giving programs offer donors the opportunity to make gifts using life insurance policies. Life insurance permits a donor to leverage his gift; for a relatively small sum in premium payments the donor can produce a large death benefit for the nonprofit. However, as with bequests, it may be many years before the nonprofit receives that death benefit. The life insurance policies given are usually either fully or partially paid-up policies.

When a donor makes an outright gift of life insurance, the nonprofit should be named as the owner and the beneficiary of the policy. The donor completely gives up ownership of the policy, waiving the right to assign or borrow against the policy and to change the beneficiary.

If the donor makes an outright gift of a paid-up policy, he or she will receive a charitable income tax deduction for the paid-up policy's replacement value, that is, the single-premium cost to purchase an identical policy. If the replacement value exceeds the donor's cost basis in the gift policy, the deduction is limited to the cost basis. The donor's deduction is also limited to 50 percent of his adjusted gross income in the year of the gift. Any unused portion of the deduction may be carried forward for the next five succeeding tax years.

On many occasions a donor may name the nonprofit as owner and beneficiary on a new or partially paid-up life insurance policy. In this case the nonprofit and the donor should agree at the outset how the remaining premiums will be paid. If the donor makes the payments directly to the charity, and the nonprofit in turn forwards them to the insurance company, the donor will receive a charitable deduction for the payments to the nonprofit. Again, the deduction is limited to 50 percent of the donor's adjusted gross income. If the donor makes the premium payments directly to the insurance company, the deduction is limited to 30 percent of his adjusted gross income. The reason for the difference is that the payment to the nonprofit is considered a gift to the nonprofit whereas the payment to the insurance company is considered *for the benefit of* the nonprofit.

If the partially paid-up policy has an accumulated cash surrender value, the donor receives a charitable deduction for the gift based on the *interpolated terminal reserve*. This is defined as the amount that reflects the daily current value of the policy at the time of the gift and will usually be slightly more than the cash surrender value. Once again, the donor's deduction is limited to 50 percent of adjusted gross income.

If a donor claims a charitable income tax deduction of $5,000 or greater for a gift of life insurance, then it must be reported on IRS Form 8283, because life insurance is considered a noncash gift. In addition, the donor must provide a qualified appraisal of the gift.

Here are some cautions to bear in mind when accepting gifts of life insurance:

- Do not endorse any one insurance company, product, or service—in order to avoid alienating the supporters of your nonprofit who may work for other insurance companies.
- Never provide a list of your donor names to an insurance agent. The confidentiality of your donor information must be protected.
- If your nonprofit is going to accept the role of owning and administering life insurance gifts, it must be sure it has adequate staff to perform the necessary duties related to administering the policies.
- Your nonprofit should develop a policy stating how life insurance policies that are in danger of lapsing will be handled.

CHAPTER EIGHT

LIFE INCOME GIFTS

L ife income gifts are key to building a sound foundation for a planned giving program. They provide an opportunity for the donor to benefit the nonprofit while receiving an income and significant tax benefits. This chapter examines the three primary types of life income vehicles—charitable gift annuities, charitable remainder trusts, and pooled income funds.

Charitable Gift Annuities

The *charitable gift annuity* allows the donor to make a gift to a nonprofit and receive an income for the donor's lifetime, and if desired, one other beneficiary's lifetime. Upon the death of the last beneficiary of the annuity, the nonprofit receives the remainder. The donor receives a charitable income tax deduction for the creation of the gift annuity.

The gift annuity is a contract between the donor and the nonprofit. In exchange for the gift, the nonprofit is legally obligated to pay the donor a fixed annuity for the remainder of the donor's lifetime. The annuity is backed by the assets of the nonprofit. (Exhibit 8.1 is an example of a gift annuity contract.)

Gift annuity rates are age dependent. The older the donor, the higher the annuity rate. The rate is also dependent on whether there are one or two annuitants and their respective ages. Charities may set their own payout rates. The

EXHIBIT 8.1. CHARITABLE GIFT ANNUITY AGREEMENT.

THIS GIFT ANNUITY AGREEMENT, made and entered into this _____ day of
_____ , 200__ , by and between _____ (hereinafter called
"Donor"), residing at _____ , _____ , _____ , and
XYZ Charity (hereinafter called "Charity"), a not-for-profit corporation located in
_____ (city), _____ (state).

1. GIFT. Donor has this day contributed and voluntarily given to Charity
the sum of _____ Dollars ($_____), receipt of which is hereby
acknowledged, to ultimately benefit _____.

2. ANNUITY. Charity, in consideration of the transfer and delivery of such gift,
shall pay to Donor during the full term of Donor's natural life the sum of _____
Dollars ($_____) annually in quarterly payments on the last day of March,
June, September, and December in each year. The obligation to pay the annuity
shall terminate with, and no amount shall be payable for, the period subsequent
to the last date for payment immediately preceding or coincident with the death
of Donor, at which date it is expressly agreed that Charity shall be discharged and
forever released from any further responsibility or obligation whatsoever that it
may have assumed under this agreement. This annuity is nonassignable by Donor.

3. REPRESENTATIONS OF CORPORATION. Charity hereby represents and certi-
fies that it is a not-for-profit corporation, publicly supported and tax-exempt, that
has been established to solicit, receive, and administer gifts and bequests for the
benefit of XYZ Charity, located and established at _____ (city), _____
(state).

4. CONTRIBUTIONS. Both Donor and Charity acknowledge that the difference
between the fair market value of the gift and the present fair market value of the
annuity to be paid to Donor constitutes a contribution from Donor to Charity.

5. IRREVOCABILITY. This Gift Annuity Agreement is irrevocable.

6. NOTICE. A charitable gift annuity provided by Charity is not issued by an
insurance company, nor is it regulated by the state division of insurance or state
insurance commissioner. It is not protected by any state guaranty fund or protective
association.

IN WITNESS WHEREOF, the parties hereto have set their hand and seals on the
day and year first above written.

DONOR

_____

XYZ Charity

By: _____
_____ , President

ATTEST: _____
_____ , Secretary

American Council on Gift Annuities is a national organization that recommends rates for nonprofits to offer to annuitants. These recommended rates are the same for both sexes and ages. There are also many types of planned giving software available that can be used to calculate a donor's annuity rate along with her charitable income tax deduction. Two of the more popular software packages are PG Calc and Crescendo.

A *deferred gift annuity* is a variant of the charitable gift annuity. Simply put, the donor makes a gift to the nonprofit, and the nonprofit agrees to pay the donor, and no more than one other annuitant, a stream of income for life beginning at an agreed-upon date in the future. At the death of the last annuitant, the nonprofit receives the remainder of the annuity. Because of the deferral period from the date of the gift until the time the payments begin, the annuity rate for a deferred gift annuity will be substantially higher than the rate for an immediate payment annuity. The donor receives a current charitable income tax deduction at the time the annuity is created even though payments are deferred until some point in the future. Deferred gift annuities are particularly popular with professionals who are seeking to supplement their retirement income.

Annuities may be funded with a variety of assets, including cash, stocks, and real estate. Caution must be exercised by the nonprofit, however, when real estate is used to fund a charitable gift annuity. The annuity rate should be negotiated with the donor with the realization that the contributed property may sell for less than its appraised value or that costs associated with selling the property may reduce the sale proceeds below the appraised value. The nonprofit should also decide how soon payments to the donor should begin, given that there may be a delay between the time the property is accepted and the time when it is sold and converted to cash to fund the annuity. It may be advisable to use a deferred charitable gift annuity when real estate will be the funding asset. The deferred annuity provides the nonprofit with time to sell the real estate before payments to the annuitant begin.

Tax Consequences of Charitable Gift Annuities

Creation of a charitable gift annuity will have consequences for the donors that will affect their income tax, gift tax, capital gains tax, and estate tax, as well as their charitable income tax deduction. These consequences are examined in the following sections.

Charitable Income Tax Deduction. The value of the charitable income tax deduction is determined by subtracting the value of the annuitant's life income interest from the value of the gift with the result being the remainder interest of the nonprofit, which is equal to the donor's charitable income tax deduction. Part of this calculation involves applying the IRS discount rate to the payments the annuitant is expected to receive over his lifetime. The discount rate is defined as 120 percent of the federal midterm rate, which changes monthly. The federal midterm rate is the average market yield on all options on the U.S. market that have a maturity of over three years and less than nine years. The donor can select the discount rate for the month in which the gift is made or the rate for either of the two preceding months. The higher the discount rate, the higher the charitable income tax deduction. If the donor uses cash to fund an annuity, the deduction is limited to 50 percent of adjusted gross income in the year of the gift. If an appreciated asset (held more than one year) is used, then the deduction will be limited to 30 percent of the adjusted gross income in the year of the gift. In each case, any unused portion of the deduction may be carried forward for the next five succeeding tax years.

Gift Taxes. If the donor establishes a charitable gift annuity for the benefit of anyone other than the donor or the donor's spouse, the donor has made a taxable gift and may be required to pay a gift tax on the value of the charitable gift annuity. The taxable gift is based on the total value of the charitable gift annuity at the time the gift is made. If the payments to the third party begin within the year the annuity is created, the donor may use his or her $10,000 (indexed after 2001) annual gift tax exclusion to eliminate or reduce the gift tax due on the creation of the gift annuity.

Capital Gains Taxes and Income Taxes. If the donor uses appreciated property to fund his charitable gift annuity, he will have to pay capital gains taxes based on the portion of the capital gain property that is used to purchase the charitable gift annuity. If the donor is the sole beneficiary or the first beneficiary, the gain can be spread out by reporting it over the donor's life expectancy. If the donor is not one of the annuitants, the donor will be taxed on all of the reportable gain, in the year of the gift. In regard to income tax liabilities, a portion of the annuity payments to the beneficiary will be tax-free return of principal, a portion will be ordinary income, and to the extent appreciated property is used, the remainder is taxed as capital gain. After the donor attains his life expectancy, as it was calculated at the time the annuity was created, the entire amount of the annuity payment is taxed as ordinary income.

Estate Taxes. If the donor is the only annuitant and the annuity ceases at the donor's death, the value of the annuity is not taxed in the donor's estate. If the surviving spouse of the donor is the remaining annuitant, the spouse's interest will qualify for the estate tax marital deduction. If someone other than the donor or the donor's surviving spouse is the remaining annuitant at the donor's death, the value of the annuity is taxed as part of the donor's estate.

State Regulation of Gift Annuities

Charities that offer gift annuities must comply with various state regulatory requirements. Because these regulatory requirements and registration procedures are not uniform across the states, nonprofit organizations should check each state's requirements before issuing gift annuities in that state. Most states that regulate gift annuities require the nonprofit that issues gift annuities to provide

- A permit issued by the State Department of Insurance
- A segregated reserve fund dedicated to sustaining the life income payments to the donors
- A copy of the nonprofit's annual financial report detailing the balances held in the reserve fund

Some states may also require the nonprofit to provide financial statements, bylaws of the nonprofit organization, articles of incorporation, and proof of tax-exempt status (see Exhibit 8.2).

If you anticipate that your nonprofit will issue gift annuities in a number of states, the American Council on Gift Annuities recommends complying with the laws of any state in which the nonprofit issues gift annuities and meeting all registration requirements and obtaining state approval before beginning to issue gift annuities. (Exhibits 8.3 through 8.6 contain examples of the common types of gift annuities.)

Charitable Remainder Trusts

Charitable remainder trusts have become increasingly popular planned giving vehicles. They can be used to create substantial financial and tax benefits for the donor and significant gifts to the nonprofit. Charitable remainder trusts may be established during the donor's lifetime or at her death. They may pay their income to the beneficiaries for life or a term of years not exceeding twenty years. To set up a qualified charitable remainder trust, the donor must make an irrevocable gift to the trust with the remainder interest going to a qualified nonprofit organization.

There are two forms of charitable remainder trusts, the charitable remainder annuity trust and the charitable remainder unitrust. With both trusts, the payout

EXHIBIT 8.2. REGULATION OF GIFT ANNUITIES BY STATE.

This chart summarizes the status of the regulation of charitable gift annuities by the fifty states and the District of Columbia as of this printing. This information is constantly changing, and regulatory initiatives now under way could change a state's current status. Check the Web site *pgresources.com* for current information on state regulations.

States That Specifically Exempt or Conditionally Exempt Gift Annuities from Regulation

(Some require notification or have other conditions that must be met)

Alabama	Kentucky	New Mexico
Arizona	Louisiana	North Carolina
Colorado	Maine	Ohio
Connecticut	Massachusetts	Oklahoma
Florida	Michigan	Pennsylvania
Georgia	Minnesota	South Carolina
Idaho	Missouri	South Dakota
Illinois	Nebraska	Texas
Indiana	Nevada	Utah
Kansas	New Hampshire	Virginia

States That Regulate Gift Annuities

Arkansas	North Dakota	Tennessee
California	New Jersey	Washington
Hawaii	New York	Wisconsin
Maryland	Oregon	

States in Which the Law Does Not Specifically Address Gift Annuities

Alaska	Montana
Delaware	Rhode Island
District of Columbia	Vermont
Iowa	West Virginia
Mississippi	Wyoming

rate is negotiated between the donor and the nonprofit at the time the trust is created. That rate will generally be a factor of the age and the number of beneficiaries on the trust. By law the rate may not be less than 5 percent or more than 50 percent. The IRS has created model forms that are templates for drafting charitable remainder trusts (see Resource 18).

The donor must name a trustee of his charitable remainder trust. The trustee may be a bank or trust company, an investment firm, or the nonprofit itself. Serving as trustee allows the nonprofit to maintain a close relationship with the donor and the beneficiaries of the trust and to control the investment allocation of the trust's asset portfolio.

EXHIBIT 8.3. ONE-LIFE CHARITABLE GIFT ANNUITY.

Deduction Calculations
SUMMARY OF BENEFITS

7.7% Charitable Gift Annuity

ASSUMPTIONS

Annuitant's age	72
Principal donated	$10,000.00
Cost basis	$5,000.00
Annuity rate	7.7%
Payment schedule	Quarterly at end

BENEFITS

Charitable deduction		**$4,220.60**
Annual annuity ($192.50 per quarter)	**$770.00**	
Tax-free portion		$199.42
Capital gain income		$199.44
Ordinary income		$371.14

Total reportable capital gain of $2,889.70 must be reported over 14.5 years, the expected lifetime of the donor at age 72.
   After 14.5 years the entire annuity becomes ordinary income.

IRS discount rate is 7.4%

Note: The information in this chart is general. Please see your tax adviser to verify all figures.

The charitable remainder beneficiary of the trust must be a nonprofit that is qualified under the Internal Revenue Code Section 501(c)(3). A donor may name more than one charitable remainder beneficiary, and the donor may reserve the right to change the charitable beneficiaries without affecting the charitable nature of the trust.

Tax Consequences of Charitable Remainder Trusts

The taxes to be considered in setting up a charitable remainder trust are income taxes, capital gains taxes, gift taxes, and estate taxes.

Income Tax. Income distributed from the charitable remainder trust to the beneficiary is taxed to the beneficiary, because the trust itself is a tax-free entity (so

EXHIBIT 8.4. TWO-LIFE CHARITABLE GIFT ANNUITY.

Deduction Calculations
SUMMARY OF BENEFITS

7% Charitable Gift Annuity

ASSUMPTIONS

Annuitants' ages	72
	72
Principal donated	$10,000.00
Cost basis	$5,000.00
Annuity rate	7%
Payment schedule	Quarterly at end

BENEFITS
Charitable deduction   **$3,505.20**

Annual annuity ($175 per quarter)   **$700.00**

Tax-free portion	$121.62
Capital gain income	$224.18
Ordinary income	$354.20

Total reportable capital gain of $3,247.40 must be reported over 14.5 years, the expected lifetime of the donor at age 72.
After 14.5 years capital gain income becomes tax free.
After 18.8 years the entire annuity becomes ordinary income.

IRS discount rate is 7.4%

Note: The information in this chart is general. Please see your tax adviser to verify all figures.

long as it receives no unrelated business income). For income tax purposes, distributions from the charitable remainder trust are taxed in the following order:

1. Ordinary income
2. Capital gain income
3. Tax-free income
4. Return of trust principal

There is no tax-free income or return of the initial principal until all ordinary income and capital gain income earned by the trust has been distributed to the beneficiary.

EXHIBIT 8.5. ONE-LIFE CHARITABLE DEFERRED GIFT ANNUITY.

Deduction Calculations
SUMMARY OF BENEFITS

11.6% Deferred Gift Annuity

ASSUMPTIONS

Annuitant's age		55
Age at date of first payment	[12/21/2010]	65
Principal donated		$10,000.00
Cost basis		$5,000.00
Annuity rate		11.6%
Payment schedule		Quarterly

BENEFITS

Charitable deduction		**$5,485.40**
Annual annuity ($290 per quarter)	**$1,160.00**	
Tax-free portion		$113.68
Capital gain income		$113.68
Ordinary income		$932.64

Total reportable capital gain of $2,257.30 must be reported over 19.9 years, the expected lifetime at the date of first payment to the donor, currently age 55.
    After 19.9 years from the year the payments begin, the entire annuity becomes ordinary income.

IRS discount rate is 7.4%

Note: The information in this chart is general. Please see your tax adviser to verify all figures.

Capital Gains Taxes. If the trust is funded with an appreciated asset, such as securities or real estate, the donor will avoid any capital gain taxes due on the gain at the time the trust is created. However, to the extent the trust does not earn sufficient ordinary income to meet the distribution due the beneficiaries at the stated payout rate, capital gains will be distributed from the trust. So, in effect, the donor may be only postponing capital gains rather than eliminating them by creating the charitable remainder trust.

Gift Taxes. If the donor and the donor's spouse, or the donor's spouse alone, are the beneficiaries of the charitable remainder trust, there will be no gift tax consequences at the time of the trust creation. If the spouse is a beneficiary of the

EXHIBIT 8.6. TWO-LIFE CHARITABLE DEFERRED GIFT ANNUITY.

Deduction Calculations
SUMMARY OF BENEFITS

10.9% Deferred Gift Annuity

ASSUMPTIONS

Annuitants' ages	55
	55
Ages at date of first payment	[12/21/2010] 65 65
Principal donated	$10,000.00
Cost basis	$5,000.00
Annuity rate	10.9%
Payment schedule	Quarterly

BENEFITS

Charitable deduction		**$4,571.00**
Annual annuity ($272.50 per quarter)	**$1,090.00**	
Tax-free portion		$81.61
Capital gain income		$136.39
Ordinary income		$872.00

Total reportable capital gain of $2,714.50 must be reported over 19.9 years,
the expected lifetime at the date of first payment to the donor, currently age 55.
　　After 19.9 years from the year the payments begin, capital gain income becomes tax-free.
　　After 24.9 years from the year the payments begin, the entire annuity becomes ordinary income.

IRS discount rate is 7.4%

Note: The information in this chart is general. Please see your tax adviser to verify all figures.

trust, the donor has made a gift to her spouse, but this gift qualifies for the unlimited gift tax marital deduction. If the donor names someone other than her spouse as a current beneficiary of the trust, it is a taxable gift for which the donor may use her $10,000 annual gift tax exclusion to reduce or eliminate the gift tax. If the value of the gift exceeds the $10,000 annual exclusion, then the donor can apply her unified estate and gift tax credit to eliminate or reduce any gift tax due. To avoid a current taxable gift, the owner may reserve the right to revoke by her will the income interest of the nonspousal beneficiary.

Estate Taxes. If the donor creates a charitable remainder trust naming himself as the beneficiary, the entire value of the trust assets as of the date of the donor's death or a portion of such value will be included in the donor's estate. However, the gift will qualify for a 100 percent charitable estate tax deduction. If the donor and the donor's spouse are the beneficiaries, the value of the trust will also be included in the donor's taxable estate but will qualify for the 100 percent marital deduction, exempting it from any estate taxes. If the trust is created so that it pays income first to the donor and then to a nonspouse, there will be estate tax consequences. There is a charitable deduction for the date-of-death charitable remainder value of the trust; however, estate tax is typically due on the life income interest of the nonspouse beneficiary who survives the donor.

Requirements Under TRA 1997. It should be noted that the Taxpayer Relief Act of 1997 establishes certain requirements a trust must meet to qualify as a charitable remainder unitrust or annuity trust. First, the act sets the maximum annual payout rate at 50 percent of the fair market value of the trust assets. This requirement discourages extraordinarily high payout rates. Additionally, the act requires that the value of the charitable remainder interest must be at least 10 percent of the net fair market value of the property transferred to the trust at the time of its creation. This requirement also deters an overly high payout rate and discourages the addition of younger or multiple beneficiaries. In addition to these requirements, a charitable remainder annuity trust must also pass a 5 percent exhaustion test. This test provides that if there is a greater than 5 percent actuarial chance that the assets of the annuity trust will be depleted so that the nonprofit will receive nothing at the death of the donor, then the donor is not entitled to a charitable income tax deduction upon the creation of the trust.

Types of Charitable Remainder Trusts

Let's look more closely at the types of charitable remainder trusts.

Charitable Remainder Annuity Trust. A *charitable remainder annuity trust* pays the income beneficiaries a fixed, guaranteed payment for life or a term of years. The payout, as mentioned earlier, must be not less than 5 percent of the initial funding amount of the trust. As with gift annuities, the payout rate is age sensitive. Unlike a gift annuity, a charitable remainder annuity trust may have more than two beneficiaries. To the extent income is not sufficient to meet the stated payout rate, the trustee may invade principal to meet the payment obligation due the beneficiaries. The annuity trust appeals to those donors who seek the security of a fixed payment. Nevertheless, fewer annuity trusts are now being created because gift annuities provide donors with many of the same benefits. However, annuity trusts are still appropriate for use by nonprofits that do not offer a gift annuity program or that are receiving gifts from donors in states in which the nonprofits are not registered to offer gift annuities.

Finally, it should be noted that once an annuity trust is established, no additional contributions can be made to it. Of course a donor may continue to contribute to the nonprofit in this way by establishing additional charitable remainder annuity trusts with it.

Charitable Remainder Unitrust. The *charitable remainder unitrust* has three variations, a straight unitrust, the net income unitrust, and the flip unitrust. Each has a different objective and affects the beneficiaries' payouts differently.

Straight Unitrust. The *straight unitrust* pays to the income beneficiary a fixed percentage of the fair market value of the trust assets, as valued annually. The trustee determines the distribution due the beneficiaries by multiplying the percentage payout rate by the fair market value of the trust's assets as valued on the annual valuation date. If the assets of the trust appreciate in value, the income beneficiary will receive a larger distribution. Conversely, if the assets of the trust have decreased in value, the beneficiary will receive a smaller distribution. To the extent income is insufficient to meet the required distribution, the trustee must invade principal to make payment to the beneficiary.

Net Income Unitrust. A *net income unitrust* pays the income beneficiaries the stated percentage or the net income earned by the trust, whichever is *less*. The trustee is not permitted to invade principal to make the distribution to the beneficiaries. Therefore, if the trust earns no net income, then no distribution is due the beneficiaries. Often the net income trust is drafted with a *makeup provision*. It provides that the income beneficiaries are entitled to a makeup of any income not distributed during the term of the trust. Thus, if the income beneficiary receives distributions that are less than the stated percentage, the makeup provision allows the beneficiary to make up the beneficiary's income in the future when the trust has net income in excess of the stated payout percentage.

Net income trusts have often been used by nonprofits when gifts of real estate are used to fund the trust. The net income trust gives the trustee time to sell the real estate before any payments are due the income beneficiary. Growth stocks are often used to fund net income trusts as well. The trustee can invest the growth stocks, which are expected to appreciate in value over time. At some point in the future the trustee converts the appreciated growth stocks to a mix of income-producing stocks and bonds. The income beneficiaries then begin receiving the net income produced or the stated payout percentage, whichever is less. This arrangement has often been popular with donors who seek a means of supplementing their retirement income. In the future, the net income unitrust may be largely supplanted by the flip unitrust.

Flip Unitrust. New regulations issued by the IRS now permit donors to employ a planned gift vehicle known as a *flip unitrust,* which incorporates a "flip" of the trust's payment method. Prior to some specified event, the trust distributes the trust's net income or the fixed percentage amount to the beneficiary, whichever is less. After the event occurs, the trust becomes a standard unitrust, and the payments to the income recipient become a straight percentage of the trust's net fair market value. Although the income stream continues to fluctuate after the flip occurs, according to the market performance of the trust's assets, the payments no longer depend upon the *income earned* by those assets.

Because the flip unitrust provides greater flexibility in determining the trust's income stream, these trusts may be recommended in the following two circumstances involving illiquid assets and deferred income.

When funding a charitable remainder trust with illiquid assets, such as real estate or closely held stock, the flip unitrust may be particularly appropriate. Prior to the sale of the non-income producing asset, the net income restriction protects the trustee from the untenable position of making distributions to the income recipient from illiquid trust assets. Once the trustee subsequently sells the property and diversifies the trust's portfolio, then, in the next calendar year, the trust begins providing an income stream based solely on the trust's fixed percentage payout.

Those donors who have little need for current income but expect that they will need such an income stream in the future may also choose to benefit charity through a flip unitrust. By selecting a future date or event as the trust's flip date (a date or event determined at the trust's creation and not at any person's later discretion), the donor receives a smaller income stream (subject to the net income restriction) until the date or event occurs. In the year following the flip date, the trust begins providing an income stream based solely on the trust's fixed percentage payout.

Examples of permissible flip events include (but are not limited to) the attainment of a specific age by the income recipient or recipients; a specified date; the birth, death, marriage, or divorce of an individual; and so forth).

Any makeup provisions used initially to recover shortfalls and distributions must be forfeited once the trust flips. In other words, after the trust has flipped, it must remain a straight percentage unitrust. Moreover, the only flip permitted is the net income unitrust to straight percentage unitrust flip. So, for example, a charitable remainder annuity trust cannot flip to a charitable remainder unitrust.

It is anticipated that the flip unitrust will replace the net income unitrust as the preferred vehicle for receiving gifts of real estate and other illiquid assets. (See Exhibits 8.7 and 8.8 for examples of a charitable remainder unitrust and annuity trust.)

EXHIBIT 8.7. TWO-LIFE INTER VIVOS CHARITABLE REMAINDER UNITRUST.

Deduction Calculations
SUMMARY OF BENEFITS

5% Charitable Straight Unitrust

ASSUMPTIONS

Beneficiaries' ages	65
	65
Principal donated	$100,000.00
Cost basis of property	$50,000.00
Payout rate	5%
Payment schedule	Quarterly
	3 months to 1st payment

BENEFITS

Charitable deduction	$35,683.00
First year's income (future income will vary)	$5,000.00

IRS discount rate is 7.4%

Note: The information in this chart is general. Please see your tax adviser to verify all figures.

Pooled Income Funds

Pooled income funds are another life income vehicle for planned giving prospects and donors. A pooled income fund is similar to a mutual fund in that a donor's gift is pooled with gifts from other donors to create a pool of funds for investment purposes. The payout rate from the pooled income fund is market sensitive and may increase or decrease, depending upon the performance of the fund. Once a donor makes a gift to a pooled income fund, she will receive income for life. The donor may claim a charitable income deduction at the time of her gift; upon the death of the donor the nonprofit receives the remainder interest.

Participating in a pooled income fund permits donors to make smaller gifts than are possible when establishing other life income vehicles. Donors may choose to employ highly appreciated securities to make their gift to a pooled income fund. They can avoid capital gains taxes on their gift and convert stock that may be paying a low dividend to a higher yielding investment in the pooled income fund.

EXHIBIT 8.8. TWO-LIFE INTER VIVOS CHARITABLE REMAINDER ANNUITY TRUST.

Deduction Calculations
SUMMARY OF BENEFITS

5% Charitable Annuity Trust

ASSUMPTIONS:

Beneficiaries' ages	65
	65
Principal donated	$100,000.00
Cost basis of property	$50,000.00
Payout rate	5%
Payment schedule	Quarterly at end

BENEFITS

Charitable deduction	$46,779.00
Annual income (fixed)	$5,000.00

IRS discount rate is 7.4%

Note: The information in this chart is general. Please see your tax adviser to verify all figures.

In recent years more and more organizations have come to prefer using charitable gift annuities and charitable remainder trusts as the life income vehicles that they offer their donors. However, the pooled income fund still has a place in a planned giving program. If the nonprofit does not offer gift annuities, the pooled income fund is a viable alternative. Also, because a gift to a pooled income fund can be much smaller than the gift required to establish a charitable remainder trust, it can be useful to those donors who wish to make a smaller gift while receiving a stream of income in return.

CHAPTER NINE

BEQUESTS AND REMAINDER INTERESTS

S o far we have discussed outright gifts and life income gifts. A third important type of planned gift is one that provides a remainder interest to the nonprofit. This chapter describes three means through which these gifts may be made— bequests, qualified retirement plan assets, and U.S. Savings Bonds.

Bequests are the cornerstone of a nonprofit's planned giving program (see Chapter Four). The majority of all planned gifts come from bequests. A bequest program is the simplest part of a planned giving program to start and administer. In fact many nonprofits receive bequests even when they do not have a formal planned giving program.

Bequests are transfers of wealth that occur upon a donor's death; they include transfers through wills and through trusts. The revocable living trust agreement has increased in popularity as an estate planning tool, and therefore an increasing number of bequests are being made through these instruments as well as through the traditional will. Many donors prefer to defer charitable transfers until death, as it permits them to maintain the use and control of their assets during their lifetime. In many cases a bequest is the only option available to the donor of a major gift.

To encourage bequests, the nonprofit should have sample bequest language available. This language can be provided to the donors' attorneys who can then incorporate it into the donor's will or trust agreement. Here is an example of the form a bequest can take: "I give, devise, bequeath (<u>fixed sum/percentage of my</u>

estate/residue) to XYZ charity, a not-for-profit corporation with principal offices located in Anywhere, USA, to be used for the purposes set out in a gift agreement on file with said charity."

The following list shows some of the forms bequests can take.

Forms of Bequests

- *Specific bequest:* a distribution of a certain amount of cash, securities, or a particular piece of personal property—for example, "$10,000," or "1,000 shares of stock," or a "Cézanne painting."
- *Percentage:* a stated percentage of the donor's estate—for example, "25 percent of my gross estate to XYG charity." A percentage of the *gross estate* is preferred, as this will result in a larger bequest to the charity than will a percentage of the *net estate,* which is the value after the estate has been reduced by estate administration expenses and the payment of any estate taxes due.
- *Residue of the estate:* the remainder of the donor's estate after specific bequests have been satisfied and taxes and costs have been paid. In many cases donors bequeath charities a percentage of the residue of the estate.

Bequests are ideally suited for a nonprofit's older donors and prospects. Donors who have consistently supported the nonprofit with annual gifts have demonstrated their commitment to its mission and are excellent prospects for bequests.

Gifts of Retirement Plan Assets

Retirement plan assets represent a tremendous potential for charitable gift planning. Owing to the fact that they face the potential for both income and estate taxation, retirement plan assets are generally an undesirable way to pass wealth to heirs (see Exhibits 9.1 and 9.2).

EXHIBIT 9.1. EXAMPLE OF RETIREMENT PLAN TAXATION.

Balance in plan	$1,000,000
Minus estate tax paid (55%)	−$550,000
[1]Minus final income tax (39.6%)	−$216,220
Remaining balance	$233,780

[1]Income tax includes a state tax credit and deduction for estate tax paid on the plan.

EXHIBIT 9.2. EXAMPLE OF BENEFITS OF GIVING RETIREMENT PLAN ASSETS.

Since retirement plan assets are so heavily taxed upon the death of the plan owner, they can be ideal for making charitable gifts.

Plan value:	$1,000,000
Gift to charity:	$1,000,000
Amount of tax:	$0
Cost of gift:	$233,780

Retirement plan assets, as listed in Internal Revenue Code Section 401(a) are the following:

- Defined contribution plans: profit sharing plans, employee stock ownership plans (ESOPs), 401(k) plans, and money-purchase pension plans (Internal Revenue Code Section 401(k))
- Individual retirement accounts (IRAs) and simplified employee pensions (SEPs) (Internal Revenue Code Section 408)
- Tax-sheltered annuities and custodial accounts (Internal Revenue Code Section 403(b))

All of these qualified retirement plans serve as trust or custodial accounts to hold an individual's retirement plan assets. The key benefit of each of these plans is that they allow the assets held in the plan to grow on an income tax–deferred basis. However, they do possess a distinct disadvantage in that on the death of the account holder, the plan assets can be subject to income and estate taxes that in combination can significantly deplete them. For this reason, they are often one of the best assets for an individual to use to make a gift.

Tax Consequences of Lifetime Transfers of Retirement Plan Assets to Charity

As the law currently stands, there can be no tax-free lifetime transfers from a retirement plan to a charity, either as an outright gift or through a deferred gift vehicle. A person can receive a distribution from her retirement plan and give it to charity. However, that distribution must be reported on the donor's income tax return, although the donor can then claim a charitable income tax deduction for her gift, which will most likely offset the income reported on her tax return so that no tax will be due as a result of the transaction.

If a donor has the option, she will be better off contributing appreciated assets during her lifetime rather than contributing a distribution from a retirement plan. There are exceptions to this guideline, however. If the donor has exceeded the annual percentage deduction limitation for gifts of capital gain property (30 percent of the donor's adjusted gross income), an outright gift of stock will not give her any additional tax benefits in that tax year. In this case, if the donor has not yet reached the limitation for cash gifts (50 percent of her adjusted gross income), she can take a distribution from her retirement plan and, as just described, use the distribution to make a charitable gift that will be tax deductible. Another exception will occur when the donor's five-year carryforward from prior charitable gifts is about to expire. In this circumstance the donor may be advised to take a large distribution from her retirement plan and then use the carryforward from prior charitable gifts to offset the distribution from the retirement plan, resulting in an effectively lower tax rate on the distribution.

In most instances a lifetime gift of retirement plan assets to fund a life income vehicle such as a charitable remainder trust, a charitable gift annuity, or a pooled income fund will not be to the donor's tax advantage. This is so because only a portion of the taxable distribution from the retirement plan used to fund the life income gift can be offset by the charitable income tax deduction that will be received.

Therefore, for most individuals the recommended action will be to leave as much as possible in their retirement plan and then have the account transfer to the charity at their death.

An exception to this general rule occurs when an individual is already past age seventy and a half and is receiving required minimum distributions from a retirement plan. This individual may benefit from the charitable income tax deduction received as a result of funding a charitable remainder trust or a charitable gift annuity.

Testamentary Charitable Gifts of Retirement Plan Assets

Retirement plan assets are not subject to probate unless the owner names his estate as a beneficiary of the assets. If he has not left them to his own estate, upon his death the retirement plan assets are transferred directly to the successor beneficiary named on forms provided by the custodian of the retirement plan. If an individual wishes to name a charity or a charitable remainder trust as the successor beneficiary of a retirement plan, he needs to indicate that on the form.

Many estate planners believe that retirement plan assets represent one of the best ways for a donor to make a charitable bequest. That is because retirement plans produce what is known as *income in respect of a decedent* (IRD). IRD is defined in U.S. Treasury Regulations Section 1.691(a)-1(b). It is the amount to which a decedent was entitled as part of his gross income but that could not be included when computing the decedent's taxable income for the tax year of the decedent's death. In short, it is an inherited payment that would have been taxable income to the decedent had he or she received it prior to death.

Distributions from a decedent's retirement plan are considered income in respect of a decedent. If the retirement plan directs the plan proceeds to the decedent's estate, they will be included on the income tax return of the estate. If they are directed to a beneficiary such as a surviving spouse or child, the retirement plan assets will be included in the gross income of that individual in the year they are received. The income tax on the retirement plan assets is in addition to any estate tax due, although the recipient will receive a deduction against taxable income for any federal estate tax paid due to the distribution of the retirement plan assets.

If the decedent directs his retirement plan proceeds to charity or a charitable remainder trust, his estate will realize significant tax savings because neither the donor's estate nor his heirs will realize any income from the plan. The income will be realized by the charity or the trust, both of which are tax exempt. Therefore no tax will be paid in the year of the distribution from the retirement plan. The highest estate tax rate is 55 percent, but the combination of estate and income taxes on IRD assets can result in a effective marginal tax rate in excess of 75 percent for taxable estates over $3 million. Using a gift to charity and taking the resulting charitable tax deduction can greatly reduce both of these taxes on retirement plan assets.

Issues in Naming a Charity as Successor Beneficiary of Retirement Plan Assets

At first glance it would seem to make good tax sense to name a nonprofit organization as a successor beneficiary of a retirement plan. However, before doing so, the donor and her advisers should examine several factors to determine whether this is in the donor's best interest as well as the charity's. The critical factors are the minimum distribution rules.

Required Minimum Distribution Rules

The rules that require individuals to start drawing benefits from retirement plans by certain times are called the required minimum distribution (RMD) rules. These rules apply to qualified retirement plans, IRAs, Roth IRAs, retirement annuities,

403(b) annuity contracts, 457(d) deferred compensation plans, custodial accounts, and retirement income accounts. For ease of discussion, these are referred to collectively here as qualified retirement plans.

In general, the RMD rules are contained in Section 401(a)(9) of the Internal Revenue Code and its corresponding regulations. On January 17, 2001, the U.S. Treasury issued proposed new regulations that greatly simplify the RMD rules pertaining to qualified retirement plans. The prior rules were extremely complex and difficult for the average person to understand. They required participants to make difficult financial decisions at age seventy and a half that often severely limited these individuals' financial flexibility in the future, even though their financial circumstances might change significantly. The determination of life expectancy, designation of beneficiaries, and the resulting RMD calculation were so complex under the old rules that compliance was a problem for most individuals. Too, under the old regulation, using an annual average return rate of 8 percent, it was estimated that 90 percent of plan owners had 90 percent of the plan intact when they reached age ninety.

The new regulations simplify the RMD rules by

- Providing a simple, uniform table that participants can use to determine the minimum distribution required during their lifetimes.
- Eliminating the requirement that participants had to decide whether or not to recalculate life expectancy each year in determining their RMD.
- Permitting (in most instances) the RMD during the participant's lifetime to be calculated without regard to the beneficiary's age.
- Eliminating the requirement that participants had to designate the beneficiary by the participant's required beginning date (RBD) for taking distributions.
- Permitting the beneficiary to be determined as late as the end of the year following the year of the retirement plan participant's death.
- Allowing participants to change their designated beneficiaries after the required beginning date without increasing the RMD.

Based on an annual average total return of 8 percent, it is estimated that 90 percent of plan owners will have 150 percent of the value of the plan intact by the time they reach age ninety.

These new minimum distribution rules took effect January 1, 2002. It is critical that they be clearly understood by donors and charitable gift planners who desire to maximize the amount of qualified plan and IRA assets available at the donor's death to fund testamentary charitable gifts with maximum tax saving benefits to heirs.

Minimum Distribution Rules' Effect on Naming a Charity as Successor Beneficiary

As discussed previously, the primary benefit of retirement plans is that they allow assets to accumulate on an income tax–deferred basis. However, the Internal Revenue Service does not allow the income to be deferred forever. An individual can receive distributions from her plan prior to reaching age fifty-nine and a half, but those premature distributions are subject to a 10 percent penalty tax as well as being taxed as ordinary income. Once the participant reaches age fifty-nine and a half, she can begin making withdrawals in any amount without penalty, but such withdrawals will be, again, subject to income tax. Furthermore, the rules require that once a participant reaches the required beginning date, she must withdraw at least a minimum amount annually. The RBD is April 1 of the year following the calendar year in which the participant turns seventy and a half or actually retires, if the retirement comes in a later year (holders of IRAs cannot delay the RBD to the time of actual retirement). Subsequent distributions must be made by the end of the calendar year in which they are due.

To ensure that participants meet the minimum distribution requirements (see Exhibit 9.3), the IRS imposes a 50 percent penalty tax on the difference between the amount that should have been distributed and the amount that was actually distributed. This penalty tax is in addition to the income tax paid on the distribution. These rules are intended to make sure that the retirement plan is used for retirement and not as a means of accumulating assets indefinitely on a tax-deferred basis for one's estate.

A retirement plan participant may designate a charity as the beneficiary of a portion or all of his retirement plan or IRA benefits, in spite of the fact that the charity (since it is not an individual) does not qualify as a designated beneficiary. Under the new rules the designation of a charity as beneficiary will have no effect

EXHIBIT 9.3. NEW RETIREMENT PLAN MINIMUM REQUIRED DISTRIBUTIONS.

Age	Approximate Payout
70	3.8%
75	4.6%
80	5.7%
85	7.2%
90	9.5%
95	12.8%

on the participant's RMD, whether or not this designation is made before or after the participant's required beginning date. After the participant's death, a charitable beneficiary can be cashed out of the plan on or before December 31 of the year *following* the participant's death. The result will be that the future RMDs of the remaining beneficiaries who are persons will not be determined until the charity is cashed out, and those RMDs can be calculated solely with respect to their life expectancies under the new regulations.

A favored method of designating a charity as a retirement plan beneficiary is to use a charitable remainder trust, because it is exempt from income tax. A distribution from an IRA or other qualified retirement plan account to a charitable remainder trust will not trigger any income tax for the trust, the estate, or any beneficiaries of the estate. The income will be taxed only as it is distributed to the persons who are beneficiaries of the trust.

Many charitable planners recommend transferring retirement plan assets to a testamentary charitable remainder trust. The primary advantages of this transfer are that, first, a charitable remainder trust is tax exempt and therefore will pay no income tax on the retirement plan distribution it receives. Second, a partial estate tax charitable deduction is available to the decedent's estate.

Retirement plan assets represent a potentially significant source of gifts to charities. However, the complex tax laws surrounding retirement plans require careful planning among the donor, the charity, and the donor's financial and tax advisers. With the proper planning, retirement plan assets can be used to carry out the donor's philanthropic intentions, benefit her family, and avoid excessive income and estate taxation.

Gifts of U.S. Savings Bonds

Many prospective donors own U.S. Savings Bonds. These bonds have unique tax treatments that make them an attractive asset for charitable bequests but not lifetime gifts.

Primarily, there are two types of savings bonds, Series EE (formerly Series E) and Series HH (formerly Series H). Series EE bonds are issued at a discount price of half of the bond's stated maturity value. For example, a savings bond with a stated maturity value of $500 is usually purchased at a discount price of $250. The bond grows in value through the accumulation of interest over time. The owner can redeem it at the maturity date for the stated value or continue to hold it and allow the interest to accumulate. Series EE bonds accumulate interest for up to thirty years after the original date of issue (the accumulation period was forty years for Series E bonds issued prior to November 1965). The owner of the Series EE bond normally is not taxed on the interest income until he redeems the bond. The amount of interest income that the bondholder must eventually report as taxable income is the difference between the bond's redemption amount and the original purchase price.

In contrast, Series HH savings bonds are issued at their face amount (with a minimum purchase price of $500 per bond) and pay interest twice each year. A popular strategy is for owners of Series EE bonds with untaxed accumulated interest to swap the Series EE bonds in a tax-free exchange for Series HH bonds. Doing so allows the owner to receive interest payments based on the full value of the Series EE bonds without having to recognize the accumulated interest on the bonds. Series HH bonds pay interest up to twenty years. At that time the bonds may be cashed in, and the bondholder will be taxed on all of the accumulated interest.

Unfortunately, both Series EE and Series HH savings bonds are not a good asset for a donor to use to make a charitable gift during his lifetime. If the donor attempts to transfer ownership during his lifetime, it will trigger taxation of all of the untaxed interest income that has been accumulating. However, savings bonds are an attractive source for testamentary gifts because the untaxed interest income is then considered income in respect to the decedent (IRD). If a donor is in the 55 percent estate tax bracket and the 39.6 percent federal income tax bracket, the IRS and the relevant state department of revenue could receive over 75 percent of a bond's interest income via a combination of state and federal income taxes. Rather than having so much of a bond's value taxed away, a charitable bequest of IRD property can provide a donor with both estate and income tax charitable deductions. Moreover, the donor gives the full value of the bond to the charity he wishes to support rather than giving the majority of the bond to the IRS.

Savings bonds can also be transferred at death to a charitable remainder trust. Doing so gives the donor's estate a partial estate tax charitable deduction for the charitable remainder value of the bequest. In addition, such a transfer at death will defer taxation on all of the bond's interest income because a charitable remainder trust is a tax-exempt entity.

It is recommended that the donor's will specifically identify the charity or charitable remainder trust that has the right to receive the savings bonds as a distribution from the donor's estate. This is best accomplished through a specific bequest, such as "all of my savings bonds shall be given to the XYZ Charity" if the bequest is to be an outright gift, or "to the Joseph Donor Charitable Remainder Trust" if the savings bonds are to be used to fund a testamentary charitable remainder trust. A specific bequest ensures that the savings bonds will be distributed to the charity so as to avoid tax on the IRD as well as to receive an estate tax charitable deduction.

For prospects and donors who have a significant accumulation of savings bonds subject to untaxed interest, transfer at death to charity provides a way for the donor to achieve his charitable goals, supporting a charity in a most tax advantageous manner.

For more information about U.S. Savings Bonds, visit the Web site *www.public debt.treas.gov/sav/sav.htm.*

CHAPTER TEN

NEW AND ADVANCED PLANNED GIVING TECHNIQUES

The previous chapters have provided an understanding of the techniques most often used in raising major and planned gifts. This chapter focuses on newer and more advanced techniques. It examines flexible endowments, charitable lead trusts, gifts of business interest, donor advised funds, and supporting organizations.

Flexible Endowment Gifts

Flexible endowment gifts are a relatively new form of planned giving. In making a flexible endowment gift the donor agrees to provide the nonprofit with an annual gift equivalent to the expendable income that an endowment would generate if it were established. These annual gifts are available for immediate expenditure by the nonprofit. It is also expected that at the same time the donor is making his annual gifts for current use, he will make additional gifts to build the principal of the endowment or that he has in place an estate gift that will fully fund the endowment at his death.

A flexible endowment is an excellent planned giving alternative for donors who may not be in a position to fully fund an endowment at the present time. Many donors have illiquid assets such as closely held stock, real estate, or partnerships, which may provide them with an income sufficient to provide the annual gifts of a flexible endowment but not the liquidity needed to fully fund an endowment. Flexible endowments also appeal to elderly donors who may already have a significant planned gift in their estate but who would also like to see their gifts benefit the nonprofit during their lifetimes.

For example, if your donor wishes to create a $100,000 endowment using the flexible endowment approach, and if your nonprofit pays out 5 percent on an endowment annually, then the donor agrees to give $5,000 each year until such time as he makes a gift totaling $100,000 separate from the annual payments. The nonprofit can spend the annual gift as if it had already received the full endowment, and the donor retains for as long as needed the assets that may eventually make up the endowment principal.

Donors can make a gift to the endowment principal in the form of a lump sum or in installments. These installments are in addition to the annual gifts. As these installment gifts are made, they generate endowment income, which has the benefit of allowing the donors to lower their annual obligation. The time by which the payment of the entire principal amount must be made can vary, depending on the donor's circumstances. If the nonprofit and the donor agree to it, the donor can defer funding the principal until after his death, by using a testamentary planned gift.

When establishing a flexible endowment, the nonprofit should account for the effect inflation will have on the purchasing power of the donor's annual and principal gifts. It is recommended that discussions with the donor should focus on how the donor's annual and principal commitment in terms of current-year dollars will be adjusted annually according to the effects of inflation. The nonprofit and the donor could agree, for instance, that the gifts will be adjusted annually according to a measure such as the Consumer Price Index. As an alternative, the donor and the nonprofit could agree that the funding level of the endowment will be adjusted according to the minimum funding level set by the nonprofit's board for this particular type of endowment gift. The nonprofit should also specify to the donor when it will consider the endowment fully funded. For example, it could be considered fully funded when the market value of the endowment's principal equals the value of the donor's original commitment, adjusted for inflation.

Principal endowment gifts may be revocable or irrevocable, depending on the purpose for which the gift was committed. If the nonprofit assumes a financial obligation on the basis of the flexible endowment gift (such as construction of a new building), then the flexible endowment agreement should be made irrevocable and its payment should be guaranteed by the donor's estate through a *will contract*. The will contract will permit the nonprofit to enforce the donor's commitment against the donor's estate.

The donor receives a charitable income tax deduction for gifts to the flexible endowment. The deduction is based on the total amount given to the nonprofit as an irrevocable gift each year, subject to applicable tax laws.

Flexible endowments provide donors with an opportunity to see their gifts to the nonprofit at work during their lifetimes. It also allows the nonprofit to recognize the donors for their generosity. The flexible endowment is a planned giving technique that offers many benefits to nonprofits. It should be examined closely to determine its appropriateness for your donors and your organization.

Charitable Lead Trusts

Charitable lead trusts are designed to make distributions to at least one qualified charitable organization for a period of time that is measured by a fixed term of years or by the lives of one or more individuals or by some combination of these two methods. After the expiration of the term, the assets remaining in the trust are paid either to the grantor of the trust or to one or more noncharitable beneficiaries designated in the trust agreement.

Charitable lead trusts are often considered the opposite of the charitable remainder trust in that the payment to the charity precedes the payment of the remainder interest. Many of the rules that govern the operation and taxation of charitable lead trusts are significantly different from those for charitable remainder trusts. One key difference is that charitable lead trusts are not tax-exempt entities as are charitable remainder trusts. Also the governing rules for charitable remainder trusts are designed to protect the remainder interest of the charity, whereas the rules governing charitable lead trusts protect the charity's income interest (see Exhibit 10.1).

History

Prior to 1969, an individual could establish a trust that would make payments to charity for a period of years, exclude the income earned by the trust during its operating life from the grantor's own income, claim a current income tax charitable deduction for the present value of the income stream to the charity, and at the end of the term of the trust, return the remainder interest to the grantor. The Internal Revenue Service and Congress decided that allowing donors to exclude trust income and receive a charitable income tax deduction provided them with a double tax benefit. The Tax Reform Act of 1969 addressed this situation by mandating that for a gift to charity of an income interest to be deductible for income tax purposes, income earned by the trust has to be taxable to the grantor. In addition, the income paid to charity has to take the form of a guaranteed annuity or unitrust interest paid at least annually.

EXHIBIT 10.1. LEAD TRUST PROJECTIONS.

Benefits and Tax Consequences

ASSUMPTIONS:

Testamentary trusts established in 2000 for 20 years.

Lead trust makes annual end-of-period payments to nonprofit.

Original principal of $4,000,000.

Beneficiary's income is $100,000.

Value of donor's estate is $10,000,000. Prior taxable gifts are $0.

Income is 4%; capital appreciation is 4%.

	6% Charitable Lead Unitrust	No Trust
Donor's estate	$10,000,000	$10,000,000
Federal estate tax (paid 2000)	3,827,594	4,920,250
Gross principal	4,000,000	4,000,000
Average annuity to nonprofit	190,338	0
Estate tax deduction	1,986,647	0
Estate tax savings	1,092,656	0
Net federal estate tax on gross principal (paid 2000)	1,107,344	2,200,000
Net principal placed in plan	2,892,656	1,800,000
Remaining estate to family	3,279,750	3,279,750
Total management fees	659,839	0
Total income tax paid	0	960,366
Principal after 20 years	3,501,738	6,550,919
Unrealized capital gain	1,903,590	2,855,643
Potential capital gains tax	380,718	571,129
Benefit to family from plan after capital gains tax	3,121,020	5,979,791
Total distributed to nonprofit	3,806,761	0

IRS discount rate is 6.4%.

The information in this chart is general. Please see your tax adviser to verify all figures.

After passage of the Tax Reform Act of 1969, charitable planners deduced that if the charitable lead trust was drafted in such a way that the grantor was not considered the owner of the trust income, no charitable income tax deduction would be available. However, neither would the grantor be treated as the owner of the trust income for income tax purposes. By excluding that income, the grantor receives the equivalent of a 100 percent income tax deduction. Moreover, even though the grantor receives no charitable income tax deduction, the trust nevertheless qualifies for gift and estate tax charitable deductions. This type of charitable lead trust has come to be known as the *nongrantor* lead trust and is a popular technique for donors who are interested in transferring assets ultimately to succeeding generations of their family while significantly reducing or eliminating the gift and estate tax costs of this transfer through the deduction allowed for a charity's income interest in a charitable lead trust.

Donors thus can employ two basic forms of the charitable lead trust: grantor or nongrantor. Each type produces tax benefits that can be matched with a donor's financial and philanthropic goals.

Grantor Charitable Lead Trusts

The *grantor charitable lead trust* is created during the lifetime of the donor for the purpose of making current distributions to charity for a term specified in the trust agreement, after which the remainder interest reverts to the grantor. The donor who creates a grantor charitable lead trust will receive a charitable income tax deduction in the year the trust is created. That deduction is an amount equal to the net present value of the income interest passing to charity. To qualify for an income tax deduction, the grantor must be treated as the owner of the trust income. Therefore all income earned by the trust, including the amounts distributed to charity, will be taxable to the grantor.

The grantor charitable lead trust may be attractive to donors who have made a commitment for a multiyear pledge. The trust can be used to fulfill the pledge commitment and to accelerate the charitable deductions that would otherwise be produced over the pledge period into the first year of the trust. Consider this example:

A donor is considering a $50,000 annual pledge to the City Philharmonic Orchestra for a five-year period. Without a charitable lead trust, she can claim a charitable contribution income tax deduction for the payments to charity only in the year they are actually made. Alternatively, if she establishes a grantor charitable lead trust and funds it with $1 million in assets with a 5 percent annuity rate and a five-year term, the annuity rate will produce the $50,000 annual distribution for a pledge period of five years, after which the trust will terminate and the assets will revert back to the donor.

The donor will receive a charitable income tax deduction equal to the present value of the income interest transferred to the City Philharmonic Orchestra. The total amount to be distributed to the charity over the five-year period is $250,000 and the present value of the income interest is calculated to be $208,370. The donor can use this deduction subject to the percentage limitations for charitable income tax deductions.

As discussed earlier, for the donor to receive the charitable income tax deduction, she must be treated as the owner of the trust. Therefore, even though income earned by the trust is distributed to the charity, for income tax purposes it is considered as having been received by the grantor.

One alternative is that a donor with a large number of municipal bonds that are tax exempt could use them to fund the charitable lead trust. The donor will not be required to include the interest from the tax-free bonds in her gross income but will still get an income tax charitable deduction. This will produce income tax savings. However, if the trustee of charitable lead trust sells the bonds, the capital gains from the sale or redemption of the bonds will be taxable to the donor.

Nongrantor Charitable Lead Trust

The *nongrantor charitable lead trust* is the more common form of charitable lead trust. Like the grantor charitable lead trust, it pays an income interest to charity for a defined measuring term; however, at the completion of the term the remainder interest is transferred to one or more noncharitable beneficiaries named in the trust instrument rather than being returned to the grantor. Typically, the grantor will name his children or grandchildren as the beneficiaries.

Upon the creation of this trust, the grantor does not receive a charitable income tax deduction; however none of the income produced by the trust is taxed to the grantor either. If the nongrantor charitable lead trust is created during the donor's lifetime, he receives a gift tax charitable deduction in an amount equal to the net present value of the annuity or unitrust income interest payable to the charity. If the trust is funded at death, the donor's estate receives an estate tax charitable deduction that is also based on the net present value of the annuity or unitrust income interest at the time the trust is funded. With careful planning of the combination of the measuring term and the annuity or unitrust payout rate, it is possible to produce a charitable gift or estate tax deduction that equals the amount transferred to the charitable lead trust. The result is that the remainder is transferred to the beneficiaries free of gift and estate taxes. Here is an example:

A donor has an estate valued at $10 million and is a loyal supporter of the City Rescue Mission and would like to continue to provide it with significant annual gifts. The donor would also like to transfer assets to his or her children in the most tax-wise manner available. He transfers $2 million in securities to a charitable lead annuity trust. The trust has a 7 percent annuity rate and a term of twenty years. At the end of the trust's term, the assets will be distributed to his children. The donor receives a charitable gift tax deduction in the amount of $1,477,400. The net taxable gift to his children is $522,600, which the donor can offset by using his unified gift and estate tax credit. As a result, the children will receive the assets of the trust twenty years hence, including any appreciation that occurs over the trust's term, completely free of gift and estate tax.

Model forms for charitable remainder trusts and pooled income funds have been provided by the IRS in revenue rulings and procedures. However, the IRS has not published any model forms that set out the mandatory governing provisions for charitable lead trusts so that they may qualify for income, gift, and estate tax deductions. Therefore it is vital that the donor and the charity work very closely with the donor's legal advisers when preparing these complex trust agreements. A sample charitable lead trust form is provided in Resource 19.

Tax Law Requirements

Certain requirements must be met by both grantor and nongrantor charitable lead trusts before the IRS will consider them to be qualified trusts. The trust must be irrevocable, and the income interest payable to the charity must be either annuity or unitrust interest in all respects. A charitable lead annuity trust is defined as one from which a specific sum, determinable with certainty at the time the trust is created, is paid not less often than annually to one or more qualified charitable organizations as described in IRC Section 170(c) for a period that is measured by a term of years or the life of one or more individuals living at the time the trust is created. Typically, the annuity amount is stated as a fixed percentage of the initial fair market value of the trust's assets. In the event the trust income is insufficient to make the annual annuity payment, the trustee must be permitted to invade principal.

A charitable lead unitrust is one from which a fixed percentage of the net fair market value of the assets (revalued at least annually) is paid, not less than annually, to one or more charitable organizations as described in IRC Section 170(c) for a period that is measured by a term of years or the life of one or more individuals who are living at the time the trust is created. The annual valuation of the unitrust interest may be made on any one date during the taxable year of the trust. If the donor makes an additional contribution to her charitable lead trust on a nonvaluation date, the trust is valued again on the date of contribution. The unitrust amount is then adjusted to reflect the additional contribution for the balance of the trust in the taxable year.

In contrast to charitable remainder trusts, which mandate a minimum payout rate of 5 percent and a maximum payout rate of 50 percent, there are no minimum or maximum annuity or unitrust payout rates applicable to charitable lead trusts. Nor does the 5 percent probability test (which ensures that there is less than a 5 percent probability that the trust will be exhausted based upon the payout rate and the number and ages of the income beneficiaries) applicable to charitable remainder annuity trusts apply to charitable lead annuity trusts.

A further distinction is that the charitable remainder trust measured solely by a term of years has a twenty-year maximum. Federal tax law sets no limit on the maximum number of years a charitable lead trust can operate. However, charitable lead trusts are required to comply with local trust law, and that may include a rule against perpetuities. As a practical matter, most donors use the term of years, as it is their desire to pass the assets on to heirs within a reasonable period of time.

Lead trusts are a complex planned giving technique with many income, estate, and gift tax consequences. Whether or not a lead trust is the appropriate technique for a particular donor will involve much analysis and discussion between the donor, the charity, and the donor's legal and tax advisers.

Gifts of Business Interests

Many prospects and donors have accumulated their wealth through operation of a business. The business may be their largest asset and best source from which to make a major gift to a charity. Methods of making a charitable gift from a business interest depend on the form of the business organization, as discussed in the following pages.

Sole Proprietorships

*Sole proprietorship*s are the most basic business form. They usually require no formal documentation or registration other than a business license. Though advantageous in that they are less complex than other forms of business organizations, the trade-off is that the sole proprietor is personally liable for the business's debts and other legal liabilities.

A sole proprietorship can be owned by an individual or by a husband and wife. It cannot be owned by a charitable organization or charitable trust. Therefore a gift of a sole proprietorship must occur as a transfer of the assets of the proprietorship. The assets of the sole proprietorship may include real property, equipment, inventory, receivables, and goodwill: that is, capital, tangible, and intangible assets. The IRS considers the assets of the business to be the assets of the owner; they are one and the same.

Transfers Through Outright Gifts. Simply transferring the assets of a sole proprietorship to a charity may be unwise because any continuation of the business may produce unrelated business taxable income for the charity. As a general rule the receipt of unrelated business taxable income will not cause the charitable recipient to lose its tax-exempt status; rather the nonprofit will pay income tax on that unrelated business taxable income. However, a nonprofit organization should be cautious here because it risks its tax-exempt status in the event that unrelated business taxable income becomes a disproportionately high share of its total revenues.

Transfers to a Charitable Remainder Trust. The transfer of sole proprietor assets to charitable remainder trusts is also not generally recommended if the trust is to continue operation of the business. The trust will lose its tax-exempt status for any year in which it generates unrelated business taxable income. In such years the trust will be taxed on all of its net income as well as on any gains from the sale of trust assets. In addition, the continued use of trust assets for the benefit of the former business owner may constitute a prohibited act of self-dealing under Internal Revenue Code Section 4941.

Transfers to a Charitable Lead Trust. A somewhat better approach is to transfer the assets of an operating sole proprietorship to a grantor or nongrantor charitable lead trust. This avoids the tax disadvantages of outright gifts and transfers to charitable remainder trusts. With a grantor charitable lead trust, all income is attributable to the grantor and is taxable to him; therefore the issue of unrelated business taxable income does not arise for the nonprofit organization. Nongrantor charitable lead trusts are taxed on their net income. They also receive a charitable income tax deduction for the amounts of income distributed to nonprofits in satisfaction of the annuity or unitrust payment. However, this deduction does not apply for unrelated business taxable income.

Transfers of Selected Assets. Because of the generally unfavorable tax consequences of the approaches just described, it may be advisable to contribute selected assets of the sole proprietorship that do not produce unrelated business taxable income, such as rents from property that is unencumbered by debt. The business may or may not be discontinued before this transfer is made. Using the assets of the sole proprietorship to make a gift may be the best option for prospects and donors who are winding down this type of business.

C Corporations

Corporations are created under state law and are established by filing articles of incorporation with the appropriate state agency. A corporation usually has written bylaws that govern its operation. The owners of the corporation are referred to as shareholders, and they receive stock certificates to evidence their ownership interest. Each shareholder's liability for debts of the corporation is limited to his or her investment in the corporation.

A *C Corporation* is a corporation governed by Subchapter C of the Internal Revenue Code. The income of the C Corporation is taxed at the corporate level and dividend distributions are taxed again at the shareholder level. The corporation is therefore a separate entity from its owners for both tax and legal purposes. Consequently, most privately held businesses are set up as C Corporations. Privately held C Corporations are not traded publicly on any established securities exchange, and therefore are commonly referred to as *closely held*. In addition, privately held corporations will often have buy-sell agreements that restrict the transferability of their stock.

Transfers Through Outright Gifts. The appropriateness of an outright gift of shares of stock in a C Corporation is contingent on the restrictions placed on stock transfers by the shareholder agreement. If this agreement does not raise any concerns, then using the stock can be a very good way to make a charitable gift. However, if the stock is not traded publicly, valuation of the gift will be an issue. In this case, the donor must obtain an independent appraisal to establish the value of the stock.

Transfers Through Deferred Gifts. C Corporation stock can be used to fund a charitable remainder trust or a charitable lead trust. A benefit of transferring this stock to a charitable remainder trust is that in the event the trust sells the stock, this approach can avoid a taxable capital gain at both the shareholder and corporate levels. The C Corporation stock can be transferred to the charitable remainder trust and, at the trustee's discretion, redeemed for cash by the corporation.

Transfers to a Charitable Lead Trust. When a donor transfers stock in a privately held C Corporation to a charitable lead trust, the source of the future income payments can be a challenging issue to resolve. The source of the unitrust or annuity payment amount may be dividends issued by the corporation on the stock or proceeds from the sale of all or a portion of the company's stock. In addition, these payments may take the form of an in-kind distribution: that is, some of the stock itself may be given to the nonprofit. In addition, charitable lead trusts are not exempt from income tax. Depending on the type of charitable lead trust (grantor or nongrantor), the corporation, the grantor, and the trustee must consider the tax consequences that will arise as the trust satisfies its payment obligations.

One challenge is how best to deal with tax on unrelated business income. If the trust is a nongrantor charitable lead trust, the trust itself will be taxed on its unrelated business income. It will also receive a charitable deduction for amounts distributed to its nonprofit beneficiary. A deduction is not allowed for amounts of income allocated to the unrelated business income realized by the trust during the tax year. In contrast, the unrelated business income tax rules have no application to a grantor charitable lead trust because the grantor is taxed on all of the trust's taxable income.

S Corporations

Until 1998, the tax laws prohibited a charity from owning any stock in an *S Corporation*. If a charity became a shareholder, the corporation immediately lost its S Corp status and became subject to many of the disadvantageous provisions of the general corporate income tax laws. Because so many corporations are classified as S Corporations, this prohibition often prevented charities and donors from working together to use S Corporation stock to make gifts. For many donors, their S Corporation stock is often the only asset they have available for a major gift.

As of January 1, 1998, the Small Business Job Protection Act of 1996 allows a charity to be an eligible shareholder of an S Corporation. However, charitable remainder trusts are still prohibited from being S Corporation shareholders. In addition, the income a charity receives that is attributable to its S Corporation stock is subject to tax as *unrelated business taxable income* (UBTI). UBTI can create an additional bookkeeping burden for a charity, and it is a concern when the charity sells the stock. The critical issue for a nonprofit organization, then, is to determine whether holding the S Corporation stock is an attractive investment when compared to the risk. The charity should ask how soon the stock can be sold and converted into marketable investments. If the charity must hold the stock for an extended period of time, it should consider whether or not the stock is likely to produce a cash flow sufficient to fulfill the gift's charitable purposes.

Most charities prefer to sell their interest in a closely held business as soon as possible after receiving it as a gift. They do this because the assets of a closely held business do not fit with most charities' investment policies. The problem of UBTI gives charities an additional incentive to sell. Therefore, before accepting such a gift, the charity should have a discussion with the donor about her expectations. She may expect the charity to hold the stock for a long period of time. Furthermore, the charity may face a very restricted market for selling the stock. Usually the potential market for the stock is limited to the S Corporation itself, existing shareholders, or pre-approved outside buyers. In addition, the charity will usually become an S Corporation minority shareholder and will be dependent upon the willingness of the majority shareholders to treat the charity fairly.

Before accepting a gift of S Corporation stock, your nonprofit should carefully review the stock and company, seeking satisfactory answers to these questions:

- Will the S Corporation distribute sufficient cash in a timely manner to pay the quarterly UBTI tax installments as they become due?
- Will the majority shareholders refrain from business practices that could harm the charity's minority interest?
- Will the charity receive a fair price for the stock as determined by a qualified appraisal at the time of the sale?
- Do any laws in your state regulate nonprofit ownership of S Corporation stock?

In summary, S Corporation stock can be beneficial to a charity if it can successfully resolve the complex financial and tax issues involved.

Partnerships

A *partnership* is a joint undertaking by two or more individuals or entities. They pool their assets in a business operation and then share in the resulting profits and losses. Partnerships may own virtually any type of assets. In most instances the partners enter into a written partnership agreement.

The tax treatment of partnerships is unique in that items of income, gain, loss, deduction, and credit pass through to the partners and are reported on their personal tax returns. The partnership itself does not pay tax, but it does file informational returns reporting the items that have been passed through. As part of the partnership agreement, the partners may place restrictions on the transfer of interest in the partnership.

There are two basic types of partnerships, the *general partnership* and the *limited partnership*. General partnerships may be established without any formal documentation or registration. In a general partnership each partner is personally liable for the debts of the partnership. In contrast, state law does require formal registration of limited partnerships. Limited partnerships have at least one general partner, who is personally liable for the debts of the partnership. They also have at least one other partner, known as a limited partner, who is liable for the partnership debts only to the extent of the assets he has contributed to the partnership. The general partner normally takes a more active role in the management of the partnership business than the limited partner does.

Transfers Through Outright Gifts. To transfer outright a partnership interest to charity, the partnership agreement must contain specific language permitting a partner to transfer his interest with or without the consent of the other partners. Absent this language, transfer of a partnership interest is invalid. As with other business interests, if the partnership is engaged in business that will produce unrelated business taxable income for the charity, the charity will be taxed on this income.

Transfers Through Deferred Gifts. Partnership interests can be difficult to transfer to a charitable remainder or lead trust because the underlying business may be involved in activities that can have an adverse impact on the donor and the trust. Charities are advised to accept the gift of a partnership interest only after a full review of the potential risk involved. For example, as described earlier, a charitable remainder trust will lose its tax-exempt status in any taxable year in which it incurs UBTI. If this change in status coincides with a year in which the trust sells appreciated assets, the trust will pay capital gains tax on the sale. To avoid such potential problems, the partnership can distribute assets directly to a partner. The partner then uses these assets to make his gift to the charitable remainder trust. The partner will not recognize any gain on the property received (other than cash and marketable securities) until he sells or otherwise disposes of the property. Therefore, depending on the asset, the partner may be able to receive a distribution from the partnership and transfer the property to a charitable remainder trust without recognition of gain. The trust will then avoid UBTI.

UBTI is also an issue for a nongrantor charitable lead trust. As mentioned earlier, although a nongrantor charitable lead trust is a taxable entity, it is entitled to a charitable deduction for amounts distributed to charity. However, this deduction is not allowed for amounts of income allocated to UBTI. In the case of a grantor charitable lead trust, however, the issue of UBTI will not arise because the grantor, who is an individual, incurs all the taxable income of the trust.

Donor Advised Funds

Donor advised funds (DAFs)have experienced significant growth in popularity in recent years, resulting in a remarkable increase in assets held in such funds. For-profit financial service firms, such as Fidelity, have offered DAFs that have attracted huge sums of money. Community foundations continue to see that the DAF is one of the most popular giving vehicles among their donors. In response to their donors' desires to exercise greater discretion about where and how their gifts will be used, more universities and other nonprofits are beginning to offer donor advised funds as well.

We will look first at what a donor advised fund is and then at the U.S. Treasury Regulations that it must meet. A DAF program is actually a collection of individual charitable funds. It is vital to donors who establish and contribute to a DAF, however, that the IRS treat their contributions as having been made to a public charity rather than to a private foundation. One of the reasons for this is that a donation to a private foundation is deductible only up to 30 percent of the donor's adjusted gross income whereas a donation to a public charity is deductible up to 50 percent that income. As a result, each DAF must be treated by the charity as a component fund owned and controlled by the charity, and not as a separate foundation. In a properly constituted DAF, the assets attributed to the fund become the legal property of the sponsoring charity, and the original donor or donors have the ability to advise the sponsoring charity on how to distribute funds from the DAF. Please note, however, that the sponsoring charity is not required to follow the advice of the donor. The charity is the owner of the property, and it must distribute the funds in a manner that it believes is compatible with its stated mission. It must be free to make its own determinations about the best use of the funds as well as to consider donor recommendations.

Donor advised funds have no basis in the Internal Revenue Code or in any statute. They are creatures of U.S. Treasury Regulations. The two key Treasury Regulations the IRS uses to determine the validity of a DAF are found in Section 1.170A-9(e) and Section 1.507–2(a)(8). (It should be noted not all the requirements set forth in these two regulations must be met to have a valid DAF.) The two tests a DAF must meet to be considered part of the assets of the public charity rather than a separate private foundation are the entry-level test and the component fund test.

Entry-Level Test

The requirements of the entry-level test must be met in order for the sponsoring public charity to be considered a single entity rather than an aggregation of separate funds. The requirements of the entry-level test are set out in Treasury Regulations Section 1.170A-9(e)(10)-(13) and are as follows:

- The DAF program must be known as a community trust or by a similar name that conveys to the public the concept of a capital endowment fund that supports charitable activities.

- All the DAFs of a sponsoring charitable organization must be subject to the same governing instrument.
- The DAF program must have a governing body or distribution committee that directs or monitors the distribution of all of the funds in the DAF in a manner that meets the charitable purposes of the sponsoring public charity.
- This governing instrument must provide the governing body with the following powers:

  The power to modify any restriction or condition on the distribution of the funds when it becomes clear to the governing body that the condition or restriction is unnecessary, incapable of fulfillment, or inconsistent with the charitable purpose of the sponsoring public charity.

  The power to replace any participating trustee, custodian, or agent for breach of fiduciary duty under state law.

  The power to replace any participating trustee, custodian, or agent for failure to produce a reasonable return on investments.

- The regular financial reports prepared by the sponsoring public charity must treat all funds held directly or indirectly by the DAF as funds owned by the charity.

Component Fund Test

A component fund test must be met for the DAF to be considered a part of the sponsoring public charity. One of the requirements is that the gift, bequest, or other transfer that creates the program must be made to a DAF that meets the previously discussed entry-level test. Moreover, to be considered a completed gift, a transfer to a DAF must be free of any material restrictions. The IRS looks at the facts and circumstances of each situation, determining whether or not the sponsoring public charity has the ability to freely and effectively use the transferred assets. In determining whether any material restrictions exist, the IRS looks at the factors set out in Treasury Regulation Section 1.507-2(a)(8), which are as follows:

- The sponsoring public charity is the owner of the assets.
- The assets are held and administered by the charity in a manner consistent with its tax-exempt purpose.
- The governing body of the sponsoring public charity has ultimate authority and control over the assets.
- The governing body of the sponsoring public charity is organized and operated so that it is independent from the donor.

This regulation also lists factors that will and factors that will not adversely affect an IRS determination that the sponsoring public charity can freely and effectively use the transferred assets. One factor that will adversely affect the determination is the existence of a transfer agreement that allows the donor to retain the right to name the recipients of distributions from the DAF or to decide when distributions will be made. In addition, the IRS examines situations in which the sponsoring public charity seeks advice from the donor or in which the donor gives advice regarding the distribution of funds from the DAF after the initial gift has been made. The IRS may look at such advice as an indirect retention of the right to name the beneficiary of the DAF. In making this determination the IRS will look for these adverse factors:

- The marketing materials used by the DAF indicate that the DAF will follow the advice of the donor.
- The sponsoring charity does not determine whether the donor's advice is consistent with its own charitable purpose.
- The DAF considers only the advice of the donor in relation to the donor's fund and has no procedures to obtain the advice of others in relation to that fund.
- The DAF follows a donor's advice nearly all the time.
- The donor requires the DAF to take or withhold action in ways that are not compatible with the charitable purpose of the sponsoring public charity, and such action or inaction would violate the private foundation rules of the Internal Revenue Code.
- The donor either expressly or implicitly requires the DAF to retain certain assets for investment.
- The DAF agreement either directly or indirectly grants the donor a right of first refusal on decisions about which investment assets are to be sold.
- The DAF agreement creates an irrevocable relationship between the DAF and the donor or an appointee of the donor.
- The donors sets any other condition on the DAF that inhibits the charity from exercising ultimate control over the assets of the DAF.

Conversely, the IRS looks for these positive factors, which show that the donor has not reserved the right to name the beneficiary of the DAF distributions:

- The sponsoring charity can demonstrate that it has made an independent investigation of the donor's advice to determine whether that advice is consistent with the charity's mission.
- The charity has established guidelines for charitable use of the DAF assets, and the donor's advice is consistent with those guidelines.
- The charity distributes funds in excess of sums received from the donor's DAF to the same charity suggested by the donor or to similar charities.
- The charity's marketing materials for the DAF state that the charity is not bound by the donor's advice.

Finally, a few factors are not an issue in the determination:

- The DAF has a name or designation that is similar to the donor's name or in some way memorializes the donor.
- The DAF funds are required to be used for a purpose that is consistent with the purposes of the sponsoring charity.
- The assets held in the DAF are separate from the general assets of the sponsoring public charity, as long as the charity has ultimate control of these separate assets.
- The donor requires the sponsoring public charity to retain the assets used to make the gift and restricts its disposition, so long as such restriction is in furtherance of the mission of the charity. However, the required retention cannot be imposed on investment income.

Essentially, all of these criteria mean that the sponsoring charity must be the owner of the assets held in the DAF and the donors must clearly understand that their role is strictly advisory. The charity must demonstrate that it has ultimate control over all assets held within its DAF program. It is therefore vital that nonprofits establish with donors that the charity is the owner of all DAF assets and that a donor's advice concerning distributions from the DAF will not always be followed. Furthermore, as the fund sponsor, the organization must manage the DAF funds and make distributions from those funds to other charities in a manner that is consistent with its charitable purposes.

The issue of donor control is the threshold issue for donor advised funds. Before implementing a DAF program, it is important that a nonprofit's management and governing board comply with the various factors that go into establishing a valid donor advised fund.

Supporting Organizations

Donors and advisers are evincing a growing interest in the use of *supporting organizations*. Supporting organizations are an alternative to the more commonly known private foundation. They have increased in popularity primarily due to the fact that under Internal Revenue Code Section 509(a)(3), supporting organizations are treated as public charities. As a result, supporting organizations and their donors are not subject to the rules and restrictions that apply to private foundations. Donors enjoy having the opportunity to direct the use of their charitable gifts, and you as a charitable gift planner may find yourself assisting in the establishment of a supporting organization for your nonprofit organization.

Basics of Supporting Organizations

Most supporting organizations are established as trusts. The trust agreement that governs the supporting organization identifies the specific charities that will receive support. Federal tax law has distinguished for many years between public charities and private foundations. Generally, it is to the advantage of the entity and its donors to be classified as a public charity rather than as a private foundation. Contributions to a private foundation are less beneficial to a donor than contributions to a public charity. Recall that gifts of cash to a public charity may be deducted up to 50 percent of the donor's adjusted gross income whereas contributions of cash to a private foundation are deductible up to only 30 percent of adjusted gross income. If the donor makes a gift of appreciated property to a public charity, it may be deducted up to 30 percent of adjusted gross income; however, gifts of appreciated property to a private foundation may be deducted up to only 20 percent. An additional distinction is that the deduction for appreciated property given to a public charity is based on the property's full fair market value, which includes any appreciation, whereas the value of a contribution of appreciated property to a private foundation must be reduced by its untaxed appreciation (capital gain), which reduces the donor's contribution to her tax basis in the property. As a result, the tax deduction for gifts of highly appreciated property to a private foundation can be effectively eliminated, as the donor's cost basis may be quite low. The tax code does provide an exception to this rule for contributions of publicly traded appreciated securities to a private foundation. These contributions can be deducted at their full fair market value, subject to the 20 percent of adjusted gross income limitation (for securities held more than one year).

Private foundations are also subjected to a variety of other tax treatments that may make them less attractive to certain donors. For example, the investment income earned by the private foundation is subject to an excise tax of 2 percent. The tax code is also structured so as to regulate the behavior of the foundation and its donors in order to prevent self-dealing and to prohibit certain types of investments. Private foundations are also required to make minimum distributions annually equal to 5 percent of the market value of their assets. In general, tax compliance for private foundations is much more complex than it is for public charities. This fact can increase the operating expenses of the foundation and also make some donors consider other alternatives, such as the supporting organization.

A supporting organization avoids the tax disadvantages of the private foundation. Even though a supporting organization is usually funded by a single individual or a family, for federal tax purposes it is treated as a public charity. As a result, contributions to a supporting organization are deducted based on the more generous rules applicable to contributions to public charities, discussed previously.

Nor does the supporting organization pay tax on its investment income; nor is it burdened with the complex tax and regulatory rules that apply to private foundations. The only requirement a supporting organization must meet is that it must provide funding for one or more specific public charities.

Operation of the Supporting Organization

After the supporting organization is established and funded, it must make distributions each year to one or more of the public charities named in the trust agreement. The distributions need not be equal nor do they have to be made each year to every charity listed. Although a private foundation is required to distribute 5 percent of its market value annually, the minimum amount a supporting organization is required to distribute each year is based on its income, not its assets. Typically, the supporting organization must distribute at least 85 percent of the net income it realizes each year. (Depending on the investment allocation of its assets, the net income of the supporting organization may actually be less than 5 percent of its market value.) Bear in mind that this 85 percent figure is a minimum requirement, and the supporting organization can distribute more.

Some donors desire even more flexibility than the supporting organization provides. They feel that the need to identify in advance the public charities that will be supported limits their flexibility. The way to provide flexibility within the form of a supporting organization is to have the trust agreement name a community foundation as one of the supported charities. The distribution from the supporting organization to the community foundation can be treated much like a donor advised fund. The supporting organization then retains the right to advise the community foundation on how the distributions from the supporting organization can be distributed to other charities. The charities the donor suggests can then change from year to year, dependent upon the donor's priorities.

The IRS requires distributions from a supporting organization to meet an attentiveness test. The supporting organization must distribute to one or more of the supported charities an amount equal to at least 10 percent of the total support received by the supported charity from all sources. However, if the charity listed in the trust agreement is one that receives a large amount of public support (such as an educational institution), it will be difficult for the supporting organization to meet this standard. Treasury regulations thus provide an alternative way for supporting organizations to meet the attentiveness test. They can distribute to one or more of their listed charities an amount sufficient to fund a significant charitable project or program that would not otherwise receive sufficient funding.

As a means of making a major gift, the supporting organization has a particular attraction for wealthy donors, especially those who are entrepreneurs who have created their wealth through their own hard work and control over their assets. Many of these donors may be reluctant to turn over large amounts of their assets to a charity for management, investment, and distribution. For these donors the supporting organization is an attractive alternative to the private foundation, as it allows them to maintain a degree of control without the private foundation restrictions.

A carefully constructed and thoughtfully conducted major gifts and planned giving program offers all nonprofits an opportunity to permit their donors to provide significant ongoing support and to create important legacies. Many planned giving vehicles can create an endowment that will support the nonprofit's mission into perpetuity. Life income vehicles can benefit your donors and ultimately your nonprofit. Bequests will often permit a donor to make a gift at death that is larger than he or she ever could have made during his or her lifetime. New and advanced techniques involving flexible endowments, charitable lead trusts, business interests, donor advised funds, and supporting organizations give donors many ways to devise meaningful gifts that match their needs, their assets, and their charitable interests. Planned giving at some level should be an essential part of every nonprofit's development program.

PART TWO

THE MAJOR GIFTS AND PLANNED GIVING RESOURCE GUIDE

RESOURCE GUIDE CONTENTS

RESOURCE 1

NONPROFIT KEY WORD SEARCH

Adolescent health issues
African American affairs
After-school/enrichment programs
Agricultural education
AIDS/HIV
Air/water quality
Alzheimer's disease
Animal protection
Art history
Arthritis
Arts appreciation
Arts association and councils
Arts centers
Arts festivals
Arts funds
Arts institutes
Arts outreach
Arts/humanities education
Arts/humanities general
Asian American affairs
At-risk youth
Ballet
Bible study/translation
Big Brothers/Big Sisters camp
Botanical gardens/parks
Business education
Business/free enterprise
Business-school partnerships
Cancer
Chambers of commerce
Child abuse
Child welfare
Children's health/hospitals
Churches
Civic and public affairs
Civil rights
Clinics/medical centers
Clubs
Colleges and universities
Community arts

Community centers
Community foundation
Community service organizations
Community/junior colleges
Continuing education
Counseling
Crime prevention
Criminal rehabilitation
Dance
Day care
Delinquency
Diabetes
Dioceses
Domestic violence
Economic development
Economic education
Economic policy
Education
Education associations
Education funds
Education reform
Elementary education (private)
Elementary education (public)
Emergency/ambulance services
Emergency relief
Employment/job training
Energy
Engineering education
Environment
Ethnic and folk arts
Ethnic organizations
Eyes/blindness
Faculty development
Family planning
Family services
Film and video
First Amendment issues
Food/clothing distribution
Foreign arts organizations
Foreign education

Forestry
Gay/lesbian affairs
Geriatric health
Gifted and talented programs
Health
Health and physical education
Health care/hospitals (international)
Health funds
Health organizations
Health policy/cost containment
Heart
Hispanic affairs
Historic preservation
History and archaeology
Home care services
Homes
Hospice
Hospitals
Hospitals (university-affiliated)
Housing
Human rights
Inner-city development
International
International affairs
International development
International environmental issues
International exchange
International law
International organizations
International peace and security issues
International relations
International relief efforts
International studies
Jewish causes
Journalism/media education
Kidney
Law and justice
Leadership training
Legal aid
Legal education

Libraries
Literacy
Literary arts
Long-term care
Lung
Medical education
Medical rehab
Medical research
Medical training
Mental health
Ministries
Minority education
Missionary activities (domestic)
Missionary/religious activities
Multiple sclerosis
Municipalities/town
Museums/galleries
Music
Native American affairs
Nonprofit management
Nursing services
Nutrition
Observatories/planetariums
Opera
Outpatient health care
Parades/festivals
People with disabilities
Performing arts
Philanthropic organizations
Prenatal health issues
Preschool education
Preventive medicine/wellness
    organizations
Private and public education (precollege)
Professional/trade associations
Protection
Public broadcasting
Public health
Public policy
Recreation/athletics

Refugee assistance
Religion
Religious education
Religious organizations
Religious welfare
Research
Research/studies institutes
Resource conservation
Rural affairs
Safety
Sanitary systems
Science
Science exhibits/fairs
Science/mathematics education
Science museums
Scientific centers/institutes
Scientific labs
Scientific organizations
Scientific research
Secondary education (private)
Secondary education (public)
Seminaries
Senior services
Sexual abuse
Shelters/homeless

Single-disease health associations
Social science education
Social services
Social/policy issues
Special education
Speech and hearing
Student aid
Substance abuse
Synagogues/temples
Theater
Trade
Transplant networks/donor banks
Trauma treatment
United Funds/United Way
Urban/community affairs
Veterans
Visual arts
Vocational/technical education
Volunteer services
Watershed
Wildlife protection
Women's affairs
YMCA/YMHA/YWCA/YWHA
Youth organizations
Zoos/aquariums

RESOURCE 2

ESTIMATING NET WORTH

ESTIMATING NET WORTH:
ONE ORGANIZATION'S SEARCH FOR TRUTH

Several months ago, the Research Department here at the University of Virginia decided to take a closer look at how we estimated an individual's net worth. Although many in our field will agree that an accurate determination of net worth is impossible (and some believe futile), here at Virginia we find it to be a necessary step in our attempts to segregate our exceptionally large database of prospects. By calculating potential gift capability based on the total known assets of an individual, we are able to assign to each a rating, ranging from $10,000 to $10 million plus. These ratings then allow us to provide a more selective solicitation strategy that is appropriate to the gift range into which each prospect falls.

For several years prior we relied upon two very straightforward formulas to arrive at these ratings. If stock holdings were an individual's largest asset, the following would apply:

Total known direct stock holdings × (1–3) = estimated net worth
5% of estimated net worth = estimated gift capability

We felt comfortable with this formula. By using a multiplier of anywhere from 1 to 3, the researcher was able to use her/his discretion as to how many unknown assets the prospect probably owned. If we believed that we had found the majority of an individual's assets, we multiplied his/her holdings by a lower number. If we felt that what we had found was just the tip of the iceberg (i.e., the prospect was a private investor), we applied a multiplier of 3. We chose to leave this formula as it was.

The problem, in our eyes, was in determining a prospect's net worth based solely on his/her real estate holdings. Our old formula for this situation was as follows:

Total real estate holdings × 5 = estimated net worth
5% of estimated net worth = estimated giving capability

While we felt that we were getting fairly accurate numbers for individuals with large real estate holdings, we believed that those with houses assessed at lower values were receiving disproportionately high ratings. Can a Professor of Architecture with a $200,000 house really afford a gift of $50,000?

In an effort to discover how our formulas for arriving at net worth compared to those of our colleagues around the country, we posted a query on PRSPCT-L. The results were quite varied and included the following:

20 × level of consistent annual giving = giving ability (over 5-year period)

10% of annual income = giving ability (over 5 years)

.5%–1.5% of liquid assets = giving ability

5% of total known assets (real estate + stock holdings +
annual income for 5 years) = giving ability (5 years)

However, after applying these formulas to examples from our database, we found that none of the above were truly feasible for us. Unless our prospect was listed on a proxy, we usually did not have his/her annual income or stock holdings. In fact, 75%–80% of the time, real estate holdings are our only source on which to base our estimates.

So we turned in a different direction. By far the most popular source recommended to us for determining net worth was an article by Rob Millar, Director of Development Services at Boston College, titled "How Much Is That Donor in Your Records?" (*Case Currents,* July/August 1995). The solution provided in this article was attractive to us for a number of reasons.

To begin, it suggests a formula based upon statistical averages obtained from the Internal Revenue Service. Compiled into percentage tables, these averages represent a breakdown of total assets drawn from tax returns for deceased individuals with estates of $600,000 or higher in 1989. This study determined what percentage each asset was of the total net worth of the estate, on average. Different percentages are also provided for estates of varying sizes. To use the tables, you simply plug in the asset you are working with and calculate a net worth.

Here is an example: you know that your prospect has real estate valued at $200,000. Looking at the table, you see that for an individual whose estate falls between $600,000–$1 million, real estate will, on the average, comprise 27.6% of his/her overall wealth. If $200,000 is 27.6% of your prospect's wealth, then she/he has an estimated net worth of $724,638 ($200,000/.276).

But once again, after applying several case studies from our database to these tables, we found that our initial problems remained unresolved. While the estimates obtained from this table initially seemed reasonable, it made no provision for individuals with estates of less than $600,000, a category into which a number of our prospects fell. Also, we were bothered by the fact that the table was based upon statistics from 1989. The Dow Jones Index has quadrupled since 1989, a fact that

Resource 2

could dramatically alter the average amount of an individual's stock holdings in relation to his/her overall wealth. This, alone, was enough to make us wary.

In the end, we chose to improvise. Because our estimates for wealthier individuals were comparable to, if not more conservative than, those arrived at by several of the formulas used by other institutions, we decided to address only the issue of prospects with lower real estate holdings. The University of Virginia, currently in a capital campaign, is focusing its efforts on major gift prospects (gifts of $100,000 and above). We therefore drew the line at real estate holdings of $400,000 and above. Those falling in this category, based upon our old formulas (5 × real estate = net worth and 5% of net worth = gift capability), were qualified as major gift prospects, and we felt fairly confident of their capability to give.

We took a closer look at our prospects that fell below the $400,000 mark. We compared the original ratings that we had assigned to these prospects based upon real estate to the actual amounts they eventually gave. We decided that our best alternative would be to lower our multiplier to 3 for those with property totaling less than $400,000:

Total real estate holdings × 3 = estimated net worth
3% of estimated net worth = estimated giving capability

These figures presented a much more accurate reflection of wealth and ability at this level than our previous numbers.

It was a long journey, but an important one. Although estimating net worth for individuals is still a nebulous practice at best, it is still a necessary one for many organizations. The solution ultimately adopted by the University of Virginia will undoubtedly not be appropriate for all, but I hope that our process of reaching it will prove helpful and informative to those of you who are facing similar challenges.

Source: Angela Vaughan, Senior Development Researcher, University of Virginia, January 1998. Copyright 1998 The Rector and Visitors of the University of Virginia. This article was initially published in the Winter 1998 issue of the official publication of the Virginia APRA. Reprinted with permission.

RESOURCE 3

WEB-BASED RESEARCH

It's All Out There . . .

I need everything there is about Bob Jones. It's all out there on the web somewhere, right? Just pull it together for me by tomorrow.

No one reading this newsletter would make (or accept) such an ill-considered request; however, here's a strategy for finding "it all" on the web. As an added bonus, everything here is a free site (although some may require you to register, and some may offer "premium" services for a fee), and they are all public records or published information.

Here's what I would do first if I got that request:

- Breathe into a brown paper bag, and
- Find out what you can from the requestor about why they think Bob Jones is a potential prospect.

With some luck, they already know something—where Bob lives or where he works. If they know nothing other than his name and, presumably, his likelihood of caring about your cause, then I offer some strategies at the end of the article. Let's be optimistic first, and assume you have some basic leads to follow. You know his address—what can you find out about him? You can almost certainly establish whether he owns or rents, how much the property is worth, what it has sold for, and when it sold. County assessors are increasingly on-line. Go to http://pubweb/acns.nwu.edu/~cap440/assess.html for a list of assessors sorted by state, then by county. It also provides phone and fax numbers. Locally, having a prospect in Greene County is a bonus. Go to http://www.co.greene.oh.us/gismapserver.htm where you can search by address or by owner and get back a wealth of detail (down to the number of bathrooms). Finding out an address's county is essential for using assessors successfully, and it's easy to find—ask the Post Office at http://www.usps.gov/ncsc/lookups/lookups.htm. With a zip code or partial address, they'll return full mailing information (including carrier codes and ZIP+4 which can be useful to those with access to marketing information) and the county in which the address is.

If the county assessor is not on-line, and you don't want to call or fax them, there is an alternative: web-based real estate tools are common, but are less reliable and may be out of date. The classic site is http://realestate.yahoo.com/realestate/homevalues/ which lets you search by exact address, street address ranges (e.g. everyone on the block), and price range (e.g. all sales in Dayton over $250,000). Don't forget to search Florida and South Carolina for holiday homes.

If you know where Bob works, his employer's website is a great starting point. More often than not, simply typing www.bobscompanyname.com will get you there. If not, some browsers, Netscape for example, will return a list of near matches, and it's very likely to have what you need there. If not, a quick trip to your favorite search engine should solve the problem. Try Yahoo.com, your browser's own home site, www.askjeeves.com, www.google.com, http://www.altavista.com/, and many more. I personally like www.dogpile.com because it searches a variety of other engines and compiles their results for you. Also excellent and fast is www.ragingsearch.com—no extraneous material, and results without ads. General search techniques could fill a book, so I suggest you go to www.about.com and check out their Internet articles; however, four quick tips that help me on-line are

- Know what search parameters your chosen engine uses. Click on their tips button to see what they want. Some are more user-friendly than others and let you use intuitive language, symbols (+ or &), or phrases in quotations; others want strict Boolean.
- Once at a site, use the site map—who knows where a webmaster decides is the right place for the info you want? Clicking on their site map reveals their filing hierarchy and lets you click straight to your area.
- Using Netscape, once at a promising site, click the button labeled "What's Related" for an instant list of other sites to explore.
- Bookmark sites you find useful, and organize the bookmark folder into subdirectories. Bookmark names are often opaque, so filing them in an appropriate directory (e.g. real estate resources, local companies, search engines) can rescue you from fruitless clicking.

Back to bobscompany.com—once at the site, you can try a variety of techniques depending on the type of company and his position. A megacorp's site may be so generic and vast that Bob isn't going to show up unless he's the CEO, but you can get a feel for how he earns his bread. If Bob ranks highly, go to "investor relations" which will get you their annual report (on-line or downloadable—getting a free copy of Acrobat Reader is vital) and corporate compensation and director bios. A search of their PR archive may get the announcement of his hiring or promotion—these usually contain education and career histories, which give you yet more leads to follow on the web. A smaller private company site often includes the history of the company and/or the founding family.

For information about companies try Hoovers (http://hoovweb.hoovers.com/) or for more financial information on public companies, visit the SEC at http://people.edgar-online.com/people/ where you can search for insider trading, IPOs, and their major filings. If Bob's a director, his stock holdings will show up here. Going to a career site such as www.nationjob.com will often give a summary of the company's own take on themselves. Two sites that are great starting points are www.business.com and http://www.ceoexpress.com.

Bob's not a corporate type? If Bob's a professional, run a search (at www.ask jeeves.com for example) to find his professional, or accrediting, organization, which may maintain searchable lists of its members. For example, the AMA gives details about areas of specialization and which medical school a doctor attended. (Go to http://www.ama-assn.org and choose Doctor Finder.) If Bob requires a license from the state to practice, the state site will often provide information. In Ohio, accountants, architects, dentists, doctors, nurses, optometrists, social workers, engineers, and more are at http://www.state.oh.us/ohio/license.htm.

Whatever Bob does, you'll want to know how much he earns. There's a variety of salary sites to look at. Try www.salary.com or http://www.jobsmart.org/tools/salary/sal-surv.htm. Feeling brave? Try the Department of Labor's Occupational Outlook Handbook: http://stats.bls.gov/ocohome.htm.

After this searching, you may know where Bob went to school. His alma mater's site is likely to have an alumni section, have an internal search function, or have a searchable set of press releases. If Bob is a notable alumnus, you may well find some excellent material here.

Need to know his political affiliation? Donations reported to the FEC are at http://www.tray.com/fecinfo/_indiv.htm. As a bonus, you can click to an image of the filing form that often shows a donor's home address and employer.

Newspapers and local community sites are indispensable: Business News not only has a Dayton edition at http://www.bizjournals.com/dayton (which lets you hunt through its archives for free), but it also lets you link to its other markets nationwide. Suburban Newspapers of Dayton gives a good local look at our community-level newspapers: http://www.sndnews.com/. Likewise, look at Active Dayton: http://www.activedayton.com—in particular their lists of the top local companies under http://www.activedayton.com/business/localbusiness/mv100/ (for public companies) or http://www.activedayton.com/business/localbusiness/mv50/ (for private companies). To find equivalent sites by region, and all the news sites you could ever want: http://gwis2.circ.gwu.edu/~gprice/newscenter.htm.

What can you do if your requestor knows nothing other than "Bob Jones gave money to XYZ so I'm sure he'll like ABC." If they can't give you an employer, a home address, or some strong lead to his whereabouts, then the reasons for their request become a) suspect, and b) essential in your quest, as they'll shape your search strategy. For example, if Bob is on their radar because of his membership in other organizations, or giving to a particular cause, then surfing over to those organizations' sites may well be your best starting point. For example, The Dayton Foundation (www.daytonfoundation.org) lets you download their annual reports.

If you have no address for Bob, try http://www.555-1212.com. This offers some of the best techniques for finding an address, including a reverse look-up (for when you have just a phone number). Another good choice is http://www.whohere.lycos.com/. An obvious problem with "Bob Jones" is his name. If you know nothing else about him, you do have a problem, but one technique is to search for his spouse (with any luck, she's called Eudoxia) and hope to track him down that way. Knowing another family member's name can be a vital cross check.

There are myriad sites out there of varying usefulness and reliability: to check a site's reliability, run a search on yourself and see what turns up. As a last resort (and often one that renews faith in serendipity), go to a general search engine (see sites suggested under searching for www.bobscompany.com), enter "Bob Jones," and see what kind of gold pans out from your prospecting. Perhaps you'll find the perfect link that begins "Bob Jones has his own university. . . ."

For more information, or refutation, please e-mail sarah.mcginley@wright.edu. Sarah McGinley is a research analyst at Wright State University.

August 2000

RESOURCE 4

RESEARCH PROFILE FORMATS

Resource 4

NORTHWESTERN UNIVERSITY

CHARTER TRUSTEE
(if applicable)

Confidential—for Internal Use Only
PROSPECT RESEARCH PROFILE
December 14, 2000

Presidential Prospect
(if Trustee)

Preferred Reunion Year: 20xx
(sometimes people have a preference for a reunion year other than the one in which they graduated)

Prospect	NU School/Year	ID NO
JOHN Q. PROSPECT	WCAS 'xx	A00000000
Spouse: Jane Prospect (nee: Doe)	WCAS 'xx	A00000001

BORN: *Full name—date of birth, in City, State*

EDUCATION:

School/Year	Degree (Major)
NU WCAS 'xx	BA (Basket weaving)
Joe's College 'xx	MBA

NU Selected Student Activities
National Basket Weaving Society
Debate Team
Alpha Beta Chi (social fraternity)

HOME:
Home Street
Home City, State Zip
Home phone number; Home fax number
(note if not verifiable through Directory Assistance)
Personal e-mail address
Include second/summer home, if applicable

BUSINESS:
Title, Business Name, Business Street
Business City, State Zip
Business phone; Business fax
Business e-mail address

FAMILY FOUNDATIONS:
John Q. and Jane Prospect Foundation
Address, phone
Any historical, asset, or giving history information available
Foundation phone; Foundation fax

JOHN Q. PROSPECT
December 14, 2000
Page 2

BUSINESS BACKGROUND & CORPORATE OR FOUNDATION AFFILIATIONS

Date	Affiliations
19xx–present	Mr. Widget Manufacturing, the nation's largest widget manufacturer (1999 sales $1 million billion), 4000 employees

- President (19xx–xx)
- Vice president of operations (19xx–xx)
- Manager, Northeast sales (19xx–xx)

Mr. Widget Manufacturing was founded by Mrs. Prospect's grandfather, Joe Doe, and was on the verge of bankruptcy when Mr. Prospect became VP of operations; he spearheaded a reorganization which helped the company become "one of the hottest manufacturing concerns in the nation" according to *Forbes* in 1998. Local trade papers have recently mentioned that Mr. Prospect is expected to gradually relinquish control of day-to-day duties to his executive vice president, (Joe Blow, NU L 'xx) and Mr. Prospect will probably be named Chairman by 2001, Mr. Blow succeeding him as President.

A 19xx article noted that Mr. Widget Manufacturing had been investigated by the US House Intelligence Committee due to the company's sale of widgets to Iraq, which might have had connections to arms manufacturing. The company's former president and Mr. Prospect's predecessor, Michael Smith, had stepped down because of a scandal involving this investigation and its connection to his service with a US government corporation. The Committee investigation remains classified and no action has been taken since it occurred.

19xx–xx	Some Other Company

- Salesman

19xx–xx	United States Army

Mr. Prospect sits on the board of the Mr. Widget Foundation, Widget International, Widget Byproduct Company, and Guns and Butter, Inc.

CIVIC AND PROFESSIONAL AFFILIATIONS AND AWARDS

Date	Civic Affiliations
19xx	Lyric Opera of Nowhere
19xx	Nowhere Zoo
19xx	Nowhere Symphony Orchestra

Resource 4

—— **CONFIDENTIAL** ——
FOR INTERNAL USE ONLY

JOHN Q. PROSPECT
December 14, 2000
Page 3

Date	Professional Affiliations
Since 19xx	Widgetmakers of America (chairman 19xx–xx)

Date	Awards
19xx	Golden Widget (Widgetmakers of America)
19xx	Nowhere's Most Prominent Businessman (Nowhere Chamber of Commerce)

FAMILY MEMBERS

Father: *(family members, names and any historical information, including*
Mother: *date and place of birth, schools attended, marriage dates, occupations,*
Spouse: *relationships to NU, etc.)*
Children:
Siblings:
Other:

INDICATIONS OF WEALTH

Most Recent Salary/Family Income:

Alumni Questionnaire/Annual Income Survey: *(if available, latest reported income range from alumni surveys)*

Other: *(any other indications, such as articles about compensation, information from proxy statements, rules of thumb for professions, American Almanac of Jobs and Salaries)*

Current Stock Holdings, per Mr. Widget proxy filed 3/11/99:

Company (date of last transaction)—shares held—direct [D]/indirect[I] × close/open price [date] = Total

Widget Int'l—2,000[D] × $33.43 [12/14/00] = $66,860
Widget Int'l—1,000[I]

Per Thomson Financial

Guns and Butter Inc. (7/20/98)—1,000[D] × $75 [12/14/00] = $75,000

Other Stock Holdings:

Mr. and Mrs. Prospect reportedly own 95% of the capital stock of Mr. Widget Manufacturing.

—— **CONFIDENTIAL** ——
FOR INTERNAL USE ONLY

Other:

Information about net worth from magazines, value of real estate holdings, large gifts to other charities, family wealth of note, "interests of wealth" such as yachting, or other information pointing to significant wealth, such as kidnappings for ransom (I'm not making this up) etc.

GIVING ABILITY

Range

Annual: $*(usually from giving to date)*
Major (3–5 years): $ *(usually from 10% of income, 10–15% of stockholdings, 15% of real estate, other formulae)*
Ultimate: $(bequest, entire estate, if applicable)

Lifetime Giving (c 1988):

Peer ratings from 1988 program

Peer Ratings (c 1998):

Peer ratings from 1997–98 program

Development Ratings:

Ratings by Development staff

Rationale:

Explanation of the factors that went into the researchers' estimation of their giving ability ranges. For example, if a prospect has mentioned that they're very committed to his/her spouse's old school or charity, or that they didn't like giving to higher ed, but they might give to NU in a smaller amount; or if their business is in transition; basically, where the numbers come from.

SELECTED ACTIVE PLEDGES AND GIFTS TO THE UNIVERSITY

FILLED IN AS NECESSARY AND AVAILABLE, all other sections deleted

Selected Active Individual Pledges

Pledge Date	Amount	Purpose	Balance Due
	0		0
	0	$	0

—— **CONFIDENTIAL** ——
FOR INTERNAL USE ONLY

JOHN Q. PROSPECT
December 14, 2000
Page 5

Selected Individual Gifts

Total Amount	# of Gifts	FY	Purpose
$ 0	0		
$ 0	0		

Selected Active Corporation Pledges

Pledge Date	Amount	Purpose	Balance Due
	0		0

Selected Corporation Gifts

Total Amount	# of Gifts	FY	Purpose
$ 0	0		

Selected Active Foundation Pledges

Pledge Date	Amount	Purpose	Balance Due
	0		0

Selected Foundation Gifts

Total Amount	# of Gifts	FY	Purpose
$ 0	0		

Matching Gift Company Connections

Are they affiliated with a matching gift company, and if so, how much does the company match and at what ratio?

Total Contributions to NU:

John Q Prospect:	$	0
Jane Prospect:	$	0
J&J Prospect Fdn:	$	0
GRAND TOTAL	**$**	**0**

CURRENT AND SIGNIFICANT NU MEMBERSHIPS AND AWARDS

Date	Membership/Award
Since 19xx	John Evans Club
19xx	WCAS Visiting Committee

—— **CONFIDENTIAL** ——
FOR INTERNAL USE ONLY

JOHN Q. PROSPECT
December 14, 2000
Page 6

PERSONAL RELATIONSHIPS

Name	Tie
Joe Blue (L 'xx)	Executive vice president of Mr. Widget under Mr. Prospect
Jim Nobody (WCAS 'xx)	Mr. Prospect's roommate at NU
Jill Nobody (WCAS 'xx)	Mrs. Widget's roommate at Joe's Law School
Professor Science	NU Professor invited to make presentation on manufacturing processes at Mr. Widget

NU AREAS OF INTEREST

Athletics, Library, WCAS *(alphabetized, unless there's a clear priority of interests)*

DEVELOPMENT CONTACT

Most Recent 3 Years

- *Month, year—Development Staff Member did thus and so to contact Mr. Prospect, and learned thus and so information and had thus and so results*
- *Etc., etc.*

Other Previous Significant Contact

-

NOTES

Most Current Reunion Survey/Alumni Questionnaire Ratings

Mr. -[Survey/Questionnaire]:
    Ranked NU:
    Evaluated NU Education:
    Characterized Attitude About NU:
    Noted:

—— **CONFIDENTIAL** ——
FOR INTERNAL USE ONLY

Resource 4

JOHN Q. PROSPECT
December 14, 2000
Page 7

Mrs. -[Survey/Questionnaire]:
    Ranked NU:
    Evaluated NU Education:
    Characterized Attitude About NU:
    Noted:

Outside Interests

Sailing, racquetball. Mr. and Mrs. Prospect have also expressed an interest in attending every basket weaving conference in the country in their Winnebago. They also enjoy rehabbing homes. Mrs. Prospect is a self-described "health nut."

Research Analysis

A summary of salient points in this report, including information about wealth and attitudes toward NU and anything that might affect the prospect's giving and mindset about NU, what to expect. The place for narrative if something just doesn't fit into any of the above categories perfectly.

Researcher: *Who wrote this*
Requested by: *Who asked for it (Research, if proactive)*

CURRENT PROSPECT ASSIGNMENTS

All this is as reported in our prospect management system in BSR Advance

Primary Officer:
Secondary Officer:
PMG:
Other:

or:

******Not Currently Assigned******

PMG Territory Officer:

CURRENT PROSPECT STAGE:

COLORADO UNIVERSITY FOUNDATION

CUF RESEARCH CORPORATE PROFILE

—Confidential—

CORPORATE NAME: CID#:
Address:
Telephone: Fax:
E-mail Address:
Website Address:

CEO—Name and Title:

Business Description:

Financial Information:

Officers & Directors:

Corporate History:

Corporate Giving to CU:
Lifetime Giving:
Total Giving FY (present year) – all campuses:
Outstanding Pledges and Designations – all campuses:
Largest Gift and Designation:
Top 5 or 6 Total Giving Designations and Amounts:

Non-CU Philanthropic Interests:
Known Corporate Relationships with CU:
Alumni/Friends:
Departmental:
Development Staff:
Faculty:
Project:

Cultivation Highlights:

Recent Noteworthy Events:

FOUNDATION NAME: CID#:

Address:

Telephone: Fax:

E-mail Address:

Website Address:

Contact:

Purpose:

Limitations:

Foundation Type:

Interest and Support Areas:

Financial Data:

Officers & Directors:

Policies & Guidelines:

Foundation Giving to CU:

Known Relationships with CU:

Alumni/Friends:

Departmental:

Development Staff:

Faculty:

Project:

Cultivation Highlights:

Recent Noteworthy Events:

NAME: CID#:
CU Campus/Year/School or College/Major:
Home Address: Business Address:
Phone:
E-mail Address:

<u>Employment Information</u>:
Current:
Career History:

<u>Corporate Directorships</u>:
Current:
Previous:

<u>Non-Profit Affiliations</u>:

<u>CU Activities and Affiliations</u>:
As a student:
As an alumnus/non-alumnus:
Awards and honors:

<u>Cultivation Highlights</u>:

<u>Noteworthy Relationships</u>:

<u>Non-CU Philanthropic Interests</u>:

<u>Giving to CU</u>:
Lifetime giving total: Last Gift: Date:
Largest single gift/pledge:
Years of giving:
Areas of support/interest:

<u>Known Assets</u>:
Bonus: Source: Date:
Household income: Source: Date:
Property: Source: Date:
Salary: Source: Date:
Securities: Source: Date:
Stock Options: Source: Date:

<u>Known Liabilities</u>:

<u>Ratings</u>:
Campaign: Source: Date:
Lifetime: Source: Date:
Net Worth: Source: Date:
Peer: Source: Date:
PPR: Source: Date:
Readiness: Source: Date:
Real Estate: Source: Date:
Research: Source: Date:
Securities: Source: Date:
Staff: Source: Date:
Wealth Estimate: Source: Date:
(CDA Wealth Estimate is not considered reliable as a major gift rating.)

<u>Financial Summary</u>:

<u>Personal Information</u>:
Birthdate: Place:
Non-CU Education:
Family: Spouse
               Children
               Others
Interests/Hobbies:
Other:

<u>Comments/Recommendations/Miscellaneous</u>:

Resource 4

HOW TO CLOSE THE GIFT

How
to Close
the Gift

The
Endowment
Campaign
for
Indiana
University
Bloomington

THE ENDOWMENT CAMPAIGN FOR INDIANA UNIVERSITY BLOOMINGTON is a national and international fundraising effort being conducted into the year 2000. This campaign seeks to add at least $150 million to the campus's endowment and to augment annual giving by at least $200 million. The Endowment Campaign is the largest fundraising campaign for a single campus in the University's history. Since it includes all components of the Bloomington campus, gifts to the Endowment Campaign will enrich every aspect of teaching and learning at IU Bloomington.

Objectives

Each Endowment Campaign volunteer needs to meet three important objectives before beginning solicitation of major gifts:

1. Know the Six Basic Closing Stages.
2. Know How to Handle Objections.
3. Know the Major Errors to Avoid in Solicitation.

Six Basic Closing Stages

Here are the six stages necessary for soliciting and closing a major gift:

1. Opening
2. Questioning
3. Listening
4. Presenting
5. Overcoming Objections
6. Asking for the Gift

1. Opening

In any person-to-person encounter, the opening, to a large extent, will determine the outcome. It does not matter whether you are asking for a luncheon date, talking with a colleague, requesting something from an assistant, or soliciting a major gift, your opening will have a definite effect on the outcome of the conversation.

One of the primary goals you are trying to accomplish in the opening is to light a fire under your prospect. It is critical that you involve the prospect in what you are saying. One of the most effective ways to do this is to talk about the prospect's favorite subject—himself or herself.

Try to get the prospect to talk about himself or herself as soon as possible. Be warm and friendly, carry a smile, and give compliments as honestly as possible, whenever possible. Remember to be as specific and sincere as you can be. Keep in mind that you never talk *to* a prospect, but rather you talk *with* him or her. Ask for responses, listen closely, and reinforce positive statements. By drawing a prospect out, you have a better chance of bringing him or her into a meaningful relationship with IU Bloomington.

The key here, as always, is involvement. Always speak from the prospect's point of view; always ask for reactions; above all, talk about his or her accomplishments. This is true whether you are dealing with an individual major donor, a foundation, or a corporation. Foundations and corporations are people. People make decisions. People carry your proposal to other people.

Make your opening as dynamic and intriguing as you possibly can.

2. Questioning

If you have done a good job of getting the prospect's attention in the opening, your task now is to keep that attention and deepen his or her involvement. That can be easily accomplished through questioning.

Questions are wonderful things. They allow you to talk *with* the prospect rather than *to* the prospect. Questions automatically force the prospect into involvement. Good questions fall into a number of categories—questions that call for a feeling response, fact-finding questions that verify your research, or challenging and new questions that help uncover your prospect's motivations and needs.

Be careful not to ask questions that require a yes or no answer. This type of question will give you little information. Ask open-ended questions. Do not ask questions like, "Do you think we need more research in the area of human attitudes and values?" but rather, "How do you think we could improve research in human attitudes and values?"

Oftentimes, you can draw a prospect out by making a statement you have heard from a respected third party, then following that by a question like, "How do you feel about this?" Try to emphasize needs and problems as much as possible.

The biggest mistake you can make at this point is to begin talking about the Campaign. During the questioning stage, it is very important that you make sure the prospect is aware of the needs of Indiana University Bloomington before you show him or her how those needs may be met.

3. Listening

Listening is probably the most difficult skill to master; however, if you are going to take advantage of all the questions you ask, you will have to do more listening and less talking. That is not easy. The only way a prospect will invest in your solution is if the prospect thinks you have understood his or her position.

A good listener is a participant who understands communication is both an active and selective process. Most people speak at the rate of 100 to 150 words per minute. You are capable of perceiving approximately 400 words per minute.

This gives you a lead time of between 250 and 300 words. You can use this lead time to evaluate what your prospect is saying—anticipating the points he or she will make, judging what has already been said, and judging the importance of each word and each statement.

The technique of listening ahead gives you an opportunity to be discerning in your listening process. Listen with a purpose. Do not interpret. Ask questions and give feedback to your prospect so that he or she knows you are hearing what is being said. You will notice that as you give feedback, your prospects will have a tendency to reinforce the topics that are most important to him or her.

Be empathic in your listening. Put yourself in your prospect's position. By doing this, you will build respect and therefore have a better chance to achieve your desired results.

Listen with your whole body, not just your ears. Lean forward into the conversation. Listen with your eyes as well; you can pick up a lot of information by watching the body language of your prospect. Your own body language and responses will show your prospect that you are alert and interested in what he or she has to say. Use phrases such as, "Let me be sure I have understood what you said" and "Let me see, do I understand this correctly?" These kinds of questions give evidence that you are listening; they encourage the prospect to listen more actively to what you are saying; they help build a common ground between you and your prospect.

Good listening, then, involves your active and meaningful participation. Your feedback to the prospect's responses helps you to qualify and understand his or her position. Probably the most important benefit of active listening is that it makes the prospect feel good about himself or herself. It makes the prospect feel that he or she has something important to say, and that you are listening intently to what is being said.

Developing good listening skills can help you become a more effective solicitor.

4. Presenting

This particular skill may seem like the easiest part of your solicitation effort; however, you must be careful not to fall into the common trap of over-simplification. The natural tendency is to emphasize Indiana University Bloomington and its needs, rather than the benefits IU Bloomington can bring to the prospect's needs. Basically, prospects want four questions answered about the University or a specific program:

1. Is it the best?
2. Will it perform the way you say it will?
3. Will it become or remain the best in the future?
4. How will I be paid back for my investment?

Knowing that your prospect wants these questions answered, you can construct your presentation to answer these questions before they are asked. One of the best ways to do this is to talk about benefits and advantages rather than about the Campaign and its needs.

When discussing the Campaign, always try to use dialogue with the prospect:

- Use people stories.
- Make your language vivid and descriptive.
- Make the benefits for donors seem real enough to touch.

Remember Bell Telephone's marvelous slogan, "Reach out and touch someone." It sells the company's benefits rather than the features of the service. Emphasizing the Campaign's benefits rather than focusing on specific features is what you are trying to do with your prospect. Your objective is to show real people solving real problems through IU Bloomington.

5. Overcoming Objections

Most of us become uncomfortable when objections are raised. Remembering that an objection is not an attack, but rather a question, will help you overcome this discomfort.

When answering an objection, always show understanding of your prospect's position. Try to gain your prospect's respect by making statements such as, "I see your point of view" or "I can understand why you would have that concern." Take the objection and turn it into a positive statement such as "Myles Brand, IU's president, feels the same way you do about this particular problem. He has talked to the administration about it and the administration has come up with a number of ideas to overcome this problem."

The main point is to let the prospect know his or her objection is acceptable, that others feel the same way, and that this type of question has helped us find constructive solutions to other problems. You can even turn the objection into the very reason the prospect should support the Campaign.

Never let the objection lead into an argument. Do not make the objection bigger than it is. Respond to it with facts and never make excuses. If the objection is weak, however, pass over it. Ignore it and move on with your proposal. It is perfectly legitimate to compromise on minor objections if, in fact, they will not be a hindrance to reaching your primary goal.

Remember that all objections are really questions, and that the prospect's investment in the Campaign will help overcome the cause of the objection. This will help you to convert the objections into reasons for giving.

6. Asking for the Gift

This skill is commonly called "the closing." After you have dealt with all the prospect's questions and concerns, it is time to ask for the gift. Most failure in a face-to-face solicitation is a result of not asking for the gift.

It is important that you know how and when to ask. If you have mastered the five previous skills, you will be able to observe when your prospect is ready for you to ask.

Always give the prospect alternatives. Never ask for a yes or no answer. Keep in mind that many prospects will say no two or three times before they say yes.

It is common practice to ask for a larger gift than is expected. This gives you a stronger negotiating position, and in most cases it helps get the gift needed. The prospect knows that this is no ordinary meeting, but that you are there to discuss serious concerns that interest both him or her and the University.

Mastering these six skills will give you a much better chance of closing major gifts for the Endowment Campaign for IU Bloomington.

Handling Objections & Closing Techniques for Major Gifts

1. Assume you already have the gift.

Do not ask for the gift; act as if you already have it.

2. Tell a story.

Use a story you have heard about another prospect who had a similar objection. The prospect in the story should overcome his or her objection and make a major gift to IU Bloomington, a specific program, or an academic unit. Always use the prospect's name in your story. Remember to make the story entertaining.

3. Reverse the question.

Have the prospect ask you a yes or no question, and then reverse it into a question that you ask. For example:

Prospect: "Will the building be named after me?"
 Solicitor: "Would you like your name on the donor plaque?"
Prospect: "If I can afford the gift to get it there. . . ."

4. Close on the major objection.

Use this technique when a prospect offers objection after objection.

    a. Hear out each objection completely.
    b. Restate and put greater emphasis on the major objection.
    c. Ask the prospect if he or she would donate, were it not for the objection.
    d. If no, deal with other minor objections in turn.
    e. If yes, work through the last objection and close.

5. Last resort.

If all else fails, you may want to try the last resort.

Solicitor: "Mr. Stockwealth, I believe Indiana University has a number of great programs, strong leadership, and real vision. All it needs to continue being one of the country's great universities is more support for its faculty and student endowments. Is there anything I did wrong that kept you from making a gift?"

Prospect: (Will bring up an objection.)

Solicitor: "Of course, I should have thought of that! Thank you for being so honest with me and clarifying your feelings. I do not know how I forgot to clear that up for you."

Then deal with the objection and close.

6. Reconsider.

As you start to leave, ask the prospect, "Won't you reconsider?"

Overcoming Obstacles

You may run into a number of problems in your solicitation presentation that will keep you from closing. Here are a few suggestions to help you overcome these obstacles:

Problem #1

Prospect says, "I have to talk to my spouse."

Strategy

a. Ask, "May we both meet with him/her?"
b. Hypothesize, "Just suppose he/she agreed."
c. Ask, "Are there any other questions to which you think he/she will want the answer?"
d. Do your research—be sure to speak with both spouses on the first visit.
e. Get the spouse involved in the Campaign before you visit.

Problem #2

Prospect imposes a time limit on the meeting.

Strategy

a. Condense your presentation.
b. Ask, "Is this the only time we will be able to spend together?"
c. Ask, "How long do you think this will take?"
d. Continue with the presentation.
e. Set new agenda and proceed.
f. Reschedule the meeting for a more convenient time.

Problem #3

Prospect offers a gift that is too small.

Strategy

a. Say, "Our expectations are greater."
b. Suggest the offered gift as first payment on a larger one.
c. Check the prospect's financial position.
d. Apologize for misleading him or her about the amount you need.
e. Take the smaller gift and upgrade later.
f. Say, "If you could make four or five gifts this size, look what we could do!"
g. Say, "Before I can accept this gift, I have to check with my Campaign chair."

Problem #4

Prospect is a non-talker or silent.

Strategy

a. Ask questions.
b. Use gestures to put the prospect at ease.
c. Look and act interested when prospect does talk, and then ask more questions.

d. Do not let the silence rest on you.

e. Get another volunteer to play devil's advocate to stimulate the conversation.

f. Go golfing, fishing, etc. with the prospect, a situation in which it is not necessary to have a lengthy conversation.

g. Ask a good friend of the prospect to volunteer information about the prospect. Ask questions the friend knows the prospect is thinking about.

h. Go into your presentation.

Problem #5

Prospect is aggressive or talkative.

Strategy

a. Let him or her talk until he or she runs down.

b. Hang tough.

c. Use a high status volunteer to counter lower status person references.

d. Do not press. Set up another meeting.

e. Ask questions to change the focus of the conversation.

f. Ask why he or she came to the meeting.

g. Look for a bridge to your presentation.

h. Ask to meet with prospect's spouse.

i. Playback.

Problem #6

Lack of coordination among team members.

Strategy

a. Clarify roles in advance.

b. Set an agenda of questions.

c. Match complementary personalities and styles.

d. Role-play and practice in advance.

e. Be flexible.

f. Work out signals.

Major Errors to Avoid in Solicitation

In your presentation, be sure to avoid the 14 critical errors that commonly occur when soliciting major gifts.

1. Not asking for the gift.
2. Not asking for a large enough gift.
3. Not listening/Talking too much.

  4. Not asking questions.
  5. Not talking about benefits to the prospect.
  6. Not being flexible/Not presenting alternatives.
  7. Not knowing enough about the prospect before the solicitation.
  8. Forgetting to summarize before moving to solicitation.
  9. Not practicing with team members before solicitation.
 10. Asking for the gift too soon.
 11. Speaking, rather than remaining silent, after asking for the gift.
 12. Settling on too small a gift.
 13. Not cultivating the prospect before soliciting.
 14. Not sending out trained solicitors.

The Indiana University Foundation is designated by the trustees of Indiana University as the official fundraising agency for the University. A not-for-profit corporation chartered in 1936 under the laws of the State of Indiana, the Foundation raises and receives gifts from the private sector, administers funds, and manages assets to enhance the quality of education at Indiana University.

Resource 5

RESOURCE 6

LETTER PROPOSAL

Date

Name
Title
Company
Address
City, State, ZIP Code

Dear _____:

We respectfully invite you to consider a gift to The University of Texas–Houston Health Science Center to support the important work of Dr. K. Lance Gould's P.E.T. (Positron Emission Tomography) Center for Preventing and Reversing Atherosclerosis.

Cardiovascular disease claims more lives than any other illness in America today.

Most victims of heart disease never know that their heart's blood vessels are silently closing, choked by cholesterol accumulating in artery walls. A few experience early warning symptoms that prompt them to seek help, but for many of the million Americans who develop cardiovascular disease each year the first symptom is a catastrophic heart attack. Those fortunate to survive or who have warning symptoms receive limited benefit from traditional therapies, which may relieve symptoms but have little effect on extending life or improving the relentless course of the disease.

Few people with cardiovascular disease have a second chance.

Some have found their way to a new approach for identifying and reversing heart disease at the P.E.T. (Positron Emission Tomography) Center for Preventing and Reversing Atherosclerosis developed by Dr. K. Lance Gould at The University of Texas–Houston Health Science Center.

The initial path to Dr. Gould was circuitous—P.E.T. coexists outside of traditional invasive procedures, and it is not yet reimbursed by many insurance companies. Those who come to see Dr. Gould are worried about their heart or health and intrigued by the knowledge that here was someone who could show them in a picture the condition of their heart and a program to preserve its health.

In short, many people know the anxiety leading to Dr. Gould and the profound relief that his program offers. Now we ask that you help in making this relief and program available to others.

An Enormous Opportunity: The Weatherhead Challenge

The work of Dr. K. Lance Gould so impressed Al and Celia Weatherhead, patients from Cleveland, Ohio, that they have made the P.E.T. Center a very generous gift and a challenge. The Weatherheads have given $3 million and pledged another $1 million, provided we raise $3 million by December 31, 1999. Last month, we met that challenge. The Weatherheads were so excited that they immediately pledged another $1.5 million provided you and others will contribute $1.5 million by December 31, 1999, in order to expand the program into the mainstream of medicine as the only documented way of preventing heart attacks and prolonging quality, productive life. To date, we have only $720,000 remaining to raise to meet the second challenge, which when met will provide Dr. Gould a total of $10 million. A gift from you at this time will bring us closer to meeting our goal.

The aim of this expansion is to make P.E.T. and reversal treatment widely accessible to women and men throughout the nation. However, at the same time the Center must expand its research program, refine the P.E.T. technology, train more doctors and nurses, and use computers to link Dr. Gould with the nation's other P.E.T. centers and their patients, creating a "virtual center" for the collection and sharing of new knowledge.

Far too many Americans know what it's like to be told they have coronary heart disease, and far too many die of sudden heart attack without showing warning symptoms. Through Dr. Gould, many have learned that they can prevent or halt the damage and return to robust health—free from fear of heart attack, stroke, or sudden death.

Dr. Gould has invested twenty-nine years in developing P.E.T. technology for the heart, the reversal program, and the knowledge that has helped many. Now you have an opportunity to help provide others a second chance for life by your generous financial support of the P.E.T. Center—support that will trigger the additional $1.5 million donation. By giving to the P.E.T. Center for Preventing and Reversing Atherosclerosis you will help change the course of cardiovascular medicine. I believe such an opportunity comes but "once in a lifetime."

We are deeply grateful for your thoughtful consideration of this request to help us meet the second Weatherhead Challenge by contributing to UT-Houston's P.E.T. Center. Gifts to support the Weatherhead Challenge may be paid in a lump sum or pledged over a five-year period. Please call me at (713) 500-3000 or Tripp Carter at (713) 500-3220 if we can answer any questions for you. Thank you.

Sincerely,

M. David Low, M.D., Ph.D.

Enclosures

RESOURCE 7

FULL PROPOSAL

Date

Name
Title
Company
Address
City, State, ZIP Code

Dear _____:

At the request of our good and mutual friend, _____ , I respectfully invite _____ to consider a leadership gift of $_____ to The University of Texas–Houston Health Science Center for a new *Nursing and Biomedical Sciences Building.* This facility will be a permanent home for our School of Nursing and will also house new classrooms, laboratory facilities, and auditoriums and conference areas available to all students in the Health Science Center.

This building has been a priority and a dream of this institution since long before my arrival in 1989. With the endorsement of The University of Texas system and generous funding commitments, we are now initiating a campaign that is fundamental to the future growth and success of UT-Houston and, when completed, will put in place a building that will become the heart of our campus and a central setting for students, faculty, and Houstonians to gather.

As is fitting for a new millennium, we will build a structure that will equip the School of Nursing to stand shoulder-to-shoulder with our nation's most admired institutions—a structure that reflects and reinforces its uses and occupants. Multilevel glass walls overlooking Grant Fay Park, one of the rare green spaces remaining in the Texas Medical Center, give the building warmth and an open and spacious feel. Students will prepare for real-life situations by practicing and perfecting their skills in virtual reality skill labs. Computer terminals located throughout the facility will allow students collaborating on research projects to instantly connect to UT-Houston's computer network. Our students' patient care skills and technical expertise will be enhanced because we are designing these features into the building's core.

As you can see, we are demanding a great deal from this new building, and we have invested an enormous amount of planning into it. If you and other trustees of the Foundation would like to learn more about the building and our School of Nursing, please let me know. I would enjoy meeting with you to go over our plans in greater detail and respond to your questions.

At the end of January, we received news that has given this campaign a tremendous start. Houston Endowment Inc., a generous and long-standing benefactor of UT-Houston, initiated the campaign with a gift of $3.6 million. This wonderful news augurs well for our efforts in the coming months, and those efforts would be immeasurably enhanced were our request to engender the gracious support of the Foundation.

We are deeply grateful for your generosity over the years and for your thoughtful consideration of this request. Please call me at (713) 500-3000 or Dr. William Taylor at (713) 500-3200 if we can answer any questions for you. Thank you.

Sincerely,

M. David Low, M.D., Ph.D.

Enclosures

A PROPOSAL
FOR THE CONSTRUCTION OF
THE NURSING AND
BIOMEDICAL SCIENCES BUILDING
AT THE UNIVERSITY OF TEXAS–HOUSTON
HEALTH SCIENCE CENTER

EXECUTIVE SUMMARY

FROM: The University of Texas–Houston Health Science Center
               P.O. Box 20036
               Houston, TX 77225-0036

CONTACT: M. David Low, M.D., Ph.D., President, (713) 500-3000
               William L. Taylor, Ph.D., Vice President, Development, (713) 500-3200
               Rodney H. Margolis, Chair, Development Board, (713) 625-3570
               Robert Cizik, Chair, Steering Committee, (713) 222-7300

PROJECT: Construction of a Nursing and Biomedical Sciences Building
               220,000 gross square feet

PURPOSE: To provide a home for the UT-Houston School of Nursing and for the
               School of Allied Health Sciences, a center for student activities, and a
               university center for faculty and community gatherings

SITE: Adjoining Grant Fay Park in the Texas Medical Center, on Holcombe
               Boulevard, adjacent to the UT-Houston School of Public Health

TOTAL PROJECT COST: $60 million

TOTAL COMMITTED: $50 million

FUNDRAISING GOAL: $10 million

THE UNIVERSITY OF TEXAS–HOUSTON
HEALTH SCIENCE CENTER
THE NURSING AND
BIOMEDICAL SCIENCES BUILDING

Introduction

Those who have carefully observed The University of Texas–Houston from its founding 25 years ago know that in the last 10 years the University has come into its own. Its teaching and research enjoy national stature; UT-Houston plays a pre-eminent role in the depth of its commitment to the underserved of our community; its professional and graduate students are among the nation's best and go on to important careers of service and accomplishment; and the University is beginning to be justly known for its leadership role in forging new models of health care education and delivery, so needed in the coming decades. Most of all, those observers note a flowering of purpose and self-confidence that marks an institution that has come of age.

As a critical part of the next 25 years, UT-Houston plans to construct a keystone building to complete its campus, providing a home for its superb nursing school, a base for a pioneering program in allied health, a university center for its students, and a welcoming front door to the Houston community.

We plan to build a Nursing and Biomedical Sciences Building next to Grant Fay Park, one of the last remaining natural spots in the Texas Medical Center. This building will be home to the School of Nursing and the School of Allied Health Sciences and will serve as an important student and faculty campus center. The building, along with the School of Public Health, which also faces the park, will form two sides of a "UT-Houston Quadrangle." Together, both buildings will complete the campus begun a quarter-century ago and celebrate the emergence of UT-Houston, which in its dedication to quality and progressive approaches to health care will continue to be a leader for many quarter-centuries to come.

The cost of the Nursing and Biomedical Sciences Building project is $60 million. A broad coalition of UT-Houston students, the State Legislature, and the University have committed $50 million to the project. It is our profound hope that Houston's philanthropic community will join this coalition by providing the final $10 million needed to complete this project.

A New Home

The UT-Houston School of Nursing

The new building will be the first permanent home for the UT-Houston School of Nursing, a school that has been on a fast trajectory. Far different from the fledgling undergraduate school its first students found 25 years ago, today the School is an important national presence focusing on master's and doctoral level training. With over 600 students and 80 faculty, it is recognized as one of the top nursing schools in the nation and is resolved to reach top ten stature. It is committed to educating the graduate-trained nurses and nurse-educators who define and lead the profession, provide the highly specialized care required today, and train coming generations of nurses to the highest standards.

- Last year *U.S. News and World Report* ranked the UT-Houston School as one of the top 40 nursing schools in the nation (in Texas, only UT-Austin's School of Nursing also ranked).
- From 1995 to 1996 the School advanced from 66th to 32nd position in the total number of dollars awarded by the NIH to schools of nursing, tying with Columbia University, Emory University, the University of Florida, and the University of Virginia. This represents an increase from $85,000 to $494,000. The School's five-year goal is to exceed $4 million in NIH support.
- Admission to the School's student body, 95% from Harris County and Texas, is highly competitive; 30% are minority students and 15% are males (a high percentage for nursing schools). Graduates perform very well on licensing exams, averaging in the 95%–100% range, and in national certification exams.
- With a strong graduate orientation, the School offers the Doctor of Science in Nursing degree, the only clinical doctoral nursing program in Texas. The School offers the only Oncology Nursing Program in Texas and the only Emergency Nurse Practitioner Program in the country.

- The School has one of the finest nurse practitioner programs in the nation, pro-ducing master's degree nurses who work with physicians to diagnose, pre-scribe, and treat patients in family practice, critical care, emergency, cancer, aging, and many other clinical areas.

For all of these achievements, however, this fine school is at a crossroads: if it is to reach its goal of becoming one of the top ten nursing schools in the nation, it must now move to its next challenge—building a facility to buttress the School's pursuit of excellence. In its 25-year history it has established a national reputation for academic excellence, attracted some of the nation's finest teachers and stu-dents, and developed a first-rate graduate nursing program.

Our faculty and students have accomplished this remarkable growth in qual-ity, even as they have learned to adapt and remodel, improvise and borrow in cramped, inadequate space. Since 1974 the School has leased space in a building designed for insurance offices, almost 50 years old, never intended for teaching and learning, and with structural and systems problems costing $80 million or more to fix. Its deteriorating condition has forced its owner, the M. D. Anderson Cancer Center, to plan to mothball or demolish the structure by 2002. The School of Nursing needs a new home.

Making an old office building work for academic purposes for over 20 years is a tribute to our nursing students' and faculty's determination to succeed. But now it is time to move beyond these years of paint, partitions, and patience into a new building expressly designed to meet educational and University needs. This graduate nursing school needs a facility with the technological infrastructure crit-ical to advanced nursing educational programs: state-of-the-art virtual reality and interactive technology, multimedia and distance learning capa-bilities, fiber-optic cabling, and easily accessed, comprehensively networked communications.

The UT-Houston School of Allied Health Sciences

The new building will also be the home of the School of Allied Health Sciences and the site of its state-of-the-art Computer Laboratory for Health Informatics. For many of us, personal medical records are spread across many caregivers—the many physicians, HMOs, hospitals, and consulting specialists we have seen. Health informatics, a specialized form of information science, seeks to devise computer-based systems to ensure that these vital facts are available precisely when and where they are needed. The School of Allied Health Sciences is a pioneer in this emerging field. Its advanced degrees and continuing education programs will enable future generations of health professionals to provide better and more efficient care.

Students from many disciplines at UT-Houston—dentistry, medicine, biomedical science, nursing, and public health—will use the facilities of the flagship Informatics Computer Laboratory to learn and develop new ways of storing, organizing, and reporting medical information. Streamlined data will be recorded and sorted in a giant electronic "filing cabinet." The goal is a system that is simple to use yet incorporates "smart" technology to search, sort, and format information— and can also act as a decision support tool. With capabilities such as this in the physician's office, the emergency room, the ICU, and at the patient's bedside, we will help meet one of the greatest needs in health care today.

The School of Allied Health Sciences will offer advanced degrees in health informatics. As the only institution in Texas to offer these programs, and the only institution in the nation to adopt a completely interdisciplinary approach to the teaching of health informatics, UT-Houston is poised to enter the 21st century in the vanguard of the field.

The new building, with its built-in networking and communications infrastructure, is an ideal base for this pioneering educational program. Intrinsically practical, the courses involve cooperation and collaboration with many of Houston's leading institutions, including Rice University, Baylor College of Medicine, The University of Houston, and branches of Texas A&M, Texas Women's University, and Prairie View A&M. The accessibility and visibility accorded the School of Allied Health Sciences within the new building will help secure its future as a center of excellence in a discipline that promises to greatly benefit patients and practitioners.

A Student and University Center

In addition to providing a home for the School of Nursing and the School of Allied Health Sciences, the new building will fill a long-felt need at UT-Houston for a central gathering place for students, faculty, and community friends. Although it is the largest and most comprehensive academic health science center in Texas, UT-Houston has never had a place where students can have a "home," with student government and other student organization offices; the registrar's, financial aid and student counseling offices; student lounges; and dining areas. Faculty, too, feel the need for a place where they can meet colleagues from all the University's six schools both individually and in committee and other faculty gatherings. The Nursing and Biomedical Sciences Building will also fill a critical role as a meeting place between UT-Houston and the University, providing areas for dining, conferences, receptions, and lectures.

The Nursing and Biomedical Sciences Building

An International Design Concept Competition

We did not decide lightly to undertake a project of this magnitude. For the past three years the University has worked hard to develop comprehensive plans for the building. Hundreds of students and faculty members have been involved in the process, which climaxed in a professionally juried, international architectural competition, led by the Dean of the UT-Austin Architecture School. In early 1997 the design concept by Patkau Architects, of Vancouver, Canada, was selected as the winner from submissions from Canada, Mexico, and the United States.

The winning design concept is flexible and will gracefully serve students and faculty for many years to come. It is innovative and responds to our challenge to the architects to design a facility that will meet today's needs with the built-in flexibility to adapt to future space and technology requirements. One of the building's most striking elements is the openness with which it embraces Grant Fay Park—large multilevel glass-walled atrium spaces, staircases, and promenades overlook the park and open onto it through decks, patios, and bridgeways. The building will be spacious but at the same time will encourage the kind of intimate, professional meetings so critical to a graduate-level environment.

A key aspect of the building will be its reliance on "green architecture," using a variety of means to reduce operating costs through passive structural and engineering features—solar panels, natural ventilation and lighting, natural construction materials, natural water conservation and reuse (both within the building and for park irrigation), and respect for the adjoining parkland in both design and construction processes.

The Building

There are certain core elements of academic buildings, and these will be present—classrooms of varying sizes and configurations, a 300-seat auditorium, deans' and faculty offices, conference and tutorial rooms, and teaching laboratories. Throughout the building there will be a major investment in state-of-the-art technology. From virtually any place in the building students and faculty will use fiber-optic cabling to "plug in" to the computer and telecommunications network—from faculty offices, study areas, graduate student carrels, student lounges, classrooms, even hallways.

Faculty will use technology built into the core of the building to facilitate their own research and their students' learning, with the ability for instant Internet communication with scholars across the globe. Classrooms and conference rooms will have immediate access to all the media technologies that advance teaching and learning. Nursing and medical school students will learn and practice their bedside skills through virtual reality skills labs with specially programmed patient dummies. Students will have individualized learning on-line with their faculty and counselors via e-mail and the Internet, as new technology allows an ever more individualized and immediate learning experience.

The student services aspects of the building will include student government and other organization offices, the registrar's and financial aid offices, student lounges, and dining areas. There will also be a penthouse-level dining, conference, and reception area overlooking the park, filling a critical need at UT-Houston for a commons area for faculty gatherings and University functions.

The Site

This site for the Nursing and Biomedical Sciences Building offers significant advantages. It forms the western side of Grant Fay Park on Holcombe Boulevard, a lovely ravine garden filled with shade trees and green spaces, an ideal setting for students, and a rare spot of green in the congestion of the Texas Medical Center. In addition, because the site includes the School of Public Health, the two buildings will complete two sides of a "UT quadrangle" around the park. This new quadrangle will be home to three UT-Houston schools (Nursing, Public Health, and the School of Allied Health Sciences) and will be the focus of many of the University's student activities and programming. Over 1,400 students in these three schools will have immediate access to the student facilities, along with more than 400 pursuing studies through UT-Houston's Graduate School of Biomedical Sciences, which is relocating to a nearby building. An additional 860 medical and dental students, although more distant, will use the new building for some of their student activities and will take academic course work in its classroom facilities.

Funding

Funding for the Nursing and Biomedical Sciences Building will come from a broad base of public and private sources, including a commitment from our students for one-third of the costs. This partnership demonstrates the unity of resolve and purpose at all levels to construct a building that serves so many important purposes for the City of Houston, the State of Texas, and The University of Texas–Houston.

Recognizing the importance of the Nursing and Biomedical Sciences Building to the academic program, and most especially to creating a better sense of community and campus for future students, UT-Houston's students have agreed

SITE PLAN.

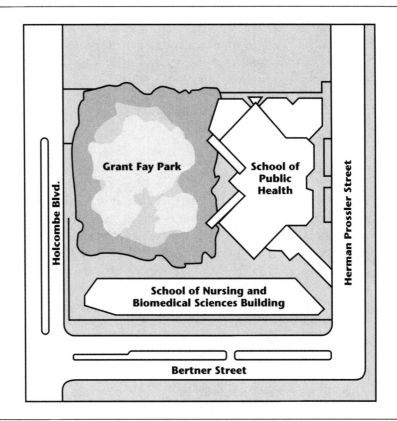

SOURCES OF FUNDING FOR THE NURSING AND BIOMEDICAL SCIENCES BUILDING.

Source	Amount	Percentage of Total	Status
Students of UT-Houston	$20.0 million	33%	Committed
Texas State Legislature	17.5 million	29%	Committed
UT-Houston	12.5 million	21%	Committed
Private philanthropy	10.0 million	16%	To be raised
Total	$60.0 million	100%[a]	

[a]Percentages do not add to 100 due to rounding.

to a substantial increase in their general use fee that will service bonding for $20 million of the construction costs.

The 75th Session of the Texas State Legislature approved the expenditure of $17.5 million bond servicing for construction of the building. An important element in legislative support of our request was our plan to secure a portion of the total cost from the private community.

UT-Houston has identified, through energy cost savings, attrition, lease revenue, and other resources, funds to service bonding for $12.5 million.

Conclusion

When we call for help in a hospital room late at night, the one who answers is a nurse. Nurses are most often the ones who attend to our needs and are often as important as the physician in restoring us to health and comfort. Less well appreciated are the increasing responsibilities that nurses are assuming in health care today. Fulfilling front-line duties previously reserved for physicians, bringing to bear very specialized knowledge in disease areas, performing important research in patient care and management, moving into very responsible positions in hospital administration—these are new and important roles for nurses, and it is imperative that they be well educated and trained. UT-Houston's School of Nursing is a leader in providing this training, and in its new home it will have the resources to better serve the Houston community.

All students at the University learn best in an environment that supports and encourages them in their lives as students—providing opportunities for talk and reflection, study and play that are so critical in students' lives and to their academic and professional success. This new building will, for the first time, address these needs in a focused way, providing a campus center for students, faculty, and staff alike and a welcoming front door to the Houston community. We believe that the building is fundamental to the future growth and success of The University of Texas–Houston, and we invite and earnestly hope for the generous support of UT-Houston's friends and supporters in making this new center possible.

NURSING AND BIOMEDICAL SCIENCES
BUILDING PROJECT: FACTS.

Sponsor: University of Texas–Houston Health Science Center

Architects: Patkau Architects, Vancouver, British Columbia, Canada

Site: Holcombe Boulevard at Bertner Street, Houston, Texas

Size: 220,000 gross square feet; 12 floors

BUDGET (in millions of dollars)

Necessary Relocation		
Human Genetics Center		
(to the Institute of Molecular Medicine)	3.50	
Graduate School Administration		
(during construction)	0.10	
Subtotal		3.60
Site clearing, asbestos abatement		2.00
New Facility		
Construction (includes contingency)	42.30	
Furnishings, fittings, and equipment	2.90	
Audiovisual equipment	5.30	
Computer equipment	3.00	
Equipment contingency	1.12	
Professional fees	0.09	
Subtotal		54.71
Total Project Budget		$60.31

Resource 7

WILLS SEMINAR PROGRAM SYSTEM

| A System for
Conducting a
Successful
Wills Seminar

By Nancy Perazelli, CFRE and Chuck Roth

7003 Oak Brook Drive
Des Moines, Iowa 50322-4838
(515) 276-9222

Foreword

In almost no other profession is successfully achieving a goal more important than in fundraising. It is through fundraising that your organization augments its ability to deliver needed services and to support relevant programs. As a fundraising executive you provide the bread and butter from which the rest of your organization derives sustenance. Without an effective development program, many good ideas, projects or services would never become reality.

The purpose of this manual is to share our knowledge, gleaned from hard experience, with you. Many fundraising professionals know firsthand the advantages of conducting a *wills seminar.* This manual describes what works and what does not and how you can get started.

As you read through these pages, you will receive a step-by-step approach to setting up and conducting a wills seminar. This means everything from planning the agenda, to identifying the prospective attendees, to working with an attorney or speaker, to writing thank-you letters to appropriate contacts, and conducting individual follow-up as necessary.

Once you have finished reading "A System for Conducting a Successful Wills Seminar," you will have the tools and information you need to start your own program. You may use this manual to accomplish your goals

> . . . if you have already tried to convince prospects to leave a bequest to your organization but were not pleased with the results you got;

> . . . if you know it can work but need the facts and a plan of action to share with your board to motivate them to move forward;

> . . . if you want to get a program started but never before had the time to compile the research necessary to learn how to go about it;

> . . . if you think it sounds like a worthwhile idea but don't know where to begin.

Good luck and best wishes for many future bequest dollars!

Table of Contents

Why Offer a Wills Seminar?

An excellent way to achieve the goals of your organization is to effectively fulfill the needs of your public. This method works particularly well when, as is the case with wills seminars, you can provide a service that may not be available from any other source. There are good reasons why wills seminars may help your organization.

Reason 1: Wills Seminars Can Help Your Organization Earn the Additional Dollars It Needs to Fund Current Programs

Organizations that engage in fundraising do so because they need resources to carry out their mission. The fundraising professional must continuously formulate new and creative ways to help people give.

Helping your organization find new funding sources is one strong reason to begin a wills seminar program. Contacts made at these seminars can lead to significant current gifts. The seminar provides a nonthreatening setting in which to get better acquainted with donors and prospects.

Reason 2: As a Key Component of the Gift Planning Program, Wills Seminars Assist Your Organization's Long-Range Planning by Providing a New Source of Income

With the increased emphasis on long-term, strategic planning, an organization relies on knowing about funding sources. A bequest awareness program, including periodic wills seminars, can help your organization cultivate prospects for long-range giving, which can in time account for a fourth, a third, and even a half of total dollars given. Recent reports concerning educational, health care, and religious fundraising make a strong case for encouraging bequests and planned gifts as part of a comprehensive long-range fundraising plan.

Reason 3: Wills Seminars Are a Means to Attract the Number Two Source of Charitable Contributions—Bequests

Many novices to the fundraising profession leap to the faulty conclusion that corporate and foundation America hold the key to a treasure house of giving. The reality is that only 5 percent of all charitable gifts generally come from corporations and foundations. Roughly an equal amount of all philanthropic giving comes from bequests. Gifts from living individuals continue to be the number one source of all charitable giving. Charitable bequests have continued to be an overlooked source of gift development for charitable organizations, despite their overall significance in charitable giving America.

Reason 4: Since a Vast Majority of American Adults Die Without the Benefit of a Will, Wills Seminars Can Fulfill a Real Service to Your Donors and Their Families

As average Americans, we work 80,000 hours in a lifetime. During this period, we accumulate 45 to 55 years of work. In spite of all the resources and assets that we collect in the process, the vast majority of us do not take the time to make a will.

National statistics indicate that 80 percent of Americans die without leaving a will.* Members of the legal profession cite several reasons for this. They speculate that people have a fear of death, they procrastinate, or they are misinformed and presume only the rich need to have wills. Whatever the excuse, it is clear that people would benefit from having a greater understanding of the importance of having their own wills.

By conducting wills seminars, you also provide a public service by informing potential donors about the benefits of bequests. Through the seminar you can explain that

- A will enables attendees to distribute their assets by their plan, not the state's;
- Attendees can retain all rights to their gifts until they die;
- Attendees can choose to make a gift to further the work of the charity that was meaningful to them during life.

Reason 5: Wills Seminars Are a Positive Way to Ensure That People Understand the Importance of Having a Will and the Need to Specify Their Charitable Bequest in That Document

In the absence of a will or other legal arrangements to distribute property at death, the state, out of necessity, must step in to administer the estate. The result can be lengthy delays before the rightful heirs receive their property. And because the state does not have any instructions from the deceased, it also means that no charitable gifts will be made.

Most people cannot make large charitable gifts while they are living because they have taxes to pay, educational expenses for children, medical expenses, and

---

* Daniel W. Vecchitto and Debra L. Thorburn, Introduction to Planned Giving, 2nd edition, JLA Publications, 1982.

other living expenses which are ongoing obligations. At the time of death, however, many adults are able to make substantial gifts to charity. A charitable bequest in a will can be introduced in your wills seminar.

These are five solid reasons why your organization and donors will benefit from conducting a wills seminar. The fundamental assumption is one that is basic to a winning formula: You can achieve your organization's goals by fulfilling a need among your donors and prospects.

Your organization can increase its level of gift income by helping people understand the importance of having wills. Throughout the rest of this manual, you will discover how to communicate that importance by conducting a wills seminar.

How to Get Started

Like any project or program, a successful wills seminar requires commitment, planning, organization, and creativity. Before you can discuss in a group setting the necessity of having a will, let alone count the dollars from those bequests you know are waiting for you, there are a number of preparations to make.

Bequest emphasis efforts practiced by numerous nonprofits educate donors, friends, and prospects on an ongoing basis. Periodically mailing information on the subject of wills and placing ads and articles in publications that remind readers of the importance of their wills can be augmented by conducting wills seminars.

Each aspect of wills emphasis efforts works together to inform donors and prospects about wills, and they remind donors of the possibility of satisfying charitable gift wishes with a bequest.

Step One: Make Sure You Have a Committed Board of Directors

Your board of directors needs to have a thorough understanding of the goals of a bequest emphasis program and what is required to achieve those goals. Without the sustained support of your board, getting the job done will be difficult.

Whether you share the highlights of this manual with them or develop a tailored presentation to enlighten them, it is worth your while to make sure you have their complete support. Wills emphasis programs take time to reap benefits, a fact that must be understood and accepted by both you and your board in order to earn the return on any investment you make today.

There are a number of ways your board of directors can demonstrate their commitment.

1. The board must support a budget adequate to cover the needs of the bequest emphasis program. This means funding for salaries, training of personnel, equipment, and travel expenses, if necessary.

2. The development officer, the chairman of the board, and each board member must have his or her own will. We have all learned that it is difficult to expect people to make a contribution to our organization if we are not willing to set the example. The same principle holds true with a will. Personal commitment is a subject that should be discussed and understood. How effectively can you communicate the importance of having a will unless you have made your own will? And, when you make that will, you will want to include a bequest to your organization.

    You will no doubt be surprised at the number of board members who have no wills. Once they understand the necessity, however, they become a good source of referrals for your wills seminar program.

    Finally, your board must have *patience, patience, patience.* Your hard work may result in getting your first wills seminar started in only a matter of weeks. Keep in mind, however, it may be a number of years before you receive the first bequest, although you will certainly be notified that your organization has been named in wills.

Step Two: Do the Preparation Necessary to Have a Working Knowledge of Your State Laws

After you have read this manual, you will understand how to prepare, structure, and present a wills seminar and conduct the follow-up with the interested prospects.

There are two other steps you may follow to help ensure you have a good understanding of the wills process.

In the back of this manual is a glossary of terms used in wills. Familiarize yourself with these. You'll be a more effective facilitator of planned gifts if you can converse intelligently about "joint tenancy" and "residuary estate," among other things.

Also remember that you do not have to be an attorney to conduct your first wills seminar. Your role is to counsel people seeking professional assistance in drawing up their personal will. You do, however, need a rudimentary understanding of the state laws of descent and distribution and how they impact individuals dying without the benefit of a will. *Research and read the laws that apply in your state.* If your constituents live in many different states, you need not know the details of all, but review a summary of state provisions for a general idea of the most common variations.

Resource 8

Step Three: Select Your Prospect Market

Before beginning any marketing program, you need to determine who and where the market is. It has been found that those over age 55 are the best prospects. These individuals have begun to think not only about retirement but their own mortality as well and have an estate, large or small. The message you communicate through the wills seminar can strike a responsive chord with this select group of older donors or friends.

Other good seminar prospects include younger persons. Their wills give them the opportunity to name a guardian for their children should both parents die simultaneously and to make a charitable distribution if they should die without children.

Once you have your sights firmly fixed on the best market, you can make contact either directly or through a sponsor, depending on how your organization is structured. Smaller organizations with limited staff may invite the participation of a local attorney, bank trust officer, and/or another organization. Remember that the program should be promoted as providing information of a general nature and that individuals should always seek the advice of their professional advisers before finalizing a will or other estate plan.

When the best way to proceed involves presenting your seminar under the sponsorship of an outside party, personal visitation is a good way to make contact with an individual who can help promote your wills seminar. For instance, a club president for a local affiliate, or local church as the case may be, could be a sponsor for your seminar.

When approaching someone outside your organization to participate in a wills seminar, here are a few tips to remember:

1. Ask about their situation and what they would like to accomplish.

2. Outline the mutual benefits to be derived from the seminar.

3. Make sure they know this is not a sales-oriented presentation.

Direct mail is another useful tool to stimulate the thinking of the contact about scheduling a wills seminar. On the following pages is a sample of a letter (Exhibit B) that could be sent to potential sponsors to pique their interest in a wills seminar. The letter explains the seminar, lays out the agenda, and emphasizes that it is free to participants. The key to the packet, however, is the response device. This is included with the letter and is very easy to use (see Exhibits A and B on the following pages).

EXHIBIT A. SAMPLE LETTER OF
INVITATION TO YOUR CONSTITUENTS.

Date

Name
Address
City, State, Zip

Dear _____ :

John Wayne, the well-known movie star, died in 1979. At his death, appraisers set a value of $12.7 million on his estate, which he intended to go to his heirs.

But his heirs have received none of it!

His estate, which is tied up in the probate process in the Orange County, California, Courthouse, has paid over $6 million in federal and state death taxes. Probate fees have consumed another $250,000.

It is sad to realize John Wayne's widow and children have received nothing!

It is just as sad to realize that 8 out of 10 American adults die without the benefit of a will.

You may have witnessed a sad situation in which an individual you know died without a will.

Without a will, there can be no charitable bequests made and heirs can be temporarily disinherited, such as happened with John Wayne's widow and children.

Would you be interested in attending a wills seminar to learn more about the benefits of having a will? Or the importance of keeping your estate plans updated? Or the benefits of a charitable bequest?

If you would like to attend a wills seminar, please fill out the enclosed RSVP card and return it in the enclosed reply envelope.

This is a free service and all you have to do is call or return the card to reserve your place. We will provide an audiovisual presentation and speakers, and bring free wills booklets for distribution during this one-hour wills seminar.

We look forward to being of service to you.

Sincerely,

(Include response card that follows.)

EXHIBIT A. SAMPLE LETTER OF
INVITATION TO YOUR CONSTITUENTS, Cont'd.

R.S.V.P. Card

Yes, I ☐ we ☐ would like to attend a wills seminar on [date] at [time] in [location].

Name(s) _____

Address _____

Phone Number (   ) _____

EXHIBIT B. SAMPLE LETTER REQUESTING
WILLS SEMINAR SPONSORSHIP.

Date

Name
Address
City, State, Zip

Dear _____ :

John Wayne, the well-known movie star, died in 1979. At his death, appraisers set a value of $12.7 million on his estate, which he intended to go to his heirs.

But his heirs have received none of it!

His estate, which is tied up in the probate process in the Orange County, California, Courthouse, has paid over $6 million in federal and state death taxes. Probate fees have consumed another $250,000.

It is sad to realize John Wayne's widow and children have received nothing!

It is just as sad to realize that 8 out of 10 American adults die without the benefit of a will.

You may have witnessed a sad situation in which an individual you know died without a will.

Without a will, there can be no charitable bequests made and heirs can be temporarily disinherited, such as happened with John Wayne's widow and children.

Would your [church, alumni group, association, club, or auxiliary] like to sponsor a wills seminar to inform [church members, alumni, or members] about the benefits of a will? Or the importance of keeping their estate plans updated? Or the benefits of a charitable bequest?

If your [church, alumni group, association, club, or auxiliary] would like to sponsor a wills seminar, please fill out the enclosed wills seminar request form and return it in the enclosed self-addressed business reply envelope.

This is a free service and all you have to do is call or return the card to sponsor a wills seminar, and we will contact you to discuss it in detail. We will provide an audiovisual presentation and speakers and bring free wills booklets for distribution during this one-hour wills seminar.

We look forward to being of service to you.

Sincerely,

(Include response card that follows.)

Resource 8

EXHIBIT B. SAMPLE LETTER REQUESTING
WILLS SEMINAR SPONSORSHIP, Cont'd.

WILLS SEMINAR REQUEST FORM

☐ Yes, we would like to sponsor a wills seminar. We are interested in the following dates:

	DAY*	MONTH	YEAR	TIME*
1st Choice	_____	_____	_____	_____
2nd Choice	_____	_____	_____	_____
3rd Choice	_____	_____	_____	_____
4th Choice	_____	_____	_____	_____

Name of Organization _____

Address _____

_____

Name of Contact Person _____

Contact Person's Address _____

Contact Person's Phone (   ) _____

*The wills seminars are presented on Monday through Thursday and we have found 6:30 or 7:00 P.M. to be the most acceptable meeting times.

Once your wills seminar program is under way, you will find referrals to be an important source for prospecting. Just like your board members who are convinced to draw up a will, others who attend your seminars and receive advice and counsel become zealous about encouraging their friends and relatives to participate. They discover that having a will provides real peace of mind. They are eager to help those close to them organize their plans as well. Because they have profited from your seminar, the chances are good they will want friends to share the experience.

Step Four: Using Publicity to Draw a Crowd

Once you have scheduled a wills seminar, you want to make sure that you have a crowd. Generating publicity through advertising and word of mouth is an important part of preparing for a wills seminar.

Effective advertising may take a number of forms. An ad that is an invitation to attend a free seminar on wills can be run in the local newspaper. Your organization's newsletter or magazine, if it reaches your prospect market, is another place to publicize your wills seminar.

A local sponsor for your seminar can also be helpful in promoting the program. After the date for the seminar is confirmed, a mini-poster along with a letter can be mailed one month in advance for the purpose of advertising the upcoming seminar. (See Examples 1 and 2.)

A selected list of friends and donors is probably the best group to approach with an invitation. In addition to using an R.S.V.P. or registration card, you may want to arrange for a volunteer or staff person to telephone persons to encourage their attendance.

EXAMPLE 1. LETTER TO SPONSOR
WITH NECESSARY PUBLICITY MATERIAL.

Date

Name
Address
City, State, Zip

Dear _____ :

Please find enclosed a copy of the wills seminar mini-poster ad that you can post in appropriate spots in order to advertise the seminar scheduled for [date].

It is always helpful to publicize the wills seminar during the three weeks prior to the actual date of the seminar. It is also helpful to have a telephone committee call prospective attenders.

I have also enclosed sample will brochures that we will have available for the people attending the seminar.

I look forward to seeing you on [date].

Sincerely,

Enclosure

P.S. I have sent a letter to the attorney, Mr. John Doe, explaining his role in the wills seminar.

EXAMPLE 2. MINI-POSTER.

WILLS SEMINAR

For everyone—bring a friend!

[Day], [Date]   [Time]

[Location]

IMPORTANT QUESTIONS TO BE ANSWERED:

Why is a will important?   Can I write a will myself?

What if I die without a will?   Can a will be changed?

SPEAKERS:

Sam Smith   Development Director
                 ABC Charity

Mary Jones   Director of Planned Giving
                 ABC Charity

John Doe   Attorney

Even if you have a will, you'll find this
Seminar INTERESTING & INFORMATIVE!

[If appropriate, include the following]

If you need transportation, please call [phone number].
Please clip the registration form below and return to
[sponsor's address] by [date].

- -

Wills Seminar Registration Form

Name Mr./Mrs./Ms. _____

Address _____

City _____ State _____ Zip _____

Phone Number (   ) _____

_____

The mini-poster is extremely useful because it can be reproduced on a photo-copy machine for mass distribution. To assure the maximum attendance we encourage publicizing the seminar at least three weeks prior to the seminar.

Here are a few examples of how the mini-poster can be used:

1. On organization entrance doors and on bulletin boards.

2. In post offices and/or local businesses in small communities.

3. At senior citizen meetings or congregate meal sites.

4. As an ad in the local paper.

5. Mailed as an invitation to people who you believe would be interested in a wills seminar.

Additional publicity idea:

6. Include an article about wills in a newsletter that goes to your constituency. At the end of the article add a "clip-out coupon" that offers information about your wills seminar.

Step Five: Role of Attorneys

When we discuss the actual seminar, you will see how an attorney may play a useful role in the program. The presence of legal counsel adds credibility to your message.

When you select an attorney, remember that some attorneys are familiar with estate planning and others are not. Try to select one who is knowledgeable in this area. You should rotate the list of attorneys used in a local area so that there are no accusations of favoritism—keep in mind that your seminar may be a good source of business for the attorney, but it is not designed for the solicitation of clients or as an endorsement of the speaker.

The attorney should receive a letter informing him or her of exactly what level of participation you expect. The letter stresses that the program is only one hour with an emphasis on wills (see Example 3 on the following page). You want to discourage an attorney from coming in with a 20-minute estate planning speech on the use of trusts in terms of someone's will that may be far above the level of the attendees. Along with the letter, send several brochures on the subject of wills. These signal to the attorney that the information level should be kept fairly basic.

EXAMPLE 3. ATTORNEY/SPEAKER CONFIRMATION LETTER.

Date

Name
Address
City, State, Zip

Dear _____ :

I am happy to have you join me for the wills seminar scheduled on [date] at [place]. The wills seminar will begin at [time].

The usual format in presenting a wills seminar is very simple. We try to stay within a one-hour limit. During the first 40 minutes I will make a brief introduction and a presentation on the benefits of having a will. Included will be a 10-minute visual presentation that focuses on the important issue that people should take the time to make out a will.

Immediately after the presentation I would like to introduce you to the audience to answer any questions in the area of wills. We generally find that the first 40 minutes stimulate a lot of questions. For this reason we are delighted to have you participate in the question and answer period during the last 15 to 20 minutes of the program.

I am enclosing samples of will brochures that we have available for the people attending the seminar.

I am not there to offer legal advice. My mission is to encourage people to (1) make out a will if they don't have a will, and (2) to use an attorney who can offer competent legal advice in drawing up a valid will.

As an organization we are concerned that many people do not have wills—an omission can bring on the anguish and problems that occur as a result of people not taking the time to draw up wills, etc. Also, those who have taken the time to draw up a will may not include a charitable bequest in the will and we want to let them know of this convenient opportunity to make a gift.

If you have any questions, please feel free to contact me prior to the program.

I look forward to seeing you at the program.

Sincerely,

Step Six: Securing the Necessary Equipment

Review the various pieces of equipment you will need to conduct your seminar. Ascertain whether or not some of the items will be available in the meeting room or if you need to bring them with you.

Be sure to use a microphone. Since most of your best prospects are elderly, it is critical that they are able to hear the presentation. They will lose interest quickly if they cannot hear you.

Depending on the audiovisual materials you are using for the presentation, you may need a slide or overhead projector and screen, a videocassette recorder and television, and tape recorder. Make sure you have an adequate supply of evaluation forms (the importance of these will be discussed later) and pens. You should also provide an assortment of free brochures on wills.

As you may have surmised, it is no small task to begin putting on wills seminars. Adequate preparation is fundamental to your success. You must have the firm commitment of your board of directors and do the preparation necessary to understand how to effectively help your prospects. After that you must identify your prospect market, thoroughly publicize the seminar, and assemble the necessary equipment.

The first seminar will undoubtedly take the longest time to prepare. Once you have your system in place, you may follow a checklist similar to the one in Example 4 on the following page and the whole process will be more expeditious.

The Wills Seminar

Once you have received the full commitment of your board, educated yourself, targeted your market, publicized your program thoroughly, and secured the equipment, you are ready to conduct your first wills seminar. But, first—a note of caution. A successful seminar depends on many factors. Here's a list of helpful tips:

1. DO try to schedule for an evening during the week (although an alumni weekend clinic, for instance, might be appropriate).
2. DO schedule an evening program for 6:30 or 7:00 P.M. For some reason 8:00 P.M. is too late and the attendance is affected. (For some groups a morning or afternoon program may be preferable.)
3. DO limit invitations to one attorney for the program.
4. DO schedule your seminar as the exclusive program for the meeting.
5. DO begin and end promptly.

EXAMPLE 4. WILLS SEMINAR CHECKLIST.

Contact

☐ Seminar presenter(s) identified _____

      Name _____

      Address _____

      Name _____

      Address _____

                                                  Date

☐ Time of seminar confirmed with presenter(s)   _____

☐ Packet with mini-poster mailed or distributed   _____

☐ Final call to contact to confirm details   _____

Attorney

☐ Attorney identified   _____

☐ Attorney name _____

        Address _____

                     _____

Advertising

☐ Invitations mailed   _____

☐ Ads placed in local newspaper or organization's magazine   _____

☐ Article and coupon in newsletter   _____

Suggested Equipment

☐ TV

☐ VCR, 1/2-inch VHS

☐ Slides or overheads

☐ Screen

☐ Microphone or lecternette

☐ Tape recorder

☐ Brochures/brochure rack/cloth to cover brochure rack

☐ Evaluation forms

☐ Pens

☐ Notepaper

☐ Two 25-foot extension cords

The Setting

A wills seminar may be conducted in the meeting room of a church, academic building, retirement center, motel/hotel, community center, office, or school. It could even be presented in a home. The key is to have enough space so that all attendees are comfortable and can see and hear clearly.

As each attendee arrives, hand him or her notepaper with a pen or pencil. This encourages note taking at the seminar.

Beverages and light refreshments can be served at the conclusion of the seminar. The refreshments are an invitation for all to linger longer and ask personal questions.

At a convenient and accessible spot in the meeting room, place a table on which to display informative publications, which attendees may take with them when they leave. It is helpful if you can have a wide selection of brochure topics to address a variety of needs or interests. The literature table displays an assortment of wills brochures that focus on the person who does not have a will as well as the person who needs to update a will.

The Agenda

It is helpful if you can work as a team with another person. One presenter serves as a moderator and can explain the purpose of the seminar, reassure participants that the program will be only one hour, and strike the right tone. A guest attorney concludes the seminar by answering questions.*

A sample agenda might include:

A. Welcome—host/moderator

B. Purpose of seminar—host/moderator

C. Mention publications available to take home and give a brief description of what is on the literature table.

D. Video (or slide presentation)

E. Consequences of not having a will and the benefits of having a will—attorney and/or host/moderator

F. Response to questions—moderator and attorney

G. Program adjourns

---

* The guest speaker could be a trust officer, financial planner, or other knowledgeable person, rather than an attorney.

Resource 8

The Program

After the host has explained the agenda, he or she can establish the tone for the attorney by making preliminary remarks.

Following is the text of an actual seminar. (State laws vary, so the details may not be accurate for your state. You will want to familiarize yourself with the laws of your state.)

> *Host/Moderator:* My message is about the number of people who do not have the benefit of a will.
>
> [Use an example from your own experience or relate the story below.]
>
> The best example I can offer of the consequences of not having a will involves a secretary who worked for a charity for about 30 years and retired at age 70. About two weeks prior to her death at age 75, she'd made an appointment to see an attorney about drawing up her first will. She procrastinated and failed to keep the appointment. Later, she died without the benefit of a will.
>
> Now, if a person dies without a will, the state steps in and determines how assets are going to be distributed. In this case, the state established that her husband and children had predeceased her. The only living next-of-kin that could be discovered was a distant cousin. So the state notified this cousin that she was going to inherit everything that the woman had accumulated during her entire lifetime.
>
> The ironic twist to this story is that the secretary had confided to a fellow employee at the office that her cousin was the "last person on earth" she would want to inherit anything of hers, since this cousin had never communicated with her.
>
> This story underscores one point: most people work hard for their assets, but in so many instances, similar to the secretary, they fail to take the necessary steps to plan for the distribution of those assets at the time of death.
>
> [NOTE: At this point the 9.5 minute videotape "The State Has Made Your Will" or a slide presentation can be presented to the audience or describe the publications available for them to take home.]
>
> *Attorney:* I am sure at this point each of you can think of your own reasons why it is important for you to have a will.
>
> Another reason is a startling national statistic that reveals as much as 80 percent of American adults die without a will, the simplest of all estate planning devices.

Resource 8

Financial planners agree it is the failure to take action, not the absence of opportunity, that is the major threat to a person's achieving their financial objectives. Since it takes a lifetime to build an estate, wouldn't you agree that it is worth taking the time periodically to review your plans?

Indeed, planning today has never been more important. It seems that people have two excuses for neglecting the right, privilege, and responsibility of making a will.

[Start the slide presentation with commentary or videotape. See the following.]

SLIDE OR OVERHEAD COPY	COMMENTARY
	The following is offered as suggested dialogue to accompany the slide presentation included with this manual. If a television and VCR are not available or the crowd is larger than would be comfortable for viewing a television screen, the slide presentation may be used in place of the videotape.
FAILURE TO PLAN— PROCRASTINATION	The first excuse is we simply "Fail to Plan." People fear death, so they simply put off making plans. But time and experience prove that where there's a will (in this instance we are talking about the last will and testament) there is a way—a way to protect family interests, to prevent estate erosion, and to provide for favorite friends and charities. But to take advantage of these opportunities—we must plan!
	The second excuse is the one we all fall victim to— "Procrastination."
	Allow me, if you will, to share with you the personal testimony of a widow which illustrates how procrastination can grip us—postponing our estate planning.
	She writes:
	"I can't count the times I said, 'If only I had it to do over again . . . I would handle myself and my money much differently.'
	"Today I know how I would go about it. I would declare a contingency day—an annual review of the

financial state of my family. And I would like to recommend such a review to every person and certainly to every husband and wife . . . then on that hypothetical day . . . I would have, and should have, asked my husband so many other questions about wills . . . about our plans for the future. But I never did any of this. The future—good or bad—was a reality I never faced.
"Signed,
"Wiser Widow"

Declaration of an official "Contingency Day" may be a forlorn hope and probably unrealistic for many of us. But every person does have the privilege of declaring a personal contingency day . . . to seriously and carefully plan for the distribution of their property at death. Making a will is a privilege allowed anyone who is of sound mind and legal age. The legal age in this state is 18 years old.

So, what is a will? A will is a written, legally binding but completely amendable document that lets you direct precisely who will receive all the property you have accumulated over your lifetime. Your will is one of the most important documents you will ever sign.

Wills can accomplish more than saving taxes and passing property to loved ones; it is your legal piece of communication which states your personal wishes and directs in an orderly manner "who" should receive "what."

Let's first consider what would happen if you died suddenly without the benefit of a will.

IF YOU LEAVE NO WILL— PROPERTY PASSES ACCORDING TO STATE LAW

1. If you leave no will—your property passes according to state law.

Under the present laws of one state your close relatives will share in your estate, but most often not in the same ratios and proportion that perhaps you would have wanted. All of us here this [morning/afternoon/evening] have wills. If you have a legally drawn will you have a will by your own design, but you haven't taken the time to draw up your own personal will—the state has prepared that will for you.

When a person dies "intestate," which means dying without the benefit of a will, he or she is simply leaving accumulated assets and wishes to "chance." This means the state will determine how his or her property is to be distributed, without knowing what those wishes are.

Let's move on and take a look at how property is distributed if there is no will.

Intestacy can be tragic, for example:

SURVIVING SPOUSE— AND CHILDREN

In the case where there's a surviving spouse and children, your spouse will inherit 100% of your estate. For instance, children will not be provided for without a will.

SURVIVING SPOUSE— NO CHILDREN

Or, if there's a surviving spouse and no children, your entire estate passes to your surviving spouse, even though this may create tax problems.

SURVIVING SPOUSE— AND CHILDREN "ONLY OF THE DECEDENT" (2ND MARRIAGE)

Problems can arise when there is a surviving spouse and the children are of the decedent only—in one state in the case of a second marriage and if the estate is over $50,000, the surviving spouse receives one-half. The other half passes to the decedent's children.

If the estate is less than $50,000, the surviving spouse receives all.

CHILDREN ONLY—

If there are children only surviving, the children will share your estate in equal portions with a separate portion divided among the issue of a deceased child.

NO SPOUSE OR CHILDREN—

In many cases, if there is no spouse or children surviving but there are living parents, they will inherit your entire estate. If parents are not living, your state will be divided in equal shares among brothers and sisters. After that your cousins or the nearest living blood relatives will receive your estate.

NO KNOWN RELATIVES—

If there are no known relatives your entire estate will be transferred to the state.

Resource 8

IF YOU LEAVE NO WILL—COURT WILL APPOINT GUARDIAN FOR MINOR CHILDREN

2. If you leave no will—and have minor children under the age of 18, you are again leaving to chance who the court will appoint as guardian for your children. Far too often, people only think of wills as a means to distribute property. But for parents of minor children, property distribution may be second in importance to assuring that love and care for the children will continue in their absence.

If you are a widowed or single parent survived by minor children, your children will need a guardian to care for them and a conservator to look after their property.

The court-appointed guardian will then care for your children, but under the supervision of the court. Annual accountings of property are required and must be filed by the conservator, and permission of the judge must be sought in order to make comparatively modest expenditures. The supervision of the court through the guardian and conservator ends at age 18, and then the child is left to fend for him- or herself at a time when he or she is usually just a senior in high school. All in all, this can be an expensive and cumbersome state of affairs and is usually a poor substitute for the supervision found in a normal parent-child relationship. This is the primary reason that people with minor children need wills to provide for the care of their children.

IF YOU LEAVE NO WILL—STATE WILL DECIDE WHO WILL BE YOUR EXECUTOR

3. If you leave no will—the state will also decide who is to manage your estate, and he or she may be the person you would have considered least capable of carrying out such a responsibility. Your executor or personal representative will be your legal representative after your death.

The responsibilities of an executor include collecting the assets of your estate, paying your creditors, managing your property, and making distributions to the persons and charities named in your will. Your executor will be legally responsible for settling your estate—and for carrying out all the provisions of your will.

If you die without a will, the person selected by the laws as your executor will be required to furnish a performance bond. A legal will avoids this expense because all attorneys who draft wills today use legal language that exempts the executor from furnishing such a bond. Reminder—it is advisable to name an alternate to act in case the designated executor refuses to act, dies, or fails to qualify.

IF YOU LEAVE NO WILL— STATE LAW WILL BE IN EFFECT IF A COMMON DISASTER OCCURS

4. If you leave no will—the distribution laws of the state will be in effect if you and your spouse should die together. If you had your own personal will, as an estate owner, you could establish the order of death in the event both you and your surviving spouse should die simultaneously.

IF YOU LEAVE NO WILL— STATE LAWS DO NOT PROVIDE FOR CHARITABLE GIFTS

5. If you leave no will—state laws do not include a provision that a portion of your estate will be given to your favorite charity. It is possible that you have been a generous donor to various charities during your lifetime. Would you want your generosity to continue after your death? It can be accomplished so simply with a will! In addition to the personal satisfaction of making a charitable bequest, the tax law continues to reward generosity by allowing an unlimited estate tax charitable deduction for any "giveable" asset which passes to a qualified charity, such as cash, stocks, real estate, jewelry, art collections, and even antiques.

There are four simple and popular ways to include a charitable bequest in your will:

1. THE PERCENTAGE METHOD—

The percentage method: this is the most flexible way to give; the gift automatically changes with the size of the estate.

Example: $4,000 is left in your estate after all final expenses and debts are paid. If you give a percentage and want to leave 80 percent to family and 20 percent to charitable interest, all beneficiaries would share according to the designated percentages.

2. FIXED DOLLAR AMOUNT—

The fixed dollar amount: this is the most common type of bequest (but not necessarily the best). Let's use the same $4,000 example. If you state $4,000 goes to my favorite son, daughter, or niece and $4,000 to a charity, there is a dilemma. With only $4,000 in your estate what happens? The first person named would get the bequest because nothing would be left in the estate to cover the second beneficiary named.

3. SPECIFIC PROPERTY—

Specific property: securities, real estate, and personal property qualify to be given as gifts to charity through a will. (However, caution—if you happen to sell a specific piece of property that you had designated as a charitable bequest before your death, there will be no gift.)

4. RESIDUE—
(THAT PROPERTY
WHICH IS LEFT)

The residue: this is a gift of whatever property is left after all other bequests have been satisfied. For instance, you might say, "After I have taken care of my family and friends, I leave the rest and the residue to the following charities . . ."

I hope I have convinced you by now that each of us here this [morning/afternoon/evening] needs a will to dispose of all the property we have accumulated during life. You may now be asking yourself about what steps need to be taken to make a proper will. An old adage says that any worthwhile journey starts with the first step.

STEP 1—
CHECK YOUR NET WORTH
ASSETS MINUS LIABILITIES

The first step is to check your net worth. This is called a personal financial inventory—assets minus liabilities is basically what Uncle Sam is going to look at when he taxes your estate.

Take an inventory and make a list of your assets—including the present fair market value as well as the cost basis. Estate planning involves the entire family, so remember, if you have a spouse who owns assets separately from you, those assets are also to be included. How are the assets owned? Individually? As joint tenants? Or as tenants in common?

STEP 2—
DECIDE ON EXECUTOR

The second step is to decide on whom you would like to appoint as your executor. Remember to always name an alternate executor or personal representative if you are naming an individual.

You may nominate your husband or wife as your executor—or a competent and experienced friend or relative—or the trust department of a bank. Or you may wish to follow the example of many who name a spouse, friend, or relative together with the trust department of a bank as co-executors.

Your thoughtfulness in selecting an executor will be well rewarded.

STEP 3—
CHOOSE GUARDIAN

The third step would be to decide on your choice of guardian or guardians if there are minor children. I recommend that you ask the permission of the chosen guardian or guardians before you appoint them in your will. This is a courtesy that should be extended because you are asking them to take on significant responsibility.

STEP 4—
SIMULTANEOUS DEATH—
WHO RECEIVES PROPERTY

The fourth step to consider is the distribution of your property in case of a simultaneous death of both husband and wife—two sisters—mother and daughter—or any combination of two people.

STEP 5—
CONSIDER CHARITABLE GIFTS

The fifth step is to consider charitable gifts in your will. In the 1991 *Giving U.S.A.* report, 89.5 percent of all the charitable dollars given to all philanthropic causes comes from individuals. Many charitably motivated individuals have included bequests in their wills as a way to perpetuate values that have been important to them for a lifetime.

Charitable bequests are also included in wills to perpetuate the memory of a loved one. You can provide for such a bequest to favorite charities by using any of the four previously suggested methods. Few people give away as much while they're alive as they can after death.

STEP 6—
TAKE PERSONAL FINANCIAL
INVENTORY TO ATTORNEY

The final and most important step is to take all of your thoughts and your financial statement in writing to your attorney. You will want to compile your financial

Resource 8

inventory in preparation for an appointment with the attorney who will be drafting your personal will.

I think you may find the booklet "Personal and Financial Affairs Record of _____ " helpful in putting together information your attorney will need to craft your will. [Distribute copies of booklet at this point.]

In it you will find a handy, compact place to keep information about your financial situation. Reviewing its contents periodically will act as a reminder that your will should also be reviewed.

As we have mentioned earlier, having your information organized lessens the time your attorney will need to draft your will. This booklet can help save your attorney time, and you money.

In conclusion, remember everyone here this [morning/afternoon/evening] has an estate plan now. For many, that plan is an ineffective one, because it's the will of the state.

Each of us may be aware of at least one family who has been torn apart by disagreements in settling an unplanned estate. It is a painful experience. Sometimes the wounds never heal and even brothers and sisters become enemies. The saddest part is that it doesn't have to happen. Don't do your family a disservice by neglecting to make a will.

Let me conclude before we take your questions with this thought—

We work to earn money.

We struggle to save money.

We learn to give money.

And it's important that we know how to leave money.

[Optional if host/moderator does slide presentation.] Thank you for your attention and interest. I would now like to introduce [attorney's name], an attorney specializing in estate planning who will respond to your questions.

The Attorney's Role

Having an attorney available to answer questions at the end of your presentation adds credibility to the seminar. Before you begin the program and again when you introduce the attorney it is a good idea to caveat your remarks. Stress to the participants that your role is not to provide legal counsel. Your objective is to make them aware of the consequences of not having a will as well as the benefits of having one. The attorney present can increase their comfort level with the whole idea of preparing a will by answering their questions. Here are typical questions the attorney will receive:

> Why should I change a will I made 20 years ago?
>
> Should I notify anyone of the location of my will?
>
> Why do I need a will if all my property is owned jointly?
>
> How long does it take to settle an estate?
>
> Should I put my son's or daughter's name on my checking and savings accounts to save taxes?
>
> What does it cost to have an attorney draft my will?
>
> Can I write my own will—and is it legal?

After these and other questions have been answered, our seminar participants should have a fairly clear idea of what to do and where to go next. They should understand that your role is limited, and they need to confer with an attorney to finalize their will.

The Evaluation Form

Before the participants at your wills seminar leave, it is important to your follow-up that you know who was in attendance. Five minutes before you dismiss them ask everyone to complete an evaluation form on the seminar. This is an excellent way to compile a list of interested individuals. It also lets you know who may want a private appointment or has further questions.

A sample of an evaluation form is featured in Example 5. These should be distributed while the presenter gives an explanation. In addition to the section that asks for reaction to the seminar, the evaluation form contains a series of questions that probe the participant's interest in learning or doing more.

The evaluation form helps augment your prospect list. The evaluation is a critical and important part of the seminar program.

The Follow-Up

One final step is necessary to put the finishing touches on each seminar—thank-yous. Your host or sponsor, the attorney, and of course, the attendees should all be thanked for their participation in the wills seminar. The letters ideally should be mailed within the week following the seminar.

Resource 8

In the case of the sponsor and attorney, the appropriate thank-you note (see Examples 6, 7, and 8) can help maintain good relations before the next seminar is scheduled. For the participants, a letter of thanks is another effective mechanism to nurture their trust in your advice and reinforce their resolve to draw up a will.

EXAMPLE 5. WILLS SEMINAR EVALUATION.

COURSE EVALUATION FORM

I felt the workshop was

___ worthwhile ___ satisfactory ___ not worthwhile.

___ I have no will but would like to make one.

___ I would consider including [charity] as part of my estate and will planning.

___ I have a will but it needs to be updated.

___ I have already included [charity] in my will.

___ I have not included [charity] in my will but would consider doing so when I update my will.

___ My will has been updated in the past year.

___ I have additional questions and would like a private appointment with
    _____ .*

COMMENTS _____

_____

_____

_____

_____

Name (Mr./Mrs./Ms.) _____

Address _____

City _____ State _____ Zip _____

Home Telephone (   ) _____

Business Telephone (   ) _____

* If your organization can accommodate such requests this question is appropriate. Otherwise it can be deleted from your evaluation form.

EXAMPLE 6. SAMPLE LETTER TO THANK SPONSORING GROUP.

Date

Name
Address
City, State, Zip

Dear _____ :

Thank you for the invitation to do a wills seminar with you on [date].

I really enjoyed the opportunity of presenting the wills seminar for your group. Hopefully, a few seeds were planted for those who did not have a will as well as for those who needed to update their wills.

Enclosed is a copy of an evaluation form summarizing the totals for those individuals who responded to the Course Evaluation Form that was distributed at the end of the wills seminar.

My best wishes to you.

Sincerely,

Enclosure

EXAMPLE 7. SAMPLE LETTER TO THANK ATTORNEY.

Date

Name
Address
City, State, Zip

Dear [Attorney's Name]:

Thank you for your help with the wills seminar held on [date and place].

You did a super job in handling the questions and I am most grateful to you for joining us.

We hope that more people will become concerned about having a will drawn up. Once this has been accomplished, hopefully more people will consider a bequest to their favorite charity.

Thanks again for taking time out from your busy schedule to assist us.

Gratefully,

Enclosure

Resource 8

EXAMPLE 8. SAMPLE LETTER TO PARTICIPANTS.

Date

Name
Address
City, State, Zip

Dear [Name of Attendee]:

It was good to see you recently at the wills seminar. I hope that your participation was a valuable experience and that you gained some sound information about wills, which you can apply today and in the future.

Although you may have conscientiously made plans for the management of your property, now and later, it is always possible to overlook important options open to you. Beginning or improving an estate plan is much easier when you have determined what information you need.

As I mentioned at the seminar, the first step is to take an inventory of what you have accumulated over your lifetime. This is where the booklet, "Personal and Financial Affairs Record of _____ ," will be helpful. You may have questions as you fill in the blanks. Please consult your adviser(s) for help. They are best qualified to know your individual situation.

Again, I appreciate your attendance and interest in the wills seminar.

Sincerely,

_____

As you can see, there are several components to an effective wills seminar. Your presentation should be well prepared and well rehearsed. As one of the presenters, you should be viewed as a knowledgeable and competent counselor who is there to help. Do not overstate your expertise, but do project your professionalism and genuine concern.

The attorney's role is to answer general questions. By including legal counsel in the program, he or she may add credibility to your comments. Finally, do not overlook the necessity for good follow-up. The evaluation forms and thank-you notes to the participants are useful tools for identifying prospects. Handling these steps well matches the importance of the presentation.

Individual Follow-Up

A friend or donor of the organization who expresses an interest in talking with you about how to make out a will is a good prospect. He or she turns to you for assistance knowing for whom you work and is presumably favorably impressed with your charity.

You may identify a prospect in a couple of ways. All those people who attended your wills seminar and completed the evaluation form indicating they were interested in a follow-up visit are prime prospects. You may also get the name of a prospect from a referral. These can be good because you have more than likely been recommended to the prospect by a satisfied friend or relative. This gives you added credibility.

The first element of follow-up is additional contact. Call or write seeking an appointment to discuss things further. You may want to encourage them to come to your office, because it uses your time more effectively and also gives them an opportunity to visit your office, which is often a "first." You can, of course, make a house call if the situation warrants, as is the case with an elderly person. This approach may also make them feel more comfortable.

When you have that first meeting or make that first call, you may be somewhat nervous. However, you are there to give assistance, not to be an attorney. Your prospect has reached out to you and is happy to have a friendly, knowledgeable helper. And it becomes easier after you have done it a few times.

Once you have the interview, it might go something like this:

Nancy: Good morning, Mr. Jones!

Chuck: Well, good morning, Mrs. Smith. You don't have to call me Mr. Jones. Please call me Chuck.

Nancy: Thank you, and I'd appreciate it if you'd call me Nancy.

Chuck: Well, thank you, Nancy. Let's go out to the kitchen and have a cup of coffee.

Nancy: All right, thank you. You have a lovely home, Chuck. Do you keep it up by yourself?

Chuck: Not quite, Nancy. I am getting up in years. I have a housekeeper, Josephine. She's been coming in for about ten years now—every Friday—and she helps keep this place looking nice.

Nancy: She certainly does a good job. [Note: You're going to exchange the pleasantries that fit with the situation.]

I appreciate your attending the wills seminar that we conducted last week. Thanks for the opportunity to come out and visit today as well.

Chuck: Well, Nancy, I thought you did a real nice job at that wills seminar. In fact, you gave me something to think about. You know, I don't have a will.

Nancy: Unfortunately, Chuck, you're not in a minority. As you recall from the program, we said that 80 percent of American adults die without the benefit of a will.

Chuck: I was really surprised at that figure.

Nancy: Most people are surprised. As we discussed in the program, the development office provides a service at no cost to you, and no obligation to our charity. I'll help you pull together the information that your attorney will need. Do you have an attorney, Chuck?

Chuck: No. Could you suggest somebody?

Nancy: Have you thought about an attorney you know or who has worked for friends or family members? If not, I can get a list with the names of several attorneys in the area who specialize in estate planning. After we conclude this visit, I will send you the list to check out for someone you think you'd like to work with.

[Note: Before I start the planning process in a face-to-face situation, I explain to the prospect or donor that there are four steps to planning a will that really work. These steps are called the "Four P's Method." Example 9 shows material I share with the prospect.]

Nancy: Chuck, before we review your situation, let me share with you a process which I call the four "P's." Let me further explain and define what I mean by the four "P's."

First "P"—Persons: Who are the persons involved in your estate? First, of course, is you. We want to remember estate planning is done for the living. Then we will list your relatives and friends.

Second "P"—Property: What are your properties? Cash, insurance, real estate, stocks, bonds, cars, furniture, antiques . . . and everything else of value comprise your property. We will list the approximate value of each and total them.

Third "P"—Plans: What are your plans, wishes, goals, and desires? Self-support for the rest of your life? Everyone wants that. Support for dependents or others for as long as they need it, even if they outlive you? Provide against possible emergencies such as illness or accident? Also under plans, we will list those charitable institutions that you have supported and are important to you.

Fourth "P"—Planners: Who can best advise you about your estate plan? These are the professionals you should consult: attorney, trust officer, CPA (certified public accountant), CLU (certified life underwriter) and possibly the director of planned giving of any organizations you might consider naming in your will.

[After explaining the meaning of the four "P's" I begin his personal financial inventory if he wants to do so.]

Nancy: It's a simple process, Chuck. I'll ask questions, and you'll get to provide the answers. Or, if you prefer, I can leave you the "Personal and Financial Affairs Record of _____ " to fill out at your convenience.

Chuck: Okay, let's go over the questions now. Where do we start?

Nancy: Let's start with the first "P." Who are the people you'd like to remember in your plan? Certainly, we want to think about you. Estate planning really involves planning for the living, as well as planning for heirs; so the first person I'd like to write down is you, Chuck. What is your date of birth?

Chuck: March 16, 1904.

Nancy: Good. That was a good year. [Note: Be careful how you address this subject, especially when dealing with women—"date of birth" is less offensive than "how old are you?"] Now, who are the other people that you want to remember in your plan, Chuck?

Chuck: I should remember my sister, Mary. You know she is pretty well off financially, but being my only sister, I would like to do something for her.

Nancy: Is Mary an older or younger sister?

Chuck: She is older. She's 89.

Nancy: And did you say that your sister lives independently of you?

Chuck: Yes. In fact, she lives in Chicago.

Nancy: Chicago is a fun place to visit. Let's see, you're heading the list and now we have added your sister, Mary. Who else would you like to provide for in your plan?

Chuck: Well, I'd like to do something for my cook, Jennie. You know, she's worked for me for about three years. Her husband has one of those construction jobs—not too secure—so I ought to do something for her.

Nancy: Is Jennie about your age?

Chuck: No, she's 28.

Nancy: She must be a fine cook. Who else would you like to provide for? Is there anyone else under the "people" section that we ought to list?

Chuck: I should really take care of my housekeeper, Josephine. You know, she's been cleaning my house for ten years now—comes every Friday and she's not too well off financially, so I want to do something for her.

Nancy: Is she about your age?

Chuck: No, she's younger—about 70.

Nancy: That's something that at 70 she is still cleaning your house. Please tell her that I noticed that your home is meticulous. I think she does a fine job.

Chuck: Well, thank you. I will pass that compliment on.

Resource 8

Nancy: Is there anyone else that we want to provide for? Anyone else you want to remember?

Chuck: No, that's about it.

Nancy: So, we have you; your sister, Mary; Jennie, your cook; and Josephine, your housekeeper.

As you recall, the second "P" to consider is the "property." This will be all the property that you own, how you hold title to that property, and what the cost of that property might have been. What is the fair market value of that property today? If this is too personal, don't hesitate to stop me. You can fill in the blanks later yourself.

Chuck, when death occurs, the IRS places a fair market value on property, or the value on the date of death. In order to ascertain the value of your estate, we need to have fair market values if possible. Do you own this home in your name or is it in someone else's name also?

Chuck: My home is in my name only.

Nancy: And what would you say the fair market value of this home would be today?

Chuck: Oh, I don't know, Nancy, could you tell me?

Nancy: [Note: They may try to get you to place a value on their property. Don't do it because you're not in the business to value their property. That's their responsibility. Here's a response.] I really can't. You know, I don't have much expertise in the area of appraising; but let me ask you this: Has a similar house within this block, or in this area, been sold recently?

Chuck: Yes, my neighbor, John Smith, sold his house about a year ago for around $170,000.

Nancy: Is it similar to your home?

Chuck: Yes, it's similar. I think that mine ought to be worth at least $175,000.

Nancy: What did you pay for your home, Chuck?

Chuck: $65,000.

Nancy: It's appreciated greatly in value. You know I noticed a beautiful red Lincoln when I came up to the door—a Lincoln Continental. Is that yours?

Chuck: You bet. That's my pride and joy. It's a 1991 Lincoln.

Nancy: It's beautiful. Red's my favorite color, so I was attracted to it.

Chuck: Thank you. That's my favorite color, too.

Nancy: Is it titled in your name, Chuck?

Chuck: Yes, just my name.

Nancy: What do you think the fair market value of that car is today?

Chuck: Oh, it's worth about $25,000. I got a real deal and paid $28,000 for it.

Nancy: OK. [Note: Fair market value isn't critical on cars, but we're going to put it down to keep it consistent.] All right, Chuck, what about your household furnishings and contents? If something happened to you and this estate needed to be liquidated—now we're not talking about replacement value; we're talking about if there were an estate sale, and everything needed to be reduced to cash—do you have any idea what your household furnishings and contents might be?

Chuck: Oh boy, you know, I have a lot of furniture all over this house. Could you tell me what it's worth?

Nancy: Well, as I said, Chuck, I really am not an authority on appraising, but most people I work with have furnishings that can amount to $3,000 to $4,000. Or I've seen household furnishings get as high as $40,000. But, most people are in the $5,000 to $10,000 range.

Chuck: I'd say the value is about $8,000.

Nancy: All right, $8,000. [Note: It's all right if the figure is not correct, but they have to put the value on their property.] What about other personal property? Do you have any stamp collections, coin collections, any antiques of high value, or jewelry?

Chuck: I really don't have any antiques or collections. But, I do have this diamond ring. It must be worth at least $4,000—at least that was what it was appraised at about a year ago. I've also got another ring back on my dresser—oh, I'd say about $5,000.

Nancy: So I'll list your diamonds at $9,000. How about your checking accounts? Do you have any bank accounts?

Chuck: Yes. I have two of them, Nancy. I used to bank at this one bank—well, I still have a checking account there. But they got a new president, and he and I don't get along. So a new branch opened up down the street and I opened an account there.

Nancy: You have two checking accounts. Are they both in your name only or with someone else? [Note: You have to keep asking because, periodically, it'll turn up, "Oh, no, I have my niece's name on the account." So, you've got to make sure we know who holds title to the property.] What would be the value of those two checking accounts?

Chuck: $25,000.

Nancy: So I will list checking accounts at $25,000. [Another note: It's not uncommon for people in this age bracket to have this much money in their checking account.] Chuck, I just wonder, when you were down at your bank, did they happen to mention that there are checking accounts that will pay you interest? Let me explain: they call them "sweep" accounts, or "NOW" accounts, where after $1,500, they sweep off the excess and it'll earn interest.

Chuck: I see, I didn't know that. That's a good tip, Nancy.

Nancy: [Note: Always look for opportunities to help the person. So, look for those opportunities and stay abreast of what's happening in the financial climate.) Are there any other bank accounts or pieces of property that you might own?

Chuck: Yes, I've got two $1,000 Series H United States Savings Bonds, Nancy. They're several years old now.

Nancy: Do you know what the present value of those two U.S. Bonds is?

Chuck: I don't know what that is.

Nancy: What about securities? Do you own any stock, Chuck?

Chuck: Yes. I worked for the ABC Insurance Company for many years. I have 10,000 shares with them that was given to me as bonuses over the years.

Nancy: I see. Are these shares of stock titled in your name only?

Chuck: My name only.

Nancy: What is the value of those 10,000 shares today?

Chuck: I got them for about $1 a share, Nancy; so my cost would be somewhere around $10,000. Today, they'd be worth . . . well, let's see . . . I just checked the paper last week. They're up to $30 a share. So, what's that? About $300,000.

Nancy: $300,000. [Note: Don't look overwhelmed, just try to take the information. This happens all the time. It's a true story.] What does this stock yield? What is your annual income from this stock?

Chuck: Eight percent.

Nancy: Oh, I'd say the ABC Insurance Company has been very good to you.

Chuck: They really have.

Nancy: Any other stock, Chuck, that we need to add to your property list?

Chuck: Yes. I've got 200 shares of Mercury common stock.

Nancy: Two hundred shares of Mercury.

Chuck: Yes, this has really been good, Nancy. You ought to look at the growth on this one. I paid $1,600 for it, and it's worth $13,200 today.

Nancy: $13,200. What is the income yield from your Mercury common stock?

Chuck: Two percent.

Nancy: Is it also titled in your name?

Chuck: Yes.

Nancy: OK. [Note: As you're going through this, you'll uncover some tremendous gift opportunities here that you can be thinking about.] Any other stock that we ought to list under the property section?

Chuck: Yes, 100 shares of Iowa Power Preferred. I really don't like to talk about this one, Nancy. I really lost my shirt on it.

Nancy: Well, you were beginning to give me a complex; in fact, I was considering giving you my own personal portfolio to manage, because you've had such success.

Chuck: This one humbled me, Nancy. I paid $10,000 for it and now it's worth only $3,600.

Nancy: And is it also titled in your name?

Chuck: Yes.

Nancy: What is the income yield from your Power Preferred?

Chuck: Three-and-a-half percent.

Nancy: Three-and-a-half. Any other stock that we ought to list?

Chuck: Yes, I have some Board of Regents bonds, Nancy. They're worth $115,000. You know, I really like these things; I get a big kick out of them. You clip those coupons and send them in. But the nice feature here, Nancy, is these bonds are free from both state and federal income taxes. That's pretty important to me.

Nancy: I'm sure it is. [Note what he is telling you. He has an income tax problem.] These Board of Regents bonds, I suspect are also titled in your name only?

Chuck: Yes.

Nancy: Do you recall what you paid for the Board of Regents?

Chuck: No, I don't, Nancy. We'd have to check with my broker.

Nancy: OK, we can do that later. And what return do you presently get on your Board of Regents?

Chuck: Three-and-a-half to 4 percent.

Nancy: Anything else that we ought to list under the property section of your inventory?

Chuck: Yes, 62 United States Series E Savings Bonds, Nancy. These are pretty old. I bought them when I first was employed.

Nancy: Do you have any idea what the present value of these bonds would be?

Chuck: Yes, the bank employee just told me last week they're worth $29,000.

Nancy: $29,000. What was the face value originally on those bonds?

Chuck: Oh, I think somewhere around $9,700.

Nancy: And these bonds are also titled in your name?

Chuck: Yes.

Nancy: Very good. Anything else that belongs under the property section of your name? How about any insurance policies. [He hands me a policy.] I see that it's owned by you, and the face value is $1,000, with your sister, Mary, listed as the first beneficiary.

Chuck: Yes.

Nancy: I also notice that you have not named a second beneficiary on this policy.

Chuck: No, I haven't Nancy. I'm not sure who to list as the second beneficiary.

Nancy: Maybe you could list one of your favorite charities as the second beneficiary.

Chuck: That's a good idea, Nancy.

Nancy: Is there any other property that we should include in your inventory?

Chuck: That's everything, Nancy.

Nancy: OK, let me ask you one other question before I do the arithmetic and total this up. Is there any indebtedness against any of this property?

Chuck: No debts.

Nancy: It's all free and clear. I'll total what you've told me about and see what your estate looks like. If my figures are correct and my arithmetic is still good, it looks like your estate totals $696,800, Chuck.

Chuck: I had no idea it was that much.

Nancy: Is that surprising to you? Well, I'm sure a lot of people don't have any idea what their assets total up to until they've taken the time to sit down and actually prepare an inventory. Now, Chuck let's talk about the third "P"—the plans.

How would you like to plan for the people you talked about? You said you have a sister, Mary, who lives in Chicago. She's 89, and financially independent at this point. You also wanted to do something for Jennie, the cook, and Josephine, the housekeeper. So, let's first decide, how would you like to provide for your sister, Mary?

Chuck: I think I'd like to give her a monthly income, Nancy, of about $500.

Nancy: Five hundred dollars a month. OK. Then, what would you like to do for Jennie, the cook? Would you like to provide her with an income or would you like to provide her with an outright bequest of a fixed amount of dollars?

Chuck: Her husband's job isn't too secure. I'd probably like to give her a cash gift, Nancy, of about $10,000.

Nancy: So a $10,000 bequest for Jennie. How about Josephine, the housekeeper? Would you like to give her an outright bequest also?

Chuck: She's been faithful for the last ten years and could really use the money. I'd say about a $15,000 cash gift.

Nancy: So a $15,000 bequest gift for Josephine. Now, those are all of the people that you mentioned that you want to care for. What about any charitable bequest? Have you considered remembering any of the charities that you have supported during your lifetime?

Chuck: Yes. There are three I've supported for many years. I'd like that support to continue.

Nancy: I would say all three of these charities would be grateful to you for your remembrance. [Note: He hasn't mentioned the charity I represent, and I've spent a lot of time with him—we'll get to that.] Now, in review, . . . you said that you'd like to provide for Mary with $500 a month. You also said you wanted to leave a cash bequest to Jennie and a cash bequest to Josephine. So, let's just recap. [Here's where you've got to get them back on target.] We have a $696,800 estate . . . and if we were to provide a $500-a-month income for your sister Mary, that would mean that you're considering an income to Mary of $6,000 a year.

Chuck: That's right.

Nancy: Two outright bequests to Jennie and Josephine totaling $25,000. So, if we add Mary's portion of $6,000 to the $25,000 we would come up with a total of $31,000. The present value of your estate is approximately $696,800, less the bequest of $31,000 this leaves an estate balance of $665,800. Let's discuss how you can make those dollars work for you today. When we started the four "P's" I indicated that we want to be sure you are adequately provided for during your lifetime.

With your permission, let me explain a plan that not only provides for you during your lifetime, but would also take care of the three favorite charities you mentioned.

Chuck: But that's an awful lot of money to leave three charities.

Nancy: I agree. Let me explain. I think you will see how you can benefit by possibly increasing your own income and still be generous to your favorite charities.

Chuck: Wait a minute, Nancy, you've certainly been good to me. I probably ought to do something for the charity you work for.

My boss died a few years ago and his family designated memorials to your charity. I sent in one of those memorial gifts. Ever since I did that, your president has sent me a letter at least every month.

Nancy: He loves to write letters—especially to generous friends like you who support our purpose. [Note: This example comes from a real experience.]

Chuck: Well, I'll tell you, it's really kept me informed about all the good work you are doing.

Nancy: Now, back to one plan I would like to submit for your consideration. The plan is called a "revocable charitable trust." Here's how it would work for you. Your advisers should be involved to ensure that your best interests are served, of course. You would transfer the $665,800 worth of assets into the Chuck Jones Revocable Charitable Trust and the trust would earn annual income for you as long as you live. The trust would earn somewhere in the range of 7 percent to 10 percent and pay you this income as per your needs and direction. Chuck, "revocable" means that you can take it back. If at any time you want the trust balance returned, you can request that the entire amount be returned to you. The trustee will act upon your demand—no questions asked. You will be free of management and investment worries, but you totally retain your economic freedom.

Chuck: But how do my favorite charities benefit from this arrangement?

Nancy: At the time of your death whatever remains in the trust will be split among the named charitable beneficiaries. Would you like for them to share equally or by percentage?

Chuck: No, not equally, I think percentage would be better. Let's divide it up this way—

> 15 percent to my church
>
> 15 percent to research
>
> 15 percent to my favorite hospital
>
> and 55 percent to your charity, Nancy.

Nancy: Chuck, that is extremely generous and on behalf of the president, the staff, and all of those we serve let me say a deep and sincere thank you for considering our charity to be a remainder beneficiary of your trust. [Note: I said "consider" because nothing is final until it is signed.]

Chuck: You're welcome, Nancy. This trust almost sounds too good to be true, but I have a feeling you know what you are talking about.

Nancy: Thanks for the compliment. It can be a "win-win" arrangement. Now let's discuss the last "P," who are the planners that we need to involve. As I indicated, we need an attorney to draft your will. I will be happy to go with you to see your attorney if that's your wish—we have all the information needed for the appointment. As I mentioned the service we provide is free, so it's whatever you'd like me to do.

Chuck: I'd feel more comfortable if you would go along, Nancy.

Nancy: I'd be happy to do that. The first thing we want to discuss with your attorney is that you have no will. When he looks at your inventory, he'll have the same information as you will have. By preparing a file for the attorney, it will eliminate any unnecessary questions. We also need to talk about your executor. Who would you like to have serve as executor of your estate, Chuck?

You just have the one older sister, and she's living outside the state. Do you have any friends that you would like to appoint as your executor? Or would you like to perhaps use a bank?

Chuck: I like this new bank I've been using.

Nancy: Do you like their trust department?

Chuck: Yes.

Nancy: That's fine. We will name that bank as your executor. And do you want the bank to act alone or do you want your sister to act as co-executor?

Chuck: Oh, I think just the bank.

Nancy: Thanks for your time, Chuck. I'll call you in a few days when the inventory is completed and we will make an appointment to see your attorney.

You perform a real service with the advice you give, and your prospect demonstrates his or her appreciation by responding in a meaningful and generous way.

Of course, this is a hypothetical conversation. Your own conversations with prospects will often extend over a number of visits, telephone calls, and written correspondence.

Equally important to remember is your role. You are a representative of a charity, so any advice given must be of a general nature only. The assistance of professional advisers should be strongly encouraged. If you have to, insist that the prospect consult his or her own adviser(s).

EXAMPLE 9. THE FOUR "P'S."

Four "P's" of Financial Planning

1. People

2. Property

3. Plans

4. Planners

   A. Attorney

   B. Trust officer

   C. CPA (certified public accountant)

   D. CLU (certified life underwriter)

   E. Gift planning officer

The Seminar at a Glance

Are you ready to conduct your first wills seminar? As you may have surmised, the process of establishing a wills emphasis program is not necessarily simple. Wills seminars can be an integral part of such a program used in conjunction with other efforts, such as informational mailings. But there is a step-by-step procedure you may follow to improve the level of planned gifts your charity is receiving. Through commitment and hard work you can get the results you desire.

Let's review some of the points we've discussed in the preceding pages. First of all, there are five good reasons to conduct a wills seminar.

1. Wills seminars can help your organization earn the additional dollars it needs to fund current programs.
2. Wills seminars, as a key component of the planned giving effort, can assist your organization's long-range planning by providing a new source of income.
3. Wills seminars are a means to tap into the number two source of charitable contributions: Bequests.
4. Since a vast majority of American adults die without the benefit of a will, wills seminars can fulfill a real public service.
5. Wills seminars are a positive way to ensure that people understand the importance of a will and the need to specify their charitable bequests in that document.

If you or your board of directors need to be convinced of the benefits of conducting wills seminars, these are five solid reasons. As in all good marketing plans, you can satisfy your organization's needs for new funding sources by providing a service important to your potential donors.

When you're ready to move forward to put a wills emphasis program together, remember there are three overall phases you need to follow: preparation, execution, and follow-up.

Preparation:

To borrow an old saying, "it pays to have all your ducks in a row," particularly before you conduct your first wills seminar.

It may take a little extra effort, but you won't regret putting in the time to be well prepared. There are five steps to follow:

Step 1: Make sure you have a committed board of directors.

Step 2: Do the preparation necessary to have a working knowledge of your state laws.

Step 3: Ascertain your prospect market.

Step 4: Use publicity to draw a crowd.

Step 5: Secure the necessary equipment.

After you have your system in place, the process of setting up a wills seminar can be handled easily.

Execution

The day of the week, timing, and agenda for your wills seminar are all important factors to consider. If a program runs too long, starts too late, or is on the wrong night, it will not matter how outstanding you think your presentation is. Your attendance at the seminar may be affected and you probably won't get the result you desire.

You should choreograph your seminar just as you do any successful fundraising event. Provide the right setting. Structure the seminar's agenda so that the program moves well and is full of interesting, useful information. And, rehearse your portion of the program so that you deliver this critical information in a confident and informed manner. We have provided you with an outline of seminar remarks. These may serve as a foundation on which you can build your own commentary.

Follow-Up

There are two sources for prospects: (1) The people who attend your wills seminar and complete the evaluation form and (2) referrals from friends and relatives who are pleased with the help and counsel they receive and want those close to them to have the same opportunity.

Either prospect is a good one. Now you need to meet personally to follow up. Prospects can become donors.

When you sit down with your potential donor, keep in mind that you are not there to give legal counsel. Rather, you should act as a friendly, knowledgeable adviser who can help the prospect prepare to seek professional help. If you do this effectively, your organization may be the beneficiary of some new bequest dollars.

And as we are all well aware, it is not the dollars themselves that are valuable. Money is only a means to achieve an end. What we really care about is the way new sources of funding can enhance our organization's programs and services.

Resource 8

EXAMPLE 10. SAMPLE INVITATION ANNOUNCEMENT.

A Special Invitation

What: A Dinner Seminar to learn about Estate Planning and Stewardship— what it is and how to use it.

Who: Presentation by [presenter's name]:

Where: XYZ Auditorium, 000 Main Street, Anywhere, State

When: [Day, Date, Time]

How: To reserve space for you and your guest at the seminar, call [contact person] at [phone number]. Since space is limited, make your reservations early.

Cost: There is no charge to those who have made reservations.

R.S.V.P. [Contact person] at [phone number] by [date].

EXAMPLE 11. SAMPLE LETTER INVITING PARTICIPANTS.

Date

Dear Friend:

[Name of organization] is pleased to announce an Estate Planning Seminar for [member, donors, etc.] and their friends. This nontechnical discussion is directed toward those persons who are genuinely interested in preparing themselves to better handle their own financial affairs in the complex economy of today.

If you would like to become better informed in this area, I believe that you will find this program rewarding. [Name of speaker], a highly qualified speaker, will lead a discussion covering wills and trusts, estate planning techniques, taxes, and charitable estate planning.

Please complete and return the enclosed card, or call me at [phone number] if you are interested in attending.

Sincerely,

What's Your Estate Planning IQ?

Take a few moments to answer the following True or False questions as a quick checkup on your knowledge of some very important financial planning techniques:

- My estate plan has been revised to reflect the important changes in federal estate, income, and gift tax laws in recent years. ☐ T ☐ F
- I am aware that I can now leave everything to my spouse free of federal estate tax. ☐ T ☐ F
- I am aware that this may not be the best tax-planning strategy and could cost my heirs in the long run. ☐ T ☐ F
- Educating my children or grandchildren will present no problems from a financial standpoint. ☐ T ☐ F
- I have no desire to benefit causes I have supported during my lifetime as part of my long-range financial plan. ☐ T ☐ F

If you answered false to one or more of these questions, you should attend our special Wills and Estate Planning Seminar.

Careful advance planning, done in conjunction with experienced professionals, can help you avoid running the risk that a court will decide who inherits your estate or that your favorite "Uncle," Sam, will "inherit" more in taxes than is absolutely necessary. This seminar surveys wills, trusts, probate, federal estate and gift taxes, and gift-giving strategies.

Space is limited! Please reserve a place by signing up. If you are unable to attend but would like information on estate planning, please call us at [phone number].

[Date]

[Time]

[Place]

Glossary of Will Terms*

Administrator The person, appointed by a court, to settle the affairs of a decedent who died without leaving a will. The duties of an administrator are similar to those of an executor, but because his or her powers and rights come from the state law, they are often more restricted than those generally given to an executor by a will. (See also *conservator* and *executor.*)

Beneficiary An individual or organization that receives funds from any source.

Bequest A transfer, by will, of personal property such as cash, securities, or other tangible property.

Charitable contribution A donation of something of value to a gift-supported charitable organization, usually tax-deductible.

Charitable deduction The value of money or property transferred to a 501(c)(3) organization is deductible for income, gift, and estate tax purposes. In most cases the term "charitable deduction" refers to the portion of a gift that can be deducted from the donor's income subject to federal income tax. A donor's charitable deduction should not be confused or equated with the value of the gift; that is, gifts for purposes of life income agreements are not federally deductible at their full value.

Conservator A court-appointed official responsible for the protection of the interest of the estate.

Deferred gift A gift to be received in the future, although the transaction housing the gift occurs in the present.

Deferred giving program; bequest program An organized effort by an institution to secure long-term commitments through various forms of gifts to be given at some future time. (See also *planned giving.*)

Descent and distribution The distribution of property to heirs and next of kin, as directed by state laws, constituting the estate of a person who dies without a will or leaves an invalid will.

Devise (*verb*) To transmit or give real property by will.

Devisee Any person receiving title to real property in accordance with the terms of a will.

Resource 8

---

* Reprinted with permission from *Glossary of Fundraising Terms,* The NSFRE Foundation, 1101 King Street, Suite 3000, Alexandria, Virginia 22314.

Devisor The donor of a gift of real property by will.

Distributee One who receives through a will or, though not named, is entitled to property by law or under the terms of a will. (Precise definition may depend on the state involved.)

Donee (or grantee) The individual, organization, or institution that receives a gift.

Donor The individual, foundation, organization, or institution that makes a gift.

Estate administrator Person or corporation with trust powers appointed by the judge to settle an estate. If no will is valid, the appointment is "Administrator." If a valid will has been probated but no executor qualified, an "Administrator with Will Annexed" is appointed by the judge; usually a bond is required.

Estate tax (federal) A tax on the net value of the estate without regard to distributive shares.

Executor (M); executrix (F) A person identified in a will to administer the estate upon the death of the maker of the will and to dispose of it according to the wishes of the same. (See also *administrator.*)

Holographic will See *will(s).*

Intestate Not having made a legal will; not disposed of by legal will. (See also *descent and distribution.*)

Joint tenancy A form of property ownership by two or more persons designated as "joint tenants with right of survivorship." When a joint tenant dies, his/her interest in the property automatically goes to the surviving joint tenant outside and beyond the power of the will of the deceased joint tenant. The property passes outside of probate.

Laws of intestacy The law governing the ownership of a deceased person's property when no specific instructions are left. (See also *intestate.*)

Personal property Cash, stocks, bonds, notes, paintings, furniture, jewelry, and other similar property.

Planned giving The integration of sound personal, financial, and estate planning concepts with the individual donor's plans for lifetime or testamentary giving. (See also *deferred gift* and *deferred giving program.*)

Pour-over will See *will(s).*

Power of attorney The legal document that grants the authority for one person (not necessarily an attorney-at-law) to act as another's agent or attorney-in-fact.

Probate The court proceedings in which the probate court has jurisdiction over (a) an executor and (b) the assets of a decedent. The purposes of probate are (1) to protect the heirs from fraud and embezzlement; (2) to protect the federal, state, and local governments so that all taxes are paid by the estate; and (3) to protect the creditors of the deceased person so that they are paid.

Probate estate The assets and liabilities of a person at death that pass according to the will or by the laws of intestacy.

Real estate Tangible land and all physical substances below, upon, or attached to land; thus, land, houses, trees, fences, oil, gas, and mineral properties are classified as real estate; all else is "personal property."

Reciprocal wills See *will(s)*.

Residuary bequest The part of a will that gives instruction for the disposal of any portion of an estate remaining after payment of debts and other obligations.

Residuary estate What remains of an estate after all bequests and devises have been executed according to the will, and after all debts and expenses have been paid.

Separate property Property owned by an individual prior to marriage, prior to moving to a community-property state, or received by gift or inheritance—to the extent it can be identified.

Tenancy An interest in land or property. "Tenancy by entireties": the owning of land or property by husband and wife, with the survivor taking all, and with interest generally nonseparable during the life of both. "Tenancy in common": the owning of land or property by several persons, with the share of the deceased passing under will or under the intestacy laws to the heirs and not to the survivors. (See also *joint tenancy*.)

Testament A written instrument by which a person disposes of his or her estate, with such disposition taking effect after death. In modern usage, "testament" is synonymous with "will" and "last will and testament." Strictly speaking, however, the terms are different in that a testament bequeaths personal property only.

Testamentary gift A gift of property to a person by will, effective upon the death of the donor.

Testate Having made a legally valid will before death.

Testator (M); testatrix (F) A person who makes or has made a legally valid will; a person who dies leaving a will or testament.

Resource 8

Will(s) Normally a legally executed written instrument by which a person makes disposition of his or her property to take effect after death. "Holographic will": a will entirely written and signed by the testator or maker in his or her own hand. "Nuncupative will": an oral will made by a person in his or her last illness or extremity before witnesses, often not honored in a court of law. "Pour-over will": a will whereby assets controlled by the will are directed to be poured over into a trust. "Reciprocal wills": wills made by two persons in which each leaves everything to the other.

About the Authors

Nancy Perazelli, CFRE

Ms. Perazelli has established a national reputation as a leading authority on planned giving, having conducted will programs for 14 years. Since 1988 she has been a gift planning officer for Drake University, Des Moines, Iowa. Before that she served as the director of planned giving for the Catholic Diocese of Des Moines.

She has served on the National Planned Giving Committee and was the president of the Central Iowa Chapter of the National Society of Fundraising Executives. In 1986, she received the Outstanding Fundraising Executive Award from the Central Iowa NSFRE Chapter.

Chuck Roth

Mr. Roth served as director of development for the Catholic Diocese of Des Moines until 1988 when he retired to pursue writing, consulting, and other interests. He was associated with the Diocese for 27 years, spending more than half of that time in fundraising.

Mr. Roth served for more than 12 years on the board of directors for the National Catholic Development Conference and was vice president of NCDC for four years.

In 1985, he assisted the National Catholic Stewardship Council (NCSC) in planning and developing the NCSC's National Planned Giving Program on behalf of the Catholic Church in the United States.

RESOURCE 9

PLANNED GIVING STRATEGIC PLAN

UNIVERSITY OF DENVER
OFFICE OF GIFT PLANNING
STRATEGIC PLAN—FY 1999

- **Phase One: Prospect/Adviser Education**
  Time allocation: Associate Vice Chancellor (AVC) 10%, Major Gift Planning Officer (MGPO) 10%.

- Financial & Estate Planning Newsletter

  - Target audience: Graduation year 1965 and earlier (alumni age 55 years and older—pre-35th reunion +), gift planning donors and prospects, DU retirees and donors of $2000+.
  - Purpose: To provide information about relevant financial and estate planning issues with a charitable planning theme to educate, identify, and cultivate prospects.
  - Topics: Two/three issues per year—15,000 per issue.
  - Detailed plan:

    - Reevaluate target audience.
    - Add photos to cover.
    - Consider periodic special edition to larger group.
    - Response card in each newsletter.
    - Systematic follow-up via letter with personal visit and/or phone call to respondents.
    - Goal: overall response rate of 0.5%.
    - Use donor testimonials/stories.
    - Provide newsletter binder for interested prospects.

- Trust Officer Luncheon

  - Purpose: Host luncheon for local trust officers featuring Chancellor giving DU update.

- Creative Estate Planning Course

  - Purpose: Provide basic estate planning information and encourage alumni to consider including DU in their estate plans.
  - Audience: Alumni celebrating 25th and 40th Reunions.
  - Timing:

    - Enrollment brochure: November.
    - Course: January–March.

  - Goals:

    - Follow-up survey with each participant; individual follow-up as determined by survey.
    - Target response rate of 5%.

- Younger Alumni
  - Target audience: Year of graduation, 1964–1974 (alumni age 46–56).
  - Purpose: Initial estate/gift planning guidance for educating and identifying future prospects.
  - Goals:
    - One mailing per year—8,000 alumni.
    - Response card in newsletter.
    - Systematic follow-up via letter with phone call.
  - Timing: January–February.
  - Strategy: Use random sample of 500 as a test market.

- Gift Planning Articles/Ads in University-Wide, Unit, and Campaign Newsletters and Publications

- Educational Seminars
  - Prospects.
  - Campaign-related seminars (Chicago, Florida, etc.—evaluate and schedule as appropriate).

- Specialized Target Mailings
  - Gifts of Securities brochure.
  - Guide to Giving—mail to identified expectancies and top prospects.

- Tax Receipt Stuffers
  - Opportunities for Giving brochure.
  - Target audience: Gifts of $500+
  - Other titles as appropriate.

- **Phase Two: Prospect Identification**
  Time Allocation: AVC 10%, MGPO 15%

- External Focus
  - Follow-up with visit/call/written documentation to all alumni, friends, and donors requesting additional information via:
    - Financial & Estate Planning Newsletter.
    - Creative Estate Planning course.
    - Annual fund gift card check-offs.
    - Telefund.
    - Alumni survey/address update cards.
    - Alumni Journal/Campaign Chronicle gift planning ads.
      Use donor testimonials as often as possible.

- Professional advisers:
  - Cultivate relationships with key attorneys, CPAs, trust officers, etc. through personal visits and other contacts in the Denver community.

- Internal Focus
  - Professional staff training sessions (4 times annually):
    - Objective: Increase familiarity of major gift officers with gift planning strategies in order to help them identify new major gift prospects.
    - Goal: One new gift planning prospect per month identified by each major gift officer.
    - Strategy: Meet regularly with major gift officers to review their potential gift planning prospects and develop cultivation and solicitation strategies.
    - Topics:

      Bequests and estate tax issues.
      Charitable remainder trusts.
      Retained life estates.
      Pooled income fund gifts.
      Gift annuities.
      Charitable lead trusts.
      Gifts of IRAs and retirement plan assets.
      Discussing gift planning with prospects.
      Identifying gift planning prospects.
      Planning options with appreciated securities.
      Ethical issues in gift planning.
      Private foundations and other giving strategies.

- **Phase Three: Prospect Cultivation and Solicitation**
  Time Allocation: AVC 60%, MGPO 70%

- Personal Contacts
  - Purpose: Identify, qualify, cultivate, solicit, and steward major and planned gifts from alumni and friends in Colorado and nationally. Such gifts include direct, outright gifts and deferred gifts such as life-income gifts and bequests.
  - Goal: Associate Vice Chancellor and Major Gift Planning Officer to focus on personally cultivating and soliciting major gift planning prospects locally and in key geographic areas:
    - AVC: 150 visits annually.
      Geographic assignment: Colorado, Arizona, Kansas (Kansas City), New Mexico, Wyoming, Utah, Oklahoma.

- MGPO: 240 visits annually.
  Geographic assignment: Colorado, Oregon, Washington, Idaho, Montana, California, Florida.
- Goal: Identify 30 new expectancies.
- Goal: Increase identified expectancies to 650 totaling $64 million in known commitments.
- Goal: Consistent contacts with identified expectancies in concert with major gift officers.
- Goal: Submit 50 personalized gift proposals/asks.
- Strategy: Assign gift planning prospects in Colorado and in key national regions.

- Gift Annuity Emphasis

  - Strategy: Market both outright gift annuities and deferred gift annuities as appropriate.
  - Purpose: Secure additional deferred gifts to the University.
  - Target: Younger alumni for deferred gift annuities and older alumni for outright gift annuities.
  - Timing: Fall–winter (focus on end-of-calendar-year giving).
  - Goals:

    - Response rate of 0.1%.
    - Systematic follow-up via personal visit/call and written proposal to respondents.

- DU 21st Century Fund/DU Flexible Endowment

  - Purpose: To provide a means of funding future endowed funds via a more aggressive mix of investments than is contained in DU's Consolidated Endowment.
  - Goal: Achieve target market value within 10 years of initial funding.
  - Strategy: Use high-profile investment manager to attract donors who want to grow current gifts into a major future endowment.
  - Target market: Younger alumni, especially local.
  - Benefits: Unique approach, growth oriented.
  - Action: Review potential costs and benefits with DU Controller, Endowment Consultant, etc., and formulate plan of action. Seek out initial donor. Develop promotional materials.

- Reunions

  - Purpose: Reestablish relationship between University and alumni in anticipation of lifetime gift at 50th reunion.

- Strategy: 40th Reunion Gift Subcommittee as part of alumni reunion effort, coupled with Creative Estate Planning Course.
- Strategy: 25th Reunion Gift Subcommittee as part of alumni reunion effort, coupled with targeted marketing efforts to this age group.
- Strategy: 10th Reunion Gift Subcommittee as part of alumni reunion effort, coupled with targeted marketing efforts to this age group.
- Gift planning staff participate in reunion events.

- Pioneer Society

  - Purpose: Recognition and donor involvement in the University, confirmation of bequest intention, identification of gifts to be credited to DU Campaign.

    - Goal: 25 new members.

  - Visit each member at least once every three years.
  - One–two on-campus events.

    - Goal: 50 attendees per event.

  - Stewardship through existing University events.

- **Phase Four: Administrative**
  Time Allocation: AVC 20%, MGPO 5%

  - Estate tracking and projections.
  - Quarterly report to Vice Chancellor.
  - Enhance expectancy file of known bequests and planned gifts.
  - Ongoing evaluation of program activities.
  - Review and revise gift planning policies.
  - Coordinate investment management and administrative tasks re life income gifts with Kaspick & Company.
  - Enhance endowment reporting/stewardship package.
  - Participate implementation of new alumni/development database software package.
  - Special projects as assigned.

RESOURCE 10

GIFT ACCEPTANCE POLICIES

Resource 10

GIFT ACCEPTANCE AND DISPOSITION POLICY OF DUKE UNIVERSITY

Table of Contents

◆

Resource 10

Gifts Governed by This
Policy Gift Policy Committee

This policy is established to govern the acceptance and disposition of all gifts made to Duke University and any of its subsidiaries or affiliated organizations, whether such gifts are *inter vivos* (lifetime) gifts or gifts from estates, other than gifts of (a) cash, (b) publicly traded equities traded on national exchanges, (c) whole life insurance policies meeting the criteria set forth in Section A of Category 3 below, (d) library books/collections donated specifically to a University library, or (e) works of art donated specifically to the University Art Museum. All gifts that fall under this policy must be approved in advance of acceptance of such gifts by the Gift Policy Committee (GPC) and in accordance with this policy. It is the responsibility of any development officer or departmental or other University official (principally in the Library, Art Museum, Real Estate Office, Medical Center Cultural Affairs Office, or Alumni & Development Records Office) presented with a gift or working with an estate to bring all gifts subject to this policy before the Gift Policy Committee prior to accepting such gifts.

The Gift Policy Committee is appointed by the President of Duke University, is chaired by the Executive Vice President, and consists of representatives from Development including the Director of Planned Giving and at least one representative from Medical Center Development, one from Duke Management Company (DUMAC), one from Alumni & Development Records, one from Endowment Investment Accounting, one from Real Estate, and one from University Counsel, subject to such changes in composition as the President may wish to make from time to time. The Director of Planned Giving will serve as Secretary to the Committee.

Gifts subject to this policy will be considered in four categories: tangible personal property, real property, life insurance, and other assets. The latter category includes, but is not limited to, such items as promissory notes, assignment of promissory notes, partnership interests, and restricted or non-publicly traded securities. The criteria for gift acceptance, the acceptance/approval process, and the disposition policy (administration policy in the case of life insurance) for each category is set forth below.

Category 1—Tangible Personal Property

A. Criteria for Acceptance

Except as provided in the following Section B regarding gifts-in-kind, the GPC will consider gifts of tangible personal property, including but not limited to works of art, manuscripts, literary works, boats, motor vehicles, and computer hardware, only after a thorough review indicates that the property is

1. readily marketable; or
2. needed by the University for use in a manner which is related to one of the purposes for which tax exempt status of the University was granted; that is, for education, health care, research, or a combination thereof.

B. Gift-in-Kind Guidelines

The GPC has delegated the authority to accept certain types of gifts-in-kind (GIKs) valued at less than $5,000 to the Office of Alumni & Development Records, including but not limited to tickets to athletic events, postage, television sets, VCRs, stereos, computers and computer software, medical equipment, and items for auction. Such gifts need not be formally presented for acceptance by the GPC, but instead may be sent directly to the Office of Alumni & Development Records for processing. Only in the event that the Director of Alumni & Development Records is unsure as to whether the GPC would accept such a gift does a GIK valued at less than $5,000 need to be brought before the GPC for formal acceptance.

Effective July 1, 1994, the GPC established a minimum value for GIKs to be recorded on the University's gift record system: gifts with a total value of less than $100 need not be processed through Alumni & Development Records or Plant Accounting. The department or program accepting a GIK valued at less than $100 may acknowledge the gift, but no further processing is required.

Any GIK with a value exceeding $100 but less than $5,000 will be recorded on the University's gift record system at $1, unless independent verification of the fair market value of the gift is provided. The receipt given by the Office of Alumni & Development Records for all GIKs will reflect the following two messages to emphasize the donor's responsibility to obtain tax advice:

1. Your [the donor's] gift may require that you complete IRS Form 8283, together with an appraisal of the donated property. Please consult your tax adviser.
2. The deduction you [the donor] receive from this gift may be limited to the lower of the cost or the market value of the goods donated. Please consult your tax adviser.

GIKs with a value exceeding $5,000 will be processed in accordance with the following Section C and will be recorded on the University's gift record system at a value to be determined by the GPC. The Director of Alumni & Development Records or the GPC may require documentation from the donor or the department or program to benefit from the GIK in order to substantiate the donor's cost and/or the market value of the goods donated.

C. Approval/Acceptance Process

1. The development officer or other appropriate departmental official will prepare a written summary of the gift proposal and submit that summary to the GPC through the Director of Planned Giving. At a minimum, the summary shall include the following information:

   a. description of asset;
   b. the purpose of the gift (e.g., to fund an endowed chair, a deferred gift, an unrestricted gift) and the department(s), program(s), or endowment(s) to benefit from the gift;
   c. an estimate or appraisal of the gift's fair market value and marketability;
   d. any potential University use and, if so, written review by the department to benefit from the asset; and
   e. any special arrangements requested by the donor concerning disposition (e.g., price considerations, time duration prior to disposition, potential buyers, etc.).

2. The GPC will review the material presented by the development officer or other appropriate departmental official and make a determination of whether to accept or reject the proposed gift (or, if necessary, to postpone a decision pending the receipt of additional information). The final determination of the GPC shall be communicated to the development officer or other appropriate departmental official by the Director of Planned Giving, and the development officer or other appropriate departmental official shall communicate the University's decision to the donor in writing.

3. If a proposed gift of tangible personal property is approved by the GPC, the Director of Alumni & Development Records will acknowledge receipt of the gift on behalf of the University. The University will not appraise or assign a value to the gift property. It is the donor's responsibility to establish a value for the gift and to provide, at the donor's expense, a qualified appraisal required by the IRS in the case of gifts of tangible personal property valued in excess of $5,000.

4. The execution and delivery of a deed of gift or other appropriate conveyance acceptable to the University, and the delivery of the property, as applicable, will complete the gift. The donor will pay the costs associated with the conveyance and delivery of the gift. In addition, the IRS requires the filing of Form 8283 by the donor for gifts of tangible personal property valued at more than $500. This form should be sent to the Office of Alumni & Development Records for execution by the University.

D. Disposition

1. Upon approval of a proposed gift of tangible personal property by the GPC, it will assign a University office the responsibility for disposing of the gift, unless the gift is intended to be put to a specific University purpose in which case no immediate disposition is necessary. Any guidelines the GPC wishes to impose on disposition, including minimum sales price and approval or rejection of any special arrangements with the donor, will be put in writing to the University office responsible for disposing of the gift at this time.
2. Upon approval of a proposed gift, the GPC through the Office of Endowment Investment Accounting will designate a Budget and Finance Responsibility code (BAFR code) for charging expenses associated with the gift pending disposition. In the absence of a known beneficiary for the gift, a Development or Medical Center Development BAFR code will be used as a holding account.
3. The Chair of the GPC must first be consulted and/or the entire GPC polled or convened before a gift of tangible personal property may be sold for less than appraised value or estimated fair market value, or fails to meet the guidelines imposed by the GPC when approving the gift, as the case may be. If in the judgment of the University office responsible for disposing of the gift a current appraisal of the property would assist in disposing of the property, the University office responsible for disposing of the gift may request permission from the GPC or its Chair to have the appraisal performed.
4. Upon sale of the property, the University office responsible for disposing of the gift will prepare a final report on the property, including a financial summary of net proceeds to the extent known, and distribute it to the Director of Planned Giving, the Office of Endowment Investment Accounting, the Office of Alumni & Development Records and the designated representative of the department to benefit from the gift.
5. The Office of Alumni & Development Records is responsible for filing Form 8282 for gifts of tangible personal property valued at more than $5,000 sold by the University within two years of the date of gift.

Category 2—Real Property

The GPC will consider gifts of real property, both improved and unimproved (e.g., detached single-family residences, condominiums, apartment buildings, rental property, commercial property, farms, acreage, etc.), including gifts subject to a retained life estate, only after a thorough review of the criteria for acceptance set forth below under the direction and supervision of the Director of Real Estate Administration.

A. Criteria for Acceptance

1. *Market value and marketability.* The GPC must receive a reasonably current appraisal of the fair market value of the property and interest in the property the University would receive if the proposed gift were approved. Development officers will inform the donor that, if the gift is completed, the IRS will require an appraisal made within sixty days of the date of gift. Development officers must understand and communicate to donors that it is the University's policy to dispose of all gifts of real estate (other than property which the University wishes to retain) as expeditiously as possible. Thus, regardless of the value placed on the property by the donor's appraisal, the University will attempt to sell at a reasonable price in light of current market conditions, and the donor needs to be informed that any such sale occurring within two years of the date of gift will be reported to the IRS on Form 8282.

2. *Potential environmental risks.* All proposed gifts of real property, including gifts from estates, must be accompanied by a Phase I environmental audit performed at the donor's expense. The only permitted exception to this requirement is for residential property which has been used solely for residential purposes for a significant (at least twenty-year) period of time. In cases where this exception applies and no environmental audit is undertaken, the donor/executor must have outside parties complete an Environmental Checklist prepared by the Office of Real Estate and may be required to execute an environmental indemnity agreement. Even in cases where a Phase I audit is submitted, the Director of Real Estate may require that the donor sign an environmental indemnity agreement.

3. *Limitations and encumbrances.* The existence of any and all mortgages, deeds of trust, restrictions, reservations, easements, mechanic's liens, and other limitations of record must be disclosed. No gift of real estate will be accepted until all mortgages, deeds of trust, liens, and other encumbrances have been

discharged, except in very unusual cases where the fair market value of the University's interest in the property net of all encumbrances is substantial.

4. *Carrying costs.* The existence and amount of any carrying costs, including but not limited to property owners' association dues, country club membership dues and transfer charges, taxes, and insurance must be disclosed.

5. *Title information.* A copy of any title information in the possession of the donor, such as the most recent survey of the property, a title insurance policy, and/or an attorney's title opinion, must be furnished.

B. Approval/Acceptance Process

1. The Director of Real Estate Administration with the assistance of the development officer will prepare a written summary of the gift proposal and submit that summary to the GPC through the Director of Planned Giving. At a minimum, the summary shall include the following information:

   a. description of real property;

   b. the purpose of the gift (e.g., to fund an endowed chair, a deferred gift, an unrestricted gift) and the department(s), or endowment(s) to benefit from the gift;

   c. an appraisal of the property and, if different, the University's interest in the property's fair market value and marketability;

   d. any potential for income and expenses, encumbrances, and carrying costs prior to disposition;

   e. any environmental risks or problems revealed by audit or survey;

   f. any potential University use; and

   g. any special arrangements requested by the donor concerning disposition (e.g., price considerations, time duration prior to disposition, potential buyers, Realtors or brokers with whom the donor would like the University to list the property, etc.).

2. The GPC will review the material presented by the Director of Real Estate and make a determination of whether to accept or reject the proposed gift of real property (or, if necessary, to postpone a decision pending the receipt of additional information). The Director of Planned Giving shall communicate the final determination of the GPC to the development officer, and the development officer shall communicate the University's decision to the donor in writing, including any conditions imposed by the GPC prior to acceptance.

3. If a proposed gift of real property is approved by the GPC, the Director of Alumni & Development Records will acknowledge receipt of the gift on behalf

of the University upon notice by the Office of Real Estate that the property has been properly recorded in the local Registry of Deeds. The University will not appraise or assign a value to the gift property. It is the donor's responsibility to establish a value for the gift and to provide, at the donor's expense, a qualified appraisal required by the IRS.

4. The execution and delivery of a deed of gift or other appropriate conveyance will complete the gift. The costs associated with the conveyance and delivery of the gift, including but not limited to recording fees and, if deemed necessary by the Director of Real Estate, a current survey, title insurance, and/or an attorney's title opinion, will be either paid by the donor or charged to the fund code of the department(s), program(s), or endowment(s) to benefit by the donation. In addition, the IRS for gifts of real property requires the filing of Form 8283 by the donor. This form should be sent to the Office of Alumni & Development Records for execution by the University.

C. Disposition

1. By resolution adopted in June 1996 by the Executive Committee of the University's Board of Trustees, the Executive Vice President may authorize the sale of real property received by gift valued at up to $1 million, provided that such property is not located on or contiguous to the University's Campus or determined by the President or Executive Vice President to be important to the University in carrying out its educational, research, and health care mission; in cases where one or more of the above criteria is/are applicable, Board of Trustee (or Executive Committee) approval of the sale is required.

2. Subject to the terms of the above resolution, it is the responsibility of the Office of Real Estate Administration to dispose of all gifts of real property, except those gifts of real property acquired by an investment pool under the management of DUMAC, at the time a gift is received. For purposes of this Policy, the term "acquired by an investment pool" shall mean, in the case of gifts designated for endowment purposes, acquired by the issuance of investment pool units credited to the designated endowment fund; in all other cases, acquired by cash transfer to the designated beneficiary of the gift. The GPC will advise the Director of Real Estate Administration of any guidelines it wishes to impose on disposition, such as minimum sales price or approving/rejecting special arrangements with the donor.

3. If the Chair of the GPC determines that it is in the best interests of the University to retain for its own use a gift of real property, he/she will recommend to the appropriate officers of the University and/or to the Board of Trustees that, in the case of gifts designated for endowment purposes, they designate

and reclassify unrestricted quasi-endowment or other available funds for the purpose of providing the designated endowment fund with an amount equal to the fair market value of the property as of the date of its receipt by the University; and that, in all other cases, they authorize liquidation of such funds for the benefit of the designated gift purpose.

4. Upon acceptance of a gift, the GPC through the Office of Endowment/Investment Accounting will designate a BAFR code for charging expenses associated with the gift pending disposition. In the absence of a known beneficiary for the gift, a Development or Medical Center Development BAFR code will be used as a holding account.

5. Until the property is sold or otherwise disposed of, the Office of Real Estate will prepare quarterly status reports and distribute them to the Director of Planned Giving and to the designated representative of the department to benefit from the gift.

6. Upon sale of the property, the Office of Real Estate will prepare a final report on the property, including a financial summary of net proceeds, and distribute it to the Director of Planned Giving, the Office of Endowment/Investment Accounting, and the designated representative of the department to benefit from the gift.

7. The Office of Real Estate Administration is responsible for filing Form 8282 for gifts of real property sold by the University within two years of the date of gift.

Category 3—Life Insurance

A. Criteria for Acceptance

The University will accept—without the necessity of review and approval by the GPC—gifts of life insurance policies, including whole life, variable, and universal life policies, which meet the following three criteria:

1. The policy is either paid up or, if not paid up as of the date of the gift:

   a. has a minimum face value of $100,000;
   b. has a payment schedule not to exceed twelve years and which assumes an interest rate not to exceed 1 percent below the prevailing prime interest rate as reported in the *Wall Street Journal* (for existing policies an "in force" illustration will be required); and
   c. requires a written pledge of a charitable contribution from the donor to the University in a total amount which equals or exceeds the total premiums

due, and with pledge payments scheduled so as to equal or exceed each policy premium payment as that payment becomes due. This written pledge also will acknowledge the absolute ownership by the University of the policy given and acknowledge the resulting right of the University to cash in the policy and apply the proceeds of the same for the benefit of the University in accordance with an existing endowment agreement, if any; and if there is no endowment agreement in effect, or if minimum funding levels for the same are not attained with the proceeds, then the pledge shall provide that the proceeds shall be applied for the benefit of the University as the Trustees of the University may deem appropriate, giving due consideration to the intent of the donor.

2. Duke University is designated as the owner and the beneficiary of the policy. (While the policy will identify the University as the beneficiary, the development officer should work with the donor to clarify the purpose of the gift—whether it be for endowment [existing or new], specific program or department, or unrestricted use—by attachment of a memorandum, letter, or endowment agreement to the policy.)

3. If intended for endowment purposes, the face value of the policy meets the minimum funding standards for endowments for its stated purpose(s) established by the Board of Trustees and in effect at the time of the gift of the policy. (Development officers need to be aware that the actual funding of an endowment funded with the proceeds of life insurance takes place following the death of the insured, and the minimum funding requirements that are in effect at the time of the insured's death will govern whether there are sufficient death benefits to fund such endowment for its stated purpose[s].)

B. Approval/Acceptance Process

1. The development officer will prepare a written summary of any proposed gift of a life insurance policy which fails to meet all of the criteria specified in Section A above and submit that summary through the Director of Planned Giving. At a minimum, the summary shall include the following information:

   a. description of the type of life insurance policy, face value, premium payment schedule, interest rate, age of insured(s), and other relevant policy information; and

   b. the purpose of the gift (e.g., to fund an endowed chair, a deferred gift, an unrestricted gift) and the department(s), program(s), or endowment(s) to benefit from the gift.

2. The GPC will review the material presented by the development officer and make a determination of whether to accept or reject the proposed gift or, if necessary, to impose any terms (e.g., the donor's pledge to make contributions to cover premiums, a revision in the payment schedule) as a condition of approval. The final determination of the GPC shall be communicated to the development officer by the Director of Planned Giving, and the development officer shall communicate the University's decision to the donor in writing, including any conditions imposed by the GPC prior to acceptance.
3. If a proposed gift of a life insurance policy is approved by the GPC, the Director of Alumni & Development Records will acknowledge receipt of the gift on behalf of the University.
4. The gift will be completed upon the execution and delivery of the life insurance policy to the University or an assignment of the policy in the event that the University is not the original owner of the policy.

C. Administration

The Office of Alumni & Development Records shall administer all gifts of life insurance policies and shall maintain records of all donor policies, contribution schedules, donor designations of death benefits, and the like. This office also shall be responsible for pledge reminders and monitoring payments of premiums.

The Office of Endowment/Investment Accounting shall be responsible for confirming the existence and cash value of all policies in force at least annually and for collecting and distributing death benefits. Upon receipt of death benefits, the Office of Endowment/Investment Accounting shall provide notice to the department(s), program(s), or endowment(s) to benefit from the gift.

Category 4—Other Assets

A. Criteria for Acceptance

The GPC will consider gifts of other assets, including but not limited to promissory notes, assignment of promissory notes, partnership interests, and restricted or non-publicly traded securities, only after a thorough review of the criteria set forth below.

1. *Market value and marketability.* The GPC must receive a reasonably current appraisal of the fair market value of the property and interest in the property the University would receive if the proposed gift were approved. Development officers will inform the donor that, if the gift is completed, the IRS will require

an appraisal made within sixty days of the date of gift. The appraisal and other information must indicate clearly and convincingly that there is a market for the asset under consideration and that the asset can be sold within a reasonable period of time.

2. *Potential environmental risks.* All proposed gifts in which the University would acquire an interest in real property must be accompanied by a Phase I environmental audit performed at the donor's expense. The only permitted exception to this requirement is for residential property that has been used solely for residential purposes for a significant (at least twenty-year) period of time. In cases where this exception applies and no environmental audit is undertaken, the donor must have an agent complete an Environmental Checklist prepared by the Office of Real Estate and may be required to execute an environmental indemnity agreement.

3. *Limitations and encumbrances.* The existence of any and all mortgages, deeds of trust, restrictions, reservations, easements, mechanic's liens, and other limitations of record must be disclosed. No gift of an interest in real estate will be accepted until all mortgages, deeds of trust, liens, and other encumbrances have been discharged, except in very unusual cases where the fair market value of the University's interest in the property net of all encumbrances is substantial or where a separate agreement to pay any such encumbrances which might be charged to the University has been executed by a financially responsible party.

4. *Carrying costs.* The existence and amount of any carrying costs, including but not limited to property owners' association dues, country club membership dues and transfer charges, taxes, and insurance, must be disclosed.

5. *Title information.* A copy of any title information in the possession of the donor, such as the most recent survey of the property, a title insurance policy, and/or an attorney's title opinion, must be furnished.

B. Approval/Acceptance Process

1. The development officer will prepare a written summary of the gift proposal and submit that summary to the GPC through the Director of Planned Giving. At a minimum, the summary shall include the following information:

   a. description of the asset;
   b. the purpose of the gift (e.g., to fund an endowed chair, a deferred gift, an unrestricted gift) and the department(s), program(s), or endowment(s) to benefit from the gift;
   c. an estimate or appraisal of the asset's fair market value and marketability;

      d. potential for income and expenses, encumbrances, and carrying costs prior to disposition;

      e. any environmental risks or problems revealed by audit or survey;

      f. credit history or financial statement of financially responsible party, if applicable (N.B.: Duke's Public Safety Department can help with credit checks);

      g. any special arrangements requested by the donor concerning disposition (e.g., price considerations, time duration prior to disposition, potential buyers, Realtors or brokers with whom the donor would like the University to list the property, etc.).

2. The GPC will review the material presented by the development officer and make a determination of whether to accept or reject the proposed gift (or, if necessary, to postpone a decision pending the receipt of additional information). The final determination of the GPC shall be communicated to the development officer by the Director of Planned Giving, and the development officer shall communicate the University's decision to the donor in writing, including any conditions imposed by the GPC prior to acceptance.

3. If a proposed gift of an asset in this Category 4 is approved by the GPC, the Director of Alumni & Development Records will acknowledge receipt of the gift on behalf of the University. The University will not appraise or assign a value to the gift property. It is the donor's responsibility to establish a value for the gift and to provide, at the donor's expense, a qualified appraisal required by the IRS in the case of assets valued in excess of $5,000 ($10,000 for non-publicly traded stock).

4. The gift will be completed by the execution and delivery of a deed of gift or other appropriate conveyance, and the delivery of the property, as applicable. The donor will pay the costs associated with the conveyance and delivery of the gift. In addition, the filing of Form 8283 by the donor is required by the IRS for gifts of assets valued at more than $500. This form should be sent to the Office of Alumni & Development Records for execution by the University.

C. Disposition

1. It is the responsibility of the Office of Endowment/Investment Accounting to dispose of all gifts of assets in this Category 4. If the asset involves an interest in real estate, it is generally expected that the Office of Real Estate will assist the Office of Endowment/Investment Accounting in disposing of the asset. If the asset is a security, it is generally expected that DUMAC will assist the Office of Endowment/Investment Accounting in disposing of the asset, subject to

DUMAC's policies then in effect for trading securities. Any guidelines the GPC wishes to impose on disposition, including minimum sales price and approval or rejection of any special arrangements with the donor, will be put in writing to the Director of Endowment/Investment Accounting at this time.

2. Upon acceptance of a gift, the GPC through the Office of Endowment/Investment Accounting will designate a BAFR code for charging expenses associated with the gift pending disposition. In the absence of a known beneficiary for the gift, a Development or Medical Center Development BAFR code will be used as a holding account.

3. Upon sale of the property, the Office of Endowment/Investment Accounting will prepare a final report on the property, including a financial summary of net proceeds, and distribute it to the Director of Planned Giving and the designated representative of the department to benefit from the gift.

4. The Office of Endowment/Investment Accounting is responsible for filing Form 8282 for assets valued at more than $5,000 sold by the University within two years of the date of gift.

Effective Date

These policies were first adopted as of May 1, 1994, and last revised as of December 18, 1996.

Exceptions

Exceptions to this policy must be approved in writing by the GPC.

Addendum No. 1: Guidelines and Procedures for the Acceptance of Outdoor Objects

This addendum establishes guidelines and procedures for the acceptance of works of art, sculpture, and other three-dimensional objects intended for outdoor display (hereafter referred to as "outdoor objects") within the confines of the University's campuses.

It shall be the general policy of the University not to accept gifts of outdoor objects for display in the core areas of the East and West Campuses. The core areas of the East and West Campuses are defined as the quadrangles and the openings that lead to the quadrangles. Normally, the only permitted exception to this general policy shall be for outdoor objects intended to be displayed in well-recognized areas set aside for such displays. Currently, benches outside the West Union Building would fall within this exception; in the future, so too would a sculpture garden outside the Art Museum, when and if such an area is established.

Other than in extraordinary circumstances, no gift of an outdoor object will be deemed acceptable if it requires the expenditure of significant sums of money by the University, either for its installation and/or its continuing maintenance, unless the proposed gift is accompanied by a separate cash gift or an endowment of sufficient size to meet these expenditures.

For outdoor objects intended to be displayed within the confines of the University's campuses, the acceptance process shall proceed as follows:

1. Upon being notified that a gift of an outdoor object has been proposed, the GPC shall first determine if the general criteria described above have been met. To assist the GPC in this evaluation, the proposal must be accompanied by the following information:

   a. a description and a picture or photograph of the object;
   b. the donor's preferences for identification of the object (i.e., any plaques or other means of identification); and
   c. estimated installation and maintenance costs, and the funding for them, if any.

   If the general criteria above have not been met or if the donor is unwilling or unable to furnish the requested information, the GPC shall decline to accept the proposed gift.

2. If the proposed gift is intended to honor an individual or an event, the GPC shall, in consultation with the Executive Vice President and/or other Senior Officers of the University, determine if the timing of the proposed gift is appropriate and, if not, the GPC shall decline to accept the proposed gift.

3. If the above criteria have been met, the GPC shall refer the matter to the President's Art Advisory Committee (PAAC) to judge the proposed gift's aesthetic merits. The PAAC is chaired by the Director of the Art Museum and also includes sufficient other members appointed by the Chair to ensure adequate representation of the University community. Currently, the other members are the University Archivist and a member of the Art and Art History Department. The PAAC shall be asked to draw one of three conclusions: (a) the proposed gift meets the University's general aesthetic standard as interpreted by PAAC, regardless of the intended site for display; (b) the proposed gift meets the University's general aesthetic standard as interpreted by PAAC, depending upon

the intended site for display; or (c) the proposed gift does not meet the University's general aesthetic standard as interpreted by PAAC. If the PAAC's conclusion is (c), it shall so advise the GPC, and the GPC shall decline to accept the gift. If the PAAC's conclusion is either (a) or (b), it shall so advise the GPC, and the GPC shall proceed to the next step below.

In the case of outdoor objects that are not works of art, such as a bench or a trellis, the GPC may decide to forgo referral of the matter to the PAAC and proceed directly to the next step below.

4. Upon receipt of a favorable determination as to aesthetic merit by the PAAC, the GPC normally will proceed to Step 5 below, but may, in certain cases in which siting is an issue, first refer the matter to an ad hoc Site Advisory Committee (typically consisting of four members: the University Architect, a representative from the Committee of Facilities and the Environment [CFE], a representative from the PAAC, and a representative from the GPC). If utilized, the ad hoc Site Advisory Committee shall report back to the GPC its recommendations as to the suitability of suggested sites and other sites, if any, deemed suitable by the ad hoc committee.

5. Based on the information and recommendations acquired in the above three steps, the GPC then shall normally either (a) reject the proposed gift if no site exists which is satisfactory to the GPC; or (b) accept the proposed gift, subject to siting approval by CFE, if there is a site or are sites satisfactory to the GPC.

6. Once a proposed gift is referred to CFE for siting approval, the University Architect pursuant to standard operating procedure shall request permission from the Executive Vice President to place the item on CFE's agenda. If the Executive Vice President should refuse permission, the University Architect shall notify the GPC, and the GPC shall decline to accept the proposed gift.

If a proposed gift of an outdoor object is placed on CFE's agenda, the sponsor of the gift (who may be a development officer or the Director of the Art Museum or his/her designee) shall then present the proposed gift to CFE outside the presence of the donor. CFE may approve, reject, or select alternative sites to any sites for display suggested prior to CFE's review. If CFE approves of one or more site(s) for display, CFE shall so notify the GPC, and the gift shall be accepted. If CFE cannot agree upon a site for display within a reasonable period of time, CFE shall so notify the GPC, and the proposed gift shall be declined.

These guidelines shall apply to proposed gifts of outdoor objects, regardless of whether or not they are intended to honor active, living, or dead faculty members, students, or staff and regardless of whether the outdoor objects represent a living person or not, including the honoree, if there is one.

UNIVERSITY OF VERMONT
GIFT ACCEPTANCE POLICY:
PLANNED/DEFERRED GIFTS

Planned/deferred gifts generally are not taken out of current earnings, but rather involve the transfer of substantial assets which affect the distribution of the donor's estate. Because they accrue to the University in the future, they do not immediately confer institutional ownership. The University may serve as sole or co-trustee of any deferred gift which requires the appointment of a fiduciary. The acceptable methods of creating deferred gifts to the University are described below.

I. Will Bequest

A bequest is a gift of any amount or form made to the University in a donor's will. Bequests may provide for a specific dollar amount in cash, specific securities, specific articles of tangible personal property, or be established as indicated in the policy on Outright Gifts. A gift in any amount may be accepted as a contribution to an existing fund so long as the terms and conditions of the existing fund so permit.

Among donors' options are residuary and contingent bequests. A residuary bequest will give the University all or a portion of the estate after all debts, taxes, expenses, and all other bequests have been paid. A contingent bequest will ensure that, despite unforeseen circumstances, specified property will pass to the University rather than unintended beneficiaries.

Donors may also establish, by will, an annuity trust or unitrust. The bequest can be arranged so as to provide a life income for a designated beneficiary or beneficiaries by directing that the bequest be used to establish a charitable remainder annuity trust or charitable remainder unitrust. If such a gift is made by will, the principal will pass to the University only after the death of the life income beneficiary.

Gifts may be made to the University through the execution of a new will, or through a codicil to an existing will. Donors may also add either a residual or contingent codicil to their wills.

Donors are encouraged to recognize that over the many years following the establishment of an endowment, the needs, policies, and circumstances of the University can change in unforeseen ways. The University Administration must have the flexibility to make use of funds in the best interest of the institution and in accord with donor interests and specifications. Thus, donors are advised to describe the specific purposes of their gifts as broadly as possible and to avoid detailed limitations and restrictions. Donors considering bequests for a specific purpose are encouraged to consult with an Advancement Officer.

When money is left to The University of Vermont & State Agricultural College as an unrestricted bequest, it is deposited into an unrestricted account to be used at the discretion of the University.

Because conditions change over time, all endowments must contain the following contingency clause: *If, in the opinion of the University of Vermont, all or part of the funds cannot be applied in strict conformance with the purpose(s) previously stated, they may use these funds for other appropriate purposes as nearly aligned to the original intent of the donor as good conscience and need dictate within the authorized powers of the University.*

II. Remainder Interest—Personal Residence/Farm

With the review and approval of the GAC [Gift Acceptance Committee], a donor can give a remainder interest in a personal residence, such as a home or condominium or a farm, to the University. The donor or other occupants may continue to occupy the residence or operate the farm without disruption for the duration of the donor's life. Thereafter, the residence or farm will either be sold or used by the University for purposes specified by the donor, if any. The procedures for evaluating proposed gifts of real property, as outlined above, also apply to gifts of a remainder interest in property.

If a life estate is retained in the property, expenses for maintenance, real estate taxes, and any indebtedness relating to the property are to be borne by the donor or the primary beneficiary.

III. Life Insurance

A. Acceptance Criteria

The University will automatically accept, without the necessity of review and approval by the GAC, gifts of whole life insurance policies which meet the following three criteria:

1. The policy is a whole life insurance policy which is either paid up or, if not paid up as of the date of gift, the University is designated as *owner* and the *beneficiary* of the policy. The policy:

   a. has a minimum face value of $100,000;

   b. has a payment schedule not to exceed ten years and which assumes an interest rate not to exceed 2 percent below prime interest rate as of the effective date of the policy; and

    c. requires charitable contributions from the donor to the University in the amount of any premiums, including unscheduled premiums, which may become due.

2. A policy on which the donor retains incidence of ownership and the University is named beneficiary only is not a completed gift. (While the policy will identify the University as the beneficiary, the Advancement Officer should work with the donor to clarify the purpose of the gift—whether it be for endowment [existing or new], a specific program or department, or unrestricted use—by attachment of a memorandum, letter, or endowment agreement to the policy.) If intended for endowment purposes, the face value of the policy meets the minimum funding standards for endowments ($25,000).

3. If a policy is a paid-up policy, its fair market value is generally its replacement cost. If premiums remain to be paid on a life insurance policy, its fair market value is equal to the interpolated terminal reserve value of the policy (an amount slightly in excess of cash surrender value), plus that part of the last premium payment that covers any period extending beyond the date of the gift.

It should be noted that an individual who donates an insurance policy arguably is required to obtain a "qualified appraisal" with respect to the policy if the donor claims a federal income tax charitable deduction of more than $5,000 for the donation.

Note: In the case of an insurance policy having a cash surrender value, the amount that is deductible for federal income tax purposes is (omitting technical details) generally whichever is less: the cash surrender value or the net premiums paid to date on the policy. Net premiums are equal to total premiums paid minus policy dividends paid back to the donor-insured.

B. Approval/Acceptance Process

1. The Advancement Officer will prepare a written summary of any proposed gift of a life insurance policy which fails to meet all of the criteria specified in Planned/Deferred Gifts policy and submit that summary to the GAC. At a minimum, the summary will include the following information:

    a. a description of the type of life insurance policy, face value, premium payment schedule, interest rate, age of insured(s), and other relevant policy information; and

    b. the purpose of the gift (e.g., to fund an endowed chair, a deferred gift, an unrestricted gift) and the department(s), program(s), or endowment(s) to benefit from the gift.

2. The GAC will review the material presented by the Advancement Officer and make a determination as to whether to accept or reject the proposed gift or, if necessary, to impose any terms (e.g., the donor's pledge to make contributions to cover premiums, a revision in the payment schedule) as a condition of approval. The final determination of the GAC will be communicated to the Advancement Officer, and the Advancement Officer will communicate the University's decision to the donor in writing, including any conditions imposed by the GAC prior to acceptance.
3. If a proposed gift of a life insurance policy is approved by the GAC, the Advancement Records Department will acknowledge receipt of the gift on behalf of the University.
4. The gift will be completed upon the execution and delivery of the life insurance policy to the University, or an assignment of the policy in the event that the University is not the original owner of the policy.

C. Administration

1. The Treasurer's Office will administer all gifts of life insurance policies and will maintain records of all donor policies, contribution schedules, donor designations of death benefits, and the like. This office also will be responsible for pledge reminders and monitoring payments of premiums. Premium bills should be addressed to the Treasurer's Office and be paid by the Treasurer of the University. Premiums paid by the donor to the University will be considered charitable deductions for the donor.
2. The Treasurer's Office will be responsible for confirming the existence and cash value of all policies in force at least annually and for collecting and distributing death benefits. Upon receipt of death benefits, the Treasurer's Office will provide notice to the department(s), program(s), or endowment(s) to benefit from the gift.

Note: Corporations may designate the University as a beneficiary of insurance policies they hold on members of their Boards of Trustees. Formal notification of the Corporation's intentions must be given, at which time a special pledge will be entered onto the system in the Corporation's name with associated credit given to the individual insured.

IV. Charitable Gift Annuity

The charitable gift annuity is a lifetime contract between the donor and the University. The donor makes a gift to the University and receives a fixed amount of income, and if desired, for another beneficiary's lifetime. Upon the death of the last beneficiary the University receives the remainder. A minimum gift of $5,000 is required to establish a charitable gift annuity. The rate of return is currently based on the tables of the national Committee on Gift Annuities, dependent upon beneficiary age. The donor may not make additional contributions to a charitable gift annuity; however, the donor may enter into additional contracts. A donor may also establish a charitable deferred gift annuity, in which case a gift is made currently, and the donor (or other beneficiary) receives an income stream beginning at a point in the future.

No testamentary gift annuity will be considered without consultation with legal counsel and the GAC.

Example: Donor gives $5,000 to the University. S/he will receive fixed payments on an annual, semi-annual, etc., schedule, even if the account does not produce that amount of income.

V. Pooled Income Fund

A pooled income fund is a fund to which each donor transfers property. The property is commingled with property transferred by other donors who have made similar transfers. All monies from all donors are pooled into one investment account. A minimum gift of $5,000 is required for participation in a pooled income fund, after which the donor may add sums of $1,000 or more to the fund. The donor only receives his or her pro rata share of the dividend and interest income. Income received by the beneficiary is variable. There is no set return amount, just the appropriate percentage of the income that the pooled monies produce.

Example: If someone gives $5,000 the University adds it to all other pooled income monies and all will share the income dividend on his/her $5,000. If the University sells stock bought with pooled money and it had gained $50 a share, this is the University's gain, not the gain of the individuals who bought into the pooled income fund.

VI. Charitable Remainder Unitrust

The primary feature of a charitable remainder unitrust is that it provides for periodic payment of income to the donor or another person specified by the donor, for life or a specified term of years, after which the trust assets pass to the University.

During the lifetime of the donor, s/he creates a formal trust agreement under which assets such as cash and/or appreciated securities are irrevocably transferred to a trustee(s) (a bank, individual, or the University), who then pays the donor or a person specified by the donor a guaranteed payment based on a percentage of the value of the assets.

During the donor's lifetime, the trust assets are managed and invested by the trustee(s) as a single fund. The donor cannot borrow or otherwise deal with the trust assets. The designated beneficiary receives payments based on a fixed percentage of the net fair market value of the trust as valued annually. The donor determines the fixed percentage, which may not be less than 5 percent, upon creation of the unitrust. Donors may make subsequent additions to the unitrust during their lifetime or by bequest upon their death.

When assets have not been "irrevocably" transferred, they are not considered as assets of the University or reported as gifts to the University in any manner.

VII. Charitable Remainder Annuity Trust

The annuity trust shares many common features with the unitrust, the principal difference being the manner used to calculate the payment to the income beneficiary. Whereas the unitrust provides for a payout that varies with each annual valuation, the annuity trust provides for fixed payments based upon the fair market value on the date the trust is initially funded. Additional contributions cannot be made to an annuity trust.

The donor during his or her lifetime irrevocably transfers assets to a trustee, who pays the donor or a person specified by the donor a fixed dollar amount annually for life. The trust can also provide income for the donor's survivors for life; however, the trust assets become the sole property of the University.

A charitable remainder annuity trust for the University may be established with a gift of $100,000 or more.

VIII. Charitable Remainder Qtip Trust

The charitable remainder Qtip trust is appropriate where the only noncharitable beneficiary is the surviving spouse. The surviving spouse must receive all of the net income each year as opposed to a guaranteed payment based on a percentage of the value of the assets of the trust estate at its initial funding (an annuity trust) or at the beginning of each year (a unitrust). In addition, the surviving spouse can receive distributions of trust principal at the trustee's discretion. The surviving spouse can be the only beneficiary entitled to receive payments of income or principal during the spouse's lifetime. However, upon the death of the surviving spouse, the remainder can be paid to the University.

IX. Charitable Lead Trust

The primary feature of a charitable lead trust is that it provides for the immediate support of the University through income generated by the assets in trust for a set period of time, after which the assets pass to a noncharitable beneficiary, such as the donor, the donor's children, or other persons the donor specifies. A charitable lead trust is conceptually the opposite of a charitable remainder trust. In a lead trust, the donor gives the University the current economic benefit of the transferred assets and retains the right to reacquire possession and control of the assets at a future date.

The donor during his or her lifetime creates an irrevocable trust agreement. The agreement may take effect during the donor's lifetime or be part of the donor's will. Assets are transferred to a trustee, with the stipulation that the income from the assets be paid to the University for the life of the trust, after which the principal or corpus of the trust reverts back to the donor or others of his or her choosing. A lead trust may be advantageous for donors who have a larger income than they currently need and who desire to transfer assets to heirs.

A charitable lead trust for the University may be established with a gift of $100,000 or more.

X. Trusts Held Outside of the University

Control of trusts which are qualified charitable remainder trusts or lead trusts managed by an outside source for the benefit of the University rests with the donor's designated trustee(s). The Office of University Advancement and the Treasurer's Office normally hold a copy of such agreements once notice has been given of the trust's existence.

XI. The University as Trustee

The University is willing to be a trustee for charitable trusts, but would rather not be sole trustee. When the University is a trustee, it will accept a charitable trust for no less than $100,000, and would prefer that the assets be managed by a financial organization recommended by the University.

Contacts

For further information, please contact: The Office of the Vice President, University Advancement, 802-656-8600.

Effective Date

August 1996

COMMUNITY FOUNDATION OF GREATER MEMPHIS GIFT ACCEPTANCE POLICIES

Revised March 18, 1999

Gifts to the Community Foundation may be made in any amount for the benefit of the Community Partnership Fund, our discretionary grantmaking program, or to donor advised, designated, or field of interest funds.

Outright Gifts

1. *Cash.* The Community Foundation accepts cash, checks, money orders, and gifts via credit card.
2. *Marketable securities.* The Community Foundation accepts gifts of publicly traded stocks and bonds. When the securities are in "street name," they are transferred to the Community Foundation's account, thereafter we may either sell or hold the securities for the benefit of the donor's fund. When the gift is in the form of physical securities, we may either sell or hold the securities for the benefit of a donor's fund.
3. *Stock in privately owned companies.* To be accepted, such stocks must have a qualified appraisal performed by an independent professional appraiser. If immediately marketable, the stocks are sold. If not, they are kept (in the safe) until they can be redeemed. Prior to approval, such gifts are reviewed by the Community Foundation staff and legal counsel.
4. *Stock in subchapter S corporations.* To be accepted, such stocks must have a qualified appraisal performed by an independent professional appraiser. Prior to approval, such gifts are reviewed by the Community Foundation staff and legal counsel.
5. *Real estate.* All real estate gifts are directed to the Community Foundation Realty, Inc. and must be approved by the board of that corporation. Prior to approval, such gifts are reviewed by the Community Foundation staff and legal counsel. Concerns include legality, mortgages, easements, restrictions, and environmental problems. Until the property is sold, the donor must provide for obligations such as taxes and insurance. (See Community Foundation Realty, Inc. Checklist.)
6. *Tangible personal property.* The property must be saleable and the donor must agree that the property can be sold unless the Foundation agrees to use the

property for a purpose related to its exempt purpose. At least one qualified appraisal by an independent professional is required. Prior to approval, such gifts are reviewed by the Community Foundation staff and legal counsel.

7. *Partnership interests and interests in limited liability companies (LLCs).* The Community Foundation does not accept gifts of general partnership interests. Prior to approval of gifts of limited partnership interests or interests in an LLC all relevant partnership and LLC agreements will be reviewed by the Community Foundation staff and legal counsel with particular attention given to the activity of the partnership/LLC and how allocations are made. Further, the underlying assets and liabilities of the partnership/LLC will be reviewed. Limited partnership interests in family limited partnerships will be considered also subject to review by the Community Foundation's Family Limited Partnership Advisory Committee. (See FLP Gift Acceptance Policy Statement.)

Deferred Gifts

8. *Bequests.* The Community Foundation receives bequests from persons who have directed in their wills that certain assets be transferred to the Foundation. The Foundation's legal name is *Community Foundation of Greater Memphis.*

9. *Life insurance.* The Community Foundation accepts life insurance policies for which the donor has relinquished ownership by assigning all rights, title, and interest in the policy to the Foundation. If the insurance policy is not fully paid up, the usefulness of the gift is judged on a case-by-case basis. If the policy is accepted, the Foundation may choose either to cash it in for the current surrender value or continue to pay the premium (e.g., the Foundation has paid the premium on a policy for which the donor provides an annual contribution equal to the premium). (See Community Foundation Statement on Gifts of Life Insurance.)

10. *Life income arrangements.* Several types of deferred giving arrangements can be established during one's lifetime or through a will and can be structured to provide a life income for oneself or a loved one. Life income arrangements include charitable remainder annuity trust, charitable remainder unitrust, and a remainder interest in a residence or farm. Charitable lead trusts provide income over a term of years or a person's lifetime to charity. (See Community Foundation Statement on Charitable Remainder Trusts.)

In conformance with the Treasury Department regulations governing community foundations, gifts to the Community Foundation may not be directly or indirectly

Resource 10

subjected by a donor to any material restriction or condition that prevents the Foundation from freely and effectively employing the transferred assets, or the income derived therefrom, in furtherance of its exempt purposes.

The Community Foundation reserves the right to refuse any gift that it believes is not in the best interest of the Foundation. E-mail Kristin Croone or call 901-728-4600, to discuss a specific type of gift.

Community Foundation Realty, Inc.

Checklist of Desired Items in Connection with Consideration or Acceptance of Real Estate Donation

All real estate gifts are directed to the Community Foundation Realty, Inc., a supporting organization of the Community Foundation of Greater Memphis, and must be approved by the board of that corporation. Prior to approval, such gifts are reviewed by the Community Foundation staff and legal counsel. Until the property is sold, the donor must provide for obligations such as taxes and insurance. What follows is a comprehensive list of issues and information that may be relevant. To facilitate the transfer, please make note of those issues relevant to the property you wish to donate. For further information or to discuss a gift of real property, e-mail Kristin Croone or call 901-728-4600.

1. Exact legal name of donor and federal I.D. number.
2. Description of property.
3. Description of any buildings or other structures located on the land.
4. Boundary survey of property with location of all structures, easements, and encumbrances appearing on the face of the survey.
5. Information regarding mortgage, if any.
6. Information regarding existing zoning status.
7. Information on all ingress/egress for the property.
8. Description of prior use of the property.
9. Description of use of surrounding property, with specific disclosure of any storage tanks or potential environmental factors affecting the property.
10. Disclosure of any contemplated or anticipated condemnations, right-of-ways, or other actions of municipalities that may affect the subject property.
11. Phase I environmental report on the property, including environmental report on any structures located on the real estate.
12. Specimen of title insurance commitment or schedule describing any liens, encumbrances, or title matters affecting the property.

13. Copy of appraisal showing the fair market value of the property current within 180 days.
14. Disclosure of amount of existing real estate taxes, insurance premiums, and assessments attributable to the property.
15. Discussion with proposed donor regarding any special arrangements for donor's fund or other sources to address ongoing expenses for taxes, insurance, assessments, maintenance, grass cutting, security, utilities, etc.
16. Specimen of proposed Seller's Affidavit disclosing any and all tenants, leases, security instruments, graves or cemetery parcels, etc.
17. Draft of proposed Warranty Deed conveying title from proposed donor to Community Foundation Realty, Inc.

Charitable Remainder Trust Gift Acceptance Policy

The Community Foundation may accept gifts from charitable remainder trusts in a form substantially similar to the forms approved by the Treasury Department or that are otherwise determined by the Community Foundation's legal counsel to be legal trusts for administration by the Community Foundation on the following terms:

1. The Community Foundation may accept charitable remainder interest from any charitable remainder trust if the Foundation determines it is in its best interest to accept the gift.
2. The Community Foundation encourages the use of a Trustee suitable to the donor, including banks or other appropriate institutions. The Community Foundation will consider serving as Trustee at a market rate if the Community Foundation is the irrevocable remainder beneficiary. Should the Community Foundation be selected to serve as Trustee, Community Foundation will provide donor's advisers with certain necessary Trustee provisions.
3. The Community Foundation encourages donors to consult their own legal counsel and tax advisers to create a charitable remainder trust. When desirable, the Community Foundation will provide sample documents and calculations for the donor and his or her advisers to review.

For more information, call 901-728-4600 or e-mail Kristin Croone.

Life Insurance Gift Acceptance Policy

The Community Foundation may accept life insurance policies as gifts to the Community Foundation on the following terms:

1. The Community Foundation shall be both the owner and the beneficiary of any policy accepted by the Community Foundation. The Community Foundation may decline to accept any insurance policy if it is not in the best interest of the Community Foundation to accept the proposed gift.
2. The donor agrees that the proceeds from the policy will be the property of the Community Foundation for the Community Partnership Fund or to be administered by the Community Foundation for such purposes as designated by the donor, subject to the policies and procedures of the Community Foundation.
3. The Community Foundation shall have no obligation to continue premium payments on insurance policies.
4. If any insurance policy lapses for non-payment prior to maturity because a donor fails to provide sufficiently for premium payments, the Community Foundation may redeem the policy and apply the proceeds from any cash settlement to the Community Partnership Fund.
5. The minimum dollar amount of the life insurance policies to be considered for acceptance by the Community Foundation is $50,000.
6. As of this writing, the Community Foundation does not participate in charitable split dollar insurance plans.

For more information call 901-728-4600 or e-mail Kristin Croone.

Family Limited Partnership Gift Acceptance Policy Statement

Prior to the Community Foundation of Greater Memphis accepting family limited partnership interests, the partnership agreement must be reviewed by Community Foundation's Advisory Committee on Family Limited Partnerships. The Committee will review the agreement's structure, function, and underlying assets. Issues to be reviewed include but are not limited to the following:

1. Value of the limited partnership interest. Generally, a minimum discounted value of the limited partnership interest, as established by a qualified appraisal of $10,000 is required.
2. The beneficiary of both the income stream and the liquidation proceeds of the limited partnership interest must be The Community Partnership Fund.
3. Costs to the Community Foundation in holding the interest such as administrative responsibilities, tax return preparation and unrelated business income tax. The donor may be asked to cover all or some of these costs, particularly the unrelated business income tax which may be generated by phantom income.

Resource 10

4. Is the Community Foundation's interest sufficiently liquid? Does the agreement provide the Community Foundation the power to redeem its interest, either through a preferred interest with a guaranteed return or a series of put options upon the expiration of which the Community Foundation has a right to absolute redemption or another method agreed upon by both parties? Do the "family" partners intend to liquidate at some point in time?

For more information, call 901-728-4600 or e-mail Kristin Croone.

RESOURCE 11

GIFT AGREEMENT TEMPLATES

XYZ CHARITY
ENDOWED GIFT AGREEMENT

◆

The _____ **Scholarship**

XYZ Charity's Name
Name of Account

DONOR(S): _____ ("Donor(s)")

AUTHORIZATION: *XYZ Charity* _____ *("Charity")*

WHEREAS the XYZ Charity ("Charity") receives, invests, administers, and manages private gifts for the benefit of XYZ Charity; and

WHEREAS the Donor(s) wishes (wish) to honor _____, and has (have) irrevocably given to the Charity the sum of $_____ for the purpose of establishing The _____ Scholarship/Fellowship ("Scholarship/Fellowship");

NOW, THEREFORE, IT IS AGREED:

"scholarship/fellowship"   1. It is the intent of the Donor(s) that income from this gift be used to support scholarships. *[criteria for selection of recipient can be spelled out here, i.e., "a student enrolled in the school who has an interest in the study of _____, and who has a record of academic excellence as demonstrated by a GPA of _____ on a 4-point scale, and that in selecting recipients, preference be given to (a woman, a graduate of _____ High School, an African American, etc.)."]* The number, amount, and recipient(s) of the scholarship will be determined by the Scholarship Committee of the School.

   -or-

"professorship/chair"   1. It is the intent of the Donor that *[criteria for selection of recipient can be spelled out here].* The use of income generated from this gift may include, but not be limited to, a salary or salary supplement for the designated holder of the professorship *[chair],* support for research, manuscript preparation, graduate research assistance, library and equipment acquisitions, and other requirements of an active scholar and teacher.

2. The use of this gift will be authorized by the Charity for the reasonable and customary requirements of authorized expenditures as indicated above in accordance with internal operating policies governing investments and administration as established by the Charity. An annual report on the status of the fund will be provided to the Donor(s).

3. The Charity acknowledges that the Donor(s) intend(s) that the original gift amount exist in perpetuity with the income being used to support the purposes of the gift. The Board of Directors of the Charity has established a spending policy which provides for the distribution of both income and a portion of the capital appreciation resulting from investment activity. This policy is consistent with the

Charity's investment philosophy to maintain the purchasing power of the original gift so that the endowments may keep pace with inflation.

4. The officers and directors of the Charity have the power, and final decision, to invest, to change investments, to accept property, to sell, to hold, or to reinvest all or any of the monies or property transferred to the Charity under the terms of this Agreement in such manner as they deem proper, and any additional gifts received in support of this purpose are subject to the terms of this Agreement.

5. In the event that the original purposes stated here can no longer be fulfilled, the Charity, through its Board of Directors, shall review the circumstances and shall modify this Agreement to the extent necessary to enable the gift to be used in a manner which coincides with the Donor's (s') original intent as closely as possible, and consistent with governing rules/regulations policies/procedures and the internal operating policies of the Charity.

6. The Agreement shall be governed by and interpreted in accordance with the laws of the State of _____.

Signed and dated this _____ day of _____, 200__.

DONOR

_____
[Name(s)]

XYZ Charity

By:_____
                    , President

INDIANA UNIVERSITY FOUNDATION
ACCOUNT AGREEMENT

```
┌─────────────────────────────────────────────────────────────┐
│                                                             │
│  For Foundation Use Only                                    │
│                                                             │
│  ACCOUNT NUMBER: _____          │
│                                                             │
└─────────────────────────────────────────────────────────────┘
```

Indiana University Foundation
Name of Account

AUTHORIZATION: School of _____ ("School") *[Department of _____*
("Department"); Indiana University _____ ("IU_____")]

SOURCE OF FUNDS: *[add source of money coming into the account]*

WHEREAS the Indiana University Foundation ("Foundation") receives, invests, administers, and manages private funds for the benefit of Indiana University in an account designated for institutional funds (the "Account"); and

WHEREAS *[state any information on how the account was created if known].*

NOW, THEREFORE, IT IS AGREED:

1. This Account shall be used for . . . *[choose from descriptions below or modify as needed].* It is further agreed that funds in this Account will not be co-mingled with donor contributions.

Choose one of the following account descriptions or modify as needed:

faculty and staff development   Expenditures may include but are not limited to continuing education, research, departmental awards, travel expenses of faculty and staff, and faculty development.

-or-

capital and equipment needs   Expenditures may include but are not limited to minor renovations to a building or rooms, improvements to the grounds, and purchase of equipment.

-or-

awards, fellowships, or scholarships   The *[award, fellowship, or scholarship]* will be given out to *[spell out specific criteria here].* The number, amount, and recipient(s) of the Scholarship will be determined by the scholarship Committee of the School.

-or-

representation funds   Expenditures from representation accounts shall meet four criteria: a direct benefit to the University, reasonable in amount, a necessary expenditure which may or may not be made from University funds, and have the appearance of proper use. Expenditures may include employee goodwill, membership dues, meals and entertainment (when the purpose is conducive to conducting university business), and memorabilia given in recognition of support of the institution.

-or-

research   Expenditures may include but are not limited to faculty and staff travel, lodging and travel of visiting scholars, lecturers and research collaborators, supplies and other items which may best serve the needs of the research program.

-or-

general purposes   Expenditures may include but are not limited to faculty and staff recruiting, faculty development, faculty travel, program promotion, and other expenses which may best serve the *[academic program or department]*.

2. The use of the funds in this account will be authorized by the *[School, Department, or Campus]* for the reasonable and customary requirements of authorized expenditures as indicated above in accordance with internal operating policies governing investments and administration as established by the Foundation, Indiana University, and the *[School, Department, or Campus]*.

3. The Foundation will annually make available the Account balance for the purpose(s) stated above. The Board of Directors of the Foundation established a spending policy which provides for the distribution of both income and a portion of the capital appreciation resulting from investment activity. This policy is consistent with the Foundation's investment philosophy to maintain the purchasing power of the original funds so that the account may keep pace with inflation. This Agreement is subject to the provisions of the Uniform Management of Institutional Funds Act (Indiana Code 30-2-12) ("UMIFA").

4. The officers and directors of the Foundation have the power, and final decision, to invest, to change investments, to accept property, to sell, to hold, or to reinvest all or any of the monies or property transferred to the Foundation under the terms of this agreement in such manner as they deem proper, and any additional funds received in support of this purpose are subject to the terms of this agreement.

5. In the event that the original purposes stated here can no longer be fulfilled, the *[Dean, Chairperson or Chancellor]*, has the power and responsibility to review the circumstances and, if appropriate, modify the purpose of the Account to enable the funds to be used.

6. This Agreement will be terminated no later than one year after all funds received for this purpose have been expended according to the terms stated here.

7. The Agreement shall be governed by and interpreted in accordance with the laws of the State of Indiana.

Signed and dated this _____ day of _____, 200__.

INDIANA UNIVERSITY SCHOOL OF _____

By: _____
[Name, Dean/Chairperson/Chancellor]

INDIANA UNIVERSITY FOUNDATION

By: _____
[Name, Executive Director, Administration]

INDIANA UNIVERSITY FOUNDATION
GIFT AGREEMENT

For Foundation Use Only

ACCOUNT NUMBER: _____

Indiana University Foundation
Name of Account

DONOR(S):_____ ("Donor(s)")

AUTHORIZATION: School of _____ ("School") *[Department of _____
("Department"); Indiana University _____ ("IU_____")]*

SOURCE OF FUNDS: *[add source of money coming into the account if funded by
transfers]*

WHEREAS the Indiana University Foundation ("Foundation") receives, invests,
administers, and manages private gifts for the benefit of Indiana University in an
account designated for gifts (the "Account"); and

WHEREAS *[state any donor wishes (i.e. in honor or memory of someone) or information on how the account was created if known]*.

NOW, THEREFORE, IT IS AGREED:

1. This Account shall be used for . . . *[choose from descriptions below or modify as
needed]*.

faculty and staff development   Expenditures may include but are not limited to
continuing education, research, departmental awards, travel expenses of faculty
and staff, and faculty development.

-or-

capital and equipment needs   Expenditures may include but are not limited to
minor renovations to a building or rooms, improvements to the grounds, and
purchase of equipment.

-or-

awards, fellowships, or scholarships   The *[award, fellowship, or scholarship]* will be
given out to *[spell out specific criteria here]*. The number, amount, and recipient(s) of
the Scholarship(s) will be determined by the Scholarship Committee of the School.

-or-

representation funds Expenditures from representation accounts shall meet four criteria: a direct benefit to the University, reasonable in amount, a necessary expenditure which may or may not be made from University funds, and have the appearance of proper use. Expenditures may include employee goodwill, membership dues, meals and entertainment (when the purpose is conducive to conducting university business), and memorabilia given in recognition of support of the institution.

-or-

research Expenditures may include but are not limited to faculty and staff travel, lodging and travel of visiting scholars, lecturers and research collaborators, supplies and other items which may best serve the needs of the research program.

-or-

general purposes Expenditures may include but are not limited to faculty and staff recruiting, faculty development, faculty travel, program promotion, and other expenses which may best serve the *[academic program or department]*.

2. The use of this gift will be authorized by the *[School, Department, or Campus]* for the reasonable and customary requirements of authorized expenditures as indicated above in accordance with internal operating policies governing investments and administration as established by the Foundation, Indiana University, and the *[School, Department, or Campus]*. An annual report on the status of the fund will be provided to the Donor(s).

3. The Foundation will annually make available the Account balance for the purpose(s) stated above. The Board of Directors of the Foundation established a spending policy which provides for the distribution of both income and a portion of the capital appreciation resulting from investment activity. This policy is consistent with the Foundation's investment philosophy to maintain the purchasing power of the original gift so that the account may keep pace with inflation. This Agreement is subject to the provisions of the Uniform Management of Institutional Funds Act (Indiana Code 30-2-12) ("UMIFA").

4. The officers and directors of the Foundation have the power, and final decision, to invest, to change investments, to accept property, to sell, to hold, or to reinvest all or any of the monies or property transferred to the Foundation under the terms of this agreement in such manner as they deem proper, and any additional gifts received in support of this purpose are subject to the terms of this Agreement.

5. In the event that the original purposes stated here can no longer be fulfilled, the Foundation, through its Board of Directors, and in consultation with the *[Dean, campus Chancellor],* shall review the circumstances and shall modify this Agreement to the extent necessary to enable the gift to be used in a manner which coincides with the Donor's(s') original intent as closely as possible, and consistent with the provisions of UMIFA and the internal operating policies of the Foundation.

6. This Agreement will be terminated no later than one year after all funds received for this purpose have been expended according to the terms stated here.

7. The Agreement shall be governed by and interpreted in accordance with the laws of the State of Indiana.

Signed and dated this _____ day of _____, 200__.

DONOR

By: _____
         [Name(s)]

INDIANA UNIVERSITY SCHOOL OF _____

By: _____
         [Name, Dean/Chairperson/Chancellor]

INDIANA UNIVERSITY FOUNDATION

By: _____
         Curtis R. Simic, President

INDIANA UNIVERSITY FOUNDATION
ENDOWED GIFT AGREEMENT

◆

The _____ **Scholarship**

```
┌─────────────────────────────────────────────────────────────┐
│  For Foundation Use Only                                     │
│                                                              │
│  ACCOUNT NUMBER: _____             │
│                                                              │
└─────────────────────────────────────────────────────────────┘
```

Indiana University Foundation
Name of Account

DONOR(S): _____ ("Donor(s)")

AUTHORIZATION: School of _____ ("School") *[Department of* _____
("Department"); Indiana University _____ *("IU__")]*

WHEREAS the Indiana University Foundation ("Foundation") receives, invests, administers, and manages private gifts for the benefit of Indiana University; and

WHEREAS the Donor(s) wishes (wish) to honor _____, and has (have) irrevocably given to the Foundation the sum of $_____ for the purpose of establishing The _____ Scholarship/Fellowship ("Scholarship/Fellowship");

NOW, THEREFORE, IT IS AGREED:

"scholarship/fellowship"   1. It is the intent of the Donor(s) that income from this gift be used to support a scholarship. *[criteria for selection of recipient can be spelled out here, i.e., "a student enrolled in the School who has an interest in the study of* _____*, and who has a record of academic excellence as demonstrated by a GPA of* _____ *on a 4-point scale, and that in selecting recipients, preference be given to (a woman, a graduate of* _____ *High School, an African American, etc.)."]* The number, amount, and recipient(s) of the Scholarship will be determined by the Scholarship Committee of the School.

2. The use of this gift will be authorized by the *[School, Department, Campus]* for the reasonable and customary requirements of authorized expenditures as indicated above in accordance with internal operating policies governing investments and administration as established by the Foundation, Indiana University, and the *[School, Department, Campus].* An annual report on the status of the fund will be provided to the Donor(s).

3. The Foundation acknowledges that the Donor(s) intend(s) that the original gift amount exist in perpetuity with the income being used to support the purposes of the gift. The Board of Directors of the Foundation has established a spending policy which provides for the distribution of both income and a portion of the capi-

tal appreciation resulting from investment activity. This policy is consistent with the Foundation's investment philosophy to maintain the purchasing power of the original gift so that the endowments may keep pace with inflation. This Agreement is subject to the provisions of the Uniform Management of Institutional Funds Act (Indiana Code 30-2-12) ("UMIFA").

4. The officers and directors of the Foundation have the power, and final decision, to invest, to change investments, to accept property, to sell, to hold, or to reinvest all or any of the monies or property transferred to the Foundation under the terms of this Agreement in such manner as they deem proper, and any additional gifts received in support of this purpose are subject to the terms of this Agreement.

5. In the event that the original purposes stated here can no longer be fulfilled, the Foundation, through its Board of Directors, and in consultation with the *[Dean, campus Chancellor]*, shall review the circumstances and shall modify this Agreement to the extent necessary to enable the gift to be used in a manner which coincides with the Donor's (s') original intent as closely as possible, and consistent with the provisions of UMIFA and the internal operating policies of the Foundation.

6. The Agreement shall be governed by and interpreted in accordance with the laws of the State of Indiana.

Signed and dated this _____ day of _____, 200__.

DONOR

By: _____
     [Name(s)]

INDIANA UNIVERSITY SCHOOL OF _____

By: _____
     [Name, Dean/Chairperson/Chancellor]

INDIANA UNIVERSITY FOUNDATION

By: _____
     Curtis R. Simic, President

INDIANA UNIVERSITY FOUNDATION
GIFT AGREEMENT

◆

The _____ Scholarship

```
For Foundation Use Only

ACCOUNT NUMBER: _____
```

Indiana University Foundation
Name of Account

DONOR(S): _____ ("Donor(s)")

AUTHORIZATION: School of _____ ("School") *[Department of _____*
("Department"); Indiana University _____ ("IU__")]

WHEREAS the Indiana University Foundation ("Foundation") receives, invests, administers, and manages private gifts for the benefit of Indiana University; and

WHEREAS the Donor(s) wishes (wish) to honor _____, and has (have) irrevocably given to the Foundation the sum of $_____ for the purpose of establishing The _____ Scholarship/Fellowship ("Scholarship/Fellowship");

NOW, THEREFORE, IT IS AGREED:

"scholarship/fellowship"   1. It is the intent of the Donor(s) that this gift be used to support a scholarship. *[criteria for selection of recipient can be spelled out here, i.e., "a student enrolled in the School who has an interest in the study of _____, and who has a record of academic excellence as demonstrated by a GPA of _____ on a 4 point scale, and that in selecting the recipients, preference be given to (a woman, a graduate of _____ High School, an African American, etc.)."]* The number, amount, and recipient(s) of the Scholarship will be determined by the Scholarship Committee of the School.

2. The use of this gift will be authorized by the *[School, Department, Campus]* for the reasonable and customary requirements of authorized expenditures as indicated above in accordance with internal operating policies governing investments and administration as established by the Foundation, Indiana University, and the *[School, Department, Campus].* An annual report on the status of the fund will be provided to the Donor(s).

3. The Foundation acknowledges that the Donor(s) intend(s) both income and principal, as required, may be used to support the purpose of the gift. The Board of Directors of the Foundation established a spending policy which provides for the distribution of both income and a portion of the capital appreciation resulting from investment activity. This policy is consistent with the Foundation's investment

philosophy to maintain the purchasing power of the original gift so that the account may keep pace with inflation. This Agreement is subject to the provisions of the Uniform Management of Institutional Funds Act (Indiana Code 30-2-12) ("UMIFA").

4. The officers and directors of the Foundation have the power, and final decision, to invest, to change investments, to accept property, to sell, to hold, or to reinvest all or any of the monies or property transferred to the Foundation under the terms of this Agreement in such manner as they deem proper, and any additional gifts received in support of this purpose are subject to the terms of this Agreement.

5. In the event that the original purposes stated here can no longer be fulfilled, the Foundation, through its Board of Directors, and in consultation with the *[Dean, campus Chancellor]*, shall review the circumstances and shall modify this Agreement to the extent necessary to enable the gift to be used in a manner which coincides with the Donor's (s') original intent as closely as possible, and consistent with the provisions of UMIFA and the internal operating policies of the Foundation.

6. The Agreement shall be governed by and interpreted in accordance with the laws of the State of Indiana.

Signed and dated this _____ day of _____, 200__.

DONOR

By: _____
      [Name(s)]

INDIANA UNIVERSITY SCHOOL OF _____

By: _____
      [Name, Dean/Chairperson/Chancellor]

INDIANA UNIVERSITY FOUNDATION

By: _____
      Curtis R. Simic, President

PLANNED GIVING NEWSLETTERS

SPRING 2000

MAKE A GIFT
THAT OFFERS YOU
AN INCOME FOR LIFE.

DRAKE UNIVERSITY ALUMNI and friends can support Drake in a way that gives the donors real financial benefits. This gift plan, the Drake Charitable Gift Annuity, lets you use your charitable dollars to strengthen Drake, feel good about your positive impact on current students, and also realize some personal financial rewards! Read on for an overview of this advantageous plan.

A gift plan that provides an income for life.

The Drake Charitable Gift Annuity allows donors to enhance Drake University with a financial contribution that gives back to the donor both tax benefits and an income for life. Through a gift annuity, you can:

- receive payments for life or designate someone else to receive the payments
- save regular income taxes
- save capital gain taxes
- provide a gift to Drake University, including a gift for a particular purpose such as funding a scholarship

How the Drake Charitable Gift Annuity works.

In return for cash, securities or other acceptable assets, Drake University will pay you, or someone else you designate, an annuity for life. The annuity can be set for two persons, if you wish, such as you and a successor beneficiary. There is no minimum age for receiving annuity payments, and the minimum amount needed to establish a charitable gift annuity is $5,000. You can also establish a deferred-payment charitable gift annuity, which will begin making payments to you at a later date (at least one year from the day you establish the gift). Deferred-payment charitable gift annuities have larger tax deductions and higher payment rates of return.

How do the payment rates work?

The payment rates are attractive. They are based on your age (if you are the sole annuity recipient) when the charitable gift annuity is established. Here are a few of the rates currently in force for a single life CGA (Charitable Gift Annuity):

Age at Date of Issue	Payment Rate
65	7.0%
70	7.5%
75	8.2%
80	9.2%
85	10.2%
90+	12.0%

If you set up a charitable gift annuity for a family member or friend, the payment rate is based on that person's age. Different payment rates apply when a charitable gift annuity is for two individuals (for example, husband and wife). For a detailed schedule of two-life rates please contact the gift planning office.

Are the gift annuity payments subject to tax?

Charitable gift annuity payments have good "spending power," because they are partly tax-free and only partly taxable. The tax-free portion varies from situation to situation but is typically 40 to 50 percent for a certain period of time (the period of "life expectancy" under the IRS tables). Here's an example:

Joan Wilson, age 70, gives $10,000 cash to Drake in return for a charitable gift annuity. Joan will receive $758 a year (a 7.5 percent payment rate) for her life. For the first 16 years ("life expectancy"), more than half of Joan's annuity will be tax-free. The balance of the annuity will be taxed as regular income. After 16 years, the annuity will be fully taxed as regular income.

Note: The figures shown in this example are for illustration purposes only. Different figures will apply to your situation.

Joan's annuity is secure, because it does not depend on the stock or bond market and is backed by all the assets of Drake University. Charitable gift annuities also provide a charitable deduction, which helps reduce income taxes for those who itemize their deductions. In the example just given, Joan receives a deduction of approximately $4,000. The deduction is figured using Internal Revenue Service tables and varies from situation to situation, depending on age.

Can stock be used to establish a charitable gift annuity?

Establishing a charitable gift annuity with marketable stock—especially stock that is highly appreciated and pays little or no dividends—can work very well. Details aside, it is possible to save capital gains taxes on the stock's appreciation and receive a much higher, more favorably taxed income.

Can a charitable gift annuity be established for someone else?

A charitable gift annuity can be established for a parent, sibling or even a friend. This can be an excellent way to provide financial support to another person. As mentioned earlier, the payment rates are based on the recipient's age. For example, an 85-year-old parent or sibling would receive a 10.2 percent rate for life.

FOR MORE INFORMATION about how the charitable gift annuity might work in your situation, please return the card enclosed with this issue of Drake Heritage or contact Drake's gift planning officers, Nancy Perazelli, CFRE, or John Smith. They will work with you and your advisers, in confidence and without cost or obligation, to help you explore giving methods that can provide for you and your family as well as for the University. Whether you simply need information on giving plans, want to compare your options, or are ready to make a gift, Nancy and John can assist you.

If you would like Nancy or John to contact you, you may indicate that on the enclosed card or contact the gift planning office.

Everyone Benefits

We can help! You can increase your income, reduce your tax burden and support Drake University, all at the same time—by making a planned gift. Planned gifts include bequests and life insurance policies as well as gifts that may generate income for the donor, such as charitable trusts and charitable gift annuities. These gifts may:

- reduce current or estate tax liability associated with charitable giving
- increase income, generated by certain types of planned gifts, to the donor or beneficiaries designated by the donor
- enable the donor to reduce/avoid capital gains tax if the gift is funded with an appreciated asset
- reduce probate and estate administration expenses

Donors of planned gifts play an important role in Drake's continued success. When you make a planned gift to Drake, you may choose to become a member of a distinguished group, the Heritage Society, established in 1991 to honor individuals who invest in Drake's future. Heritage Society members are listed in Drake's annual Honor Roll of Donors and receive special invitations to University events. Most important, they enjoy the personal satisfaction of strengthening an outstanding university and directly benefiting students. We want to help you achieve your personal, financial and charitable goals. For additional information visit our website at: *www.drake.edu/alumni/gifts.html.*

Drake University Gift Planning Office

2507 University Avenue
Des Moines, IA 50311

Toll free: 1-800-443-7253, x2500
Local: 515-271-2500

E-mail: nancy.perazelli@drake.edu
or john.smith@drake.edu

Make a gift that offers you an income for life!

☐ Please send me the free brochure *Giving Through Gift Annuities.*

☐ Please provide me with more information about wills and estate planning.

☐ I have a question. Please call me. The best time to call is: _____ a.m./p.m.

☐ I am considering a provision for your organization. Please contact me.

☐ I have already included your organization in my estate plan through
    ☐ my will   ☐ a trust arrangement   ☐ an insurance policy
    ☐ other _____

Please print.

Name   Telephone

Address

City   State   Zip

E-mail

Mail this card to: Drake University Gift Planning Office, 2507 University Avenue, Des Moines, IA 50311. One can also request information from our website at: www.drake.edu/alumni/gifts.html.

Summer 1999   Volume 1 Number 3

...next steps...

*A Newsletter of Estate Planning and Philanthropy
from the Indiana University Foundation*

Alan M. Spears
*Director, Office of Major
and Planned Gifts
Indiana University Foundation*

In This Issue

The Charitable Bequest:
• *Go to It with a Will*

Music by Bequest:
• *Dean Wilfred Bain*

Things to Keep In Mind:
• *The Arbutus Society*
• *Mind Your Language*
• *Gift Agreements*

Foundation Profile:
• *George Bledsoe*

Dear Alumni and Friends:

I'd like to take a moment to thank all of you who have given to Indiana University. Without your support it would be impossible to maintain the degree of excellence that is the hallmark of an IU education. If you choose to make a planned gift, there is a more tangible way for us to show our thanks—the Arbutus Society.

Making *any* planned gift to IU entitles you to membership in the Arbutus Society. You can find out more on page 7. If you have not told us about a planned gift arrangement you have made, we would love to know about it. The enclosed reply card is double-sided for this purpose.

This issue of *Next Steps* is about charitable bequests. Like many of our alumni and friends, you may want part of your estate assets to be used to benefit IU. We understand, however, that you have other estate objectives—providing for family

members, for instance, is probably at the top of your list. But good estate planning involves a *balancing* of priorities: With careful planning, you can better provide for your family, save taxes, and do more for your favorite charities.

One of the most popular ways to achieve this balance is a charitable bequest. By leaving a legacy in this way, you can make a material difference to the future of Indiana University. The potential tax savings are an extra incentive.

Feel free to send for our new booklet, *Charitable Bequests—How To Get the Most Out of Yours.* You can also call me at (812) 855-8311, or toll-free at (800) 558-8311.

Sincerely,

Alan M. Spears
Director, Office of Major and
Planned Gifts
Indiana University Foundation

The Charitable Bequest: Go to It with a Will

1999: Is It Time to Review Your Will?

There are many reasons why taking another look at your will may be a good idea. You may have changes in your own circumstances—a move to a new state, a change in marital status, the death of a loved one, or the birth of a child or grandchild.

And here's another reason: You should make sure that your will has not been affected by recent changes in the tax law. For example, the exemption for federal estate taxes has been raised this year—from $625,000 to $650,000. And it will go up to $675,000 next year. These are minor changes, but they do afford you some relief if you are liable for estate tax.

Finally, you may be thinking about making a bequest to a favorite charity, or adding a charity to your list of beneficiaries. Remember that all charitable bequests are deductible for estate tax purposes, so you get the satisfaction of doing great things for your favorite causes and the added benefits of tax deductions.

Forms of Bequest: Outright Bequests

There are several ways you can provide for Indiana University in your will. The most common and straightforward method is to bequeath a specific amount to the IU Foundation. For example, a friend of the university may direct, in her will, that $10,000 be paid to IU at her death.

On the other hand, you may prefer to direct that a percentage of the value of your estate (for example, 10% of the net value of your estate) be paid to IU at your death. This way, the University will share in increases or decreases in the value of your estate.

Of course, you can bequeath almost any type of property (e.g., stocks, bonds, royalties, a residence or

Next Steps

This newsletter is published three times a year by the Office of Major and Planned Gifts.

Indiana University Foundation
President
Curt Simic
Director, Office of Major and Planned Gifts
Alan M. Spears
Director, Publications
Jana Wilson
Editor
Nick Riddle
Designer
Terry Howe
Photographer
Tyagan Miller

Questions? Comments?
Address Corrections?
Please let us know!
Office of Major and Planned Gifts

Indiana University Foundation
P.O. Box 500
Bloomington, IN 47402-0500
(800) 558-8311

other real estate) to IU. A bequest of property can often have unique tax advantages for both your estate and your beneficiaries. And a bequest of a specific property is often uniquely helpful to the mission of the University.

Another alternative would be to bequeath all or part of your "residuary estate" to Indiana University. This ensures that IU will receive all or part of whatever is left in your estate after all priority bequests have been satisfied.

Examples of Outright Bequests

Which areas of Indiana University have benefited from bequests?

Virtually every school, program, and unit, on all eight campuses.

A bequest can provide funds for many different areas of IU, including:

- Undergraduate scholarships
- Graduate fellowships
- Professorships and faculty chairs
- Research and travel grants
- Library acquisitions
- Lecture series
- "Bricks and mortar" projects
- Landscaping
- Special programs

As a member of the Well House Society, Sally K. makes annual gifts to Indiana University of about $2,000. To be sure these gifts will continue after her death, her will directs that $40,000 be paid to the Indiana University Foundation endowment fund. The income earned through the investment of this bequest will equal or exceed Sally's annual gifts and Well House membership will be perpetuated forever.

Bob C. wants to remember several friends and family members, but wants the bulk of his estate to pass to Indiana University. His will leaves modest dollar amounts to each individual beneficiary and names the IU Foundation as the residual beneficiary of his estate.

Mark T. wants at least 80% of his estate to pass to his wife. But he also wants to benefit his two children, his church, and IU. His skillfully prepared will leaves 5% of the value of his estate to each child and to each charity and directs that the balance of his estate be paid to his wife.

Music by Bequest

Former Dean's Gift Performs for the Benefit of IU Music Students

Wilfred Bain was one of the architects of Indiana University as it exists today. As dean of the School of Music from 1947 to 1973, he worked tirelessly to develop the school into a globally renowned center of excellence.

"Under his direction," said Herman B Wells, "the school built a solid foundation and began an upward trend toward the worldwide reputation it now enjoys." During his deanship, the number of IU students majoring in music increased from 225 to 1,700, and the school's faculty expanded from 25 to 150. At his behest, the school began to offer doctoral degrees and specialized study, while still emphasizing the importance of a complete musical education.

The Musical Arts Center on the Bloomington Campus is one example of the legacy left to IU by a man who was passionate about music. "I cannot understand how people can live without music," he once said. "It is a matter of the spirit. It is a matter of communication."

Wilfred Bain was born in Quebec, Canada, in 1908. He came to the United States to attend Houghton College in New York State, earning a Bachelor of Arts degree there in 1929. After receiving a Bachelor of Music degree in Voice from Westminster Choir College in Princeton, New Jersey, he returned to Houghton College as Associate Professor of Music in 1931.

In the meantime, he felt it necessary to continue his education. In 1935 he received a Master of Arts degree in Music from New York University, followed by a Doctor of Education in Music from the same institution in 1938.

He arrived at Indiana University in 1947, after nine years as Chairman of the Music Department of North Texas State College in Denton, Texas. Having begun to develop an interest in opera production at Denton, Dean Bain brought his wealth of ideas and energy to Bloomington. By the end of the first year of his deanship, he had established the IU Opera Theater, which mounted its first production, Offenbach's *Tales of Hoffmann,* on May 15, 1948. The following year, he began a tradition at the Opera Theater with the first annual production of Wagner's *Parsifal.*

Dean Bain's efforts to find a permanent home for the Opera Theater led to the acquisition of East Hall, complete with stage, loft, and orchestra pit, at his insistence. After East Hall met its end in a fire, he began the campaign that culminated in the building of the world-famous Musical Arts Center on the same site.

When Dean Bain died in 1997, he left a provision in his will to ensure that the fellowship he established in 1994 would continue in perpetuity. The Dean Wilfred Bain Opera Fellowship Fund makes annual awards to voice students at IU School of Music who possess special singing talent and who wish to prepare for a professional career in opera. Candidates are chosen by a committee which includes Dean Bain's widow, Elisabeth Myers Bain, herself a donor to IU.

Under Dean Bain's provision, the principal—that is, the lump sum named in his will—remains untouched, and the interest earned from investing this sum is transferred to the fund. This way, the original bequest will always be there, working to produce an annual profit that gives singers of exceptional promise the chance to realize their full potential.

"I came from a background in performance," said Dean Bain, shortly before his death. "I believed in performance. Still do. I wanted to bring that to IU. And that turned out to take some building."

Thanks in part to his generous bequest, the building that Dean Bain accomplished in his lifetime continues into the future.

Other Types of Bequest

In the Unlikely Event: Contingent Bequests

Many people may feel that they cannot afford to make an outright bequest to Indiana University because of family needs and objectives. A well-prepared and practical will anticipates the improbable by naming contingent beneficiaries.

For example, John K. bequeaths $10,000 to his brother Mike, and also names the IU Foundation as a *contingent beneficiary* to take the bequest if Mike is not living at the time of John's death.

Putting It Off: Deferred Bequests

Alternatively, your bequest to IU can be deferred. This allows for the payment of income to another beneficiary for life or for a period of years.

For example, you can bequeath money or property to a trust. The trust agreement can direct the trustee to hold and invest the property and to pay an annual income to a family member for as long as he or she may live. The property will be distributed to the Indiana University Foundation only after the death of the family member. This kind of arrangement may be ideal for providing support to a relative who lacks financial management skills.

Then again . . . you can bequeath money or property to IU on the condition that we use the

Two Attractive Alternatives to a Bequest

You may find that naming the Indiana University Foundation as the beneficiary of an existing life insurance policy is the easiest and most cost-effective way of making a generous estate gift to the University. As with a bequest, you retain complete control over the policy during your life. You can borrow against the policy, cash it in, or change the beneficiary whenever you wish.

Or you can name the IU Foundation as the death beneficiary of a bank account, certificate of deposit, or retirement account—or even of a bond or stock certificate. Again, you remain the sole owner and, at your death, the property will pass directly and immediately to the Foundation.

bequest to make lifetime annuity payments to a family member. That way, you can use a single property or fund to provide lifetime security for family members *and* a deferred benefit for Indiana University.

Make Life Less Taxing

Bequests to qualified charities have always been a good way to reduce estate and inheritance taxes. Every dollar of your estate that passes outright to Indiana University will be fully deductible for federal estate tax purposes. Even if you make a deferred bequest to the University, part of your bequest will escape the harsh federal estate tax.

Estate tax rates range from 37%–55% of the value of your taxable estate, so it's easy to see how important the charitable deduction can be for your heirs. If the value of your estate (after deductions) will exceed the federal estate tax exemption ($650,000 in 1999), you may want to consider the tax savings you can gain through a carefully planned bequest to Indiana University.

If you would like to discuss a possible bequest or other estate gift to Indiana University, please make a note of it on the enclosed reply card and return it to our office. Of course, there is no cost or other obligation for this service. For more information about charitable bequests, please request a complimentary copy of our new booklet, *Charitable Bequests—How to Get the Most Out of Yours.* Simply complete and return the enclosed reply card or call the Foundation office at (812) 855-8311.

Things to Keep in Mind

Arbutus Society

The generosity of our friends and donors deserves recognition. The Arbutus Society honors those who inform us that they are including Indiana University Foundation in their estate plans. This can be through a charitable bequest or any other planned giving arrangement, such as a charitable gift annuity or charitable remainder trust.

Named for the official flower of Indiana University, the Society organizes an annual event exclusively for its members. Throughout the year, members are also invited to lectures, exhibits, receptions, performances and other special events.

Here's what some of our special Indiana people have to say about their charitable bequests:

I always wanted to make a gift to IU. I loved my days there as a student—I even met my husband there. By leaving a bequest I can fulfill my desire to make a meaningful gift, without worrying about the impact on my finances. It's great to know that I will be leaving a personal legacy at a place that has meant so much to me over the years.

New members also receive, with their confirmation letter, a supply of note cards featuring the Maryrose Wampler artwork of "*The Trailing Arbutus.*"

It is our great pleasure to recognize the more than 500 current charter members of the Arbutus Society for their foresight in supporting Indiana University through planned giving.

And remember—*any* planned gift qualifies. To join, please complete the enclosed reply card. You can also call the Indiana University Foundation at (812) 855-8311, or toll-free at (800) 558-8311.

Mind Your Language

The Indiana University Foundation is the official entity designated by the trustees of IU to receive and administer gifts for the University. If you wish to include a provision in your will to benefit Indiana University, please use the following language:

"I give, devise and bequeath the (sum of/percentage of/residue of my estate) to Indiana University Foundation, a not-for-profit corporation with principal offices located in Bloomington, Indiana, to be utilized for the benefit of Indiana University as specified in a gift agreement on file at said Foundation."

Gift Agreements

The IU Foundation provides all of its donors with a gift agreement. The sole purpose of this agreement is to assure you that your gift will be used exactly as you intended. The document does not place you under any legal obligation—you can modify the gift agreement if your plans change. This is why gift agreements are especially useful to our alumni and friends who have included IU in their will.

If you would like more information about the IU Foundation's gift agreements, fill out and return the enclosed reply card. Alternatively, call us at (812) 855-8322, or toll-free at (800) 558-8311.

Not long ago, my attorney explained to me the effect that taxes were going to have on my estate. He asked if I would like to make any charitable bequests as a way of reducing these taxes. It was an idea that I'd never considered before—and I'm glad I did! I've been a regular donor to IU for years, and the people at the IU Foundation showed me how to structure a bequest that will continue my annual contributions forever. It's been wonderful to leave some money to IU, rather than see it go to Uncle Sam.

I never thought about estate taxes until my mother died last year. My family never felt wealthy, but with the growth in the stock market several of my mother's investments were larger than I realized. Our attorney told me she could have left some money to charities that she cared about rather than pay all those taxes. That really made me stop and think. Now I've included IU in my will, and I feel better and better every time I think about it.

Foundation Profile

A New Movement, a Familiar Theme

"It's not just a pleasure, it's an honor," says George Bledsoe, newly appointed director of development for the IU School of Music. "I'm looking forward very much to my new assignment. The school's outstanding reputation is recognized around the world. I'm privileged to be a part of the administrative and faculty team that will maintain and enhance that reputation."

George has been on the IU team for a while now, as senior development director in the Office of Major Gifts at the IU Foundation. "I was a generalist before, focusing on the needs of all schools and colleges and campuses," says George. "Now I'll be focusing on the private support needs of the School of Music."

For George, the move is a return to an old, beloved theme. "I received my bachelor's degree in music from IU. Seven years later I earned a Master of Music in choral conducting. It was a great experience."

Since coming to the Foundation in 1996, after twenty-five years in private business, he has found that the rewards of working for his alma mater are many. "Being of service to the University is wonderful. It brings me a great deal of satisfaction to be facilitator between the donor and the University. I find that very rewarding."

"Many people think of gifts to the University as just outright cash. But there are many different ways to support IU—planned giving, estate planning, gifts of art or personal libraries—and often at levels far greater than they think possible without affecting their lifestyle or their heirs."

George will continue to spread the word from his new offices in Merrill Hall. His appointment to the School of Music brings him full circle from his earlier student days, a fact that fuels his enthusiasm.

"It's time for me to help look after and enhance the very things that attracted me to the School of Music in the first place," he says, "its faculty, its facilities, and its incredible record of training and inspiring the musicians of the future."

Fill in the information below to inform us of a planned gift you have made to benefit Indiana University, or use the other side of this card to request further information on charitable bequests.

Please briefly describe and/or attach the relevant document page(s) describing your planned gift to IU.

Name

Spouse's Name

Address

City   State   Zip

Phone Number(s)

Signature   Date

○ You may publish my name as a member of the Arbutus Society.

○ I would like to know more about gift agreements. Please have a planned giving professional call me.

The Arbutus Society

Indiana University Foundation

You can fill in the card below to request further information on charitable bequests, or use the other side of this card to inform us of a planned gift you have made to benefit Indiana University.

Name

Address

City   State   Zip

Phone Number(s)

○ Please have a planned giving professional call me.

○ Please send me the booklet *"Charitable Bequests—How To Get the Most Out of Yours"*

RESOURCE 13

SAMPLE PLANNED GIVING BROCHURES

THE CHARITABLE GIFT ANNUITY

a great way to

give and receive

Barnes-Jewish Hospital Foundation

Perhaps you are like many friends and supporters of Barnes-Jewish Hospital Foundation:

You want to provide for your future financial security, reduce your taxes, perhaps even include a charitable gift in your financial and estate plans. If these are among your objectives, you may very well want to look at our gift annuity program.

Mrs. Brown is a good example. Her husband, a supporter of BJH, died three years ago. Now, at age 75, her major objective is to establish a dependable income to ensure her financial security. She has always wanted to make a substantial gift to Barnes-Jewish in her husband's memory, but feels that she simply cannot give up any of her present assets.

Mrs. Brown learned that she can transfer cash or stock to Barnes-Jewish Hospital and receive dependable—and favorably taxed—fixed payments for as long as she lives. Her payments represent a substantially higher return than she's currently getting from her money market funds and CDs. What's more, she can even deduct a portion of her gift on her income tax return.

A favorably taxed income, immediate tax saving, the satisfaction of memorializing her husband's name and helping to assure the future of health care in our community . . . these are the rewards Mrs. Brown can gain by participating in BJH Foundation's gift annuity program.

How a Gift Annuity Works for You

In exchange for your gift of cash or securities, Barnes-Jewish Hospital Foundation will agree to pay a specified dollar amount to you (and/or to another beneficiary) each year for as long as you (or another beneficiary) may live. In most cases, annuity payments will be made on a quarterly basis, although other installment options are available.

Your gift will be held in a special reserve fund to help assure the Foundation's ability to make the annuity payments. Upon the death of the annuity beneficiary, the current value of the gift will be transferred to the Foundation. The income will be used for the general purposes of Barnes-Jewish Hospital, or for a specific doctor or program you may wish to support.

The annuity payments are based on the age of the annuitant(s) at the time you make your gift. The table below shows the percentage of income the Foundation will pay at various age levels.

For example, if you are 65 years old and make a gift of $10,000 to this program, the BJH Foundation will agree to pay you an annuity of $700 a year for as long as you may live. If you are 80 years old the payments will be $920 per year. Among the few advantages of growing older are the higher rates you can expect with a gift annuity!

A Gift Annuity Saves You Taxes

A portion of each and every annuity payment you receive will be taxable, but the balance will be free of both federal and state income taxes. The exact amount of the payment that will be tax-free depends upon the age of the beneficiary but, in most cases, at least one-third of each payment will be tax-free.

Charitable Gift Annuity Income Payout Rates

Age	Rate
65	7.0%
70	7.5%
75	8.2%
80	9.2%
85	10.5%

Note: Please call (314) 286-0449 for payout rates on ages not shown here.

In addition, every gift made to our gift annuity program qualifies for an immediate income tax charitable deduction. The deduction generally is equal to the fair market value of the property transferred to us minus the value of the annuity that the donor receives. Valuing the annuity depends on the number and age(s) of the annuitant(s), and the current level of interest rates. We will be happy to supply a free illustration for your specific circumstances. Just call Randy Flachsbart at (314) 286-0449 for information.

A Gift Annuity Is Flexible

Where to direct the income. Arranging a gift annuity for yourself is only one of the possible beneficiary designations. If you are like many friends of the Foundation, you may want an annuity that will be paid to you and your spouse for as long as either of you may live.

Choosing the gift property. You can transfer securities, as well as cash, to our gift annuity program. Indeed, funding your gift with appreciated securities can be an excellent means of minimizing capital gains taxes. If you own securities that are providing little or no income, our gift annuity program is an opportunity to convert your investment into a high and favorably taxed income.

Additional Rewards to Consider

Estate and inheritance taxes. Property transferred to the gift annuity program generally will not be subject to estate or inheritance taxes at your death. Gifts to the program can also significantly reduce the cost of administering your estate.

Social Security benefits. Because a portion of each annuity payment you will receive is tax-free, a gift annuity can help you to avoid income taxation of your Social Security benefits.

An Annuity Can Increase Your Income

To see how a gift annuity can increase your income, consider the following example:

Thomas, age 70, transfers $10,000 cash to Barnes-Jewish Hospital Foundation in exchange for an assured lifetime annuity of $750 a year. At his age and at the current level of interest rates, he can deduct about $3,700 on this year's income tax return (approximately 37 percent of the value of his gift). If his federal income tax bracket is 36 percent, the charitable deduction will provide an immediate tax savings of about $1,330 ($3,700 × 36 percent).

Factor in the $1,330 tax savings and the net outlay for Thomas is only $8,670. This means his $780 lifetime annuity—assuming quarterly installments—represents an assured 9 percent return on his after-tax outlay for as long as he lives.

What's more, part of each quarterly annuity payment will be tax-free. Thus, the annuity Thomas is to receive will probably be substantially more than what he could earn from a certificate of deposit, money market account or corporate bond fund. And Barnes-Jewish Hospital Foundation will ultimately receive the remainder of the gift (about 50 percent of the initial gift value).

A gift annuity is truly a gift plan that can help you do more for yourself and still make a gift that will have an impact on health care in our community.

An Invitation to Investigate Further

In today's fluctuating market and lower yield investment environment, an assured high income for life is an opportunity worth exploring—especially when the income is favorably taxed. And that's what you get with a gift annuity. That's not all, however. A gift annuity also gives you the opportunity to make a personal statement about your commitment to quality of health care through Barnes-Jewish

Hospital. It's nice to know you can make a difference in the lives of others while also making a difference in your own.

For more information about how you can benefit from a gift annuity, we urge you to send for your booklet, *Planning with Gift Annuities—How to Do More for Yourself and Barnes-Jewish.* Simply use the enclosed reply card. You'll note there is even a check-off box to request a no-obligation, personalized illustration to spell out your potential tax and financial benefits for any contribution you may wish to consider making to our gift annuity program. We look forward to hearing from you about this exciting opportunity.

Barnes-Jewish Hospital Foundation
www.bjc.org
Randy R. Flachsbart
Director, Planned Giving
Phone: (314) 286-0449
Fax: (314) 286-0599
E-mail: rflachsbart@bjc.org
600 S. Taylor Avenue, Suite 120
St. Louis, Missouri 63110-1035
Mail Stop: 90-94-206

> *Our mission is to improve the health of the people and communities we serve.*

Resource 13

PLANNING YOUR WILL

Your will is a unique document! During your life it has little or no meaning. You can change or revoke it and it has no effect on your financial, business or social situations. But at death, your will becomes tremendously important. It will be submitted to a court for a determination of its validity. When the court accepts your will as valid, its terms will control the disposition of assets you have accumulated through a lifetime of effort.

Certainly, your will can have a profound effect on the financial well-being of family members, friends and institutions. In all events, it will be a permanent reflection of your personal life values and your love and concern for family, friends and community.

A will is one of the most important documents you will execute during your life.

Three Key Elements

Whether your will is simple or complex, it is—first and foremost—a legal document. To be effective it must meet the requirements of state law. Even a small mistake in the drafting, execution, or witnessing of your will can make it completely invalid and ineffective.

Secondly, your will can—and should—be much more than a cold, sterile legal document. A will can be a final message reflecting your personal life values . . . a way of leaving a lasting legacy by which others may remember you.

Perhaps of greatest importance, your will should be practical. Within the parameters of the available assets, it should accomplish your objectives, meet the needs of your beneficiaries and permit an efficient and economical settlement of your estate.

Legal Requirements

Although every state has different rules for the execution of a will—and there seem to be exceptions to every general rule—the typical requirements of a valid will are:

- The will must be in writing and signed by the testator—the person executing the will. (We will use this term throughout the booklet, even though the correct legal term for a woman who makes a will is testatrix.) Many states specifically require that the signature of the testator be at the end of the document.
- The testator must be mentally competent at the time the will is executed.

- The testator must sign the will in the presence of two or three disinterested persons and must affirmatively state to these persons that the document is his or her last will and testament.
- Each witness must sign his or her name (usually in the presence of each other and the testator) and affirm that the testator did sign the document and acknowledge it as his or her last will and testament.

Commonly Asked Questions

Although you should always rely on your attorney to be sure your will is validly executed, you still may have questions that lurk in your mind. Here are some of the more common ones asked of our staff:

Do you need to change your will when you move to a different state? Technically, a will must meet all the requirements of the state where the testator resides at the time of his or her death. And if the will disposes of real property, it also must be executed according to the laws of the state where the property is located. However, some states will now admit a will to probate if it meets the requirements of the laws of the state where the testator resided at the time the will was executed.

Whom should you select as witnesses to your will? Ideally, a person witnessing a will should not have an interest in the will as beneficiary, trustee or executor and should not be related to the testator either by blood or by marriage. Certainly, a witness should be a person of good character and truthfulness who is likely to outlive the testator and remain in the state.

Can you use a fill-in-the-blanks type of will to avoid attorney costs? The answer is "Yes"; but this often can be a tragic mistake. It is wise to rely on an attorney for the drafting and execution of your will.

Can a minor execute a will? Most states provide that a person must be 18 years of age or older in order to execute a valid will.

Revoking or Amending

Your will can be changed easily and inexpensively by executing a "codicil"—a separate document that is executed with the same formalities of a will. In most cases, a codicil is used to make minor modifications in an existing will. The old will remains intact and is simply amended by the codicil.

If you need to make major changes you'll probably want to execute a completely new will. Usually a new will revokes all previously executed wills . . . but it is prudent to provide explicitly in your will that all former wills are revoked.

The best way to revoke a will is by executing a new will. However, a will can be revoked in most states by burning, tearing or obliterating the document or by simply writing "canceled" on the pages of the existing document. Of course, the acts must be done with the intention of revoking the will. If a will is revoked by a physical act and a new will is not executed, the estate will be distributed under the intestacy laws of the state where the decedent resided at the time of death.

A will also can be revoked by operation of law. In most states, divorce will revoke the benefits provided for the divorced spouse, but may not revoke provisions made for other beneficiaries. And, in some states, a will is wholly or partially revoked by the marriage of the testator, or the birth of a child to the testator, after the execution of his or her will.

Restrictions on Asset Disposition

Although you generally have freedom to dispose of assets to beneficiaries of your own choosing, state laws do impose some restrictions. The best example is the rule that a married person cannot disinherit his or her spouse. If a will makes no provision for the testator's spouse (or makes inadequate provision), the spouse generally can elect to take a specified portion of the estate against the terms of the will. Typically, a surviving spouse can claim one-third or one-half of the value of the estate.

What about children? People often ask us whether each child must receive a certain portion of the estate. As a general rule, children do not have an absolute right to receive any part of the estate unless the parent dies without a will ("intestate").

A few states restrict a person's right to name charitable institutions as beneficiaries of the estate. Usually, these restrictions are applicable only if the will was executed within 90 days of the testator's death or if the charitable bequests amount to more than one-half the value of the estate. In recent years, however, some such laws have been stricken down by the courts as unconstitutional.

In a real sense, then, we are free to leave our estates to persons or institutions of our own choosing—with the important exception that a surviving spouse cannot be disinherited.

Practical Considerations

Let's turn now to the practical side of a will . . . an area where the person making the will, rather than the attorney, has primary responsibility. And let's look first at the various forms of bequest that are available to you.

Most Popular Forms of Bequests

Specific Sum. Chances are good that your present will leaves specific sums of money to one or more designated beneficiaries and then directs that all the rest of your estate be divided among other designated beneficiaries. It may say something like this:

I give and bequeath the sum of $10,000 to _____ , my brother.

I give and bequeath the sum of $5,000 to _____ , a not-for-profit corporation located in the City of _____ and the State of _____ .

Percentage of Value. Many attorneys recommend "percentage-of-estate-value" bequests rather than monetary bequests. This causes all beneficiaries to share in increases or decreases in the value of the estate after the will is executed.

Contingent Bequests. What will happen if a beneficiary named in your will dies before you? It may go to an unintended relative or "lapse" and pass to your residual estate. Either way, your objectives may be frustrated. The best approach is to name contingent beneficiaries to take a bequest if the primary beneficiary predeceases you.

In-Kind Bequests. In appropriate cases, your will can bequeath specific real or personal property to a beneficiary. Keep in mind, however, that if the property is not in your estate at the time of your death, the bequest may become void and the beneficiary will not receive any part of your estate.

Residuary Bequests. It is important to note that the specific bequests provided for in your will are paid and satisfied first. Then, whatever is left of your estate after all specific bequests, taxes and estate costs have been paid will be distributed to the residuary beneficiaries. The balance of the estate may be bequeathed to a beneficiary in language similar to the following:

All the rest, reside and remainder of my estate, I give, devise and bequeath in equal portions to my children, _____ and _____ .

Selecting the Executor of Your Estate

Many people name their spouse or a child as the executor of their estate. And, unless the estate is large or complex, this is generally a good decision. (In actual practice, much of the work is done by the attorney.) However, depending on the nature of your estate, there may be good reason to nominate a friend as your executor . . . or to name a bank or trust company to settle your estate.

In choosing an executor, keep in mind that settling an estate can be a complex and demanding task. Assets must be collected and preserved, claims must be settled, debts collected and tax returns filed. The will must be probated, and court proceedings are essential. In most cases, all this is accomplished in one or two years, an accounting is filed, the estate is distributed to your designated beneficiaries and the executor is discharged.

It is important to make sure your executor has the power and authority needed to settle your estate. This can be a technical area of will planning, and you should rely on your attorney to provide the right power and authority for your executor.

The Art of Planning an Effective Will

There are five basic steps that generally should be taken in making a new will or reviewing an existing will.

First: *Make a detailed inventory of your estate . . .* a comprehensive listing of assets and liabilities, including personal effects. Write down the income each asset produces and other characteristics of each asset.

Second: *Make a list of your objectives in terms of what you want your estate plan to accomplish* rather than how much each beneficiary is to receive. For example, you may want to provide practical financial security for your spouse, a fund to protect a child against a temporary financial misfortune or a fund to assure an education for a grandchild.

We hope that one of your objectives will be to provide a lasting statement of support for one or more important charitable institutions such as ours. In most cases, there will be many ways to provide this support and still accomplish your other estate objectives.

Third: *Seek the advice of an attorney* as to how your estate can be arranged to accomplish your objectives. Trusts, contingent bequests, lifetime gifts and other arrangements may be suggested. Ask questions. Be sure you understand all the techniques for disposing of your estate in an effective manner.

Fourth: *Make your own decisions.* It is your estate and you have a right to dispose of it in any manner you desire.

Fifth: *Communicate your decisions to your attorney* and rely on the attorney to draft a will to accomplish your objectives.

A Final Word

In years past, wills were extremely personal—often emphasizing the personal philosophy of the testator and explaining his or her motive for making each and every bequest.

Today, the opposite seems to be true. Many wills are "boilerplate" documents that are largely impersonal. Certainly, there's nothing wrong with an impersonal will. On the other hand, there's nothing wrong with a will that is a warm and solemn message to family and friends.

If you feel that you have something important to say to your children, for example, it makes sense to write your message carefully and include it in your will. Certainly, care should be taken to be sure the message does not create confusion as to the disposition of your estate.

Many people demonstrate their love and concern for family members by making specific bequests of personal effects. Bequeathing a piece of jewelry to a daughter, a piece of furniture or art to a son or a library collection to an old friend can add greatly to the personal nature of your will.

You also may want to include a bequest to one or more charitable organizations that have added meaning to your life. It's a way of "giving back" and continuing to help make a difference in the lives of others. We can help you plan your bequest to provide the greatest personal satisfaction and tax and financial rewards.

This booklet is based on general tax and legal principles.
Always consult your attorney for specific advice. If you have
questions about any of the suggestions made in the booklet or
would like to discuss methods of including us in your estate
plans, please call or write us at your convenience.

Grace H. Timberlake, Esq.
Office of Development
NYU Medical Center
550 First Avenue, New York, NY 10016
212-263-5794 • 800-422-4483
E-mail: Grace.Timberlake@med.nyu.edu

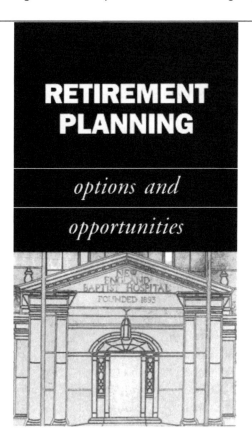

RETIREMENT PLANNING

options and

opportunities

NEW ENGLAND BAPTIST
HOSPITAL
A member of CAREGROUP

FINANCIAL PLANNING FOR RETIREMENT

For many, retirement is a time of dramatic change. The person who has gone to the office every morning, five days a week for forty years or more, suddenly has absolute freedom to do as he or she wishes. Experts tell us that the keys to a happy and successful retirement are good health, financial security, enthusiasm for life, and careful planning prior to retirement.

During the retirement years, financial support generally must come from a combination of:

1. Social Security benefits;
2. pension or other retirement benefits;
3. investment income; and/or
4. continued employment.

Certainly, common sense mandates that we carefully plan for a financially secure retirement and that we be aware of the role taxes can play in our retirement plans.

In this booklet, we will review some of the many tax benefits Congress has provided to help us achieve a financially sound retirement. In Section One, we will discuss tax planning after retirement; then in Section Two, we will emphasize the great importance of tax planning in the year of retirement. Section Three points out how carefully planned charitable gifts can be an important part of our financial plans for retirement.

SECTION ONE: Income Taxes After Retirement

Income tax planning can be very important for persons who now are retired and living on a relatively fixed income.

The typical retired couple (both over age 64) can have up to $14,650 of income in 2000 completely sheltered from any federal income tax through a combination of their personal exemptions, the "standard deduction," and the additional standard deduction for persons 65 and over. This tax-free amount will increase each year as the personal exemption and standard deduction are adjusted for inflation.

Income in excess of these amounts is taxable at the standard rates of 15%, 28%, 31%, 36%, and 39.6%.

The basic income tax rules remain essentially the same after retirement. Dividend and interest income is fully taxable. Salaries and business income remain taxable both before and after retirement. Long-term capital gains are generally taxed up to a top rate of 20% (with certain exceptions). And interest received on municipal bond investments remains wholly free of any federal income tax.

Taxation of Social Security Benefits

Up to 50% of a taxpayer's Social Security benefits are includable in gross income if a married couple's income base exceeds $32,000 ($25,000 for single taxpayers). An even higher tax applies when married Social Security recipients have an income base over $44,000 ($34,000 for single taxpayers). Above these levels, up to 85% of the taxpayer's Social Security retirement benefits may be included in gross income.

This can be especially harsh for Social Security recipients who continue to work. If age 64 or under, they lose part of their Social Security benefits, plus the earnings from their job may push them over the threshold at which their Social Security benefits will be taxed.

Withdrawals from a Traditional IRA Are Usually Taxable

Funds you withdraw from a traditional IRA are usually taxable as ordinary income in the year the withdrawal is made, unless you have made nondeductible contributions to the IRA. However, you can choose the year for making withdrawals or you can simply not withdraw any funds from the account in the early years of retirement thus allowing tax-deferred accumulation to continue. However, withdrawals must begin no later than April 1 of the year following the year you attain age 70½.

Pension Benefits Generally Are Taxable

As a general rule, your pension and other retirement benefits will be fully taxable unless you made nondeductible contributions to the plan. As a general rule, you can recover your own contributions tax-free over your life expectancy (unless your contributions were tax-deductible), and the balance of the benefits are taxed as ordinary income. The administrator of your retirement plan can provide the exact amount of the contributions you made.

For example, at retirement, Paul B. elects to receive a lifetime pension of $12,000 a year. During his working years, he contributed $40,000 to the pension plan. For tax purposes, Paul has a life expectancy of 19 years and must recover his contributions over this period. *The result:* $2,105 will be excludable each year from the $12,000 pension benefit Paul receives. The balance of each year's pension benefit will be taxable.

Sale of a Principal Residence

Gain on the sale of a principal residence is treated more favorably than other types of capital gain. Effective for home sales on and after May 7, 1997, both the old rollover-of-gain deferral rule and the former age-55 exclusion of up to $125,000 have been replaced by a new, broader exclusion. A seller of any age who has used the home as a principal residence for at least two of the last five years can exclude from gross income up to $250,000 ($500,000 if married filing jointly) of gain realized on a home sale. Further, this provision is reusable every two years.

Capital improvements made to a residence increase the cost basis and reduce the gain that could be taxable when the property is sold.

There are some standard approaches to minimizing income taxes on retirement income:

- Capital gains can be avoided by retaining appreciated property for life. The property takes a stepped-up cost basis at the death of the owner equal to its value at death.
- Social Security benefits can be tax-free in any year in which adjusted gross income (including half of the Social Security benefits and tax-exempt income) is less than $32,000 ($25,000 for a single taxpayer).
- Withdrawals from a traditional IRA are usually taxable income in the year of withdrawal. But income earned on IRA contributions is not taxable as currently earned.
- Interest earned on municipal bonds continues to be exempt from federal income taxes. If you are in a 31% tax bracket, a tax-free income of 6.5% is equivalent to a 9.4% taxable income.
- You can itemize your deductions if, and to the extent, your deductible interest expenses, taxes, medical costs, casualty losses, and charitable gifts exceed the standard deduction and the additional deduction available to elderly taxpayers. Timing your deductible costs and charitable gifts—so that deductions are "bunched" into years of higher income—can be financially rewarding.

SECTION TWO: Tax Planning in the Year of Retirement

Many of your friends will find that their income is unusually high in the year of retirement. Bonuses, accrued vacation or sick pay, and other special forms of income often are received in the year of retirement. For many, this is an excellent time to make a tax-favored charitable gift and otherwise establish the maximum itemized deductions.

The year of retirement is also the time for making important decisions about retirement benefits . . . and tax consequences should play a major role in making these decisions.

Experts in financial planning generally agree that most Americans should establish a retirement income that is approximately 75% of their pre-retirement income.

Retirement Plan Elections

Many qualified retirement plans give the participant two basic elections: a lump-sum payment or a life-time annuity. Moreover, a plan participant generally can roll a distribution into an IRA. So there are three basic alternatives: (1) take a lump-sum payment; (2) transfer a distribution to an IRA; or (3) elect a lifetime annuity or other form of periodic benefit. Each alternative has its own special tax consequences.

- A lump-sum payout, at the election of the taxpayer, can be taxed under a special and favorable provision if the participant was born before January 1, 1936.
- A distribution that is rolled over directly to an IRA is not subject to taxation until withdrawals are made from the IRA, and then are taxed as ordinary income. There are two basic advantages to this election: income earned on the investment of the retirement benefits is not subject to current taxation, and withdrawals from the IRA often can be planned so as to result in the lowest possible tax.
- Periodic payments generally are taxable as ordinary income in the year they are received. Because payments generally are made on a regular monthly basis, we lose the ability to time withdrawals for the most favorable tax consequences.

Investments After Retirement

In most cases, the retired person will want to invest the bulk of his or her assets with a primary goal of producing a good income. In many cases, the growth investments of pre-retirement years will be sold and the proceeds invested in higher income-producing securities or other properties.

Capital gains taxes can sometimes be minimized through the use of installment sales or by spreading the sale of appreciated properties over several years. And because a charitable remainder trust (described on a later page) has the important advantage of permitting the sale of appreciated property without any capital gains tax consequences, it can play a major role in your retirement plans.

SECTION THREE: Charitable Gifts in Your Retirement Planning

The Charitable Remainder Trust

A charitable remainder trust frequently can be a very important element in a sound and practical retirement plan. Charitable trusts and retirement planning really go hand in hand. A trust created for the eventual benefit of our institution can pay a good lifetime income to the creator of the trust and/or to other beneficiaries designated by the creator. In addition, the trust produces immediate income tax savings for the person creating the trust.

In many cases, this is exactly what the person planning for retirement wants—a regular income that will be paid for as long as he or she lives and an immediate tax saving that is available prior to retirement (or in the year of retirement) when he or she is in a high income tax bracket.

There are three other factors that make the charitable remainder trust an attractive retirement income plan.

First, the lifetime income paid to the creator of the trust and/or to other beneficiaries often can be favorably taxed or even completely tax-free. Keep in mind that an 8% tax-free yield is equivalent to an 11.6% yield if you are in a 31% federal income tax bracket.

Second, there is no capital gains tax when you transfer appreciated property to a charitable remainder trust. This factor makes the charitable trust an excellent method of converting a low-yield, highly appreciated investment into a high-income producing investment without paying a capital gains tax.

Third, with careful planning, a charitable trust can, in effect, accumulate income while the beneficiary is in a high tax bracket and pay this income after the beneficiary has retired and is in a lower tax bracket.

Charitable remainder trusts are very flexible and are tailored to meet the needs and objectives of the creator of the trust. Some examples of how a trust for our institution can be a valuable part of your retirement planning:

- William B. took his retirement benefits of $120,000 in a lump sum and transferred the full amount to a charitable trust that will pay him $10,000 a year, completely tax-free, for as long as he lives. The charitable deduction allowed for the gift to the trust actually saved substantial income taxes in the year of retirement, but the guaranteed and tax-free income . . . and the desire to provide a significant deferred gift to our institution . . . were the major reasons William created the trust.
- Edward J. established a charitable remainder trust when he was 56 years of age. He does not want any income until he is 65, but he did want an immediate tax savings from the charitable deduction. Because income is being accumulated for Edward, the annual payment when he retires will be a significant percentage of his net after-tax investment in the trust.
- Franklin P. bought undeveloped real property almost twenty-five years ago. At retirement, he wanted to convert this investment to one that would provide a high income. By transferring the property to a charitable trust, Franklin completely avoided a capital gains tax, established a good retirement income (that is designed to keep pace with inflation), gained immediate income tax benefits and minimized potential estate tax liability.

Other Charitable Gifts in Retirement Planning

Retirement is a time for reviewing your estate, tax, gift, and financial plans.

As you review your will, we hope you will consider the good you can accomplish by including our institution as one of your beneficiaries. Or if you find that one or more life insurance policies are no longer needed for your personal financial security or the financial security of your family, do consider the personal satisfaction and the tax benefits that can be realized by transferring ownership of the policy to our institution.

You may want to name our institution as the death beneficiary of your IRA or other qualified retirement plan. Because IRA and other retirement benefits are taxed as ordinary income to the beneficiary—and are also subject to estate taxation—an individual beneficiary may actually keep only about 30%–40% of the benefits, whereas our institution (because it is tax-exempt) will keep the full amount of the benefits.

If you would like more information about the tax and financial consequences of a charitable remainder trust, or if you would like to discuss a bequest, life insurance gift, or other tax-rewarding charitable gift that can complement your personal retirement planning, please feel free to call or write us at your convenience.

This booklet is based on general tax and legal principles.
Always consult your attorney for specific advice. If you have
questions about any of the suggestions made in the booklet or
would like to discuss methods of including us in your estate
plans, please call or write us at your convenience.

NEW ENGLAND BAPTIST HOSPITAL
A member of CAREGROUP
Alan H. Robbins, MD
President
John A. Dresser
Chief Development Officer
125 Parker Hill Avenue
Boston, Massachusetts 02120
617-754-6880
Fax 617-754-6397

Resource 13

LIFE INCOME PLANS
Ways to Give and Receive

Life income gift plans have become a very popular way for donors to make major gifts. Typically, the donor makes the irrevocable gift to a special fund and reserves the right to receive an income from the gift property for his or her life (or the donor may direct that an income be paid to one or more designated individuals for as long as they may live). The gift property passes to the charity, or becomes available to the charity, only after all the income rights have terminated.

Life income gifts are made for many reasons. One big reason is personal satisfaction. Donors are able to support major causes in ways that otherwise would be impossible. And there is another big reason—tax and financial rewards. In many cases, life income gift plans can enhance the investment, retirement, tax, and estate plans of the donor.

The purpose of this booklet is to highlight these life income plans. Technically, they are known as:

- charitable remainder annuity trust,
- charitable remainder unitrust, and
- gift annuity program.

These plans are similar in that each provides income payments to the donor or other designated beneficiaries. But they differ in the amount or nature of the income payments, the allowable income tax charitable deduction, the type of property that can be given, and other tax and financial consequences that result from the gift.

The Charitable Remainder Annuity Trust

You can create a trust that will hold and invest property and pay you and/or other designated beneficiaries a specified dollar amount each year for as long as you or the other beneficiaries may live.

You can select the amount of your annual income payments. It must be at least 5% of the value of your gift but it could be up to 8% or 9% of your gift. Nothing will be paid to our institution until all the income rights have terminated. At that time we receive all the property held by the trustee.

Every Trust Is Tailored for the Donor

Every charitable remainder annuity trust is planned and drafted to accomplish the specific objectives of the donor. For example:

You can name the income beneficiaries. You can name yourself, or anyone you wish, as the income beneficiary of the trust. You can direct that the income benefits be paid to you for your life and then to your spouse for his or her life. Or you can name one or more of your children as beneficiaries. But there must be at least a 10% projected residual for the charity.

You can set the exact amount that will be paid each year. You have a broad right to fix the dollar amount to be paid out every year. And it will be paid from principal if income is not sufficient. Typically, a donor will fix the annuity from 5% to 9% of the value of the property placed in the trust.

You can decide how long the income will be paid. Income can be payable for the life of one beneficiary, the lives of two or more beneficiaries, or for a specified period of years (up to 20 years).

You pick the property that will be transferred to the trust. There are advantages to funding your trust with appreciated property, especially if the property is producing little or no income. But there may also be advantages to funding your trust with cash, certificates of deposit, closely held stock, or other properties. We can tell you the tax consequences that will result from the property you select to fund the trust.

You name the trustee. You can name anyone you wish as trustee—your bank, your attorney, a family member, etc.

You name the charitable beneficiary. A qualified charitable institution must be named as remainder beneficiary of the trust. But you can name more than one charity if you wish. And you can place restrictions on how the charity may use the gift.

Planning Pointers for the Annuity Trust

Clearly, the annuity trust can be the best plan for the donor who wants to receive a fixed and guaranteed income that he or she cannot reasonably outlive. In many cases, the annual income payments can be tax-free or favorably taxed. And the annuity trust arrangement will generally produce the largest income tax charitable deduction.

The Charitable Remainder Unitrust

The charitable remainder unitrust differs from the annuity trust in one very important way—rather than a fixed-dollar income, the unitrust arrangement must provide for income payments that vary with the investment success of the trust. Specifically, the unitrust must direct that the trust assets be valued each year and that a specified percentage of the value be paid to the individual beneficiary or beneficiaries. If the value of the trust assets goes up, the annual payments go up. But the reverse is also true—the annual payments will decrease if the value of the trust assets decreases. One other difference: you can make additions to the unitrust, but not to an annuity trust.

Other than that, the unitrust is quite similar to an annuity trust. The donor can select the individual beneficiaries, fix the percentage of value that will be paid to these beneficiaries, and direct the period of time during which income benefits will be paid. The trust can be funded with almost any kind of property, and the donor can name anyone he or she wishes as trustee. The donor can name one or more qualified charities to receive the trust property when the income rights terminate, or direct that the trust be continued for the benefit of the charitable beneficiaries.

There is an interesting variation possible with a unitrust that is not available with an annuity trust. The unitrust agreement can direct that each annual payment be the lesser of (a) the specified percentage of value in that year, or (b) the income earned by the trust in that year. If option (b) is selected, the trust agreement will generally provide that, if less than the specified percentage of value is paid in any year, the deficit will be made up in a subsequent year in which income exceeds the specified percentage of value. This variation makes the unitrust useful as a retirement planning tool.

Planning Pointers for the Unitrust

The charitable remainder unitrust is the preferred plan for persons who want an income that is likely to increase in an inflationary economy. As the value of trust assets increases so do the annual income payments.

The income-only unitrust can be advantageous when the trust is to be funded with property that produces a low income and may be difficult to sell. Income payments can be deferred until the property is sold and the reinvested sales proceeds are producing a good income.

The Charitable Gift Annuity

The easiest way to make a tax-favored deferred charitable gift is through a gift annuity program. You transfer money or securities to the charity in exchange for its commitment to pay you a specified annuity for as long as you live. There's no trust agreement or other complexities . . . just the charity's simple written promise to pay a specified dollar amount to you and/or other beneficiaries each year for the lives of the beneficiaries.

The amount of income or annuity that will be paid generally depends on the age of the beneficiary (or beneficiaries). In most cases it ranges from 7% (for a 65-year-old beneficiary) to 12% (for a 90-year-old beneficiary).

Persons making a contribution to a gift annuity fund may arrange to postpone annuity payments for a period of years. For example, a 55-year-old donor may postpone any annuity payments until he is 65 years of age and retired. The delay in making payments permits the charity to increase dramatically the amount of the annuity that will eventually be paid.

Planning Pointers for the Gift Annuity

The simplicity and certainty of the gift annuity makes it attractive to many donors. In most cases, a gift made for an annuity can be only $5,000, whereas a much larger gift must generally be made to fund a charitable remainder trust.

Donors like the fixed payments for life, the fact that part of the payments may be tax free, and that the effective yield is extremely attractive.

The deferred gift annuity can be especially attractive to middle-aged professionals (ages 50–65). Like an IRA, it can be an excellent way to build a sound retirement income.

Tax Consequences of Life Income Gifts

Each of the deferred gift methods we have discussed provides at least four basic tax benefits:

First, the present value of the deferred gift to the charity can be deducted as a charitable contribution to the donor's income tax return.

Second, the gift generally does not give rise to an immediate capital gains tax even though the gift property has substantially appreciated in value.

Third, the gift property can be sold by the charity, the fund, or the trust without incurring a capital gains tax.

Fourth, the gift will avoid or minimize federal estate taxes at the death of the donor.

In many cases, there will be a fifth tax advantage that can result from a carefully planned deferred gift—the annual income payments can be tax-free or favorably taxed.

The Allowable Charitable Deduction

The exact amount of charitable deduction allowable for a deferred gift depends on several different factors. The value of the gift and the nature of the gift property are obviously important factors. So is the amount of income payable to individual beneficiaries, the period of time during which payments will be made, and the form in which the deferred gift is made.

Favorably Taxed Income

A life income gift can often be arranged to provide a tax-free or favorably taxed income to the beneficiary.

A trust (annuity trust or unitrust) will generally provide the most favorably taxed income arrangement. The income payments can be tax-free if the trust itself has no ordinary income and no capital gains. For example, if the trustee invests all the trust assets in municipal bonds and does not realize any capital gains, the income payments will be tax-free to the donor or other beneficiaries.

The income payments made through a charitable gift annuity will almost always be partially tax-free. Historically, 30%–50% of the annual payment is free of income taxes.

Avoiding Capital Gains Taxes

A life income gift can be arranged to avoid or reduce the liability to the donor. And the trust or charity can sell the property without incurring any capital gains tax. This means that the full value of the property will be available to provide an income for the beneficiary . . . and the property eventually passing to the charity will not be depleted by capital gains taxes.

A Life Income Gift to Accomplish Your Objectives

A life income gift to our institution can be—and should be—carefully planned to accomplish the individual investment, retirement, or estate objectives of the donor. Here are some examples.

Building an Immediate Retirement Fund

Frank W. is 65 years of age and expects to retire within the next few months. He has accumulated stock in his employer's corporation that is now worth more than $200,000. His cost basis is only $30,000. The stock pays a very small dividend and is a rather risky investment. Frank wants to sell it and invest the proceeds for a high income.

A sale of the stock would, of course, result in a federal and state capital gains tax liability and selling expense. (Frank figures the depletion could be as much as $47,600, leaving only about $152,400 to invest for a retirement income).

Frank could transfer the stock to a charitable remainder trust that would pay him $16,000 a year for as long as he might live. The gift in trust would result in an immediate income tax charitable deduction to shelter Frank's income from taxes.

Building a Future Retirement Fund

The simple and practical gift annuity can be an excellent method of making a life income gift and building a good future retirement income.

Richard C. is 55 years of age. He intends to transfer $5,000 a year to a charitable institution that agrees to pay him a high and favorably taxed annual annuity starting when he reaches age 65. He can deduct a substantial portion of each annual $5,000 gift to the charitable institution. And he can supplement his retirement income with the annuity payments at age 65.

Minimizing Taxes and Other Costs

Each of the life income plans can be very effective in minimizing estate taxes and settlement costs.

Nancy J. transferred property worth almost $500,000 (about one-half of her estate) to a charitable remainder annuity trust that is expected to pay an income of about $40,000 a year to her daughter for as long as the daughter (then 63 years old) might live. This deferred gift will save $100,000 or more in federal estate taxes and settlement costs at Nancy's death. She could have chosen a gift annuity or a unitrust for her daughter with rather similar tax rewards.

Providing a Favorably Taxed Income

A charitable gift annuity is a very popular way to gain a favorably taxed income. Historically, approximately 30%–50% of each annuity is received tax-free. For example, a 70-year-old person could give $10,000 to a charitable institution and receive a guaranteed annuity of $690 a year for his or her life. About 43% of the value of the gift would be deductible as a charitable contribution and 50% of the annuity would be tax-free.

A completely tax-free income can be arranged by transferring cash or a non-appreciated asset to a charitable remainder trust. So long as the trust had only tax-free income, the income payments would be tax-free.

Establishing an Educational Fund

A charitable remainder trust can be created to pay an income to one or more children for a specified period of years. For example, a grandfather could create a trust that would pay 10% of the value of the trust assets to a grandchild each year for ten years.

Because trusts can be created for a specified number of years (up to 20) they are an ideal way to build an educational fund or a career-starting fund for a minor child. A deferred gift annuity can also be used to build an educational fund for a minor child. The charity can pay the child the commuted value of the lifetime annuity at a time when the child needs educational funds.

We Can Provide More Information

Life income gifts can be very important for our future, and richly rewarding to the donor. We would welcome an opportunity to discuss how a life income gift can work for both you and us.

This booklet is based on general tax and legal principles.
Always consult your attorney for specific advice.
If you have questions about any of the suggestions
made in the booklet or would like to discuss methods
of including us in your estate plans, please call or
write us at your convenience.

For more information please contact:

David Blackman
Senior Development Officer
for Planned Giving
Museum of Fine Arts, Boston
465 Huntington Avenue
Boston, Massachusetts 02115
Tel: (617) 369-3816
Fax: (617) 247-6761
E-mail: dblackman@mfa.org

PLANNING WITH GIFT ANNUITIES

how to do more for yourself and charity

photo by Andrew Brilliant

PLANNING WITH GIFT ANNUITIES

Each year thousands of caring individuals use the charitable gift annuity to provide major financial support for important charitable organizations. In many cases, this time-tested technique has permitted gifts that otherwise would not have been financially prudent.

Elizabeth, age 70, is a good example. Although she has always wanted to make a significant gift to her favorite charity, she feels she cannot afford to lose any income. Through a gift annuity arrangement she is able to give $10,000 to the charity which, in turn, commits itself to pay her an income of $750 a year for as long as she might live. This is a higher return than she has been earning on her $10,000 and her annuity will be favorably taxed. Elizabeth's gift also will result in an immediate and significant income tax savings.

The Gift Annuity Is Popular and Flexible

Certainly, the ability to make a gift without loss of income—and with very favorable tax results—is a major reason for the popularity of the charitable gift annuity. But a carefully planned gift annuity can accomplish other important personal and financial objectives as well.

Perhaps you will see your own objectives mirrored in one or more of these cases:

- Patrick, at age 58, has an income more than adequate for his needs, but wants to reduce his current tax liabilities and also add to his future retirement income. A deferred gift annuity—explained later in this booklet—would be an excellent technique for him.
- Helen wants to provide a solid and favorably taxed lifetime income for a dear friend. She finds that she can make a gift to a charity that she and her friend have long supported, gain an immediate tax deduction and arrange to have the charity pay a good annuity to her friend for as long as the friend may live.
- Frances is preparing for retirement and wants to sell property that is producing little or no income and invest the proceeds in a way that will produce a high and dependable income. The charitable gift annuity permits her to accomplish this objective without incurring an immediate capital gains tax.

Although our gift annuity program is very simple, direct and certain, it also offers a great deal of flexibility. For example:

- You can name yourself or any other person as the annuity beneficiary or you can create a joint-and-survivor annuity for two beneficiaries.
- You can direct us to start making annuity payments immediately or at some later time.
- You can fund the annuity with cash or another form of property—generally with very favorable proration of capital gains taxes.

We'll address these planning options later in this booklet. Now let's discuss some general questions that are frequently asked about the program.

Answers to Commonly Asked Questions

How is the annuity amount determined?

In most cases the amount of the annual annuity is based on the age of the donor (or other beneficiary) and the amount or value of the gift made to our program. The older the beneficiary, the higher the annuity rate.

(The table on a later page shows sample annuity payments and charitable deduction for single-life gift annuities.)

Is any part of the gift made to your gift annuity program tax-deductible?

Yes, a portion of the amount you transfer to our gift annuity program is deductible as a charitable contribution on your federal income tax return. Typically, you can deduct from 30 percent to 50 percent of the amount you transfer to this program.

Let's say you transfer $5,000 to the program and, at your age, exactly one-half of the gift is tax-deductible. If you are in a 36 percent federal income tax bracket, the gift will reduce your current income taxes by $900.

Can the annuity payment change?

No. The annuity is fixed at the time the gift is made. You don't have to worry about the volatility of the stock market. Your payments are fixed for life.

How does the charitable gift annuity differ from fixed-income investments?

First off, a charitable gift annuity is not an investment. It is part gift and part annuity. But when you factor in the tax deduction, your effective rate of return is often substantially higher than the return you can get from passbook savings, money market funds or even your CDs.

The charitable gift annuity is attractive because it enables you to make a difference in the lives of persons served by the charity of your choice . . . and to enjoy the lifetime income and tax deduction earned by your generosity.

How are annual annuity payments taxed?

A portion of each payment is taxable as ordinary income, but part of each payment—generally about 30 percent to 50 percent—is tax-free over your life expectancy. The percentage excludible depends on your age. If you outlive your life expectancy, subsequent payments become taxable as ordinary income.

How will annuity payments be treated in determining the taxation of my Social Security benefits?

Only the taxable portion of annuity payments is treated as income in computing the potential tax on Social Security benefits. The favorable taxation of gift annuity payments can be a real advantage to many retired persons who are receiving Social Security benefits . . . especially now that up to 85 percent of the benefits may be taxable.

What factors should I consider in deciding whether to make a contribution to a gift annuity program?

All gifts made to our gift annuity program are irrevocable. Certainly, it would be a mistake for any person to make a significant gift if there was any real possibility that the gift property would be needed for personal financial security.

Annual Annuity and Charitable Deduction for $10,000 Single-Life Gift Annuity

Age of Annuitant	Annual Annuity*	Charitable Deduction*
65	$ 700	$3,371
70	$ 750	$3,707
75	$ 820	$4,060
80	$ 920	$4,444
85	$1,050	$4,885
90	$1,200	$5,435

This assumes quarterly payments and an adjusted federal interest rate of 7%. The charitable deduction will vary with the current federal interest rate and the frequency of payments (annual, semi-annual, quarterly, etc.). The annual annuity will be somewhat lower for two-life gift annuities. We'll be happy to provide you with the exact figures for your situation.

Planning Options

Providing a Lifetime Income for a Family Member or Friend

A person making a contribution to our gift annuity program can name—within reasonable limitations—any person he or she wishes as the annuity beneficiary. Indeed, the donor can direct that the annuity be paid to one person for life and thereafter to a second beneficiary for as long as the second beneficiary may live.

Keep in mind that it is the age of the beneficiary—not the age of the donor—that will determine the amount of the annuity and the charitable deduction.

Example: Helen has been giving $18,000 a year to help support her 80-year-old sister. In Helen's 36% federal income tax bracket, she needs an income of about $28,127 a year to provide this support.

Helen makes a gift of $200,000 to a qualified charity and the charity commits to pay the sister $18,400 a year for as long as she lives. Because part of the gift is deductible, Helen significantly reduces her current income taxes and provides a guaranteed source of income that will pay her sister even after her own death.

Equally important to Helen is the satisfaction she receives by making a generous gift to an important charity.

The Deferred Gift Annuity Can Increase Retirement Income

Our gift annuity program permits the donor to postpone the starting date of the annuity for a specified period of time—generally until the time he or she expects to retire. Since annuity payments are postponed, both the amount of the annuity and the allowable charitable deduction are significantly increased. Recent changes in the tax law give you more flexibility in determining your start-up date, which should make the deferred gift annuity even more attractive.

Example: Patrick, a successful doctor, doesn't need more income right now, but he is concerned about having enough income in his retirement years. In his 39.6% federal tax bracket, he would welcome an immediate tax deduction. After talking with his financial advisers and our staff, he decides to contribute $25,000 for a gift annuity that will start in ten years—when he will be 68 and expects to retire.

Starting at age 68, Patrick will receive an annuity of approximately $2,975 a year . . . every year for life. He can immediately deduct about $12,850 as a charitable contribution and in his tax bracket this will save about $5,000 in income taxes. *(Calculations are based on a federal interest rate of 7 percent. Interest rates change each month so your deduction may be different.)*

Periodic Gifts Can Be Made to Supplement Your Retirement Plan

Our gift annuity program can work somewhat like an IRA. Periodic gifts to the program will produce a cumulative retirement income, and each gift will reduce your current year's income tax liability.

Example: Richard, now 55 years old, is in a position to give $5,000 a year to us. To help assure his own financial future, he decides to make these gifts to our gift annuity program and directs that all annuity payments be deferred until he is age 65.

A portion of each annual gift will be tax-deductible. Over the 10-year period, this will reduce Richard's income tax liability significantly. When Richard reaches age 65, he will start receiving annuity payments that will continue for as long as he lives.

Funding Your Gift with Appreciated Property Can Save More Taxes

Generally, there is no immediate capital gains tax when you transfer appreciated property to our gift annuity program.

Example: Let's say you own securities now worth $25,000. Your cost basis is only $10,000. You have owned the securities for several years, but since they provide very little income, you are thinking about selling them and investing for a high income.

A sale of the securities will result in a federal capital gains tax of about $3,000, so you will have only $22,000 (or less when state taxes and transaction costs are considered) to invest for an income. With a 5 percent return, you will earn $1,100 a year.

At age 75, you can gain a much higher income of about $2,050 a year by giving the securities to a gift annuity program. You also will gain an immediate income tax charitable deduction for your contribution.

Funding a gift annuity with appreciated property will cause part of each annuity payment to be taxed as a capital gain. However, in most cases, transferring appreciated property to our gift annuity program is very advantageous for the donor.

A Bequest to Our Gift Annuity Program

Most gift annuities are completed during the life of the donor, but you also can make a bequest to our program and direct that an annuity be paid to a designated beneficiary for his or her lifetime. If you intend to make such a bequest, please tell us so that we understand how the annuity is to be paid. This option underscores the flexibility of our programs. We invite you to explore the many possibilities.

This booklet is based on general tax and legal principles.
Always consult your attorney for specific advice. If you have
questions about any of the suggestions made in the booklet or
would like to discuss methods of including us in your estate
plans, please call or write us at your convenience.

For more information, contact:

Laureen B. Cahalane
Manager, Planned Giving and Leadership Gifts
Tel: 617.589.0243
Fax: 617.589.0363
Email: lcahalane@mos.org
Museum of Science
Science Park
Boston, MA 02114-1099
www.mos.org

Resource 13

THE CHARITABLE REMAINDER TRUST

a gift and

an income

THE COLUMBUS FOUNDATION

The Center for Charitable Giving ™

THE CHARITABLE REMAINDER TRUST
A Gift and an Income

Almost every charitable gift can be considered an investment. The gift may be an outlay of time, money or property—whatever the form, it can bring you deep personal satisfaction . . . the joy of knowing that you have helped ensure the financial future of charitable causes you feel are important.

However, a charitable gift that is made through a unique trust arrangement can also be a sound financial tool. With careful planning, a charitable remainder trust can provide both a good, solid lifetime income and immediate tax benefits for the donor and his or her family.

Understanding the Charitable Remainder Trust

The charitable remainder trust is a popular and time-tested method of making a generous deferred gift to a charitable institution that you personally want to support.

You, the donor, irrevocably transfer money or property to a trust that you have created. The trust agreement (drafted by your attorney) directs that a specified income be paid each year to you and/or other individuals named in our agreement. In most cases, the trustee will be directed to make the income payments for as long as you or other designated beneficiaries may live. After the income benefits terminate, the principal of the trust is paid to your designated charitable beneficiary(ies).

Steps in a Charitable
Remainder Trust

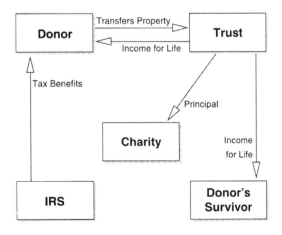

The chart shows the four steps in a typical charitable remainder trust.

First, the donor transfers property to the trust and gains several immediate tax benefits.

Second, the trustee invests the assets placed in the trust and pays an annual income to the donor for his or her life.

Third, the trust can pay an income to a designated survivor after the donor's death or concurrently with the payments to the donor.

Fourth, when all income rights have been satisfied, the principal of the trust will be distributed to our institution or held in trust for the benefit of our institution.

An Illustration

A simple example is probably the best way to explain the charitable remainder trust. Mary W. transfers property worth $100,000 to a trust and directs that $5,000 be paid to herself each year for as long as she lives. The property will be retained by the trustee during Mary's life, and both income and principal will be used to make the annual payments. After Mary's death, the trust will end and the property remaining in the trust at that time will be paid to our institution.

Mary, of course, gains a good and solid lifetime income. She also gains an immediate and substantial tax saving because she can deduct, as a charitable contribution, the present value of our institution's right to receive the trust property at some later time.

A charitable remainder trust also can produce other important tax and financial benefits.

Mary will not incur a capital gains tax even if she transfers highly appreciated property to the trust and the property is immediately sold by the trustee. In short, she can convert a low-income producing property to a high-income producing property free of any capital gains tax liability. In addition, Mary is assured an income of $5,000 annually from the trust for as long as she lives.

Benefit 1—A Lifetime Income

As was previously indicated, every charitable remainder trust provides an annual income to the donor or other beneficiaries designated in the agreement. The income can be a specific sum of money (a so-called annuity trust), or it can be a percentage of the value of the trust in each year (a so-called unitrust). In most cases, the income payments will be made for the life of the beneficiary, but they can also be made for a fixed period of years.

Typically, a donor will reserve an income that is 5 percent to 8 percent of the value of the trust. But the amount of income is always a decision made by you, the donor, to accomplish your personal objectives.

Some donors want to establish an income that will vary with the investment success of the trust. Under this arrangement, the trust assets will be valued each year and a specified percentage of the value in each year will be paid to the donor or other beneficiary. A unitrust can be a hedge against future inflation.

Other donors who prefer the stability of a fixed-dollar amount of income for as long as they may live may want to choose the annuity trust.

Benefit 2—An Immediate Income Tax Charitable Deduction

The most obvious tax benefit produced by the charitable remainder trust is a federal income tax charitable deduction. Even though the charitable institution will receive absolutely no benefits until the termination of all the income interests, the donor can immediately deduct—on his or her federal income tax return—the present value of the deferred charitable interest.

Computing the charitable deduction is rather cumbersome and complex because it depends in part upon the particular federal interest rate in the month of the gift and the two preceding months. Generally speaking, the higher the federal interest rate, the larger the charitable deduction. We can provide you with the exact figures.

Converting an Asset to Produce a High Income

Peter, age 65, owns a parcel of real estate that is now worth $150,000. The property provides absolutely no income, but it has appreciated tremendously in value since Peter bought it some years ago for $25,000.

Peter could sell the property, but he would incur combined costs (realtor's commission, selling costs, capital gains tax) of about $34,500. If he invested the after-tax sales proceeds of about $115,500 in CDs earning 5 percent, he would realize an income of $5,775 a year.

On the other hand, Peter can transfer the appreciated property to a charitable remainder trust that will pay him $10,500 (7 percent) a year and also give rise to a substantial income tax charitable deduction.

Assuming that Peter's charitable deduction results in a tax savings of $20,000 in his federal income tax bracket, and that this sum is invested at 5 percent, Peter's total annual income will be $11,500 ($10,500 + $1,000) . . . almost $5,725 a year more than if he sold the property and invested the after-tax sales proceeds.

Of course, the charitable organization designated by Peter in the trust agreement would receive the principal of the trust at his death.

Benefit 3—Avoidance of Capital Gains Tax

Under today's tax laws, a charitable remainder trust can be especially rewarding if it is funded with appreciated property. The reason: there will be absolutely no capital gains tax liability either when you transfer the property to the trust or when the property is sold by the trustee.

Perhaps you own securities that provide little or no income, but have appreciated significantly in value. You can transfer the securities to a charitable remainder trust that will pay you a high income for your lifetime . . . and you will pay no capital gains tax, even though, in most cases, your charitable deduction will be based on the full fair market value of the property.

The ability to convert a low-income producing asset into a high-income producing asset without incurring a capital gains tax is a distinct benefit that can be gained through a carefully planned charitable remainder trust.

Planning Your Charitable Remainder Trust

Although the tax benefits of a charitable remainder trust are extremely generous, it is important to determine whether the trust will fit into your broad estate, tax and financial plans. Happily, the charitable remainder trust is extremely flexible.

You name the income beneficiaries. You can name yourself, or anyone you wish, as the income beneficiary of the trust. If you wish, you can direct that the income benefits be paid to you for your life and then to your spouse for his or her life. Or you can name one or more of your children as beneficiaries. You can even direct that the income be divided among all your children at the discretion of the trustee.

You set the exact amount that will be paid each year. You have a broad right to fix the dollar amount to be paid out every year. Typically, a donor will fix the annual income at 5 percent to 8 percent of the value of the property placed in the trust.

You elect a fixed or variable income. While the fixed-dollar income (annuity trust) has received more emphasis in this booklet, you may very well prefer a variable income (a unitrust) designed to keep pace with inflation.

Indeed by using a unitrust, you can effectively defer part of the annual income payments until you are in a lower tax bracket.

You select the property transferred to the trust. There may be real advantages to funding your trust with appreciated property, especially if the property produces little or no income. But there may also be advantages to funding your trust with cash, certificates of deposit, closely held stock or other properties. We can tell you the tax consequences that will result from the choice of properties transferred to the trust. But the decision is yours.

You name the trustee. You can name anyone you wish as trustee—your bank, your attorney, a family member, etc. You also can fix the commission that will be paid to the trustee or direct that the trustee serve without compensation.

A High Income for Retirement

Richard W. transfers undeveloped real estate worth $100,000 to a charitable remainder unitrust that will pay him, for his lifetime, 6 percent of the value of the trust, or income, whichever is less, with a make-up provision.

Because Richard, now 55 years of age, does not need immediate income, the trustee will retain the real estate that has great growth potential but produces no income.

Ten years from now, the property is expected to be worth $250,000. At that time, the trustee intends to sell the property and invest in bonds paying 8 percent a year. Richard will receive all this income—$20,000 a year—until the deficiencies of prior years are fully paid, and will thereafter receive 6 percent of the appreciated value of the trust (about $15,000) each year of his life.

Richard will receive a very substantial retirement income when he reaches age 65. And he also gains an immediate tax deduction that will significantly reduce his current income tax liability.

He is, of course, delighted that his retirement plan also will provide a gift of about $250,000 to a charitable institution he has long supported.

A Final Word

The charitable remainder trust can be tailored to meet your individual needs and objectives. It can be a vital and rewarding part of your investment plans, your retirement plans and your estate plans. It can be a means of increasing your own spendable income or providing a reliable income for another person.

We will be pleased to give you further information about the tax benefits and flexibility of the charitable remainder trust. There is, of course, no cost or other obligation. Feel free to call or write us at your convenience.

This booklet is based on general tax and legal principles.
Always consult your attorney for specific advice. If you have
questions about any of the suggestions made in the booklet or
would like to discuss methods of including us in your estate
plans, please call or write us at your convenience.

THE COLUMBUS FOUNDATION
The Center for Charitable Giving

For more information please contact:

Terry Schavone, Vice President for Advancement
The Columbus Foundation
1234 East Broad Street
Columbus, OH 43205
614-251-4000   •   Fax 614-251-4009
E-mail: info@columbusfoundation.org
Web: www.columbusfoundation.org

RETIREMENT PLAN ASSETS

leaving more to your

family and charity

THE
Saint Paul
FOUNDATION

RETIREMENT PLAN ASSETS
Leaving More to Your Family and Charity

Retirement planning. It's a hot topic and becoming hotter as 77 million baby boomers prepare to enter, and perhaps redefine, retirement.

Traditional IRAs, 401(k)s, Keogh plans—they've all become part of our everyday lexicon. Today, a record number of people have become participants in tax-favored retirement plans. And for many individuals retirement assets may comprise the largest component of their estates.

While just about all of us have become concerned with the accumulation of retirement assets, far too few of us have thought about the ultimate distribution of those assets and their tax consequences at that time. Taxation can be surprisingly harsh, depleting much of the retirement accumulation.

As more and more people coordinate their financial, estate and gift planning, a technique that is rapidly gaining acceptance is the strategic use of "tax-plagued" retirement assets to make charitable gifts. Many people have found that they can reduce taxes and leave more for both family members and favorite charitable organizations by creatively using such retirement assets.

The purpose of this booklet is to answer some of the most frequently asked questions about the charitable use of retirement assets. We hope it will stimulate you to explore the benefits of this new and unique planning technique.

Why give retirement plan assets? Isn't their purpose to provide for a secure retirement?
At first blush it may seem inappropriate to make a charitable gift of assets originally intended for retirement purposes. And, indeed, for some people it may well be inappropriate. But for others, especially those whose retirement assets have grown substantially over the years, charitable giving may offer an attractive alternative to having the assets chewed up by taxes. Surprisingly, as much as 70 percent of a retirement account can be lost needlessly to taxes. A planned gift to a qualified charitable organization may reduce or eliminate those taxes and, at the same time, better provide for family members. The key is to integrate your giving with your overall financial and estate planning.

Why are retirement assets so heavily taxed? Because of the way the tax law is structured. To encourage individuals to save, the law allows you to make tax-deductible contributions to retirement plans such as IRAs or 401(k) plans. What's more, assets in these accounts are allowed to grow income tax free. To be sure, these are excellent tax breaks.

The downside comes, however, when the individual withdraws the retirement assets. The assets generally are taxed as ordinary income based on the recipient's current bracket, which could be as high as 39.6 percent. Moreover, withdrawals before age 59½ are subject to an additional penalty tax of 10 percent unless certain exceptions apply. And if you don't begin to take withdrawals after you reach age 70½—whether you need the money or not—another penalty tax is triggered. The gloomiest scenario occurs when an individual dies with undistributed retirement plan assets. Unless left to a surviving spouse, the assets may be subjected to federal estate taxes—at rates up to 55 percent! Worse yet, the residue also may be subject to income taxes when distributed to heirs. The combined taxes can deplete the retirement account by as much as 70 percent. Heirs are often caught off-guard by this tragic reduction of their inheritance.

Why are retirement assets subject to income taxes for heirs? The tax law classifies certain assets as IRD (income in respect of a decedent). While the term sounds complicated, it simply refers to assets that would have been taxed as income had the decedent lived to receive them.

Examples include deferred compensation, post-death bonuses, payments on accounts receivable, income from exercise of stock options, unused vacation pay, interest on savings bonds or CDs, and other forms of accrued but unreceived income. Of such assets, retirement accounts are often the largest IRD component.

Since IRD assets have never been taxed as income during life, they become subject to taxation when received by heirs after death. For income tax purposes, they are taxed to the person who is entitled to receive them from the decedent's estate. With federal income tax rates as high as 39.6 percent, and with some state income tax rates in double digits, the bite taken out of retirement benefits can be quite significant.

How can I integrate charitable gifts of retirement assets with my financial and estate planning? First, there should be a genuine desire on your part to make a major gift to our institution. Assuming such a desire, the basic strategy is to reverse what most people do. Rather than leave retirement assets to your family, use those assets to make your gift and leave other assets—ones that are "tax plagued"—to family members. The upshot is that you can reduce your tax liability on your retirement assets; and by leaving other assets such as appreciated securities to family members, your heirs receive a stepped-up basis on the value of the property (for tax purposes) at your death. This will reduce their capital gains tax liability later on should they decide to sell those assets.

Example: Roger A., a widower, plans to leave a charitable bequest to us in his will with the remainder of his estate to go to his children. A very typical plan.

Paradoxical as it sounds, it may make more sense to make his charitable bequest out of his retirement assets and leave other assets to the children. Even though the bequest is made with IRD money, it will not be taxed because the charity is exempt from federal taxation. Thus, the retirement assets will escape the clutches of the estate tax, plus the children have no "hidden" income tax liability. And, by leaving other assets such as highly appreciated securities to his children, they will not have to pay federal income tax when they receive those assets, even though the appreciation during Roger's life has never been taxed. They also will receive a stepped-up basis which will reduce any capital gains tax should the securities be sold later on.

What kinds of retirement assets can be used to make a charitable gift? First off, the assets must be part of a qualified retirement plan or IRA. A qualified retirement plan is one that receives favorable income tax treatment during the participant's life. You pay no income tax on the contributed funds or on their growth in value while they are in the plan. You pay income tax only when you withdraw the funds.

Generally speaking, qualified plans are classified either as defined benefit plans or as defined contribution plans. Defined benefit plans—rapidly becoming an "endangered species"—pay a specific benefit to retirees. Since the payments terminate with the beneficiary's(ies') death(s), there usually is no residue to leave to charity.

On the other hand, defined contribution plans, by far the most popular kind of plan today, are highly suitable for charitable gifts. When a participant dies, often there is an undistributed portion still in the plan; and that undistributed portion can be transferred to other beneficiaries, including one's favorite charitable organizations.

Profit-sharing plans, money-purchase pension plans, 401(k) plans and traditional IRAs are all examples of defined contribution plans that can be used effectively for charitable purposes. Our development staff will be happy to answer any questions you may have about the appropriateness of your retirement plan for making a charitable gift.

Can social security benefits be used to make charitable gifts? Social Security benefits are an integral part of just about everyone's retirement planning. Unfortunately, Social Security cannot be used to make charitable gifts, but may make it possible to use other assets to make your gift.

How do I donate retirement assets? The easiest way to donate retirement plan assets is to designate us as a beneficiary. All you need do is contact the administrator of your plan. The administrator will send you the correct forms to sign. If you are married, your spouse must waive his or her right to survivor benefits from the plan (not the case for IRAs).

When you designate us as a beneficiary, as with a charitable bequest, you have considerable flexibility. You can give a specific amount to us, or a percentage to us and other beneficiaries. You can name your spouse as the primary beneficiary and us as the secondary beneficiary. There are many possibilities.

Another way to give from your retirement account is to have those assets transferred at death to a charitable remainder trust. If the beneficiary is a spouse, it's possible (by combining this strategy with the unlimited marital deduction) to eliminate all federal estate taxes attributable to the retirement account.

Example: George T. creates a testamentary charitable remainder unitrust in his will that will pay his wife, Barbara, 7 percent of its annual value for as long as she survives him. At her death, the remaining trust assets will pass to our institution. He directs that the trust be funded with his IRA account.

Since Barbara's interest qualifies for the estate tax marital deduction and the charity's remainder interest also qualifies for the state tax charitable deduction, the entire value of the trust will be deductible from George's estate.

The IRA benefits will be payable to the trust which is a tax-exempt entity. Although the IRA funds constitute income in respect of a decedent, there will be no income tax generated under this arrangement. George has been able to address multiple estate planning goals and eliminate all income and estate taxes attributable to the IRA funds.

It's also possible to use a charitable remainder trust to provide tax relief for certain non-spousal beneficiaries (who do not have the availability of the marital deduction). For example, you can designate that your beneficiary receive the income from the trust (either a fixed or variable income can be arranged), with the remainder interest going to us, but only after the termination of all income rights. Your estate will be entitled to an estate tax charitable deduction for our remainder interest and any income tax liability will be spread out over the life of the income beneficiary.

Can I roll over my retirement account into a charitable remainder trust? This is one of the most frequently asked questions received by our professional development staff. The answer, unfortunately, is no.

A charitable remainder trust, however, can be used to offset taxation of retirement plan assets when they are withdrawn.

Here's how it works: You fund a charitable remainder trust with after-tax dollars taken from your retirement account. You select the amount of income you wish to receive for the rest of your life from the trust (usually between 5 percent and 7 percent). The income can be a fixed annual amount or a fixed percentage based on the annual valuation of the trust. Most importantly, you receive an income tax charitable deduction for our remainder interest. This deduction will offset a large part of the tax on the lump sum distribution from your retirement account. So the deduction acts essentially as "a wash." Also on the plus side, you lock in a very favorable income for life, and you have the satisfaction of knowing that your gift ultimately will go to support a cause in which you deeply believe.

How can I benefit from a gift of retirement assets? The first step: Contact us to explore the possibilities. But also be sure to contact your financial advisers. The tax laws on retirement planning are quite complex and constantly changing. Our development staff is prepared to work with you and your advisers to ensure that your gift generates the best personal and financial benefits.

This booklet is based on general tax and legal principles.
Always consult your attorney for specific advice. If you have
questions about any of the suggestions made in the booklet or
would like to discuss methods of including us in your estate
plans, please call or write us at your convenience.

THE *Saint Paul* FOUNDATION
600 Norwest Center
55 Fifth Street East
Saint Paul, Minnesota 55101
651-224-5463   •   800-875-6167
Fax 651-224-9502

Resource 13

ESTATE PLANNING TODAY

a guide to a more

effective plan

The Basilica of Saint Mary

ESTATE PLANNING TODAY

Every person who owns money or property that will not be consumed during life has an estate. And every property owner has a right to dispose of that estate as he or she wishes . . . to decide the persons or institutions that will one day receive those estate assets.

The purpose of this booklet is to point out some of the common problems encountered in the distribution of an estate, and to explain time-tested methods of planning an effective and economical distribution of an estate. It is important to note that, in most cases, estate planning involves a great deal more than simply executing a will. Many assets do not pass under a will and must be separately planned.

Three Basic Considerations

Before getting into the various methods of planning an estate, there are three basic factors that should be briefly mentioned.

First, as noted, many assets do not pass under the terms of a will. These assets are often called "nonprobate assets," as distinguished from "probate assets" that do pass under a will.

Second, practically every estate faces several major sources of depletion, often in the form of taxes; one purpose of a good estate plan is to avoid or minimize this depletion.

Third, property can be left directly to an individual or institution or to a trust that benefits several individuals or institutions.

One all-important consideration that must be emphasized: the basic purpose of an estate plan is to carry out your personal objectives.

Probate and Nonprobate Property

Let's start by distinguishing between probate property and nonprobate property.

Robert B. has a typical estate. He is married and his house and bank accounts are jointly owned with his wife, Agnes. He has a modest portfolio of stocks, bonds and mutual funds in his own name. Robert has recently retired and has named Agnes the beneficiary of his retirement plan. He owns two life insurance policies, one payable to Agnes, the other to his son, Robert, Jr.

At Robert's death, his property will pass as follows:

- Jointly owned property passes to surviving owner immediately and automatically.
- Retirement death benefits pass to beneficiary named in plan agreement.
- Life insurance proceeds pass to the beneficiary named in each policy.
- Stocks, bonds, mutual funds and other separately owned property pass under the terms of Robert's will.

Certainly an effective estate plan must coordinate the disposition of each of these assets. A will is only part of a complete plan. In Robert's case, his probate assets are only a small percentage of the total value of his estate.

The Depletion of an Estate

The typical estate faces four major sources of depletion.

Probate Costs. Court costs, attorneys' fees and executors' commissions can amount to 8 or 9 percent of a typical estate valued at $100,000 or less, and may average 4 or 5 percent of a $1,000,000 estate. If the estate is complex or ambiguous, costs can be substantially higher.

Federal Estate Tax. If the total value of an estate is $675,000 or more, the federal estate tax can be a major source of depletion. Federal estate tax rates start at 37 percent of the value of a decedent's "taxable estate" and go as high as 55 percent. Happily, there are ways (to be discussed) to dramatically reduce this harsh tax.

State Death Taxes. Almost every state exacts a toll on property passing from a decedent. The severity and nature of state death taxes varies from state to state. In many states, the tax rates can range from 2 to 8 percent for smaller estates and can reach as much as 16 or 20 percent for larger estates.

Sacrifice Sales. Taxes and probate costs must be paid soon after death and they must be paid with cash. If an estate lacks the liquidity to pay these costs (and to provide for the support of the decedent's family), it may be necessary to sell property at a sacrifice price.

An effective estate plan should try to minimize these major sources of estate depletion.

Developing an Effective Estate Plan

The first step in developing an effective estate plan is to decide exactly what you want to accomplish. The second step is to prepare a detailed inventory of assets available to accomplish your objectives. The third step is to learn about the various planning tools which can help you accomplish your objectives.

Step One: Determine Your Objectives

It is important to look at your ultimate objectives—not in terms of dollars, but in terms of what you want to accomplish.

If you are married, you may want to provide security for your spouse. If you are a parent, you may want to provide financial protection for your children or simply provide a token of your love. If you think about it, you also may want to remember certain friends in your estate plans or make a final expression of your commitment to one or more charitable organizations whose missions you have supported.

Take the time to write down all your ultimate estate objectives. Again, forget about dollars. Just think about what you want to accomplish for both yourself and your beneficiaries. Consider various contingencies that can affect your estate plan—changes in the size of your estate or the needs of your beneficiaries and the possibility of a beneficiary predeceasing you.

Step Two: Prepare an Estate Inventory

Typically, most assets can be classified as securities (stocks, bonds, vacation property and investment realty), bank accounts (savings, checking, CD, money market), personal property (art, collections, jewelry, furniture, cars, etc.), life insurance (cash value, term, universal, group, etc.) and retirement benefits. Write down everything on your list.

Step Three: Understand the Tools

One early decision you will need to make in developing your estate plan is whether you want to leave property outright or in trust.

Trusts or Outright Bequests. Certainly, if the beneficiary is a minor or ill or incapacitated, a logical answer would be to leave property in trust. Trusts should also be considered if

. . . you feel that the beneficiary might have a difficult time handling an out-right bequest.

. . . you want to ensure that the property, or the income from the property, will be available to provide security for the life of the beneficiary.

. . . you want your property or the income from the property to be available to one person, but to definitely pass to another person or institution at some later time.

Trusts are extremely flexible. Your attorney can draft a trust that will accomplish your objectives. You name the trustee, the income beneficiaries and the ultimate beneficiaries. You define what each beneficiary is to receive and also the rights and obligations of the beneficiaries and trustee.

Do Lifetime Gifts Make Sense? Let's assume you decide to leave part of your estate in trust and part outright. Your next decision might be whether to give the property during your lifetime or after your death.

This can be an easy decision if there is any possibility that you will need the property for your own security. But if your estate is sufficiently large that you can prudently give part of it now, a current gift should be considered.

Many people find lifetime gifts are more helpful and personally satisfying to their beneficiaries than testamentary gifts. Tax savings may also be a good reason to consider lifetime gifts. We will discuss this later.

Consider a Revocable Living Trust

There are two basic methods you can use to direct the disposition of your estate at death:

- your will can direct the disposition of probate assets, with separate dispositions made for nonprobate assets; or
- you can create a revocable living trust to control the disposition of both probate and nonprobate assets.

There are advantages and disadvantages to each method. The revocable living trust, as the name implies, is created during life and can be changed or revoked at any time. In the trust agreement, you set forth exactly how trust property is to be disposed of at death, very much like a will.

As the creator of the trust you transfer properties to the trust so that the trust becomes the legal owner of the property. You can reserve the right to receive all the trust income; you can also change the trust, remove property from the trust, or cancel the entire arrangement at any time. You can even serve as trustee—with a substitute trustee taking over the responsibility in the event of death, disability or incapacity.

What does the revocable living trust accomplish that will make it worth your effort?

First, it will avoid probate costs. Since the trust is the legal owner of the property, assets transferred during life are not subject to probate.

Second, the revocable living trust will avoid delays that are almost inherent in the settlement of an estate. Income and principal will be available to your beneficiaries immediately.

Third, the trust can be the cornerstone of a comprehensive estate plan. During your life, you can name the trust as beneficiary of your life insurance and retirement death benefits. You also can direct in your will that certain assets be paid to the trust at your death. The end result: the trust will receive practically all your assets—both probate and nonprobate assets.

Fourth, because the trust is a private document, your estate plan will never become public knowledge as it does with a will.

What are the disadvantages of the revocable living trust? First, it may be more expensive than a will; and, second, there may be complexities in transferring assets to the trust and managing the trust during your lifetime.

Still, you may want to consider the revocable living trust, especially if you have decided that trusts can be helpful to your beneficiaries or if you have substantial estate assets that may need professional management.

Planning Your Will

Space does not permit any detailed discussion of the requirements of a valid will or methods of bequeathing property. We *can,* however, point out that

- Your will must meet all the technical requirements of the state where you reside. Rely on your attorney; and, if you move to another state, ask an attorney in the new state to review your will.
- You can bequeath a sum of money or a specific property to a beneficiary of your choosing or a specified percentage of the value of your estate to a beneficiary.
- You can create a trust through your will or during your life.
- In your will, you can nominate an executor or executrix to manage the settlement of your estate. You can choose a family member, a friend, your attorney or a bank or trust company. If you wish, you can nominate co-executors and often define the power of the executor.
- You can name one or more residuary beneficiaries such as a charity to receive property not specifically bequeathed.

Your Bequest to Charity

Please consider the good you can accomplish by leaving a portion of your estate to the charity of your choice. Your charitable bequest can be a sum of money, a specific property, a percentage of the value of your estate or all or part of your residuary estate. If you would like to discuss a memorial bequest or if you simply would like assistance in planning your bequest, please call or write us. There is no cost or obligation.

Minimizing Federal Estate Taxes

If the value of your estate may exceed $675,000, you will need to consider the potential impact of the federal estate tax in developing your estate plan.

Harriet K. is a widow, 68 years of age, and in excellent health. She has an estate, mostly securities, valued at about $900,000. She intends to leave $50,000 to charity and the balance of her estate equally to her three children.

Of course, Harriet's charitable bequest will be wholly deductible for federal estate tax purposes. But the balance of her estate will be taxable. The tax bite: $66,750.

Harriet can reduce potential estate taxes by making lifetime gifts of $10,000 a year to each of her three children. ($10,000 is the maximum annual gift that can be made free of the federal gift tax.) Over three years she can make tax-free gifts of $90,000, reducing the potential estate tax liability to $22,400 (if death occurs in 2002).

Harriet also can bequeath $200,000 to a charitable remainder trust. The trust can provide a good and favorably taxed income to her children for a period of years (or even for the lives of the children), with the trust property eventually passing to the charity. Because the present value of the charity's deferred interest is deductible for federal estate tax purposes, there will be no estate tax at Harriet's death.

Simply put, if your estate *may be* subject to the federal estate tax, you can reduce the tax dramatically with proper planning. You may want to consider making lifetime gifts or bequeathing property directly to charity or to a charitable remainder trust that will pay a lifetime income to your other beneficiaries and eventually pass to a charitable organization. There are many possibilities.

The Rewards of Estate Planning

Effective estate planning does take time and effort. And it frequently involves making some hard decisions. However, the rewards will more than justify the costs. A carefully developed estate plan will provide greater financial security for you and your family and make it possible to support worthwhile charitable organizations.

We urge you to consider the rewards and to contact us if we can help.

This booklet is based on general tax and legal principles.
Always consult your attorney for specific advice. If you have
questions about any of the suggestions made in the booklet or
would like to discuss methods of including us in your estate
plans, please call or write us at your convenience.

Our Vision
Seek the well-being of the city to which I have sent you. Pray for it to the Lord.
For in seeking its well-being you shall find your own.

Jeremiah 29:7

Our Mission
The Basilica of Saint Mary is a community rooted in the Gospel of Jesus Christ. As
the Co-Cathedral of the Archdiocese of Saint Paul and Minneapolis it is our mandate to model, to inspire and to . . .

- provide quality liturgy, faith formation, pastoral care and hospitality;
- preach justice and provide emergency relief to the poor;
- pursue interfaith relationships;
- contribute to the celebration of the sacred arts in this community.

The parish is marked by hospitality and a rich diversity of age, ethnic, racial, social
and economic backgrounds.

Cover artwork by Jack Vawter, deceased member of the Basilica Heritage Society.

For more information, please contact:

Terry H. Ashmore
Director of Development
Basilica of Saint Mary
Post Office Box 50010
Minneapolis, Minnesota 55405-0010
tel: (612) 333-6023
fax: (612) 371-9776
e-mail: thashmore@mary.org
web-site: www.mary.org

Resource 13

GIFTS OF LIFE INSURANCE

Life insurance. At first blush the thought of it may not exactly send shivers of excitement down your spine. However, if you have a sincere desire to make a major financial contribution to our institution, life insurance can be an excellent tool for helping to accomplish your philanthropic and other financial objectives. Indeed, life insurance can empower many individuals to make charitable gifts they never would have dreamed possible.

Life insurance can be an excellent means of providing a major future benefit for an important charitable organization such as ours. And it generally can be made at a relatively modest after-tax cost to the donor.

In addition to an outright gift of an insurance policy, there is another important charitable use for life insurance. Oftentimes, an individual is strongly motivated to make a significant gift to charity, but is constrained from doing so by family considerations. The concern: if a lifetime gift is made, the family will be deprived of assets they might eventually need. "Capital replacement" is a technique that has evolved to address this issue.

In this booklet we will first address the ways of using life insurance as an outright gift to charity, and then we'll discuss the capital replacement technique.

Low-Cost Major Gift Opportunities

As noted, life insurance provides you with an excellent opportunity to make a major future gift to our institution at modest after-tax cost to yourself. If it is a gift of an existing policy, there is *no out-of-pocket cost.* Plus there are other tax benefits. By assigning to us—complete and outright—the ownership of your life insurance policy you generally will get an income tax charitable deduction equal to the present value of the policy or its net cost, whichever is less. Furthermore, you can arrange to deduct any future premiums that may be due on your policy.

How an Outright Gift Works

It's really quite simple to make a gift of life insurance. If you are the insured-policyowner you simply transfer physical possession of your policy to us and file an absolute assignment-of-ownership form with your insurance company. Your company then will send an endorsement to us showing that we are the sole owner and beneficiary of the policy.

Consider the situation of Bob, the owner of a $100,000 life insurance policy with a cash value of $12,000. He can assure that our institution will receive $100,000 at his death by assigning the policy to us and making annual future gifts for the payment of premiums.

Bob can deduct $12,000 immediately for income tax purposes (perhaps a somewhat smaller sum if his cost basis in the policy is less than the cash value). He also can deduct later gifts to us to pay the premiums, and the proceeds from his policy will not be subject to the federal estate tax at his death.

Other Effective Ways to Give

There are other gift arrangements of life insurance you may also want to consider.

- You can simply name our institution as the beneficiary of a policy . . . although you may not deduct the value of the policy. Or, if you feel that the policy proceeds must be paid to a family member, you can name us as the contingent beneficiary. We will receive the proceeds only if your primary beneficiary is not living at the time of your death.
- You may also purchase a new policy and then transfer ownership of the policy to us. All the premiums you pay are tax-deductible charitable gifts. A very popular arrangement is to purchase a policy that will be paid-up in five or six years. In many cases the after-tax cost of a generous future gift will be only about 20 percent of the benefit provided to our institution . . . without decreasing the estate you want to leave to other beneficiaries.
- You may want to consider the tax and financial rewards that can be gained by transferring a policy to a charitable remainder trust. The trust will pay an income to your beneficiary for life. At the death of the beneficiary, any remaining proceeds will pass to us.

    This form of trust will produce immediate tax savings for you because the present value of our time-delayed interest will be immediately deductible as a charitable contribution. Furthermore, the policy proceeds will avoid probate and will not be reduced by estate administration expenses. The policy proceeds will immediately be available to begin paying an income to your spouse, child, or other named beneficiary.

A Word of Caution

In some states, a charitable organization is not considered to have an "insurable interest" in a donor. This means that the charity cannot apply for and be the original owner of a policy on the donor's life. Instead, the donor should apply for the policy and then transfer ownership to the charity as suggested in this booklet.

Replacing Assets Donated to Charity

One deterrent for any individuals wanting to provide major financial support to our institution is fear of depriving their family of needed assets. This presents a classic dilemma of competing family and philanthropic objectives. Fortunately, "capital replacement" (also known as "wealth replacement") is a technique that has evolved to help such individuals achieve both objectives. It can also provide significant income tax and estate tax savings.

Capital replacement involves the combined use of

- a charitable remainder trust,
- a life insurance policy, and
- an irrevocable life insurance trust.

Although it may sound complex, capital replacement is a very effective way to achieve both family and philanthropic financial goals, while minimizing income and estate taxes, and—in some cases—capital gains taxes.

Consider the following example, which demonstrates the rewards and benefits of capital replacement techniques.

Case Study

Mary, age 72, owns marketable securities worth $100,000. She purchased the securities many years ago for $20,000, and the holdings are producing income of around $2,500 each year (a 2.5 percent return). Mary has considered selling the securities and reinvesting the proceeds to obtain a higher income, but she is not happy about the capital gains tax that she would have to pay. Ultimately, Mary would like to split the property or the sale proceeds in her will among her three grandchildren. Furthermore, Mary is committed to making a significant gift to our institution, but not at the expense of her grandchildren.

A logical solution: First, Mary transfers the securities to a charitable remainder trust that will pay her a 5 percent income (about twice what she had been receiving) for as long as she might live. Mary can deduct on her tax return the present value of the charity's interest in the trust. She will also avoid the capital gains tax.

Second, Mary will use the tax savings to purchase a $100,000 insurance policy on her life, naming her grandchildren as beneficiaries. The policy will be owned by an irrevocable life insurance trust, and Mary will make future premium payments from a portion of the income she will receive from the charitable remainder trust.

Finally, at Mary's death, our institution will receive the principal of the charitable remainder trust; Mary's grandchildren will receive the $100,000 insurance proceeds; the charitable remainder trust will be dissolved; and the irrevocable life insurance trust will either terminate or hold and invest the insurance proceeds for the benefit of the grandchildren.

Consider These Benefits

- Mary fulfills her life-long desire to make a substantial gift to our institution.
- She maintains the size of the estate passing to her grandchildren.

- She avoids a capital gains tax by transferring the appreciated securities to the charitable remainder trust.
- Mary takes an income tax deduction in the year she transfers the securities to the charitable remainder trust.
- Neither the transferred securities nor the life insurance proceeds will be included in Mary's gross estate for federal estate tax purposes, saving her heirs thousands of dollars.
- Mary's grandchildren will receive the life insurance proceeds income tax-free.

Essentially, Mary will be able to make two major gifts with the same asset—one to her grandchildren and one to our institution!

This diagram illustrates the steps involved in this mutually beneficial arrangement.

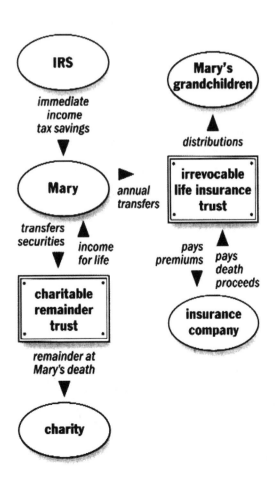

Mary transfers appreciated securities to a charitable remainder trust.

The trust pays Mary a lifetime income, based on the payout percentage specified in Mary's trust agreement.

Mary receives an immediate income tax charitable deduction for the present value of the charity's remainder interest (subject to broad limits), and avoids a capital gains tax on the appreciation in value of the securities.

Mary uses the income from the trust and the tax savings to pay the premiums on a life insurance policy placed in an irrevocable life insurance trust.

At Mary's death, her grandchildren receive the face amount of the policy, and our institution receives the principal of the charitable remainder trust.

As you can see, the arrangement is not as complicated as it may have first appeared. You will, however, want to seek the advice of knowledgeable estate planning professionals. Many professionals today are well aware of this planning technique. They are in the best position to advise you of the appropriateness of this plan for your own situation.

A Final Word

We hope this booklet has helped you in exploring the many unique and rewarding charitable uses for life insurance. We will be pleased to help you plan a satisfying and tax-rewarding gift of life insurance or to develop a plan for capital replacement.

If you have questions about any of the suggestions made in this booklet, we can provide additional information. Please call us at your convenience.

*This booklet is based on general tax and legal principles.
Always consult your attorney for specific advice. If you have
questions about any of the suggestions made in the booklet or
would like to discuss methods of including us in your estate
plans, please call or write us at your convenience.*

J. P. LaMontagne, CTFA
Director, Gift and Estate Planning
(619) 296-8420, Ext. 177

San Diego
Blood Bank
Saving Lives Since 1950

GIFTS OF PROPERTY

opportunities

and benefits

UNIVERSITY OF
Miami

GIFTS OF PROPERTY
Opportunities and Benefits

Over the years, every conceivable type of property has been the subject of a major charitable gift. Tobacco, animals, crops and rum were common gifts in the early days of our nation. Today, the most popular gifts of property are stocks and bonds, life insurance and real estate.

Gifts of Marketable Securities

Many people give marketable securities to the charitable institutions they wish to support. Stocks listed on one of the major exchanges or actively traded over the counter can be transferred to a charitable institution quickly and easily. And there are definite tax advantages in giving securities that have appreciated in value since the time they were acquired by the donor.

Income Tax Charitable Deduction

In most cases, the full fair market value of the stocks, bonds and mutual fund shares given to charity will be allowable as a charitable deduction. For example, if you give stock that is now worth $10,000, you can deduct this full amount on your income tax return even though you may have bought the stock for substantially less.

The value of the stock—and the amount of the deduction—is the mean between the highest and lowest selling price on the date of the gift, or the mean between the bid and asked price on the date of the gift.

When is the date of the gift? It is the day the duly endorsed stock certificate or bond is delivered to the charity, transferred to its brokerage account, or is postmarked. If possible, you should make your gift on a day when the market value of the stock is relatively high.

Caution: There is an important exception to the general statement that the full fair market value of the stock or bond is deductible. If a sale of the security on the date of the gift would give rise to ordinary income or short-term capital gain—as distinguished from a long-term capital gain—the charitable deduction is limited to your "adjusted cost basis" for the security.

Avoidance of Capital Gains Taxes

A gift of securities to our institution is not considered a sale of those securities, so it does not result in any capital gains tax. This is an important secondary tax reward provided by Congress to encourage gifts of appreciated stocks and bonds.

No matter how much the stocks, bonds, and mutual fund shares have appreciated in value, a charitable gift will not make any part of your profit taxable. This means you get a charitable deduction even on profits that have never been taxed to you.

Example: Jim owns 100 shares of XYZ stock that he bought in 1981 at a cost of $1,143 (including broker commissions). On December 19 of this year he instructs his broker to transfer the stock to our account and the gift is completed on that day. XYZ stock sold for a high of 83.250 and a low of 82.500 on December 19.

Jim can deduct $8,287 as a charitable contribution (the mean between the high and low price of 100 shares on the date of the gift). And he completely avoids a capital gains tax on the $7,144 appreciation in the value of the stock.

The after-tax cost of the generous gift of $8,287 will depend on Jim's federal income tax bracket (with a 20 percent cap on the capital gains tax rate):

	31% Tax Bracket	36% Tax Bracket
Value of gift	$8,287	$8,287
Charitable deduction saves	−2,569	−2,983
Capital gains tax avoided	−1,029	−1,029
After-tax cost of gift	**$4,689**	**$4,275**

Our Institution Is Tax-Exempt

When our institution sells the XYZ stock, we are able to use all of the proceeds. We do not pay any capital gains tax, no matter how much the property has appreciated in value.

Therefore, Jim, in a 36 percent combined tax bracket, can give our institution $8,287 at an after-tax cost of only $4,275—less than 52 percent of the value of the gift to us.

Limitations on the Tax Deduction

The deduction allowable for a gift of long-term, appreciated securities cannot exceed 30 percent of your adjusted gross income. Thus, if your income is $90,000, the maximum deduction that can be claimed in the year of the gift will be approximately $27,000. Any excess gift over that limitation can be carried over and deducted in subsequent years.

A donor can avoid this 30 percent limitation by a tax election to deduct only the original cost of the stock. If this election is made, the deduction can be as much as 50 percent of your adjusted gross income (the same as for a cash gift).

Gifts of Closely Held Stock

A charitable gift of closely held stock presents a unique opportunity for some of our friends, especially if the closely held corporation has substantial accumulated profits. The reason is that after the gift has been made, the corporation can buy back the stock and retire it. This gives the stockholder approximately the same percentage of control he or she had before the gift was made.

Of course, the fair market value of the closely held stock is deductible as a charitable contribution, and there is no capital gains tax no matter how much the stock has appreciated in value. But the great popularity of this giving technique lies in the fact that the donor can get a charitable deduction without being taxed on the cash distribution in redemption of the stock.

We can provide more information about this giving technique that can produce future estate tax benefits, and can also play an important role in business tax planning. Call us at your convenience.

Gifts of Real Estate

In recent years, gifts of real estate to charitable institutions have become quite popular. A major reason for this popularity is the fact that most real estate has so appreciated in value during the past 20 years that a sale would produce big capital gains taxes.

When real estate is given to our institution, capital gains taxes are completely avoided and the full fair market value of the property is deductible as a charitable contribution. (We are assuming that the real estate qualifies as long-term appreciated property and that the donor is not in the business of selling real estate.)

Example: Paul owns a 30-acre plot of vacant land that he bought for $30,000 and that is now worth $400,000. If he sells the property, he could incur state and federal capital gains taxes and selling costs that might consume up to 30 percent of his profit.

Resource 13

A gift of the property to a qualified charitable institution will avoid the huge capital gains tax and selling costs. Moreover, the $400,000 charitable deduction will produce an income tax savings of $144,000 in Paul's 36 percent tax bracket. (A portion of Paul's large deduction would likely be non-deductible in the current year but would carry over to future years.)

Gift of Fractional Interest in a Vacation Home

Our federal tax laws permit a charitable deduction for gifts of fractional interests in real estate. This type of gift can be especially rewarding if you own a vacation home that you use only part of the year.

Example: Mary and Jim own a $180,000 vacation home that they use for only two months of the year. They can give our institution a 50 percent interest in the property, gain a tax deduction for approximately $90,000 (one-half the value of the property) and still have a right to use and occupy the property for six months every year.

Gift of a Remainder Interest in a Residence or Farm

A provision of the tax law allows an immediate income tax charitable deduction for a gift of a remainder interest in your home or farm. You may retain an absolute right to occupy the home or farm for your life (or you can give family members a right of lifetime occupancy). The property passes to us only after those lifetimes.

The immediate charitable deduction allowable for this future gift is the present value of our right to receive the property at some later date. The age of the life tenants is the primary factor in determining the present value of our deferred interest and the resulting allowable charitable deduction.

We will be pleased to provide an approximate charitable deduction and to discuss with you the other financial factors involved in this form of gift.

Gifts of Life Insurance

Many of our friends have life insurance policies that are no longer needed for their security or the security of their families. A good example might be a policy for a child's education, with the child now grown.

When an existing policy is given to us, the owner can immediately deduct, as a charitable contribution, the current value of the policy (or the net cost of the policy if this is less than current value). Of course, future premium payments are also deductible after ownership has been transferred to charity.

Gifts of Tangible Personal Property

Antiques, artwork, jewelry, book collections—these are just a few of the kinds of tangible personal property that friends have used in making charitable gifts to us. The full fair market value of such assets is deductible providing the gift asset is used for our charitable exempt purpose. Otherwise, the deduction is limited to its adjusted cash basis.

An interesting aspect of the 1997 Taxpayer Relief Act may increase the appeal of tangible personal property gifts. While the maximum capital gains tax rate for other long-term appreciated assets was scaled back from 28 percent to 20 percent, the maximum rate was unchanged for tangible personal property. The upshot is that a well-planned gift of tangible personal property may generate a larger capital gains tax savings than other long-term appreciated property (28 percent vs. 20 percent), assuming, of course, it is used for our charitable exempt purposes. Our staff can help plan your gift so that you don't inadvertently lose your maximum tax benefits.

Life Income Plans—Gifts with a Retained Income

In addition to outright gifts, long-term appreciated property is often used to fund what are called "life income gift plans." A life income plan is an arrangement whereby income will be paid to the donor and/or designated beneficiaries for their lifetimes. Our institution will eventually receive the gift property—or be able to use the gift property—only after all income benefits have terminated.

A life income gift plan may take the form of a charitable remainder trust, a gift annuity or a pooled income fund. The plan best for you depends upon a variety of factors: the size of your gifts, your age and your desire for either a fixed or variable income.

Under a well-arranged life income gift plan, you often can increase your spendable income, substantially reduce your taxes, and, at the same time, be recognized for making a gift that will have a substantial impact on our future.

Example: Tom invested $10,000 in a growth stock ten years ago. Today it is worth $110,000 but it still pays a minuscule dividend. Now that he is retired, he needs more income. He can sell the stock, but that will trigger a hefty capital gains tax of about $20,000 (the $100,000 gain × 20 percent capital gains tax). That leaves only $90,000 to reinvest.

Instead, Tom gives us the stock to fund a charitable remainder trust. There is no capital gains tax, so the full $110,000 can be used to reinvest and provide him with a much higher income stream. Under this arrangement (assuming a 7 percent payout) he will receive $7,700 a year for the rest of his life, an income tax deduction of about $47,320 (assuming his age is 70 and the mid-term federal rate is 7 percent), and the asset is effectively sheltered from the federal estate tax. Tom increases his retirement income, gets tax savings from his income tax deduction and reduces his potential estate tax liability. Our institution will ultimately receive what's left in the trust (the remainder interest), but not until Tom has enjoyed all of his benefits. A win-win for both parties.

You Can Depend on Us

Let us know if you are interested in exploring the many opportunities and benefits of a gift of property to us. Our professional development team is highly qualified and will be happy to meet with you and your advisers to craft a plan that will best meet your needs.

This booklet is based on general tax and legal principles.
Always consult your attorney for specific advice. If you have
questions about any of the suggestions made in the booklet or
would like to discuss methods of including us in your estate
plans, please call or write us at your convenience.

UNIVERSITY OF MIAMI

For more information, please contact:

Tom Dieters
Executive Director of Planned Giving
5807 Ponce de Leon Boulevard
Coral Gables, FL 33146
(305) 284-1527   •   (800) 529-6935
fax: (305) 284-4985

GUIDE TO GIVING

Contents

Resource 14

The Indiana University Foundation is designated by the trustees of Indiana University as the official fundraising agency for the University. A not-for-profit corporation chartered in 1936 under the laws of the State of Indiana, the Foundation raises and receives gifts from the private sector, administers funds, and manages assets to enhance the quality of education at Indiana University.

A Message from Curt Simic

Every year, Indiana University benefits from the generosity of thousands of people. Their reasons for giving vary as widely as their interests and their financial circumstances. What they all have in common is the desire to help make a great university even greater, to enable it to better serve the state and the nation.

You share that desire, and IU is pleased to count you among its supporters. Yet your situation, like everyone else's, is unique; your motivations, your goals, and your available resources combine to make your situation unlike that of any other donor. What may seem to be the most obvious way to make your gift may not be the best way for you.

Fortunately, there are many options for setting up a gift to IU. I am sure one of them will suit your purposes. This booklet is designed to help you become familiar with these choices and, I hope, help you identify the ones that are right for you.

While philanthropic impulses may have prompted your decision to support the University—indeed, few gifts are as personally rewarding as a gift to education—you should also consider the potential tax advantages provided by certain types of gifts. Some arrangements offer you other financial benefits—life income, for instance, or professional management of your assets.

The fundraising professionals at the IU Foundation are here to answer any questions or concerns you or your financial advisers may have. We want you to be confident, right from the start, that you have all the information and informed advice you need. In short, we want you to know that you are choosing the best path.

Curtis R. Simic

Curtis R. Simic
President, Indiana University Foundation

The Basics

You will find a wide variety of giving options in this booklet. Some are simple, others more complex. The general information in this section may be useful to you whichever ones you choose.

Designating Your Gift

What you choose to support is entirely up to you. You may designate your gift for any purpose that contributes to Indiana University's three-fold mission of teaching, research, and service, and that is acceptable to the trustees of the University or the board of directors of the IU Foundation. Among the most useful gifts, however, are those designated for "wherever the need is greatest." These unrestricted gifts offer much-needed flexibility to an otherwise rigid state-appropriated budget. They allow the University to take advantage of unexpected opportunities and meet challenges that arise after state budgets are set. Donors who make unrestricted gifts can be confident that their gifts will be put to the best possible use.

Endowed Funds: The Gifts That Keep On Giving

An endowment is an investment in the future. When you use your charitable gift to establish an endowment, the gift is invested with two goals in mind: to make the principal grow faster than inflation, and to provide spendable income for whatever specific purpose you have designated. The principal is never invaded, and any earnings over a certain amount—usually five percent—are channeled back into the fund to keep it healthy and growing. Well-managed endowments can generate income indefinitely. That fact makes them uniquely valuable to the University, and therefore especially attractive to donors who wish to leave a legacy at IU.

Gift Agreements

Whenever a gift fund is set up, it is wise to create a gift agreement. The agreement sets out your specific criteria for how the University will utilize your gift. It ensures that the gift will always be used exactly as you intend. It also may set out provisions for alternative uses, should it become impossible or impractical for the University to carry out your original intention (as when, for instance, advances in knowledge render a given field of study obsolete). For these reasons, the IU Foundation now requires that all new funds have a written gift agreement on file. The Foundation staff will work with you to draw up the agreement.

Donor Recognition

Indiana University appreciates its supporters. Regardless of what form your gift to the Indiana University Foundation takes, it may qualify you for one of IU's donor recognition groups. The best reward for your contribution, of course, is the knowledge and satisfaction that you have made a difference in the lives of the individuals your gift touches. Nevertheless, the University wants to publicly thank its major donors and recognize them for their philanthropy. Below are the University-wide recognition groups. In addition, the different schools may have their own donor societies.

The Presidents Circle. The Presidents Circle honors the University's most generous benefactors, those who make irrevocable gifts at leadership levels. Lifetime giving of $100,000 or more qualifies a donor for inclusion in the Presidents Circle. One may also become a member if others donate $100,000 or more in his or her honor.

The Arbutus Society. The Arbutus Society recognizes those individuals who inform the IU Foundation of their intention to invest in the future of Indiana University through planned or deferred gift arrangements.

The Well House Society. The Well House Society is unique among college and university donor recognition groups. Donors make annual gifts that are *unrestricted,* that is, they may be used for whatever purpose Indiana University's president and the IU Foundation's board of directors deem best. Alternatively, Well House Society donors may choose to combine their unrestricted gift with one directed to a school, department, or program of their choice. Because a very small percentage of gifts for the University are unrestricted, the Well House Society gives IU a vital source of flexible funds.

Outright Gifts

Most gifts to the IU Foundation for the benefit of Indiana University are simple, outright transfers of property. They range from $30 checks for the Annual Fund to multimillion-dollar real estate transactions. Regardless of their size or method, however, all have tax advantages for the donor, with the added appeal that the University can put an outright gift to work immediately.

Gifts of Cash

The most common type of gift is the gift of cash—and with good reason. It is simple, straightforward, and as easy as writing a check. And, because charitable gifts qualify for federal tax deductions, the real out-of-pocket cost of a cash donation is usually much less than its face value: you save whatever tax you would have owed on the amount of the gift. Likewise, some state tax laws offer additional deductions or credits for gifts to education.

For record purposes, a gift of cash is considered made on the date it is mailed or hand delivered. Please make checks or money orders payable to the Indiana University Foundation, the designated fundraising agency for Indiana University.

Features & Benefits

- Simple and quick
- Charitable income tax deduction
- IU can make immediate use of your gift
- Estate tax and probate savings

Gifts of Appreciated Property

Charitable gifts of appreciated property—whether real estate or capital gain securities—can provide even greater tax benefits than a cash gift of equal value. You may take a charitable deduction for the full fair market value of the property, while avoiding capital gains taxes. The IRS currently allows you to deduct the full fair market value of the property up to 30 percent of your adjusted gross income for the year. Any amount over that ceiling can be carried forward for future deduction, for up to five years, subject to the same percentage limitations.

A gift of appreciated property is considered made on the day the transfer is completed. Please contact the IU Foundation for specific instructions.

Features & Benefits

- Opportunity to make a substantial gift to IU
- Charitable income tax deduction
- IU can make immediate use of your gift
- Avoid capital gains tax
- Estate tax and probate savings

Gifts of Tangible Personal Property

A gift of tangible personal property—such as furniture, art works, jewelry, antiques, books, coin or stamp collections, and so on—is deductible for its full fair market value (up to 30 percent of your adjusted gross income) if it meets two conditions: 1) it must be documented by a legitimate appraisal, and 2) it must satisfy the "related use" standard.

"Related use" means that the University must be able to use the gift in a way that is related to or furthers its educational mission. For example, books donated to the library will meet the standard, as will classroom or office furniture, or computers, or business machines. A painting will meet the standard if it is displayed for viewing, but will not if the University sells it. Property that does not satisfy the "related use" standard may still be deducted, but only for your cost basis in the property, subject to a limit of 50 percent of your adjusted gross income. The five-year carryover rule for the deduction applies in both cases. Please note, however, that in order to protect its tax-exempt status, the University must severely limit the non-related-use gifts that it accepts.

A gift of tangible personal property is considered to be made on the date when ownership or legal title is transferred. To make the formal transfer, you may write up a simple "letter of intent to donate" that identifies the property and includes a signed statement of your intent to transfer it to the Indiana University Foundation.

Features & Benefits

- Opportunity to make a unique and substantial gift to IU which may be of significant value to teaching, learning, or research
- Charitable income tax deduction
- IU can make immediate use of your gift
- Avoid capital gains tax
- Estate tax and probate savings

Bargain Sales

You may have property that has appreciated in value, but you only want to give part of that value to the IU Foundation. You may make a "bargain sale" of the property to the Foundation for less than its fair market value, usually your cost basis. You thereby get cash in hand to recoup your original investment, while getting a charitable deduction for the donated difference. You should note, however, that some of the cash recovered will be treated as a capital gain.

For record purposes, the date of the sale is considered to be the date of the gift. Bargain sales require careful planning. Please consult your tax adviser, legal counsel, or other financial planner, and contact the IU Foundation's Office of Planned Giving Services for further information.

Features & Benefits

- Possible recovery of original investment
- Opportunity to make a substantial gift to IU
- Charitable income tax deduction
- Reduction in capital gains tax
- Increased cash flow
- Estate tax and probate savings

Gifts of Closely Held Stock

If you are a business owner and you contribute closely held stock, you may take a charitable deduction for the stock's appraised fair market value. Besides increasing your cash flow, you also avoid the potential capital gains tax on the appreciated value of the stock. The corporation may buy back the stock, but so long as the IU Foundation is not legally obligated to sell back the stock, you may enjoy significant tax savings.

For record purposes, the date of a gift of closely held stock is considered to be the date the stock is transferred.

Features & Benefits

- Opportunity to make a substantial gift to IU
- Charitable income tax deduction
- Avoid capital gains taxes
- Positive impact on cash flow
- Estate tax and probate savings
- Excellent estate planning opportunity for yourself and your heirs

Life Income Plans

You can make a substantial gift to Indiana University while still earning income from the donated assets. These life income plans are some of the most flexible and fruitful options available to donors. They allow you to provide income for yourself, your heirs, or both; avoid significant capital gains and estate taxes; and satisfy your wish to make a substantial gift to IU.

This is how it works: You fund the trust with a significant, irrevocable gift to the IU Foundation to benefit Indiana University. (The gift must be irrevocable to qualify for the federal charitable deduction.) The Foundation invests the gift, and you or your designee receive income for as long as you choose: for a definite term of not more than 20 years, or for the rest of your life. At the end of that time, the remaining principal benefits the University in whatever way you specify.

You may establish a trust using assets such as real estate, stock, or cash. Funding it with appreciated long-term property enables you to protect your profit or reinvest for a higher yield, while avoiding capital gains taxes. You thereby maximize the value and the benefit of the property, both as income and as a gift.

There are two basic types of life income trusts: annuity trusts and unitrusts. The annuity trust pays a fixed *dollar amount,* while the unitrust pays a fixed *percentage.* With the annuity trust, your income will be the same each year, regardless of the value of the trust. With the unitrust, your income will go up or down as the value of the trust itself fluctuates.

Annuity Trusts

A charitable remainder annuity trust pays a fixed amount (at least five percent of the fair market value of the trust assets when the trust is established) to you or your beneficiaries at least once a year. The payout is determined when you set up the trust, based on such factors as your age, the number of beneficiaries, your desired income, and the length of the trust term. If the trust earns more income than the agreed amount, the additional earnings are reinvested. If the earnings are less, withdrawals from the trust's principal make up the difference. Once the annuity trust is created, you may not make additional contributions to it.

You will receive an income tax deduction for the value of the charitable remainder interest in the trust at the time you set it up (calculated from tables based on your age), and you avoid capital gains taxes on the transfer of appreciated long-term assets such as real estate or securities. Because the assets are effectively removed from your estate, you also avoid estate taxes.

Features & Benefits

- Opportunity to make a substantial gift to IU while receiving life income
- Fixed payout offers the security of guaranteed income
- Can unlock appreciated assets for diversification or increased yield
- Professional asset management
- Can receive an attractive equivalent rate of return
- Immediate tax deduction
- Avoid capital gains taxes
- Estate tax and probate savings

Unitrusts

A charitable remainder unitrust differs from an annuity trust by paying a fixed percentage—at least five percent—of the fair market value of the trust's assets each year, rather than a fixed sum. That means the income will fluctuate from year to year as the trust's value fluctuates, but because the long-term market pattern is usually one of growth, you can generally expect payments to increase over time. In this way a unitrust can be an effective hedge against inflation.

Choosing a lower percentage may actually increase your income over time because it allows the principal to grow more quickly. As the principal increases, so will the amount of your payment. The difference can be significant. And the more the principal grows, of course, the larger the ultimate gift to Indiana University will be, and the more completely it fulfills your philanthropic goals. You may also make additional contributions to a unitrust.

Your charitable deduction depends on the fair market value of the initial assets you transfer, the payout percentage you choose, the number and ages of beneficiaries, and other such factors. As with an annuity trust, you effectively remove the funding assets from your estate, and you likewise avoid capital gains taxes.

Features & Benefits

- Opportunity to make a substantial gift to IU while receiving life income
- Variable percentage payout may protect against inflation as your trust's assets grow
- Larger gift to IU than might otherwise be possible
- Professional asset management
- Receive an attractive "real" rate of return on your assets
- Can unlock appreciated assets for diversification or increased yield
- Immediate tax deduction
- Avoid capital gains taxes
- Estate tax and probate savings

Pooled Income Funds

Another kind of trust is called a pooled income fund. It allows separate donors to pool their gifts for investment purposes. Two or more donors must irrevocably transfer property into the trust, contributing the remainder interest in the property to the IU Foundation. The Foundation then acts as trustee, investing the combined fund and distributing the annual proceeds to the donors in direct proportion to the assets each one contributed. The actual dollar amount is not specified: it depends on the amount earned by the fund. You may designate yourself as beneficiary, or anyone else living at the time the fund is created.

Your charitable deduction would be the present value of the remainder interest in the property, as determined by IRS tables, on the day you transfer it. You may add to the fund at any time.

Features & Benefits

- Opportunity to make a substantial future gift to IU
- Competitive rate of return
- Professional asset management
- Income for yourself or other beneficiary

- Can unlock appreciated assets for diversification or increased yield
- Immediate tax deduction
- Avoid capital gains taxes
- Estate tax and probate savings

Charitable Gift Annuities

One of the most common and popular ways to make a planned gift is with a charitable gift annuity. It is a simple contract between you and the IU Foundation. In exchange for an irrevocable gift, the Foundation agrees to pay one or two annuitants a fixed dollar amount each year for life. The amount is based on life expectancy: the older you are at the time of the gift, the greater the amount can be. The payments are guaranteed by the general resources of the Foundation.

Charitable gift annuities can be funded with cash, real estate, or appreciated securities. You receive a tax deduction based on your age, the payout rate, and the federal discount rate. If you use an appreciated asset, a portion of each payout will be capital gain, which is therefore spread out over your lifetime. Likewise, a part of each payment would be a tax-free return of principal, increasing the after-tax value of each payment. And because you have effectively removed the assets from your estate, you avoid estate taxes.

A similar type of annuity is the deferred charitable gift annuity. The arrangement is essentially the same; the difference is that the IU Foundation waits to begin your fixed payout until some specified point in the future (at least one year). In either case, at your death the proceeds of the gift annuity become available for Indiana University to use in whatever way you wished.

A deferred charitable gift annuity can be an excellent way to supplement your retirement income. The Foundation receives the gift today and invests it for years; you receive a current tax deduction, but you don't receive the payments until you retire, when you may be in a lower income tax bracket.

Features & Benefits

- Fixed payout offers the security of guaranteed income
- Attractive rate of return
- Can unlock appreciated assets for diversification or increased yield
- Professional asset management
- Opportunity to make a substantial gift to IU
- Favorable income tax position now and at retirement
- Immediate charitable tax deduction
- Estate tax and probate savings

Resource 14

Other Planned Gift Arrangements

Life income plans are not the only kind of planned gift. Many others exist that offer particular advantages for specific circumstances. The following pages present a sampling of the most popular. If you believe your own situation requires something not described here, a specialist from the Office of Planned Giving Services at the IU Foundation will be happy to discuss other options with you.

Charitable Lead Trusts

A charitable lead trust is like a charitable remainder trust in reverse. You select the assets used to fund the trust and decide how long it will last, and the IU Foundation receives income from the trust while it exists. There is no minimum payout. When the trust terminates, its assets return to you or your designated beneficiary.

This type of trust can be useful if you want to reduce your current income but wish to retain the assets for your family. A charitable lead trust can be a means to transfer substantial amounts of wealth from generation to generation, free (or largely free) of estate, inheritance, and gift taxes.

A charitable lead trust is a complex giving vehicle with many income, estate, and gift tax consequences. You should discuss your goals with your legal and financial advisers to determine whether a charitable lead trust would suit your plans. You are also encouraged to contact the planned giving professionals at the IU Foundation for more detailed information.

Features & Benefits

- Reduces current income while retaining assets
- Can be a low-cost means of transferring property to heirs
- Opportunity to make a substantial current gift to IU
- Potential estate, inheritance, and gift tax savings

Gifts of Real Property Subject to Life Estate

Your personal residence or farm may be the single most valuable asset you own. If it has appreciated significantly in value, you could owe tremendous capital gains taxes if you or your heirs sold the property. An alternative is to give the property to the IU Foundation subject to life estate, which simply means that you or your designees retain the use of the property for life.

You gain an immediate tax deduction for the remainder interest in the property, and you escape the potential capital gains taxes. Best of all, you get to make a substantial gift for Indiana University without disrupting your lifestyle.

Gifts of this kind require detailed language tailored to your specific situation and needs, and the advantages and benefits vary accordingly. The Foundation's planned giving staff will be happy to work with you and your advisers to help you arrange the best plan for you.

Features & Benefits

- Opportunity to make a substantial gift to IU while retaining lifetime use
- Immediate tax deduction
- Avoid capital gains taxes
- Estate tax and probate savings
- Can provide a favorable income tax position

Wealth Replacement with Life Insurance

When you make a gift to the Indiana University Foundation for the benefit of Indiana University, you may use a life insurance trust to replace the value of the donated assets. In this way, you can protect the interests of your heirs while still fulfilling your philanthropic goals. The life insurance provides the dollar amount, and the trust, provided it is irrevocable, removes the proceeds from your estate for tax purposes.

In this arrangement, you create a trust to buy insurance on your life, with your children as beneficiaries. You can use the tax savings from your charitable gift, or the payout from a life income arrangement, to cover the premiums. After your death, the proceeds from the policy pass to the trust free of estate taxes, thereby replacing the value of the original charitable gift.

Wealth replacement life insurance trusts can be set up in several different ways, and all have strict technical requirements. You should discuss them with your financial and legal advisers before deciding to pursue this option. The Foundation's planned giving staff will be happy to answer your questions.

Features & Benefits

- Restores asset value to your estate at relatively low cost
- Opportunity to make a substantial gift to IU without consequence to your heirs
- Estate tax and probate savings

Resource 14

Wills and Estate Plans

A carefully prepared will or estate plan is the best way to ensure that your loved ones are provided for after your death, and that your preferred charities are supported as you intend. They allow you to retain full use of your assets during your lifetime and still make a significant gift for Indiana University. They are technical documents that should therefore be drafted by an attorney, but they may be revised and updated whenever you like, as your wishes and circumstances change.

Types of Gifts

By far the most common means of making a charitable gift is through a personal trust or will. It's no wonder: such gifts allow you to contribute to Indiana University at a level you might never have managed during your lifetime.

Your bequest can take a variety of forms. Here are a few samples for you to consider.

Specific Bequest. The most popular type of charitable bequest, a specific bequest provides that the IU Foundation receive a specific dollar amount, percentage of your estate, or piece of property.

Residuary Bequest. A residuary bequest provides that the IU Foundation receive all or a stated portion of your estate after all other bequests, debts, taxes, and expenses have been distributed.

Contingent Bequest. A contingent bequest can ensure that if circumstances make it impossible to carry out your primary provisions (as when your spouse or other heirs do not survive you), your assets will then pass to the IU Foundation for Indiana University rather than to unintended beneficiaries.

Trust Under Will. You can bequeath a portion of your estate to be held in trust for a specified purpose, as stated in your will.

Bequest Language

Because the Indiana University Foundation has been designated by the trustees of Indiana University as the official entity for receiving and administering gifts for IU, please incorporate the following language into your will:

"I give, devise, and bequeath the (sum of/percentage of/residue of my estate) to Indiana University Foundation, a not-for-profit corporation with principal offices located in Bloomington, Indiana, to be utilized for the benefit of Indiana University as specified in a gift agreement on file at said Foundation."

Appreciation and Recognition

If you decide to include a gift to Indiana University Foundation for the benefit of IU in your will, we invite and encourage you to let the Foundation know about your decision ahead of time, for several reasons. First, so you can complete a gift agreement and ensure that there will be no question as to how your gift will be used. Second, so that IU and the Foundation can make note of the gift as they plan for the future. And finally, so that we may recognize your generosity and show our appreciation, if you so desire, by including you in the roster of major donors to Indiana University.

For more information, please contact:

Office of Planned Giving Services
Indiana University Foundation
P.O. Box 500
Bloomington, IN 47402
(800) 558-8311 or (812) 855-8311

Resource 14

PERSONAL FINANCIAL PLANNER

Personal Financial
Affairs Record
of

_____

Information contained here is current as of

_____

date

We are pleased to present this booklet to you as a convenient method of record-ing information about your personal financial affairs. The information you collect in your *Record of Personal Financial Affairs* can have several practical uses:

- summarize your present financial position,
- inform your attorney and other advisers of your assets and objectives, and
- assist your family members in the event of your absence or incapacity.

We recommend that you first review the booklet to determine the information that will be needed to complete it. Then collect the certificates, documents, records and other information you will need to record accurate financial data.

Preparing your *Record of Personal Financial Affairs* may reveal areas where you will want to make changes or take some additional action. After these actions are taken, make it a point to keep the booklet up-to-date. An annual review is strongly recommended.

The time you spend completing this booklet can be very rewarding. You will have the satisfaction of knowing that your financial affairs are in order and that you have taken steps to assure the effective management of your assets.

If we can be of assistance to you, please feel free to call.

Individual and Family Background

Legal residence _____

Occupation _____

Social Security # _____

Date and place of birth _____

☐ Married   ☐ Single   ☐ Divorced   ☐ Widowed

Date and place of marriage _____

_____

Prior marriages (date and place) _____

_____

Children

Name	Birthdate	Natural, Adopted or Stepchild?
_____	_____	_____
_____	_____	_____
_____	_____	_____
_____	_____	_____
_____	_____	_____
_____	_____	_____

Other close relatives (if any)

Name _____

Relationship _____

Address _____

Name _____

Relationship _____

Address _____

Employment, Compensation and Benefits

Employer _____ Date of hire _____

Position/title _____ Salary $ _____ per _____

Bonus/commission _____

Check all that apply:

☐ Medical Insurance

☐ Group Life Insurance

Amount $ _____

Primary beneficiary _____

Secondary beneficiary _____

☐ Disability Insurance

☐ Individual Retirement Account

☐ Pension/Profit Sharing/401(k) Plan

Value of death benefits _____

Beneficiary _____

Form of payout elected _____

☐ Other Employment Benefits (describe)

_____

_____

Wills and Trusts

Have you executed a will? _____ Date of execution _____

By whom was it drafted? _____

Name and address of executor of will _____

_____

Special instructions to executor or beneficiaries _____

_____

Has your spouse executed a will? _____ Date of execution _____

By whom was it drafted? _____

Name and address of executor of will _____

_____

Have you created a living trust agreement? _____ How many? _____

Are these agreements ☐ revocable? ☐ irrevocable?

Are any of the trusts related to a pour-over provision in your will? _____

Names and addresses of the trustees

_____

_____

_____

Names and addresses of the beneficiaries

_____

_____

_____

_____

Approximate value of trusts $ _____

Nature of properties included in trusts _____

_____

Name and address of the attorney drafting these agreements _____

_____

Have you executed ☐ power of attorney? ☐ health care proxy? ☐ living will?

Inventory of Accumulated Wealth

Residential Real Estate

Location #1 _____

Description _____ Approximate value $ _____

Mortgage $ _____ Mortgagor _____

If the property is not in your name alone, who is/are the co-owner(s)? _____

_____ Is there a right of survivorship? _____

Location #2 _____

Description _____ Approximate value $ _____

Mortgage $ _____ Mortgagor _____

If the property is not in your name alone, who is/are the co-owner(s)? _____

_____ Is there a right of survivorship? _____

Nonresidential Real Estate

Location of property #1 _____ Description _____

Approximate value $ _____ Mortgagor _____ Mortgage $ _____

Is property leased? ____ Name of lessee _____ Duration of lease? _____

Annual rent $ ____ If the property is not in your name alone, who is/are

the co-owner(s)? _____

Is ownership ☐ tenancy-in-common? ☐ joint tenancy? ☐ community property?

Location of property #2 _____ Description _____

Approximate value $ _____ Mortgagor _____ Mortgage $ _____

Is property leased? ____ Name of lessee _____ Duration of lease? _____

Annual rent $ ____ If the property is not in your name alone, who is/are

the co-owner(s)? _____

Is ownership ☐ tenancy-in-common? ☐ joint tenancy? ☐ community property?

Stock

Shares	Purchase Date	Cost	Value

Name of co-owner, if any _____

Special dividend arrangements are _____

_____

Bonds

Denomination	Purchase Date	Cost	Value

Mutual Fund Shares

Shares	Purchase Date	Cost	Value

If any shares are not solely owned by you, the co-owner(s) is/are

_____

Life Insurance Policies

Policies on Your Own Life

Policy number _____

Company _____

Principal amount $ _____

Cash value $ _____

Beneficiaries _____

Loans against the policy $ _____

Location of policy _____

Policies You Own on the Life of Another

Policy number _____

Company _____

Principal amount $ _____

Cash value $ _____

Beneficiaries _____

Loans against the policy $ _____

Location of policy _____

Bank Accounts and Certificates

Checking Accounts

Bank	Account Number	Co-Owner	Avg. Balance

Savings Accounts

Bank   Account Number   Co-Owner   Avg. Balance

_____

_____

_____

Certificates of Deposit

Institution holding _____

Amount $ _____

Maturity date _____

Co-owners _____

Institution holding _____

Amount $ _____

Maturity date _____

Co-owners _____

Business Interests

Nature of Ownership

Do you have ownership in a business or profession?

_____

Is the business   ☐ a proprietorship?
                     ☐ a partnership?
                     ☐ a corporation?
                     ☐ a family limited partnership?
                     ☐ a limited liability company?

If you do not have sole interest, what is the percentage of your ownership?

_____

The other owners of the business or profession are:

Name   Age   Percentage of Ownership

_____

_____

_____

Sale of the Business After Death

Is your estate committed to sell the business after your death? _____

Indicate the parties to this agreement _____

Date of agreement _____

Sources of funds to carry out transaction _____

What is the value of the business _____ Your interest in it _____

Tangible Personal Property

Do you maintain a list of your valuable possessions? _____

Where is the list located? _____

Indicate the major items of value within each category:

Automobiles _____

Home furnishings _____

Jewelry _____

Antiques and art _____

Other tangibles _____

Other assets (describe) _____

_____

_____

Liabilities

I owe money or am financially obligated to _____

Amount $ _____ Location of note _____

Due date _____ Collateral _____ Terms of payment _____

I owe money or am financially obligated to _____

Amount $ _____ Location of note _____

Due date _____ Collateral _____ Terms of payment _____

I owe money or am financially obligated to _____

Amount $ _____ Location of note _____

Due date _____ Collateral _____ Terms of payment _____

Personal Advisers

Indicate the name, address, and telephone number of your:

Physician _____

_____

Clergyman _____

_____

Insurance agent _____

_____

Attorney _____

_____

Trust officer _____

_____

Accountant _____

_____

Investment broker _____

_____

Financial planner _____

_____

Other _____

_____

Location of Key Documents

Birth certificate _____

Marriage certificate _____

Prenuptial agreement _____

Divorce papers _____

Naturalization (citizenship) papers _____

_____

Passport _____

Employment records (including benefits)

_____

Tax returns _____

Last will and testament (original) _____

_____

Funeral/burial instructions _____

Deeds to real estate _____

Stock certificates, bonds, mutual fund shares

_____

_____

_____

Living will _____

Power of attorney _____

Health care proxy _____

Safety deposit box _____

Business buy-sell agreements _____

Additional Notes

_____

_____

_____

_____

_____

_____

_____

_____

_____

_____

_____

_____

_____

Resource 15

*Front Photo: Kay and Arthur Laro Fountain in the lobby
of the Albert B. and Margaret M. Alkek Hospital.
Mrs. Laro graciously provided funds for the
fountain through a planned gift.*

Development Office
1515 Holcombe Boulevard
Houston, Texas 77030-9989
713-792-3450 • 1-800-525-5841

PLANNED GIVING HONOR ROLL

DRAKE UNIVERSITY NATIONAL ALUMNI ASSOCIATION
ALUMNI AWARDS DINNER

(Photo)

A Drake education represents both a wonderful achievement and the means by which individuals can achieve far more. Thanks to Drake, we can believe in our own great potential and we can believe in the institution that empowers so many to accomplish so much. Tonight we celebrate the diverse achievements of Drake alumni and salute the ways they have shown their faith in the University. By believing in Drake, we make possible the great achievements of the generations to come.

To respect the privacy of participants, photographs, names, and descriptions of individuals have been omitted.

Master of Ceremonies

[Name]

[Photo]

[Biography]

_____

_____

_____

_____

_____

_____

_____

_____

_____

Evening Agenda

6:00 PM   Reception

7:00 PM   Welcome
[Name]
President, Drake University
National Alumni Association

7:15 PM   Scandinavian Smorgasbord

8:00 PM   Program
Introduction of Special Guests
and Reunion Class Chairs

**Recognition of Members
of the Heritage Society**
[Name]
National Chair, Heritage Society

Presentation of Alumni Awards
[Name]
Master of Ceremonies

Remarks
[Name]
Drake University President

Closing Remarks
[Name]

Resource 16

[Photo]

Distinguished Service Award
[Name]
[Biography]

"[Quote]

_____

_____

_____ "

Young Alumni Loyalty Award

[Name]
[Biography]

[Photo]

"[Quote]   "

[Photo]

Young Alumni Achievement Award

[Name]

[Biography]

"[Quote] _____

_____

_____

_____

_____

_____

_____ "

_____   _____

_____   _____

_____   _____

_____   _____

_____   _____

_____   _____

_____   _____

_____   _____

_____   _____

_____   _____

_____   _____

_____   _____

_____   _____

_____   _____

_____   _____

_____   _____

_____   _____

_____   _____

_____

Alumni Loyalty Award

[Name]

[Biography]

_____   _____

_____   _____

_____   _____

_____   _____

[Photo]

_____   _____

_____   _____

_____   _____

_____   _____

_____   _____

"[Quote]_____

_____   _____

_____   _____   _____

_____   _____   _____

_____   _____   _____

_____   _____   _____

_____   _____

_____   _____   _____"

_____

_____

_____

_____

_____

[Photo]

Alumni Loyalty Award
[Name]
[Biography]

"[Quote] _____
_____
_____
_____
_____
_____
_____ "

Alumni Achievement Award

[Name]
[Biography]

[Photo]

"[Quote]
"

[Photo]

Alumni Achievement Award
[Name]
[Biography]

"[Quote]

                                                                         "

Drake National Alumni Association *Board of Directors, 1999–2000*

President

Chair

**Vice President
for Fundraising**

**Vice President
for Programming**

**Vice President for
Student Recruitment**

Secretary

**Chair of
Chapter Council**

Members at Large

Chapter Chairs

Central Iowa

Chicago

Dallas

Denver

Kansas City

Nashville

Omaha

St. Louis

Twin Cities

College/School Chairs

Arts and Sciences

*Business and Public
Administration*

Education

Law School

*Pharmacy and
Health Sciences*

*Journalism and
Mass Communication*

Special Members

Drake University
Student Alumni
Association

Drake Nursing
Alumni Association

Drake Alumni
Association of Des Moines

Drake Athletics

Reunion Chairs

Class of 1950

Class of 1960

Class of 1975

Class of 1980

Class of 1990

Class of 1995

DRAKE HERITAGE SOCIETY

Established in 1991, the Heritage Society honors donors of planned gifts (those of other than outright cash, such as bequests and life insurance policies). Members are listed to the right, with new members in boldface type. Members indicated by an asterisk made additional planned gifts in the 1999-2000 fiscal year.

[Names]

_____

_____

_____

_____

_____

_____

_____

_____

_____

_____

_____

_____

_____

_____

_____

_____

_____

_____

_____

RULES REGARDING
CHARITABLE TAX DEDUCTIONS

PREPARED BY ALAN M. SPEARS,

EXECUTIVE DIRECTOR,

OFFICE OF MAJOR GIFTS

AND PLANNED GIVING PROGRAMS,

INDIANA UNIVERSITY FOUNDATION,

ON THE BASIS OF

INTERNAL REVENUE SERVICE INFORMATION

(As of December 2001)

Income Tax Charitable Deductions

I. *Total amount of the charitable deduction*
   A. Cash: face amount
   B. Securities and real estate owned over one year: fair market value
   C. Securities and real estate owned one year or less: cost basis or fair market value, whichever is less
   D. Tangible personal property
      1. "Related use," owned over one year: fair market value
      2. "Related use," owned one year or less: cost basis or fair market value, whichever is less
      3. "Unrelated use," owned over one year: cost basis or fair market value, whichever is less
      4. "Unrelated use," owned one year or less: cost basis or fair market value, whichever is less
   E. Inventory (excluding inventory contributed for research and other special cases): cost basis or fair market value, whichever is less

Note: The above amounts apply to public charities, pass-through foundations, and private operating foundations. If the gift is made to a private, nonoperating foundation, the amount of the deduction is the face amount for cash and the fair market value for publicly traded securities, but for all other property the deduction is limited to cost basis (or fair market value if less than cost basis).

II. *The amount of the charitable deduction that can be reported in any one year depends on the type of property contributed and the type of nonprofit organization to which the donor makes the gift*
   A. Type of property contributed
      1. Cash and all ordinary income property: 50 percent of adjusted gross income (AGI)
      2. Appreciated long-term capital gain property: 30 percent of AGI
   B. Type of organization
      1. Public charities: educational institutions, churches, tax-exempt hospitals, governmental units, publicly supported organizations such as the American Red Cross or a symphony orchestra, broadly supported and private operating foundations—50 percent or 30 percent of AGI, depending on type of property
      2. Private nonoperating foundations
         a. Cash and ordinary income property: 30 percent of AGI
         b. Long-term capital gain property: 20 percent of AGI

III. *Carryovers,* when the total allowable deduction cannot be reported in a single year. Donor has year of gift plus five carryover years in which to use it. (Carryovers apply to private nonoperating foundations as well as to public charities and operating foundations.)

IV. *Pledges.* The deduction is taken in the year the pledge is paid, not when it is made. The IRS takes the position that a written commitment or a promissory note is merely an intention to pay and not a payment. This is true even if the donor makes provision in his or her will to ensure that any outstanding balance on the pledge will be covered by bequest.

If all or a portion of the pledge is unfulfilled at the time of the donor's death, and the donor's promise is enforceable against his estate, the payment of the pledge qualifies for an estate tax deduction.

V. *When a gift is completed*

  A. *Gift by check.* The effective date of the contribution is the day the check is mailed or hand-delivered, provided there are no restrictions on the cashing of the check. A check dated December 31, 1999, mailed and postmarked the same date, is deductible in 1999. It does not matter that the charity receives the check in the new year and that it is actually charged to the donor's account in January. However, a check dated in December but not mailed or handed to the charity until January cannot be deducted on the prior-year return. Neither can a check that is mailed in December but postdated so that it cannot be cashed until the next month.

  B. *Gift of securities.* If the certificate is registered in the name of the donor and properly endorsed or accompanied by a separate stock or bond power assignment, the date of the gift is the date on which the security is hand-delivered or mailed.

If the certificate is in "street name" and held by the donor's broker, the date of the gift is the day when, on proper instructions from the donor, the broker charges the donor's account and credits the charity's account with the particular shares or bonds donated.

If the donor has a certificate re-registered in the name of the charity, the date of the gift is the date on the certificate. This procedure is not advisable for year-end gifts, as re-registration by the transfer agent can take several weeks.

  C. *Gift of real estate.* The gift is complete on the day when the signed deed is delivered or mailed to the charitable organization.

VI. *Valuation of securities.* For publicly traded securities, the deduction is the mean between the "high" and the "low" on the date of the gift. For unlisted securities (for example, those sold over the counter), it is the mean between the "bid" and "asked" prices. In short, the deduction is the average value of the securities on the day the donor relinquishes control. Value is not dependent on the net proceeds actually received by the charity when the securities are sold.

The valuations of some securities—such as certain municipal bonds and closely held stock—are not quoted and may not be readily ascertainable. A broker can usually ascertain market values of bonds. Closely held stock presents a different set of problems and must be valued by a qualified appraiser's accounting procedures that take into consideration a number of factors about the company.

VII. *Volunteers' expenses*

    A. *Gifts of services.* The value of a volunteer's time is not deductible. For example, if an attorney who normally charges clients $150 per hour gives two hours of free legal service to the charity, the attorney may not deduct $300. Neither may volunteers who serve on committees and boards deduct the value of their time. Likewise, newspapers that grant free advertising space and radio and television stations that offer free broadcast time are not allowed a deduction. These are all treated as gifts of services and thus are not deductible.

    B. *Out-of-pocket expenses.* Out-of-pocket expenses incurred by a volunteer while working for the charity are deductible. Examples of deductible items are telephone calls, stationery, postage stamps, and travel between home and the places where the volunteer renders services. A volunteer who uses a personal automobile may deduct the actual costs of gas, tolls, and parking (but not insurance or depreciation) or may calculate a flat 12 cents a mile. If the volunteer attends an out-of-town convention representing the charity in an official capacity, lodging, meals, and transportation are also deductible. These items are not deductible if the volunteer attends the convention merely to enhance knowledge and skills.

VIII. *Substantiation requirements (gift receipts)*

    A. Gift of $250 or more—no goods or services provided to the donor

        1. Donor must obtain a receipt from the nonprofit to support the deduction. A canceled check is insufficient.

        2. Receipt must state that no goods or services were provided to the donor.

        3. The $250 requirement applies to each gift. The gifts to a single charity are not cumulative.

    B. Gift of $75 or more—goods or services provided to the donor.

1. Nonprofit is required to provide a receipt, informing the donor of the amount of the contribution that is deductible.
2. The receipt could contain one of three statements:
    a. If the value of the premium does not exceed $71 (adjusted for inflation each year) or 2 percent of the gift, whichever is less, the receipt could say something like "Under IRS guidelines, the value of the benefits is within the allowable limits; therefore, the full amount of your payment is a deductible contribution."
    b. If the benefits exceed these *de minimis* limits, the receipt must provide a good faith estimate of the value of those benefits and indicate the deductible amount.
3. Intangible benefits such as a name on a building or endowment are not counted.

C. Failure to provide the required information can subject the charity to penalties—$10 per contribution and up to $5,000 per fundraising event.

IX. *Substantiation requirements*

A. Form 8283: Information About Donated Property
1. *Form 8283 is required* if the total value of all property contributed, other than cash, exceeds $500. Depending on the value and type of property contributed, the donor may need to complete Section A, Section B, or both.
2. Types of contributions reported in Section A
    a. Publicly traded securities
    b. Real estate and tangible property (paintings, boats, and other items) valued between $500 and $5,000
    c. Closely held securities (not traded publicly) valued between $500 and $10,000
3. Types of contributions reported in Section B
    a. Real estate and tangible property (paintings, boats, and other items) valued between $500 and $5,000. Section B must be completed if the aggregate claimed value of all similar items exceeds $5,000, even if the value of each single item is less than $5,000.
    b. Closely held securities (not traded publicly) valued in excess of $10,000.
4. *Qualified appraisal.* To receive a charitable deduction for gifts of property covered by the requirement, the donor must obtain a qualified appraisal and attach an appraisal summary to the tax return on which the deduction is first claimed.

    A qualified appraisal must meet the following criteria.

a. It is completed not earlier than 60 days prior to the date of contribution.

b. It is prepared by a qualified appraiser—a person who is professionally qualified to appraise the type of property being valued. The appraiser should be independent of both donor and donee. The appraisal cannot be done by anyone affiliated with the charity.

c. It does not involve a prohibited type of appraisal fee. The fee should not be based on a percentage of the appraised value of the property. It should rather be a flat fee based on the time and expenses of the appraiser.

5. *Appraisal summary.* The appraisal summary should be made on Section B of Form 8283 and include the following information as required.

a. Donor's name and taxpayer identification number (Social Security number in the case of an individual)

b. Description of the property

c. Date of acquisition

d. Donor's cost or other tax basis for the property

e. Nonprofit's name, address, and tax identification number

f. Date on which the nonprofit received the property

g. Name, address, and tax identification number of the appraiser (Section B only)

h. Fair market value of the property

i. The appraiser's declaration that he or she is qualified and did not charge a fee under a prohibited method (Section B only)

   After completing the form but before filing it with the tax return, the donor should have it signed by the nonprofit. The nonprofit should retain a copy.

B. Form 8282: Information About Sale of Donated Property

1. *Form 8282 is required* if the nonprofit sells or otherwise disposes of the property (real estate valued in excess of $5,000, closely held stock valued over $10,000) within two years after receiving it.

2. The nonprofit must file the form.

3. Information reported on form

a. Name and tax identification number of the donor

b. Name, address, and tax identification number of the charity

c. Description of the donated property

d. Date of gift and date of disposition

e. Appraised value

f. Selling price or amount received from other type of disposition

4. Donor is entitled to a copy. The nonprofit should send a copy of this information to the donor.

C. Form 1040: Income Tax Return

1. Documents and information to be included for outright gifts
   a. For cash contributions of more than $3,000 to any one charity, state name of charity and amount given.
   b. For noncash gifts over $500, attach Form 8283.

2. Documents and information to be included for irrevocable deferred gifts
   a. Name of charity, type of gift vehicle, and amount contributed
   b. Form 8283 for noncash gifts over $500, same as for outright gifts
   c. Computation form showing value of remainder interest
   d. Copy of the trust agreement, gift annuity agreement, or instrument of transfer

D. Form 709: Gift Tax Return

1. Form 709 is required in the following circumstances:
   a. For gift annuities where gift value exceeds $10,000. Also if the annuitant is neither the donor nor the donor's spouse and the actuarial value exceeds $10,000.
   b. For bargain sales where gift value exceeds $10,000
   c. For charitable remainder trusts, pooled income fund gifts, and retained life estates where charity has a future interest, whatever the amount
   d. For charitable lead trusts in most instances
      Note: The donor should file Form 709 even when no gift tax is due.

2. Documents and information to be included: name of nonprofit, type of gift, amount contributed, and computation form showing value of remainder interest or other charitable interest

X. *Corporate contributions.* Same rules as for individual contributions, but with the following differences.

A. The maximum amount of charitable deductions the corporation can use in one year is 10 percent of taxable income.

B. Corporations may contribute inventory for research purposes or for the care of the ill and needy and deduct up to twice the manufacturing costs (see Section XI for details).

XI. *Corporate gifts of inventory.* Normally, if a corporation donates inventory to a charity, the deduction is limited to the cost basis (the actual manufacturing cost if the company produced the item). There are, however, two exceptions:

A. For a contribution of newly manufactured scientific equipment to colleges and universities for research and experimentation, including research training, the corporation is allowed a deduction of either cost basis plus 50 percent of the appreciation or twice the corporation's cost basis, whichever is less.

The contribution must be to the physical and biological sciences—engineering, medicine, chemistry, physics, zoology, or the like. The increased deduction does not apply to gifts to the social sciences and humanities. Further, the following requirements must be met:

1. The corporation must have manufactured the equipment.
2. The contribution must be made no later than two years after the property was completed.
3. The original use of the property must be by the donee.
4. The donee cannot sell the property for money, services, or other equipment.
5. The donee must provide the corporation with a written statement that the use of the property will fulfill the requirements.

B. For a contribution of inventory to be applied for the care of the ill, the needy, or infants, corporations may also receive a deduction of either cost basis plus 50 percent of the appreciation or twice the corporation's cost basis, whichever is less.

Gift and Estate Tax Charitable Deductions

1. *Gift tax* is levied on a person's right to transmit property during his or her lifetime. The amount of the tax depends on the size of the gift.
2. *Estate tax* is levied on the right to transmit property at death. The amount of the tax depends on the size of the estate the deceased leaves.
3. *Historical background.* The federal government adopted the estate tax first, followed by the gift tax. The purpose of the estate tax was to raise revenue and redistribute wealth. The purpose of the gift tax was to reinforce the estate tax by discouraging people from giving property during their lifetime in order to avoid the estate tax. Until 1976, the estate and gift taxes were largely independent of each other. If a person made a taxable gift during his or her lifetime, the tax was computed using the gift tax rate schedule. If the gift was made at death, the tax was imposed on the estate of the deceased and was computed using the estate tax rate schedule. It was generally advantageous for a wealthy person to give away as much as practical while living because the total tax would be less.

   The 1976 act eliminated the dual tax system and thereby removed most of the incentive for transferring property during one's lifetime. The two tables were replaced by a single progressive rate schedule that applies to the cumulative total of all transfers during life and at death. Thus if a person made $400,000 of taxable gifts during life and died with a taxable estate of $600,000, the transfer tax could be computed on a total taxable estate of $1,000,000.

   Another revision brought about by the 1976 act was the substitution of a single "unified" credit for the lifetime $30,000 gift tax exemption and the $60,000 estate tax exemption. Today, a person may transfer $1,000,000 of bequests to noncharitable beneficiaries without incurring tax. This will increase progressively to $3,500,000 by 2009. In 2010 the Estate Tax is repealed.
4. *Annual gift tax exclusion.* An individual may give another individual up to $10,000 in cash or property each year without having to report the gift or incurring a gift tax. There is no limit to the number of individuals to which such gifts may be made. Husbands and wives may join together and give up to $20,000 (indexed for inflation under 1997 law) to any individual without tax (this is known as *gift-splitting*).

   To qualify for the annual exclusion, the gifts must be present-interest gifts. That is, the donee must have a right to benefit from the property now.
5. *Marital deductions.* Gifts of any size between spouses are not subject to gift tax. Likewise, the first spouse to die can now leave an unlimited amount to

the surviving spouse completely free of federal estate tax. The amount passing to the surviving spouse can qualify for this marital deduction if it is given outright or under certain approved trust agreements.

6. *Deductibility of lifetime gifts to charity.* A donor is allowed an unlimited charitable gift tax deduction for lifetime gifts to qualified charities. However, the donor is required to complete a gift tax return (Form 709) if making a future-interest gift such as a charitable remainder trust or a gift annuity.

7. *Deductibility of bequests to charity.* A donor is allowed an unlimited charitable estate tax deduction. If the bequest is in the form of a charitable remainder trust with survivor as income beneficiary, the deduction is for the present value of the remainder interest. If a surviving spouse is the only income beneficiary, the combination of the marital deduction and charitable deduction will eliminate estate tax on the property.

RESOURCE 18

TEMPLATES FOR DRAFTING TRUSTS

CHARITABLE REMAINDER ANNUITY TRUST

◆

Inter Vivos (Between Two Living Persons), Consecutive and Concurrent Interests

On this _____ day of _____, 200_, I, _____, (hereinafter referred to as "the Donor"), of _____, County of _____, State of _____, desiring to establish a charitable remainder annuity trust, within the meaning of Section 5 Rev. Proc. 90-32 and Section 664(d)(1) of the Internal Revenue Code of 1986, as amended from time to time (hereinafter referred to as "the Code") hereby create the _____ Charitable Remainder Annuity Trust and designate the XYZ Charity (hereinafter referred to as the "Trustee") as the initial Trustee.

1. *Funding of Trust.* The Donor hereby transfers to the Trustee the property described in Schedule A attached hereto, and the Trustee acknowledges the receipt of such property and agrees to hold, manage and distribute such property of the Trust under the terms set forth in this Trust instrument.

2. *Payment of the Annuity Amount.* In each taxable year of the Trust, the Trustee shall pay to _____ and _____ (hereinafter referred to as "the Recipients"), in equal shares during their lifetimes an annuity amount equal to the following percentage: _____ (_) percent of the net fair market value of the Trust assets valued as of the date of transfer to the Trustee of the property indicated on Schedule A. The annuity amount shall be paid from income in equal quarterly installments on or after March 31, June 30, September 30 and December 31, and, to the extent income is not sufficient, from principal. If necessary, a fifth payment will be made on or before the date by which the Trustee is required to file the Federal Income Tax return for the Trust, to bring the total payment to the actual amount to which the Recipient was entitled for that year pursuant to this paragraph. Any income of the Trust for a taxable year in excess of the annuity amount shall be added to principal. If for any year the net fair market value of the Trust assets is incorrectly determined, then within a reasonable period after the value is finally determined for federal tax purposes, the Trustee shall pay to the Recipients (in the case of an undervaluation), or shall collect from the Recipients (in the case of an overvaluation), an amount equal to the difference between the annuity amount which the Trustee should have paid if the correct value had been used and the annuity amount which the Trustee actually paid.

3. *Proration of the Annuity Amount.* In determining the annuity amount to be paid under Paragraph 2, the Trustee shall prorate the same on a daily basis for a short taxable year in accordance with the Treasury Regulation Section 1.664-2(2)(1)(iv)(a) and, for the taxable year of the death of the survivor Recipient in accordance with Treasury Regulation Section 1.664-3(a)(1)(iv)(b). In the case of a taxable year which is for a period of less than 12 months, the amount required to be distributed under Paragraph 2 hereunder shall be the fraction of such percentage of which the numerator is the number of days in the short taxable year of the Trust

and of which the denominator is 365 (366 if February 29th is a day included in the numerator).

4. *Distribution to Charity.* Upon the death of the survivor Recipient, the Trustee shall distribute all of the then principal and income of the Trust (other than any amount due either the Recipients or their estates, under the provisions above) to the XYZ Charity, a charitable organization, to be used for _____. If the Charity is not an organization described in each of Sections 170(b)(1)(A), 170(c), 2055(a), and 2522(a) of the Code at the time when any principal or income of the Trust is to be distributed to it, then the Trustee shall distribute such principal or income to such one or more organizations described in each of Sections 170(b)(1)(A), 170(c), 2055(a), and 2522(a) as the Trustee shall select in its sole discretion.

5. *Additional Contributions.* No additional contributions shall be made to this Trust after the initial contribution.

6. *Prohibited Transactions.* If the Trust is continued after the termination of all noncharitable interests, there shall be distributed amounts at least sufficient to avoid liability for the tax imposed by Section 4942(a) of the Code. Except for payment of the annuity amount and notwithstanding any other provisions of this Trust, the Trustee shall not engage in any act of self-dealing, as defined in Section 4941(d) of the Code, and shall not make any taxable expenditures, as defined in Section 4945(d) of the Code. The Trustee shall not make any investments that jeopardize the charitable purpose of the Trust, within the meaning of Section 4944 of the Code and the Treasury Regulations thereunder, or retain any excess business holdings, within the meaning of Section 4943 of the Code.

7. *Taxable Year.* The first taxable year of the Trust begins with the date the Trust is first funded with property and shall end on December 31 of that year. Subsequent taxable years shall be on a calendar year basis.

8. *Governing Law.* This Trust having been delivered in the State of _____, the laws of the State of _____ shall govern the validity and interpretation thereof, notwithstanding the residence in another jurisdiction of the Donor or of any persons who may have an interest in this Trust. For purposes of this Paragraph 8 in any conflict with Section 664 of the Code and the Treasury Regulations thereunder, that Code Section and the corresponding Treasury Regulations shall govern.

9. *Trust Not Liable for Estate or Inheritance Taxes.* No gift, legacy, inheritance, estate, or generation-skipping transfer taxes which may be assessed against the property of this Trust by reason of the Donor's death or transfer of property to this Trust shall be paid out of any property held in trust hereunder. If the payment

of any such taxes is due, the surviving Recipient shall provide for payment of such taxes that may arise as a result of his or her survivorship interest from sources other than property held by this Trust and failure to do so shall cause his or her income interest to terminate as if he or she predeceased the Donor.

10. *Limited Power of Amendment.* The provisions of this Trust shall be irrevocable and not subject to amendment, alteration, or revocation by anyone, except the Trustee shall have the power and duty, acting alone, to amend the Trust in any manner required for the sole purpose of ensuring that the Trust qualifies and continues to qualify as a charitable remainder annuity trust within the meaning of Section 664(d)(1) of the Code and the corresponding Treasury Regulations.

11. *Powers.* In administering this Trust, the Trustee shall have all of the trustee powers and discretions conferred upon it by the laws of the State of _____. These include those powers described in _____ Code Section _____ (as amended from time to time), including but not limited to the power to:

(A) sell, exchange or otherwise dispose of any asset held in this Trust at either public or private sale, for cash or on credit;

(B) invest and reinvest the funds of the Trust in any kind of property, real or personal, including (by way of example and not limitation) stocks of any class, shares of regulated investment companies ("mutual funds"), bonds and debentures, real estate investment trusts, shares or interests in common trust funds, and life insurance policies, all notwithstanding any laws or rules of law that would otherwise require the diversification of trust investments solely to types appearing on a statutory list, or prohibit the holding of underproductive property.

(C) vote shares of stock or other corporate securities, in person or by proxy, on any and all corporate matters, and to exercise conversion privileges, warrants, and options, and to hold shares of stock and any other corporate securities in the name of a nominee, without disclosure of a fiduciary relationship;

(D) prosecute, defend, compromise, abandon, or pay any claim by or against it; to employ agents, attorneys, brokers, or other counsel, or employees to aid it in performance of its duties hereunder, and to pay them reasonable compensation for their services; and the Trustee shall not be liable for any negligence, omission, or mistake of any such agent, attorney, broker, or other counsel or employee selected or retained by it with reasonable care;

(E) borrow money for any Trust purpose (including the payments to be made to the Recipient or other beneficiaries under this Trust) either without security or secured by part or all of the Trust property; and to allocate receipts and disbursements between income and principal in accordance with Chapter _____ of the (State) Trust Code, as amended.

12. *Trustee Compensation and Bond.* The Trustee shall not receive any compensation for services rendered under this agreement, excepting a reasonable investment management fee. Such fees shall be charged to income first, but if income is insufficient, to principal. Any such fees paid shall in no way reduce the annuity amount required to be paid to the Recipient under this Trust. No bond or other security shall be required of the Trustee for the faithful performance of its duties in such capacity.

13. *Investment of Trust Assets.* The Trustee's powers and discretions referenced in Paragraph 11 shall not include any power or discretion that is in conflict with Code Section 664 and the Treasury Regulations thereunder or any specific provision of this Trust. No provision of this Trust shall be construed to restrict the Trustee from investing the property held in Trust hereunder in a manner that would result in the annual realization of a reasonable amount of income or gain from the sale or disposition of such property.

14. *Effective Date.* This agreement shall be effective upon the receipt of the Trustee of the property or title to the property listed in Schedule A.

IN WITNESS WHEREOF, the parties hereby execute this Trust on this _____ day of _____, 200_.

                                        DONOR

                                        _____

                                        XYZ Charity

                                        By:_____
                                                            , President

ATTEST:

_____
Corporate Secretary

CHARITABLE REMAINDER UNITRUST

On this _____ day of _____, 200_, I, _____, (hereinafter referred to as "the Donor"), of _____, County of _____, State of _____, desiring to establish a charitable remainder unitrust, within the meaning of Rev. Proc. 89-20 and Section 664(d)(2) of the Internal Revenue Code of 1986, as amended from time to time (hereinafter referred to as "the Code") hereby create the _____ Charitable Remainder Unitrust and designate the XYZ Charity (hereinafter referred to as the "Trustee") as the initial Trustee.

1. *Funding of Trust.* The Donor hereby transfers to the Trustee the property described in Schedule A attached hereto, and all property that may be added to the Trust at any time. The Trustee acknowledges the receipt of such property and agrees to hold, manage and distribute such property of the Trust under the terms set forth in this Trust instrument.

2. *Payment of the Unitrust Amount.* In each taxable year of the Trust, the Trustee shall pay to _____ (hereinafter referred to as "the Recipient") wholly for the Recipient's lifetime a unitrust amount equal to the following fixed percentage: _____ ( ) percent of the net fair market value of the Trust assets valued as of the last business day of the first calendar month in each taxable year of the Trust (the "valuation date"). The unitrust amount shall be paid from income in equal quarterly installments on or after March 31, June 30, September 30 and December 31, and to the extent that income is not sufficient, from principal. If necessary, a fifth payment will be made on or before the date by which the Trustee is required to file the Federal Income Tax return for the Trust, to bring the total payment to the actual amount to which the Recipient was entitled for that year pursuant to this paragraph. Any income of the Trust for a taxable year in excess of the unitrust amount shall be added to principal. If for any year the net fair market value of the Trust assets is incorrectly determined, then within a reasonable period after the value is finally determined for federal tax purposes, the Trustee shall pay to the Recipient (in the case of an undervaluation), or shall collect from the Recipient (in the case of an overvaluation), an amount equal to the difference between the unitrust amount which the Trustee should have paid if the correct value had been used and the unitrust amount which the Trustee actually paid.

3. *Proration of the Unitrust Amount.* In determining the unitrust amount to be paid under Paragraph 2, the Trustee shall prorate the same on a daily basis for a short taxable year in accordance with Treasury Regulation Section 1.664-3(a)(1)(v)(a), and for the taxable year ending with the death of the Recipient in accordance with Treasury Regulation Section 1.664-3(a)(1)(v)(b). In the case of a taxable year which is for a period of less than 12 months, the amount required to be distributed

under Paragraph 2 hereunder shall be the fraction of such percentage of which the numerator is the number of days in the short taxable year of the Trust and of which the denominator is 365 (366 if February 29th is a day included in the numerator).

4. *Distribution to Charity.* Upon the death of the Recipient, the Trustee shall distribute all of the then principal and income of the Trust (other than any amount due the Recipient or the Recipient's estate, under the provisions above) to the XYZ Charity, a charitable organization, to be used for _____. If the XYZ Charity is not an organization described in each of Sections 170(b)(1)(A), 170(c), 2055(a), and 2522(a) of the Code at the time when any principal or income of the Trust is to be distributed to it, then the Trustee shall distribute such principal or income to such one or more organizations described in each of Sections 170(b)(1)(A), 170(c), 2055(a), and 2522(a) as the Trustee shall select in its sole discretion.

5. *Additional Contributions.* The Donor or any other person may at any time make additional contributions to this Trust with the consent of the Trustee. If any additional contributions are made to the trust after the initial contribution in Trust, the unitrust amount for the taxable year in which the assets are added to the Trust shall be _____ percent (__) of the sum of (1) the net fair market value of Trust assets (excluding the assets so added and any income from, or appreciation on, such assets) and (2) that proportion of the value of the assets so added that was excluded under (1) which the number of days in the period that begins with the date of the contribution and ends with the earlier of the last day of the taxable year or the Donor's death bears to the number of days in the period which begins on the first day of such taxable year and ends with the earlier of the last day in such taxable year or the day of the Donor's death. The assets so added shall be valued at the time of contribution. If any property is added to the Trust by the Will of any person, the obligation to pay the unitrust amount with respect to such property shall commence with the date of death of such person, but payment of the unitrust amount with respect to such property may be deferred from the date of such person's death to the end of the taxable year of the trust in which the full amount of such property is finally transferred to the Trust. Within a reasonable time after the occurrence of said event, the Trustee shall pay to the Recipient (in the case of an undervaluation), or shall collect from the Recipient (in the case of an overvaluation), an amount equal to the difference between the unitrust amount which the Trustee should have paid if the correct value had been used and the unitrust amount which the Trustee actually paid. In the case where there is no valuation date after the time of contribution, the assets so added shall be valued as of the time of contribution.

6. *Prohibited Transactions.* If the Trust is continued after the termination of all noncharitable interests, there shall be distributed amounts at least sufficient to avoid liability for the tax imposed by Section 4942(a) of the Code. Except for payments of the unitrust amount and notwithstanding any other provisions of this Trust, the Trustee shall not engage in any act of self-dealing, as defined in Section 4941(d) of the Code or make any taxable expenditures, as defined in Section 4945(d) of the Code. The Trustee shall not make any investments that jeopardize the charitable purpose of the Trust, within the meaning of Section 4944 of the Code and the Treasury Regulations thereunder, or retain any excess business holdings, within the meaning of Section 4943 of the Code.

7. *Taxable Year.* The first taxable year of the Trust begins with the date the Trust is first funded with property and shall end on December 31 of that year. Subsequent taxable years shall be on a calendar year basis.

8. *Governing Law.* This Trust having been delivered in the State of _____, the laws of the State of _____ shall govern the validity and interpretation thereof, notwithstanding the residence in another jurisdiction of the Donor or of any persons who may have an interest in this Trust. For purposes of this Paragraph 8, in any conflict with Section 664 of the Code and the Treasury Regulations thereunder, that Code Section and the corresponding Treasury Regulations shall govern.

9. *Trust Not Liable for Estate or Inheritance Taxes.* Notwithstanding anything herein to the contrary, the assets of the Trust shall not be subject to claim for any federal, state or other gift, estate, inheritance, succession or generation-skipping transfer taxes or duties which may be assessed against the estate of the Donor, and the Donor agrees to make no inconsistent provision in his or her will.

10. *Limited Power of Amendment.* The provisions of this Trust shall be irrevocable and not subject to amendment, alteration, or revocation by anyone, except the Trustee shall have the power and duty, acting alone, to amend the Trust in any manner required for the sole purpose of ensuring that the Trust qualifies and continues to qualify as a charitable remainder unitrust within the meaning of Section 664(d)(2) of the Code and the corresponding Treasury Regulations.

11. *Powers.* In administering this Trust, the Trustee shall have all of the trustee powers and discretions conferred upon it by the laws of the State of _____. These include those powers described in _____ Code Section _____ (as amended from time to time), including but not limited to the power to:

> (A) sell, exchange or otherwise dispose of any asset held in this Trust at either public or private sale, for cash or on credit;

(B) invest and reinvest the funds of the Trust in any kind of property, real or personal, including (by way of example and not limitation) stocks of any class, shares of regulated investment companies ("mutual funds"), bonds and debentures, real estate investment trusts, shares or interests in common trust funds, and life insurance policies, all notwithstanding any laws or rules of law that would otherwise require the diversification of trust investments solely to types appearing on a statutory list, or prohibit the holding of underproductive property.

(C) vote shares of stock or other corporate securities, in person or by proxy, on any and all corporate matters, and to exercise conversion privileges, warrants, and options, and to hold shares of stock and any other corporate securities in the name of a nominee, without disclosure of a fiduciary relationship;

(D) prosecute, defend, compromise, abandon, or pay any claim by or against it; to employ agents, attorneys, brokers, or other counsel, or employees to aid it in performance of its duties hereunder, and to pay them reasonable compensation for their services; and the Trustee shall not be liable for any negligence, omission, or mistake of any such agent, attorney, broker, or other counsel or employee selected or retained by it with reasonable care;

(E) borrow money for any Trust purpose (including the payments to be made to the Recipient or other beneficiaries under this Trust) either without security or secured by part or all of the Trust property; and to allocate receipts and disbursements between income and principal in accordance with Chapter _____ of the (State) Trust Code, as amended.

12. *Trustee Compensation and Bond.* The Trustee shall not receive any compensation for services rendered under this agreement, excepting a reasonable investment management fee. Such fees shall be charged to income first, but if income is insufficient, to principal. Any such fees paid shall in no way reduce the unitrust amount required to be paid to the Recipient under this Trust. No bond or other security shall be required of the Trustee for the faithful performance of its duties in such capacity.

13. *Investment of Trust Assets.* The Trustee's powers and discretion referenced in Paragraph 11 shall not include any power or discretion that is in conflict with Code Section 664 and the Treasury Regulations thereunder or any specific provision of this Trust. No provision of this Trust shall be construed to restrict the Trustee from investing the property held in Trust hereunder in a manner that

would result in the annual realization of a reasonable amount of income or gain from the sale or disposition of such property.

14. *Effective Date.* This agreement shall be effective upon the receipt of the Trustee of the property or title to the property listed in Schedule A.

IN WITNESS WHEREOF, the parties hereby execute this Trust on this _____ day of _____, 200_.

DONOR

_____

XYZ Charity

By:_____
                              , President

ATTEST:

_____

By,

CHARITABLE REMAINDER UNITRUST

◆

Income-Only, with Flip Provisions, and Without "Makeup" Provision Inter Vivos (Between Two Living Persons), Consecutive Interests

On this _____ day of _____, 200_, I, _____, (hereinafter referred to as "the Donor"), of _____, County of _____, State of _____, desiring to establish a charitable remainder unitrust, within the meaning of Section 4 of Rev. Proc. 90-31 and Section 664(d)(2) and (3) of the Internal Revenue Code of 1986, as amended from time to time (hereinafter referred to as "the Code") hereby create the _____ Charitable Remainder Unitrust and designate the XYZ Charity (hereinafter referred to as the "Trustee") as the initial Trustee.

1. *Funding of Trust.* The Donor hereby transfers to the Trustee the property described in Schedule A attached hereto, and all property that may be added to the Trust at any time. The Trustee acknowledges the receipt of such property and agrees to hold, manage and distribute such property of the Trust under the terms set forth in this Trust instrument.

2(a). *Payment of the Unitrust Amount.* Subject to the conditions contained in paragraphs 2(b) and 2(c) below, in each taxable year of the Trust, the Trustee shall pay to _____ during his or her lifetime, and after his or her death to _____ (hereinafter referred to as "the Recipients") for such time as he or she survives, a unitrust amount equal to the smaller of (i) the Trust income for such taxable year (as defined in Section 643(b) of the Code and the Treasury Regulations thereunder), and (ii) the following fixed percentage amount: _____ ( ) percent of the net fair market value of the Trust assets valued as of the last business day of the first calendar month in each taxable year of the Trust (the "valuation date"). The unitrust amount shall be paid from income in equal quarterly installments on or after March 31, June 30, September 30 and December 31, and to the extent that income is not sufficient, from principal. If necessary, a fifth payment will be made on or before the date by which the Trustee is required to file the Federal Income Tax return for the Trust, to bring the total payment to the actual amount to which the Recipient was entitled for that year pursuant to this paragraph. Any income of the Trust for a taxable year in excess of the unitrust amount shall be added to principal. If for any year the net fair market value of the Trust assets is incorrectly determined, then within a reasonable period after the value is finally determined for federal tax purposes, the Trustee shall pay to the Recipient (in the case of an undervaluation), or shall collect from the Recipient (in the case of an overvaluation), an amount equal to the difference between the unitrust amount which the Trustee should have paid if the correct value had been used and the unitrust amount which the Trustee actually paid.

2(b). The method of computing the unitrust amount payable to the Recipients as set forth in the foregoing provisions of Paragraph 2(a) shall continue until _____. Commencing on _____ *[the beginning of the following taxable year],* the method of computing the unitrust amount payable to the Recipients shall be converted to the method provided for in the following Paragraph 2(c).

2(c). Commencing on _____, and continuing for each taxable year of the Trust, the Trustee shall pay to _____ during his or her lifetime, and after his or her death to _____ for such time as he or she survives, a unitrust amount equal to ___% of the net fair market value of the assets of the Trust valued as of the Valuation Date of each taxable year of the Trust. The unitrust amount shall be paid in equal quarterly amounts from income and, to the extent that income is not sufficient, from principal. Any income of the Trust for a taxable year in excess of the unitrust amount shall be added to the principal.

3. *Proration of the Unitrust Amount.* In determining the unitrust amount to be paid under Paragraph 2, the Trustee shall prorate the same on a daily basis for a short taxable year in accordance with Treasury Regulation Section 1.664-3(a)(1)(v)(a), and for the taxable year ending with the death of the Recipient in accordance with Treasury Regulation Section 1.664-3(a)(1)(v)(b). In the case of a taxable year which is for a period of less than 12 months, the amount required to be distributed under Paragraph 2 hereunder shall be the fraction of such percentage of which the numerator is the number of days in the short taxable year of the Trust and of which the denominator is 365 (366 if February 29th is a day included in the numerator).

4. *Distribution to Charity.* Upon the death of the survivor Recipient, the Trustee shall distribute all of the then principal and income of the Trust (other than any amount due the Recipients or the Recipients' estates, under the provisions above) to the XYZ Charity, a charitable organization, to be used for _____. If the Foundation is not an organization described in each of Sections 170(b)(1)(A), 170(c), 2055(a), and 2522(a) of the Code at the time when any principal or income of the Trust is to be distributed to it, then the Trustee shall distribute such principal or income to such one or more organizations described in each of Sections 170(b)(1)(A), 170(c), 2055(a), and 2522(a) as the Trustee shall select in its sole discretion.

5. *Additional Contributions.* The Donor or any other person may at any time make additional contributions to this Trust by gift or bequest with the consent of the Trustee. In any taxable year in which additional contributions are made to the Trust, the unitrust amount for the year in which the additional contribution is made shall be equal to the lesser of: (a) the Trust income for the taxable year, as defined in section 643(b) of the Code and the regulations thereunder, and (b) _____% of the sum of (1) the net fair market value of Trust assets as of the valuation date (excluding the assets so added and any income from, or appreciation

on, such assets) and (2) that proportion of the fair market value of the assets so added that was excluded under (1) that the number of days in the period that begins with the date of the contribution and ends with the earlier of the last day of the taxable year or the day of the Recipient's death bears to the number of days in the period that begins on the first day of such taxable year and ends with the earlier of the last day in such taxable year or the day of the Recipient's death. In the case where there is no valuation date after the time of contribution, the assets so added shall be valued as of the time of contribution. However, any additional contributions received as described in this paragraph are also subject to the conditions of paragraphs 2(b) and 2(c) hereinabove, which define the circumstances when a change of payout method shall be initiated by the Trustee.

6. *Prohibited Transactions.* If the Trust is continued after the termination of all non-charitable interests, there shall be distributed amounts at least sufficient to avoid liability for the tax imposed by Section 4942(a) of the Code. Except for payments of the unitrust amount and notwithstanding any other provisions of this Trust, the Trustee shall not engage in any act of self-dealing, as defined in Section 4941(d) of the Code or make any taxable expenditures, as defined in Section 4945(d) of the Code. The Trustee shall not make any investments that jeopardize the charitable purpose of the Trust, within the meaning of Section 4944 of the Code and the Treasury Regulations thereunder, or retain any excess business holdings, within the meaning of Section 4943 of the Code.

7. *Taxable Year.* The first taxable year of the Trust begins with the date the Trust is first funded with property and shall end on December 31 of that year. Subsequent taxable years shall be on a calendar year basis.

8. *Governing Law.* This Trust having been delivered in the State of _____, the laws of the State of _____ shall govern the validity and interpretation thereof, notwithstanding the residence in another jurisdiction of the Donor or of any persons who may have an interest in this Trust. For purposes of this Paragraph 8, in any conflict with Section 664 of the Code and the Treasury Regulations thereunder, that Code Section and the corresponding Treasury Regulations shall govern.

9. *Trust Not Liable for Estate or Inheritance Taxes.* Notwithstanding anything herein to the contrary, the assets of the Trust shall not be subject to claim for any federal, state or other gift, estate, inheritance, succession or generation-skipping transfer taxes or duties which may be assessed against the estate of the Donor, and the Donor agrees to make no inconsistent provision in his or her will.

10. *Limited Power of Amendment.* The provisions of this Trust shall be irrevocable and not subject to amendment, alteration, or revocation by anyone, except the Trustee shall have the power and duty, acting alone, to amend the Trust in

any manner required for the sole purpose of ensuring that the Trust qualifies and continues to qualify as a charitable remainder unitrust within the meaning of Section 664(d)(2) of the Code and the corresponding Treasury Regulations.

11. *Powers.* In administering this Trust, the Trustee shall have all of the trustee powers and discretions conferred upon it by the laws of the State of _____. These include those powers described in _____ Code Section _____ (as amended from time to time), including but not limited to the power to:

(A) sell, exchange or otherwise dispose of any asset held in this Trust at either public or private sale, for cash or on credit;

(B) invest and reinvest the funds of the Trust in any kind of property, real or personal, including (by way of example and not limitation) stocks of any class, shares of regulated investment companies ("mutual funds"), bonds and debentures, real estate investment trusts, shares or interests in common trust funds, and life insurance policies, all notwithstanding any laws or rules of law that would otherwise require the diversification of trust investments solely to types appearing on a statutory list, or prohibit the holding of underproductive property.

(C) vote shares of stock or other corporate securities, in person or by proxy, on any and all corporate matters, and to exercise conversion privileges, warrants, and options, and to hold shares of stock and any other corporate securities in the name of a nominee, without disclosure of a fiduciary relationship;

(D) prosecute, defend, compromise, abandon, or pay any claim by or against it; to employ agents, attorneys, brokers, or other counsel, or employees to aid it in performance of its duties hereunder, and to pay them reasonable compensation for their services; and the Trustee shall not be liable for any negligence, omission, or mistake of any such agent, attorney, broker, or other counsel or employee selected or retained by it with reasonable care;

(E) borrow money for any Trust purpose (including the payments to be made to the Recipient or other beneficiaries under this Trust) either without security or secured by part or all of the Trust property; and to allocate receipts and disbursements between income and principal in accordance with Chapter _____ of the (State) Trust Code, as amended.

12. *Trustee Compensation and Bond.* The Trustee shall not receive any compensation for services rendered under this agreement, excepting a reasonable investment management fee. Such fees shall be charged to income first, but if

income is insufficient, to principal. Any such fees paid shall in no way reduce the unitrust amount required to be paid to the Recipients under this Trust. No bond or other security shall be required of the Trustee for the faithful performance of its duties in such capacity.

13. *Investment of Trust Assets.* The Trustee's powers and discretion referenced in Paragraph 11 shall not include any power or discretion that is in conflict with Code Section 664 and the Treasury Regulations thereunder or any specific provision of this Trust. No provision of this Trust shall be construed to restrict the Trustee from investing the property held in Trust hereunder in a manner that would result in the annual realization of a reasonable amount of income or gain from the sale or disposition of such property.

14. *Effective Date.* This agreement shall be effective upon the receipt of the Trustee of the property or title to the property listed in Schedule A.

IN WITNESS WHEREOF, the parties hereby executive this Trust on this _____ day of _____, 200_.

DONOR

_____

XYZ Charity

By:_____
President

ATTEST:

_____

Corporate Secretary

On this _____ day of _____ , 20__ , (name of donor) (hereinafter referred to as "the donor"), of the city of _____ , county of _____ , state of _____ , desiring to establish a charitable lead trust hereby create the _____ charitable lead annuity trust and designate the (name of the foundation or bank that will serve as trustee) as the trustee.

WITNESSETH:

In consideration of the mutual covenants herein contained, the Donor hereby conveys, assigns, and delivers to the Trustee the property described in "Schedule A" annexed hereto and made a part hereof, the receipt of which the trustee acknowledges and is hereinafter collectively sometimes called the "Trust Estate,"

IN TRUST, for the following uses and purposes and subject to the terms, conditions, and powers hereinafter set forth:

FIRST: *Trust Distributions.* The Trustee shall invest, reinvest, and administer the Trust Estate, collect the income therefrom, and after deducting all proper expenses dispose of the net income and the principal as follows:

A. *Payment of Annuity Amount.* The Trustee shall pay to _____ (hereinafter referred to as "the Charitable Organization"), a corporation organized and existing under the laws of the state of _____ , if the Charitable Organization is an organization described in all of Sections 170(b)(1)(A), 2055(a), and 2522(a) at the time of such payment, for its general charitable purposes in each taxable year of the Trust until _____ , if the years from the commencement date of the Trust (the "termination date") an annuity amount equal to _____ percent (the "payout percentage") of the net fair market value of the assets of the Trust as of the commencement date. If the Charitable Organization is not an organization described in Sections 170(b)(1)(A), 2055(a), and 2522(a) at the time when any principal or income of the Trust is to be distributed to it, then the Trustee shall distribute such principal or income to such one or more organizations described in Sections 170(b)(1)(A), 2055(a), and 2522(a) as the Trustee shall select in its sole discretion.

The annuity amount shall be paid in _____ *[annual or equal semi-annual, quarterly, monthly, or weekly]* amounts from income and, to the extent income is not sufficient, from principal. Any income of the Trust for a taxable year in excess of the annuity amount shall be added to principal. If the net fair market value of the Trust assets is incorrectly determined, then within a reasonable period after the value is finally determined for federal tax purposes, the Trustee shall pay to the Charitable Organization (in the case of an undervaluation) or receive from the Charitable Organization (in the case of an overvaluation) an amount equal to the difference between the annuity amount(s) properly payable and the annuity amount(s) actually paid. The payout percentage shall in no event exceed that percentage (and thus, if necessary, shall be reduced to that percentage), to the nearest one-tenth percent, immediately less than the percentage which would cause the discounted present value of the annuity amount to be 60% of the net fair market value of the Trust assets as finally determined for federal tax purposes.

B. *Proration of the Annuity Amount.* In determining the annuity amount, the Trustee shall prorate the same on a daily basis for a short taxable year and for the taxable year ending __ years *[same number of years as in paragraph A]* from the date of commencement of the Trust.

C. *Distribution to Donor Issue.* Upon the termination date, the Trustee shall distribute all of the then principal and income of the Trust (other than any amount due the Charitable Organization) to the descendants of the Donor then living upon the principle of representation.

D. *Additional Contributions.* No additional contributions shall be made to the Trust after the initial contribution.

E. *Prohibited Transactions.* The Trustee shall make distributions at such time and in such manner as not to subject the Trust to tax under Section 4942. Except as otherwise expressly provided herein, the Trustee shall not engage in any act of self-dealing, as defined in Section 4941(d), and shall not make any taxable expenditures, as defined in Section 4945(d). The Trustee shall not make any investments that jeopardize the charitable purpose of the Trust, within the meaning of Section 4944 and the regulations thereunder, or retain any excess business holdings, within the meaning of Section 4943(c).

F. *Taxable Year.* The taxable year of the Trust shall be the calendar year.

G. *Limited Power of Amendment.* The Trustee shall have the power, acting alone, to amend the Trust in any manner required for the sole purpose of ensuring that the Trust qualifies and continues to qualify as a charitable lead annuity trust within the meaning of Sections 170, 2055, and 2522.

H. *Investment of Trust Assets.* Nothing in this Trust Agreement shall be construed to restrict the Trustee from investing the Trust assets in a manner that could result in the annual realization of a reasonable amount of income or gain from the sale or disposition of Trust assets.

I. *Reference to Sections.* Every reference in this Article FIRST to "Section" or "Sections" refers to a Section or Sections of the Internal Revenue Code of 1986, as amended, and all corresponding subsequent laws of the United States of America (referred to as the "Code").

J. *Intention to Qualify as a Charitable Lead Annuity Trust.* It is intended that this Trust qualify as a "charitable lead annuity trust" within the meaning of Sections 170, 2055, and 2522. The Trustee shall administer the Trust in such a manner as to comply with the provisions of the Code and all regulations which may be promulgated from time to time thereunder. If the Trustee determines that any amendment or reformation might jeopardize the status of the Trust as a qualifying charitable lead annuity trust, the Trustee may, in the Trustee's absolute discretion, request a written opinion of counsel that such amendment or reformation is necessary to the qualification of the Trust. Nevertheless, no such request or opinion shall prevent any amendment or reformation from being effective as of the moment necessary to assure qualification as a charitable lead annuity trust.

K. *No Liability for Transfer Taxes.* The Trust shall not be subject to any claim for estate, transfer, succession, legacy, inheritance, generation-skipping, or similar taxes (including any interest and penalties thereon) payable in respect of any trust or decedent's estate, including property deemed to be part of such trust or estate for tax purposes. The Donor covenants (1) to pay all such taxes out of assets other than assets of the Trust, and (2) to provide validly, by will or otherwise, that the Trust shall not be subject to any claim for such taxes. Any beneficiary, the Trustee, or both is authorized to enforce this paragraph. If for any reason the Trust becomes liable for such taxes, the interest of any descendant of Donor, which might otherwise arise as a consequence of the circumstances giving rise to those taxes, shall take effect only if that descendant furnishes the funds to pay those taxes. If the descendant fails to furnish the funds, that beneficiary shall, to the extent such interest gives rise to those taxes, be deemed to have predeceased those circumstances.

SECOND: *General Provisions Regarding Trustee.*

A. *Successor Trustee.* Each Trustee is authorized to resign at any time by giving written notice. If an Individual Co-Trustee is to be replaced, an individual will be appointed.

B. *Method of Resignation, Removal, Appointment, or Acceptance.* Each appointment, removal, resignation, or acceptance of appointment shall be by duly acknowledged written instrument delivered, in the case of an appointment or removal, to the individual or corporation appointed or removed, and, in the case of a resignation or acceptance, to the Donor and to the Charitable Organization.

C. *Number of Trustees.* At no time shall there be more than two Trustees. There may be more than one Trustee only in those instances when there is a Corporate Trustee and the Trust Estate includes real property or is not qualified to do business (hereinafter referred to as "Foreign Assets"). At such time or times an Individual Co-Trustee may be appointed to act only for the period during which the Trust holds property attributable to such Foreign Assets.

D. *Individual Co-trustee Vested with Foreign Assets.* Each Individual Co-trustee shall be vested with, and only with, sole title to and management of each Foreign Asset and shall pay over to the Trust, at least annually, the net income of the Trust attributable to such Foreign Assets.

E. *Trustee Fees.* Each Trustee shall be entitled to deduct and retain, without court approval, such compensation as may be allowed from time to time by law.

F. *Trustee Bond and Accounts.* No Trustee shall be required to give any bond, surety, or other security for the performance of the Trustee's duties; and the Trustee shall not be required to file periodic accounts in any court.

G. *Reference to Original and Successor Trustees.* Except as otherwise expressly provided in this Agreement, the word "Trustee," wherever used in this Agreement, shall be deemed and construed as referring to such Trustee or trustees as may at the time be acting.

THIRD: *Administrative Powers.* In addition to all other powers conferred by law or otherwise, the Trustee shall have the following discretionary powers and authority with respect to any and all property, real or personal, at any time held hereunder, without regard to any legal restrictions otherwise applicable to fiduciaries (whether pertaining to investments, location of property in a particular jurisdiction, or to other matters):

A. *Investment.* (1) To retain any property; (2) to invest and reinvest in any property without regard to the effect any such investment may have upon the diversification of investments held hereunder; (3) to hold any part of the Trust Estate in cash or uninvested for any period which may seem advisable; and (4) at any time and from time to time to join in or consent to or become a party to any agreement, reorganization, readjustment, merger, consolidation or exchange, to deposit any securities or property thereunder, or to exercise rights and options to subscribe to new securities, and to take, receive, and hold any securities or property resulting therefrom. The word "securities" as used in this Article shall include (but without limitation) corporate bonds and stocks of any kind, shares of investment companies, trusts, and discretionary common trust funds, and any and all unsecured obligations.

B. *General Disposition and Management.* (1) To convey, sell, exchange, or otherwise dispose of any property at public or private sale, and at such prices, at such time or times, and for such purposes, as may seem advisable; (2) to lease, operate, develop, or exploit any property; (3) to borrow money, from the Trustee or from others, to provide funds for any purpose, without resorting to the sale of any asset, and, for the purpose of securing the payment thereof, to pledge, mortgage, or otherwise encumber any property; (4) to extend the time of payment of any liens or encumbrances which may at any time be encumbrances upon any property, irrespective of by whom the same were made; (5) to foreclose, reduce the rate of interest on, or consent to the extension of mortgages on real property, or to accept a deed in lieu of foreclosure; (6) to join in a voluntary partition of any property; (7) to demolish or cause to be demolished any structure on any real property if the same seems desirable; (8) to abandon any property deemed to be worthless; and (9) to effectuate any and all of the foregoing on such terms and conditions, and regardless of whether or not the periods thereof extend beyond the statutory period for leases made by fiduciaries or the period of the Trust, as may seem advisable.

C. *Distribution in Kind.* To distribute and to accept in kind, or partly in kind, the property to be allocated, transferred, or distributed hereunder; and to determine the kinds and the values of any property for such purposes.

D. *Proxies.* To vote and give proxies, discretionary or otherwise, in respect of securities.

E. *Nominees.* To cause securities to be registered in the name of a nominee, without the addition of words indicating that the securities are held in a fiduciary capacity.

F. *After Jurisdiction.* To remove any property from any jurisdiction and to keep such property in any other jurisdiction for convenience of administration.

G. *Maintain, Insure, and Pay Taxes on Property.* To such extent, if any, as may seem necessary or desirable, to keep and maintain any property in good state of repair and upkeep; to effect insurance upon any property; and to pay the taxes, upkeep, repairs, carrying charges, maintenance, and premiums of insurance.

H. *Principal and Income.* So far as legally permissible, to allocate to income or to principal or partly to each any dividend, of whatever kind or nature, and any other money or property received hereunder, and to determine all questions as to what portion of expenses shall be credited or charged to income and what to principal.

I. *General.* (1) To settle, compromise, and adjust any and all claims in favor of or against the Trust, including any claim for taxes; (2) to execute and deliver such instruments as may be necessary to carry out any power hereunder; and (3) generally to have all powers with respect to property as if the Trustee were the absolute owner thereof.

FOURTH: *Donor Will Perfect Title in Trustee.* The Donor shall execute all further instruments necessary to vest the Trustee with full title to the property hereby transferred.

FIFTH: *Governing Law.* This Trust has been delivered to and accepted by the Trustee in the state of _____ and shall be governed and construed in all respects according to the laws of that State; PROVIDED, HOWEVER, (1) that the Trustee is prohibited from exercising any power or discretion granted under the laws of that state that would be inconsistent with the qualification of the Trust as a charitable lead annuity trust under the Code and the corresponding regulations; and (2) that any Corporate Trustee may, at any time and from time to time, in its absolute discretion, determine that the Trust shall similarly be governed and construed according to the laws of the state where such Trustee has its principal office.

SIXTH: *Binding on Successors; Incorporation.* This Agreement shall extend to and be binding upon the executors, administrators, successors, and assigns of the parties hereto. This Agreement contains all the terms of this Trust and all agreements concerning the Trust and Trust Estate between the Donor and the Trustee. There are also no other agreements between the Donor and the Trustee relating to the Trust, and all previous understandings or agreements are hereby declared to be null and void.

SEVENTH: *Commencement Date of Trust.* This Trust shall be considered to commence on the date when all of the following have occurred:

A. This Agreement has been executed by all parties and dated; and

B. Some assets have been transferred to the Trustee, as Trustee of this Trust, but not earlier than the date of this Agreement.

IN WITNESS WHEREOF the parties hereto have executed this Agreement in three (3) counterparts (each of which shall be deemed an original) on the date first above mentioned.

DONOR

_____

XYZ Charity

By: _____
    President

Resource 19

STATE _____)
) SS
COUNTY OF _____)

On the _____ day of _____ , 20____ , before me, a Notary Public in and for said County and State, personally appeared _____ , to me known and known to me to be the person whose name is subscribed to the within Instrument, and acknowledged that [s]he executed the same.

WITNESS my hand and official seal.

_____
Notary Public
Residing in _____

My Commission Expires:

_____

STATE _____)
) SS
COUNTY OF _____)

On the _____ day of _____ , 20____ , before me, a Notary Public in and for said County and State, personally appeared _____ , to me known and known to me to be the person whose name is subscribed to the within Instrument, and acknowledged that [s]he executed the same.

WITNESS my hand and official seal.

_____
Notary Public
Residing in _____

My Commission Expires:

_____

REFERENCES

American Association of Fund-Raising Counsel Trust for Philanthropy. *Giving USA, 1998.* New York: American Association of Fund-Raising Counsel Trust for Philanthropy, 1998.

American Association of Fund-Raising Counsel Trust for Philanthropy. *Giving USA, 1999.* New York: American Association of Fund-Raising Counsel Trust for Philanthropy, 1999a.

American Association of Fund-Raising Counsel Trust for Philanthropy. *Giving USA Update,* 1999b, 2 (entire issue).

American Association of Fund-Raising Counsel Trust for Philanthropy. *Giving USA, 2000.* New York: American Association of Fund-Raising Counsel Trust for Philanthropy, 2000.

American Association of Fund-Raising Counsel Trust for Philanthropy. *Giving USA, 2001.* New York: American Association of Fund-Raising Counsel Trust for Philanthropy, 2001.

Arenson, K. W. "$100 Million Donation to Cornell for Medicine." *New York Times,* May 1, 1998, p. A27.

Ashton, D. *The Complete Guide to Planned Giving.* Cambridge, Mass.: JLA, 1991.

Barth, S., "Finding the Needle in the Haystack: Use Computer Screening and Database Analysts to Discover the Hidden Major-Gift Prospects Among Your Alumni." *CASE Currents,* June 1998, pp. 32–36.

Baxter, F. R. "Prospect Management." Unpublished paper, University of California-Berkeley, 1987.

Berry, M. "Native American Philanthropy: Expanding Social Participation and Self-Determination." In Council on Foundations, *Cultures of Caring: Philanthropy in Diverse American Communities.* Washington, D.C.: Council on Foundations, 1999.

Campbell, D. A., Jr. "The Capital Campaign: Soliciting the Lead Gift(s)." Paper presented at the annual Council for Advancement and Support of Education District VI conference, St. Louis, Mo., Jan. 1985.

Capek, M.E.S. *Women and Philanthropy: Old Stereotypes, New Challenges.* Princeton, N.J.: Princeton University Press, 1997.

Conrad, D. L. *How to Solicit Big Gifts.* San Francisco: Public Management Institute, 1978.

"Exploring Women and Philanthropy: Interview with Gwinn Scott." *Counsel* (newsletter of Marts & Lundy Inc.), Summer 1998, pp. 1–2.

Frost, S. E. *Blueprint for Marketing: A Comprehensive Marketing Guide for Design Professionals.* Portland, Ore.: See, 1995.

Fund Raising School. *Principles and Techniques of Fund Raising.* Indianapolis: Indiana University Center on Philanthropy, 1995.

Gibson, E. B. "Raising the Bar for Major Gifts: Special Report. *Counsel* (newsletter of Marts & Lundy Inc.), Spring 1999, pp. 1–3.

INDEPENDENT SECTOR. *Giving and Volunteering in the United States, 1996.* Washington, D.C.: INDEPENDENT SECTOR, 1996.

Kateman, M. "Planning to Market and Marketing the Plan: An Overview of Marketing Planned Gifts." Paper presented at the 12th National Conference on Planned Giving, Anaheim, Calif., Oct. 13, 1999.

La Rocque, P. "More Precise Writing." Handout given with presentation at the Council for Advancement and Support of Education Writing Institute, Philadelphia, Dec. 1992.

Lange, S., and Hunsaker, C. "Information Systems: Managing the Database." In A. Kihlstedt and R. Pierpont (eds.), *Capital Campaigns: Realizing Their Power and Potential.* New Directions for Philanthropic Fundraising, no. 21. San Francisco: Jossey-Bass, 1999.

Millar, R. G. "How Much Is That Donor in Your Records? Step-by-Step Advice for Figuring Net Worth and Giving Ability." *CASE Currents,* July-Aug. 1995, pp. 38–42.

Miller, A., and Nayyar, S. "The New Hands-On Philanthropy: Women Are Going the Distance to Make Their Money Count." *Working Woman,* July-Aug. 1998, pp. 52–57.

National Committee on Planned Giving. *NCPG Directory of Council Members.* Indianapolis: National Committee on Planned Giving®, 2001.

Price, A. P., and File, K. M. *The Seven Faces of Philanthropy: A New Approach to Cultivating Major Donors.* San Francisco: Jossey-Bass, 1994.

Ruderman, S. "Panning for Gold." *Contributions,* May-June 2000, pp. 9–12.

Shaw, S. C., and Taylor, M. A. *Reinventing Fundraising: Realizing the Potential of Women's Philanthropy.* San Francisco: Jossey-Bass, 1995.

Smith, B., Shue, S., Vest, J. L., and Villarreal, J. *Ethnic Philanthropy.* San Francisco: Institute for Nonprofit Organization Management, University of San Francisco, 1994.

Steenhuysen, J. "Capturing the Donor's Attention: Using Generational Information to Effectively Market Gift Plans." *Journal of Gift Planning,* 1999, *3*(4), 13–17, 49–53.

United Auto Workers. "Focus On: The Distribution of Wealth." [http://uaw.org/publications/jobs-pay/1097/stat1097-03html]. Fall 1997.

U.S. Bureau of the Census. [http://www.census.gov]. Mar. 23, 1999.

White, D. E. *The Art of Planned Giving.* New York: Wiley, 1995.

Women's Philanthropy Institute. (Fact sheet.) [http://women-philanthropy.org]. July 31, 1999.

INDEX

A

Ability to give. *See* Giving capacity
Accountability system, as prospect management subsystem, 44, 45
Accountants. *See* Professional advisers
Advancement listening, 69
Advertisements, for marketing planned giving, 144–146
African Americans, philanthropy among, 14–15
Age: and continuous lifetime giving, 89–90; of major gift donors, 2; segmentation by, 125–127
American Association of Fund-Raising Counsel (AAFRC) Trust for Philanthropy, 1, 14, 61, 80
American Council on Gift Annuities, 181, 183
Annenberg, W. H., 64
Annual reports, information on planned giving in, 142
Annuities. *See* Charitable gift annuities
Appraisals: of real property, 168; of tangible personal property, 153–155, 160

Approach system, as prospect management subsystem, 44–46
Arenson, K. W., 67
The Art of Planned Giving (White), 76
Ashton, D., 102
Asking for gift: effect of, on giving, 53–54; timing of, 48; when soliciting lead gifts, 67–68; when soliciting major gift from individual, 50, 51
Asset inventory booklets: as planned giving marketing tool, 134; sample, 489–500
Asset screening, 16
Attentive listening, 69
Attorneys. *See* Legal counsel; Professional advisers

B

Baby boomers, 127
Bargain sales of real property, 170–171
Barth, S., 16
Barton, D. W., Jr., 59
Baxter, F. R., 38, 40, 41
Bequest expectancies. *See* Bequests

Bequests, 80–92; amount nonprofits receive from, 80, 194; board's role with, 80; direct mail appeal for, 91, 92; face-to-face visits to promote, 89; forms of, 195; as means for providing remainder interest, 194–195; prospective donors of, 89, 90, 195; recognizing gifts made through, 80, 84–88, 91; sample gift acceptance policy on, 364; stewardship of donors of, 91; U.S. savings bonds as asset for, 201, 202–203; will brochures encouraging, 80, 81–83, 409–415; will seminars promoting, 91, 281–330
Berry, M., 14
Board of directors: bequest gift leadership from, 80; gift acceptance policy approval and review by, 95, 101; planned giving program involvement by, 93–94, 95, 120; women on, 12
Brochures: charitable gift annuities, 404–408, 431–437; charitable remainder trusts, 438–444;